Davidson College

THE EXPEDIENT UTOPIAN:
BANDARANAIKE AND CEYLON

THE EXPEDIENT UTOPIAN: BANDARANAIKE AND CEYLON

JAMES MANOR

Fellow, Institute of Development Studies
University of Sussex

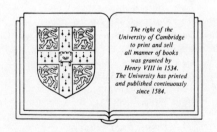

The right of the
University of Cambridge
to print and sell
all manner of books
was granted by
Henry VIII in 1534.
The University has printed
and published continuously
since 1584.

CAMBRIDGE UNIVERSITY PRESS

CAMBRIDGE

NEW YORK   PORT CHESTER   MELBOURNE   SYDNEY

Published by the Press Syndicate of the University of Cambridge
The Pitt Building, Trumpington Street, Cambridge CB2 1RP
40 West 20th Street, New York, NY 10011, USA
10 Stamford Road, Oakleigh, Melbourne 3166, Australia

First published 1989

Printed in Great Britain at The Bath Press, Avon

British Library cataloguing in publication data
Manor, James
The expedient utopian: Bandaranaike and Ceylon.
1. Sri Lanka. Bandaranaike, Solomon, 1899–1959
I. Title
954.9′302′0924

Library of Congress cataloguing in publication data
Manor, James.
The expedient utopian : Bandaranaike and Ceylon / James Manor.
p. cm.
Bibliography
Includes index.
ISBN 0-521-37191-0
1. Bandaranaike, S. W. R. D. (Solomon West Ridgeway Dias).
1899–1959. 2. Sri Lanka – Politics and government. 3. Prime
ministers – Sri Lanka – Biography. I. Title.
DS489.83.B3M36 1989
954.9′303′0924 – dc 19
[B]   89-724 CIP

ISBN 0 521 37 191 0

VN

for T.L.D.

The Hon. S. W. R. D. Bandaranaike: There is a very beautiful and great legend in which that human yearning for better things is enshrined. It is the story of the Garden of the Hesperides. At the Western verge of the world there is a garden where golden apples grow. It is guarded by the Hesperides, the daughters of the Night, and this is the manner of their vigil – Hand in hand they dance round the apple tree:

> And none may taste the golden fruit
> Till the golden new time come;
> Many a tree shall spring from shoot,
> Many a flower be withered at root
> And many a song shall be dumb.
> Broken and still shall be many a lute
> Or ere the new times come.

I ask my countrymen, Honourable members of this House, to discard that mutual suspicion and the mutual tearing of each other to pieces and to join each other in that constructive cooperation which I hope will enable us to reach that golden age.

Mr Philip Gunawardena: You will have to wait long, at the rate you are going.

Mr Bandaranaike: I do not think that golden age is very far off. If my diagnosis of world movements is correct, we can all join in ushering in that golden age and pluck for our people the golden fruit of prosperity, of progress and of happiness.

State Council debate, August 1936

Mr Bandaranaike: You know, my dear fellow [smiling broadly], I have never found anything to excite the people in quite the way this language issue does.

Interview, 1956

CONTENTS

Preface   *page* ix
List of abbreviations   xii
Map of Ceylon   xiii

Introduction   1
1 Youth, 1899–1919   14
2 Scholar, 1919–1925   36
3 Novice, 1925–1931   56
4 Councillor, 1931–1936   91
5 Minister, 1936–1946   125
6 Heir presumptive, 1946–1951   168
7 Outcast, 1951–1956   204
8 Arbiter, 1956–1959   254
9 Legend   319

Select bibliography   328
Index   333

PREFACE

The island of Sri Lanka was officially known as 'Ceylon' until 1972, and since the latter name applied throughout the period covered in this book, 'Ceylon' will be used here. This is done for the sake of historical accuracy, and not out of any nostalgia for a name that was a product of the colonial era.

The word 'Ceylonese' is used here to refer to all of the island's indigenous inhabitants. The term 'Sinhalese' refers to the majority linguistic group (69.4 per cent of the population in 1953), and the term 'Sinhala' refers to the language which they speak. The word 'Tamil' refers both to the language spoken by the largest minority and to the people who speak it. They comprised 22.9 per cent of the population in 1953 – and they can be broken down into 'Ceylon Tamils' or residents of the island over many centuries (10.9 per cent of the island's population), and 'Indian' or 'estate Tamils' brought as tea estate labourers in the British period (12.0 per cent).[1]

My understanding of Bandaranaike's story was greatly enriched by the oral testimony of many witnesses to the events discussed here. I conducted several hundred hours of interviews, mainly in Sri Lanka. Except in cases where only one person could have known something, I have generally obtained corroboration from documents or at least one other interview. When only a single oral source was available, I have tested the plausibility of his or her assertion against circumstantial evidence. Some interviewees insisted that their identities remain confidential because they feared that their comments might make them vulnerable to retribution from one quarter or another. Despite the difficulties that this presents to specialists seeking to assess the validity of such remarks, I have felt compelled to honour my informants' wishes. I am prepared, with certain reservations, to discuss these sources with scholars.

---

[1] *Census of Ceylon, 1953* (Colombo, 1958) vol. 1, pp. 107–28. Most Muslims on the island also speak Tamil as their first language. But they are not seen, nor do they see themselves as 'Tamils' and they will be seen here as members of a separate 'Muslim' category.

I have also – on a very small number of occasions – curtailed or withheld comments on highly sensitive topics, which are of marginal importance in a political biography, particularly when I felt that a discussion might place certain informants at serious risk.

I am grateful to the Nuffield Foundation, the British Academy and the Research Board of the University of Leicester for grants in support of research for this book. I am particularly indebted to the US National Endowment for the Humanities for a fellowship which enabled me to devote a full year to the project, and to the University of Leicester for giving me leave during that year. These agencies made it possible for me to pay three extended visits to Sri Lanka in 1977, 1978 and 1980. The Twenty-Seven Foundation also provided support for the preparation of the manuscript.

Several libraries and archives provided indispensable help. In Sri Lanka these included the National Archives of Sri Lanka (where, among other things, the staff warded off a deadly snake), the library of what is now called the University of Peradeniya, the Presidential Archive, the library of Parliament (under its various names), the Colombo Museum Library and the Bandaranaike Memorial Museum. In England, I received assistance from the libraries of the Institute of Commonwealth Studies and the School of Oriental and African Studies in London; the Bodleian Library, the libraries of Rhodes House, the Oxford Union Society and Christ Church at Oxford; and the University Library, the Centre for South Asian Studies Library, and Gonville and Caius College Library at Cambridge. I am especially grateful to the University of Leicester Library for acquiring microfilms of Colombo newspapers.

A great many people were very generous to me. It is possible here only to mention a small number of them. I wish to thank Mrs Sirimavo Bandaranaike and Sunethra Bandaranaike for allowing me to see the papers of S. W. R. D. Bandaranaike and the diaries of Sir Solomon Dias Bandaranaike, and to J. R. Jayewardene for making his papers available to me. In both cases, permission was granted for the first time. I am indebted to a Colombo research student, who wishes to remain anonymous, for many hours of assistance with translations of Sinhala newspapers and other documents. The overwhelming majority of documents for a study of this man, who had extreme difficulty reading Sinhala, and who always wrote and thought in English, are in the latter language.

I am also particularly grateful to R. St. L. P. Deraniyagala, Sir Senerat Gunawardena, the late A. P. Jayasuriya, Mr and Mrs A. L. Dias Bandaranaike, Nimal Karunatilake, Tissa Wijeyeratne and James T. Rutnam. Among the many scholars who provided crucial assistance, I am especially grateful to Richard Gombrich, K. M. de Silva, Hugh Tinker, C. R. de Silva, Eric Meyer, Gananath Obeyesekere, Jane Russell, Michael Roberts and W. Howard Wriggins. Several of the people listed here will disagree with views expressed in this book and they should not be held responsible for any errors that follow.

ABBREVIATIONS

BP   S. W. R. D. Bandaranaike Papers, National Archives of Sri
Lanka
CDN   *Ceylon Daily News*
CI   *Ceylon Independent*
CML   *Ceylon Morning Leader*
LSSP   Lanka Sama Samaja Party
MEP   Mahajana Eksath Peramuna
NASL   National Archives of Sri Lanka
PRO   Public Record Office, Kew, England
SLFP   Sri Lanka Freedom Party
TC   *Times of Ceylon*
UNP   United National Party

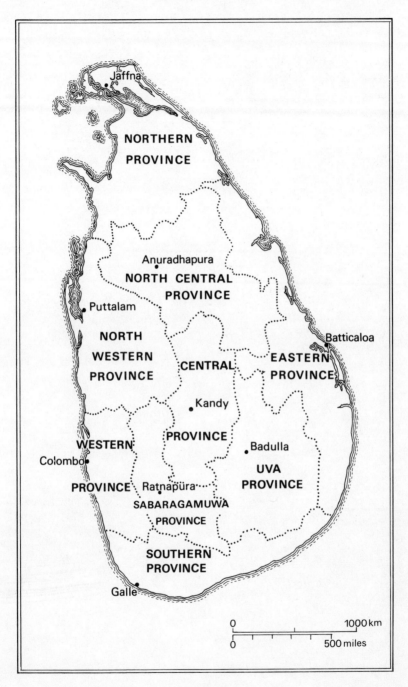

NORTHERN
PROVINCE

Anuradhapura

NORTH CENTRAL
PROVINCE

Puttalam

NORTH
WESTERN
PROVINCE

CENTRAL

EASTERN
PROVINCE

Batticaloa

Kandy

PROVINCE

WESTERN

Badulla

Colombo

UVA
PROVINCE

PROVINCE

Ratnapüra

SABARAGAMUWA
PROVINCE

SOUTHERN
PROVINCE

Galle

| 0 | | | | | | 1000 km |
| 0 | | | | | | 500 miles |

Map of Ceylon

INTRODUCTION

This is the story of one man's quest for pre-eminence and power, and of the uses to which he put them. It is also an account of his impact on his society and his nation's politics, and of their influence on him. It is not a simple story. S. W. R. D. Bandaranaike was both a utopian idealist and an ardent opportunist, a progressive and a parochialist, an egalitarian and an imperious snob. He was a rationalist with a fascination for the paranormal, an occasionally radical free thinker who helped to conserve many central elements of the existing order. He was vain and often shameless in the pursuit of power, but when he finally reached the top he was recklessly over-generous.

Our main concern in this study is the man at the centre, but his story – like his life – moves out from the centre into ever-widening circles. After an opulent, lonely childhood surrounded only some of the time by a troubled family, he moved to boarding school in Ceylon and then on to Oxford where he spent five years as a rather isolated onlooker on the margin of the British establishment. Soon after his return home in 1925, he entered politics which brought him into contact first with the leaders of powerful elites and interests and eventually with more humble, local-level elites who provided him with links to the great mass of under-privileged villagers. In this study, we follow Bandaranaike where he leads us. Each new arena that he enters, each new group and social stratum that he meets, will be dealt with as and when he encounters them. The same is true of the major topics and themes that arise: his psychological development, his relations with leading politicians, his attitudes and actions on questions such as caste, religion, parochialism, socialism and land reform. Several important socio-economic issues and groups will therefore appear in this discussion later and less often than they would in a general history of the island, but this is instructive, since it indicates how tardy and half-hearted the national political elite was in tackling many of the problems in Ceylonese society.

Bandaranaike was the central, pivotal figure in Ceylon's modern political transformation. When he entered politics, power lay mainly in

1

the hands of the island's British rulers and a very small group of wealthy, high caste, highly westernized, mainly Christian and mostly unelected Ceylonese – among whom his own family enjoyed pride of place. The colonial regime was far more uncompromising than its counterpart in India in its handling of the culture, sensibilities and needs of the island's population. It conducted its affairs almost entirely in English, and the accommodations that it made with indigenous religions and the provisions that it made for the material welfare of the common man were minimal. In 1925, there was no income tax and no general land tax. Less than 10 per cent of the adult male population could read.[1] By the time Bandaranaike was assassinated in 1959 after over three years as Prime Minister, much had changed. The island's government was freely elected on the basis of universal suffrage by voters who included substantial numbers of people from disadvantaged groups. They had a genuine choice between two major parties which between them had created a whole range of programmes to assist ordinary people. By 1959 Sinhalese and Buddhist interests, far from being ignored, were indulged.

Bandaranaike played a crucial part in much of this: in the opening of the political system to people from less prosperous and less westernized backgrounds, and from less exalted castes; in the creation of a two-party system; in the institutionalization of welfare state policies which by 1959 gave Ceylon remarkably high life expectancy and literacy rates (75 per cent of adults – males and females – could read) and a low infant mortality rate.[2] He had also been instrumental in entrenching extreme Sinhalese Buddhist sentiments and interests at the centre of the political arena. The dangers posed by these interests – which in our time have come to threaten the very survival of representative government and national integrity – had already become apparent by 1959. Severe communal riots had occurred the previous year in which the Tamil minority had suffered grievously, and Bandaranaike's murder was planned by one Buddhist monk, who had been a key supporter in his election campaign, and carried out by another.

Throughout his life, Bandaranaike wrestled with the problem of authority – both his own and that of others. Each time he moved into a wider arena, this problem arose in a new form. His childhood was dominated by his difficulties with the authority first of his father whom he mocked, resented and feared, and then of a tutor who acted as his father's

---

[1] M. Roberts, '*Elite* Formation and *Elites*, 1832–1931', in K. M. de Silva (ed.), *University of Ceylon History of Ceylon*, vol. iii (Peradeniya, 1973), p. 275.

[2] The literacy rate is from 1960. *World Bank Development Report 1983* (New York, 1983), pp. 192–93 and 196–97.

surrogate. At school and at Oxford, he was intensely preoccupied with what he saw as his 'struggle' to establish his 'superiority', his authority among his fellow students. Throughout his adult life, he was unable to accept the authority of any superior. He denied the legitimacy of British rule in Ceylon – a posture which helped him to reject his father's public role as a pillar of the British regime – although for long periods he maintained an uneasy truce with colonial officialdom. As a young politician, he could not accept the authority of the leading Ceylonese nationalists who were suspicious of a young man whose father and grandfather had scorned them. The result was two decades of alternating cooperation and strife, even when (after 1936) he served in a team of ministers led by a senior nationalist – D. S. Senanayake, the architect of the island's independence in 1948. That phase ended in 1951, when Senanayake with his allies and kinsmen drove Bandaranaike out of Ceylon's first post-independence Cabinet.

His difficulties with authority also intruded into his personal and intellectual life. He was so intensely preoccupied with status and power in personal relations that he was never able to form a friendship of equals. He was never comfortable in relationships based on anything except at least modest deference to his position. This meant that in adulthood he was assailed by the loneliness which he had known in his youth. The same need to assert his authority was apparent in his frequent, rather forced efforts to exhibit erudition. He read for pleasure, but also because he could not bear to be less well informed than those around him. When in the 1950s he discovered an aide reading Camus – of whom he had never heard – he was visibly perturbed and could not rest until he had devoured several of the author's works.[3] John Ratsinghe, the hero of the detective stories which Bandaranaike wrote, was a Sinhalese Sherlock Holmes who served his creator as Holmes had served Conan Doyle – as a 'fantasy self' whose towering intellect made him a figure of immense, if casual authority.[4] Late in life, he dreamed of going into semi-retirement as a constitutional head of state to write an epic novel which was to be a Ceylonese *War and Peace* – a project which he actually began.[5] All of this bespoke a desire to establish his authority in the cultural as well as the political sphere.

D. S. Senanayake and his highly westernized associates had displaced Bandaranaike's forebears as the leading Ceylonese in the power structure by mobilizing elites from the upper-middle stratum of society. In order to

[3] Interview with Nimal Karunatilake, Colombo, 7 September 1980.
[4] L. Edel, 'The Figure under the Carpet', *New Republic*, 10 February 1979, p. 28.
[5] See the fragments of manuscript for the novel *Karma* at the Bandaranaike Museum, Colombo.

dislodge them, Bandaranaike had to activate a broader array of less privileged, less prosperous groups. It turned out to be an onerous task. His main difficulty was in gaining acceptance among Sinhalese Buddhists who were suspicious of a scion of an older, more exalted and alien elite. He had, after all, been brought up as a Christian and had embraced Buddhism, a more indigenous lifestyle and Sinhalese chauvinism only in his thirties. When he finally gained broad popular support and with it national leadership at the election of 1956, he did so largely by default – because there was no one else to whom the linguistic revivalists could turn.

His election as Prime Minister did not end his struggle with the problem of authority, it only altered its character. He no longer had to strive after power, but he had to decide what to do with it and this proved far more taxing than he had anticipated. After so many years of regarding others' claims to authority as illegitimate, he emerged with the eccentric notion that to appear legitimate, a leader had to be exceedingly, indeed excessively generous to pressure groups over which he ruled. He thought that acts of extravagant magnanimity would enhance his own strength and bring social harmony out of a dangerously inflamed situation. Instead, he squandered his power and ensnared himself in a succession of increasingly serious crises. His misjudgements opened the way to the disastrous communal riots of 1958 and then to the vicious delusions of the erstwhile supporters who conspired in his assassination.

This book is not intended to suggest that history is made or dominated by great men. Leaders have important roles to play, but their influence is curtailed by larger forces, structures and circumstances. So this study does not seek to explain the whole of Ceylon's history during Bandaranaike's lifetime. It concentrates on one hugely important politician in those years, and on those political, cultural, social and economic forces which had a substantial bearing upon his story. It is worth stressing, however, that in the period discussed here it was possible for political leaders to have a much greater impact upon Ceylon's politics and society than in the years since Bandaranaike's death. He was a member of that generation of Asian and African politicians who guided their nations through the transition from imperial rule to independence and helped to develop new modes of politics. All of these leaders were presented with unprecedented but temporary opportunities to shape political perceptions and processes. They took power while important socio-economic groups were still crystallizing and discovering how to assert themselves politically. Therefore this generation of leaders deserves particular attention.

Obviously this 'generation' – which included such diverse figures as Nkrumah, Nehru, Sukarno, Ho, Nasser, Nyerere, Makarios, Lumumba and Bandaranaike – is far from homogeneous.[6] The differences among them outweigh the similarities. These many unique personalities emerged from radically different cultural and socio-economic backgrounds, encountered a wide variety of colonial regimes, and evolved strikingly different ideologies and political organizations. Nonetheless, there are certain common elements in their careers, certain broad tendencies in their behaviour which ought to be recognized.

In their struggles against imperialism, they tended towards heady, moralistic rhetoric, accounts of self-sacrifice, idealized visions of the future under self-rule and an inordinate faith in the power of ideas and precepts to change individuals and society. This was to be expected, since in most cases they faced years, even decades, in opposition with little hope of obtaining political resources. Ideals, parables, symbols and slogans were necessarily their main, and sometimes their only, weapons. Later and particularly after independence, when decisions were between shades of gray and not between freedom and bondage, many transitional leaders were reluctant to abandon the old rhetoric. They tended to indulge in degrees of hypocrisy, *naïveté* and egotism. Again, this was understandable. It was less the result of venality on their part than a logical outgrowth of the culture of anti-colonial politics on which they had battened for so long. It would therefore be unfair to judge them too harshly for these failings – though failings they remain.

It is more important to understand the problems which arose out of these tendencies. However enthusiastically one might agree with their views on the immorality of imperialism, however moved one might be by their accounts of sacrifice, we must not overlook the dangers which these ideas posed to the leaders who articulated them, to the followers who heard them, and to many fledgling political systems in the early post-independence years. Almost without exception, these leaders tended to fall short in the eyes of their followers. Their idealized visions of the future had created unrealistic expectations. Some, like Nehru, anticipated

[6] It can also be argued that it is more appropriate to include Bandaranaike's name in a list of second generation post-independence leaders who succeeded the men named in the text – a list containing names like Sadat, Moi, Marcos and Indira Gandhi. After all, Bandaranaike did not achieve supreme power until eight years after independence. But it should be remembered that he spent over two decades in high politics before independence in 1948, and that that experience shaped his outlook in much the same way as it influenced the first generation leaders named in the text. He also had a substantial influence on pre-independence politics in Ceylon and – first as a minister and then as an opposition leader – he did much to shape events immediately after independence.

this,[7] but most, including Bandaranaike, did not. Since in many new states the political system and the person of the national leader were intimately bound up with one another, popular frustration with a leader often created antipathy towards the system itself and *vice versa.* Leaders often reacted to an unexpected upsurge of discontent by turning to autocratic methods.[8] Even in nations like Ceylon where (in Bandaranaike's time at least)[9] this did not reach serious proportions, leaders whose perceptions had been shaped in the pre-independence years found such popular discontent difficult to manage.

Bandaranaike also made a habit of striking moralistic postures, albeit in an eccentric manner. He had, for a start, a strange notion of what moralizing was. He tended to equate it with lyricism. This does not mean that he seldom spoke of rights and wrongs in politics, but he appears to have ascribed moral content to poetic images which he often used as a substitute for political or moral argument. He also tended to borrow his moralistic rhetoric rather unthinkingly from others. There was cause for concern here, for when a politician starts with a confused notion of what moralizing is, and then indulges in it rather casually, a certain complacency and hypocrisy can creep into his work.

One sign of this – in his case and in the careers of many other transitional leaders – was laxity in the use of language. Bandaranaike, far more than any other pre-independence politician in Ceylon, threatened to initiate 'struggles' (usually boycotts or civil disobedience) against the British and summoned his countrymen to undertake 'sacrifice' for the nation. Yet this nearly always entailed an abuse of language, since he did not seriously intend such things to happen. Indeed, in the three decades before independence in 1948, there was not the faintest flicker of an anti-British 'struggle' and there was precious little 'sacrifice' by nationalists. As we shall see, there were good reasons for this, and it is partly understandable that an exuberant young politician who was impatient with other, more staid Ceylonese leaders should adopt rhetoric which was in widespread (and genuine) use a few miles across the straits in India. It also stirred the crowds that heard it – a temptation to recklessness that he always found hard to resist – but in the long run, when the 'struggles'

[7] The main sign of this in Nehru's case was his refusal to accept a ministerial post in the Congress-controlled United Provinces in 1937, when the British system of dyarchy was still in effect. He knew that people expected far too much and that ministers' powers were too limited. Whether he was as keenly aware of this after independence is doubtful.
[8] For a stimulating discussion of the strategies open to such leaders, see W. H. Wriggins, *The Ruler's Imperative: Strategies for Political Survival in Asia and Africa* (New York, 1969).
[9] For a discussion of rather different trends thereafter, see J. Manor (ed.), *Sri Lanka in Change and Crisis* (London and New York, 1984).

never materialized, it undermined public confidence in him. It also contributed to a dangerous divergence of public rhetoric from political reality in the island.

When Bandaranaike spoke of 'sacrifice', he often referred to the things that he himself had given up. It was a promising theme among the island's Buddhist majority, people who were raised on the story of 'the selfless generosity' of Prince Vessantara 'who gave everything away'. This is 'the most famous story in the Buddhist world' and in Ceylon 'it is still learnt by every [Buddhist] child . . . even the biography of the Buddha is not better known'.[10] In several ways, Bandaranaike fit plausibly into this general mould. People knew that he had been raised a Christian amid opulence at the pinnacle of the Ceylonese social order, and educated at Oxford among the future masters of the Empire. And yet he had abandoned the expensive fashions, pastimes, food and drink of the anglicized elite, and the certainty of a comfortable life as a government official and laird of the family estate. He now dressed and lived simply, and had taken up the language, the religion and the cause of the common man.

There was, however, a good deal less to these 'sacrifices' than met the eye. He was in fact mightily bored by the westernized elite, their tastes and many of their pastimes (though he never lost interest in tennis or billiards, and he remained an ardent competitor in the Kennel Club shows). A career as a civil servant seemed both tedious and *passé*, since for his generation electoral politics was the way to real power. Nor had he ever found Christianity particularly appealing. None of these were real 'sacrifices'. Nonetheless, throughout his career, the theme of renunciation yielded abundant political returns and betrayed a somewhat disingenuous turn of mind.

Many transitional leaders in Asia and Africa felt impelled by their nations' need for an ethos, a sense of cohesion and grandeur, to provide them with a philosophy or 'ism'. Kenneth Kaunda developed 'humanism', Kwame Nkrumah's 'Nkrumaism' later became 'consciencism', and Julius Nyerere offered his less pretentious 'African socialism'. Thakin Nu's 'Burmese Way to Socialism' and Sekou Toure's *commannocracie* are other examples. Bandaranaike never went that far, but he often aired his views on literature, philosophy and world history. In the colonial period, this enabled him to demonstrate that Ceylon's British residents had no monopoly on erudition – indeed precious few of them were as superbly educated as he. Later, this impulse carried him into lofty pronouncements

---

[10] M. Cone and R. Gombrich, *The Perfect Generosity of Prince Vessantara* (Oxford, 1977), p. xv.

on the Sinhalese Buddhist cultural heritage and on the tide of world
history which in his view was running in the direction of the non-
Western civilizations and of the common man. Most of his comments
were unoriginal and far from profound, but they soothed feelings of
inferiority among the Sinhalese who were reassured that a man who had
spent time at Oxford, which seemed the very summit of Western
intellectual life, found their much maligned cultural tradition as rich and
appealing as that of the West.

Most transitional leaders in Asia and Africa had their naïve moments.
Many of them put too much faith in the power of precepts, parables and
ideals to motivate their countrymen. After coming to power, they often
assumed rather blithely that the heterogeneous coalitions that had
supported their struggles could be maintained with relative ease. They
also believed in the idea of progress, which was natural, since without it
they could hardly have survived long periods in opposition. The eventual
success of their movements reinforced their optimism about the future
and confirmed their belief that society could be changed for the better,
and that they, their movements and the post-colonial state were proper
agents for change. They were inclined to take major risks in social
engineering since their experiences suggested that history consisted of
happy endings. In other words, they were less sensitive than they might
have been to the ironies and tragedies that afflict human endeavours. This
helped them to inspire their countrymen, but it led many of them into
deep water.

Bandaranaike, whose optimism in this vein was both disarming and
unsettling, vividly exhibited these traits. In one way, this is surprising. He
had, after all, spent five years at Oxford with men who had only recently
been in the trenches. But whatever disillusionment and pessimism the
First World War instilled in that generation of Englishmen, it seldom
came to the surface in the Oxford of the early 1920s. Even if it had, it is
unlikely that Bandaranaike would have imbibed much of it since he
arrived there with expectations that were derived, quite explicitly, from
Tom Brown at Oxford. And after much pain and effort he saw to it that what
he called 'My Great Adventure'[11] ended in a triumph worthy of Tom
Brown himself. He emerged with a good degree in classics but without
much grasp of the ancients' sense of tragedy.

He therefore returned to Ceylon with his boyhood faith in happy
endings intact and projected it onto his own career and his nation's quest
for freedom. Ceylon's easy achievement of self-rule in 1948, without
struggle and with little sacrifice, and his own success at the election of

[11] S. W. R. D. Bandaranaike, *Speeches and Writings* (Colombo, 1963), p. 3.

1956, bolstered this optimism. As Prime Minister, he spoke constantly of the present age of transition and of progress towards a better world. Here, however, he differed from most other Asian and African leaders by adopting a rather passive role. His government sought to enact numerous reforms, but Bandaranaike proved far less forceful in his use of power than he had been in pursuit of it. In speaking of himself merely as a midwife assisting at the birth of a new order, he credited the process of change with much greater inevitability than it actually possessed and underestimated the importance of human agency in history. The passivity which this outlook bred ultimately took a grievous toll on Bandaranaike, his government and Ceylon's social cohesion.

To say that Bandaranaike had many things in common with other members of this transitional generation is not to claim that he was an archetypal figure among them. But a wealth of documents and oral testimony make it possible to build up an unusually full picture of his personal development and political career, warts and all. The warts are not difficult to find because he was less guarded and self-conscious than most other transitional figures and because the colonial authorities, his political opponents and a free and generally hostile press were never loath to point them out. This offers clear advantages to a biographer who believes that these transitional leaders were, by and large, no more and no less fallible than most other human beings – however inspirational or vile they may appear in legend. My purpose is neither to debunk nor to deify – there has been quite enough of both already.

Whatever else may be said of Bandaranaike, he was no flat, one-dimensional character. This is hardly surprising, since to be a colonial is to be prey to contradictions and counter-pressures: to be torn between things local and things cosmopolitan, between Asian and European perceptions, between anti-colonialism and British values and ways. Add to that Bandaranaike's own highly complex personality and the result is a life that was a tangle of incongruities. On close examination, some of these turn out to be more apparent than real, but many were or became patent contradictions. The influence that he achieved ensured that many of these incongruities left their marks on the island's politics.

As the title of this book suggests, he was fond of invoking utopian imagery in presenting his political goals to audiences (and probably to himself), yet he also carried short-term and often short-sighted opportunism to excess. There is a certain incongruity between these two themes, but in practice they were far from contradictory. *Naïveté*, which was a product of his brand of utopianism, and cynicism, born of his pursuit of expediency, tend to generate similar insensitivities. The utopian visions that Bandaranaike summoned up were literary rather than political in character. His reference to a scene in the Garden of the Hesperides which precedes the preface to this book (and which he used on numerous occasions between 1936 and 1958) is a good example. Such images are so lyrical and vague that they provide no guidance at all to someone faced with day-to-day moral or political choices. His utopian turn of mind therefore actually facilitated his earnest pursuit of expediency by freeing him from the constraints which a more clearly defined set of political beliefs would have imposed.

Bandaranaike's exalted social status also produced paradoxical results. His family stood at the apex of the island's old social order and as near to the pinnacle of the old political order as any Ceylonese was allowed to stand. And yet more than any other politician in modern Ceylon (given the failure of leftist parties) he was instrumental in envisioning and, to a lesser degree, in generating change – in drawing disadvantaged groups into politics and in promoting the evolution of a new and distinctly different social and political order. He did so because he wanted to win votes, but also because he had egalitarian sentiments and desired greater social justice for the common man, to whom he felt a vague but genuine attachment. Bandaranaike's enthusiasm for reform – in taxation and local government, in land policy and language policy, in the legal and electoral systems and so on – arose partly despite his exalted social position, but also because his high status freed him from insecurities that might have inhibited empathy with the needs of ordinary people.

This is not to say that he was immune from the Sinhalese and Ceylonese elite's preoccupation with status, but he arrived at this egalitarianism by way of a monumental conceit. Once he had convinced himself, after his years at school and at Oxford, of his 'superiority' and that his 'destiny' was 'greatness',[12] he came to regard all Ceylonese – and, for good measure, nearly all Britishers – as his inferiors. 'He began', as a perceptive observer jokingly put it, 'with the assumption that he was God and that all others were mere mortals.'[13] He was therefore most offended by those in Ceylon who lived most pretentiously, that is, by the island's British residents and by the higher caste and upper-middle-class Ceylonese. Since ordinary folk – and most especially the disadvantaged – were largely free of such pretentions, they naturally attracted his sympathy. Ironically, then, an overweening hauteur inclined him to seek justice for common folk.

His decision to plunge into the kind of politics where one appealed to

[12] See chapters 1 and 2.
[13] Interview with Nimal Karunatilake, Colombo, 28 August 1977.

ordinary people for their votes deeply offended his father and yet, at a more fundamental level, it was squarely within the family tradition. Sir Solomon Dias Bandaranaike was for years the Maha Mudaliar or chief of the extensive network of Ceylonese headmen which assisted British administration. He regarded popular politics as demeaning for someone of his son's social rank, and many of the changes which the young man advocated were assaults on the social and political order over which his father had presided. On the other hand, the son's intense pursuit of pre-eminence and power was something that Sir Solomon understood. No one was happier at Bandaranaike's rise to the post of minister of the Crown than the old knight. Nor did it escape the father – whose ancestors down the centuries appear to have changed from Hindus to Buddhists to Roman Catholics to Dutch Reformed to Anglicans in turn with succeeding ruling regimes[14] – that a further shift in religion and in political strategy made sense in an era of rapid change.

Bandaranaike was also a man caught rather incongruously between cultures. His education and upbringing were in English, a language in which he took immense delight, and over which he had sufficient command to be the finest debater in the Oxford Union of his day. Yet in early adulthood he also acquired an intuitive understanding of the underside of colonialism, of the fears and aspirations of many ordinary Sinhalese for their language, religion and culture. He developed a genuine attachment, mainly at an aesthetic level (at which he operated far more than is normally supposed, and far more than was politically healthy) to the Sinhalese cultural tradition, especially to the elegance of its architectural heritage. He therefore tended to share the anger of Sinhalese revivalists at any disparagement of that tradition. At the same time, however, he never ceased to identify very substantially with the cultural and political traditions of Britain. Although he was probably not conscious of it, this entailed a partial acceptance of the disparagement which so annoyed him.[15] He never broke with his countrymen's tendency to use things British as the yardstick for assessing things Ceylonese. He never forgot, nor let others forget, that he had excelled at the Oxford of Anthony Eden and Evelyn Waugh.

In attempting to synthesize elements of British and Sinhalese culture, in his thirties he developed a coolly rationalistic, intellectualized Buddhism to which he was – contrary to popular belief among the

---

[14] This is conceded by many members of the Bandaranaike family. See the comments of one of them, Y. Gooneratne, *Relative Merits: A Personal Memoir of the Bandaranaike Family of Sri Lanka* (London, 1986), pp. 3–6.
[15] I am grateful to Ashis Nandy for raising this point.

Ceylonese elite – genuinely attached. This dispassionate, rather Nehruvian outlook set him apart from most Buddhists in Ceylon whose
devotion to gods of Hindu origin (and, in some cases, to demons and
sorcery) was viewed by Bandaranaike as a pollution of the pure book-
learned Buddhism that he espoused.

It also set him apart from one side of
himself which he revealed in his fictional and autobiographical writings,
which was fascinated by the macabre, the horrific and the paranormal.
His rationalism predominated through nearly all of his adult life, but in
1959 when the disintegration of his political position placed him under
excruciating stress, it cracked. He consulted a medium who diagnosed his
troubles in occult, supernatural terms. He then astonished close aides by
taking part in ceremonies which Buddhist purists regarded as dis-
reputable in an attempt to undo his fate.

Bandaranaike was not one to cling fiercely to any particular political
line. The posthumously published little blue book of his 'Thoughts'
contains the following quotation which stands in contrast to the
vehemence of Mao in his little red book:

What is truth?
Whatever may be the eternal verities, truth itself is in many ways a relative thing.
What is true today may not have been true yesterday, and may not be true
tomorrow. What is true for one person need not necessarily be true for another.
Very often, the whole truth lies neither entirely on one side, nor on the other. It is
very often, a rather puzzling compound of many things.[16]

This outlook facilitated his countless, often brazen shifts of position on
political issues, despite his insistence that he was 'Committed to the
Hilt.'[17] This produced contradictory reactions among onlookers. On the
one hand, it made him seem hopelessly inconstant. On the other, it was in
a curious way reassuring. Since it was known that he argued whatever
case he happened to be making in forceful terms, he developed a
reputation as a *poseur*, and this made it impossible for many people to take
his vehemence and his views seriously, to credit the claims of his critics
that he was a genuine Sinhalese bigot.

Bandaranaike often appeared to possess a dangerously puffed-up ego,
but, over the long term, other forces within him checked it from
becoming the damaging force which many feared. This produced some
surprising and, at times, incongruous results. He had, for example, a great
need for popular acclaim and was at his happiest and least lonely when he
captured and held crowds with his rhetoric. This was, in the words of an
aide, 'like a drug to him',[18] but he consistently regarded the cult of

---

[16] M. A. de Silva, *The Thought of S. W. R. D. Bandaranaike* (Nugegoda, n.d.), p. 27.
[17] S. W. R. D. Bandaranaike, *Towards a New Era* (Colombo, 1961), p. 197.
[18] Interview with a close Bandaranaike aide of the 1950s, Colombo, 1 September 1980.

personality as unseemly. He would almost certainly have disapproved of the cult which was developed after his death to bolster the political fortunes of his widow who had never enjoyed much influence while he had lived. He also understood the need for impersonal and non-partisan political institutions. It would never have occurred to him to elevate himself above the state and the nation in the manner of Nkrumah who allowed himself to be described as 'the source of its [Ghana's] honor'. Nor would he have tried to smother public debate as Nkrumah did when he said: 'All Africans know that I represent Africa and that I speak in her name. Therefore no African can have an opinion that differs from mine . . .'[19] And although Bandaranaike appeared so often to be the egotistical opportunist and self-aggrandizer in the pursuit of power, when he achieved supreme power it seems almost to have bored him. His actions as Prime Minister revealed that it was not power that he had been after all those years, but status, deference, a general acceptance of his pre-eminence as legitimate. He understood this, but he must be judged largely to have failed in this mission, both because the situation which he inherited as Prime Minister had been inflamed by the bunglings of his predecessors and because of his own miscalculations. That failure opened the way to ghastly national tragedy which overtook the island in the 1980s. And yet the popular desire for reform and social justice which he helped to crystallize is also part of his legacy. It is a measure of the importance and ambiguity of Bandaranaike's role in Ceylon's modern history to say that he did more than anyone else to institutionalize these two largely contradictory themes – chauvinism and reform – as core elements of the island's politics.

---

[19] J. Lacouture, *The Demigods* (New York, 1970), p. 136.

1

YOUTH, 1899–1919

Solomon West Ridgeway Dias Bandaranaike was born on 8 January 1899 at Horagolla, the large coconut estate of his father, Sir Solomon Dias Bandaranaike.[1] He was his parents' first child and, as it turned out, their only son. Two of his names were taken from his father, but the other two were derived from those of Sir Joseph West Ridgeway, the then Governor of Ceylon and the boy's godfather – for the Bandaranaikes, in this predominantly Buddhist society, were Anglicans.

It was no ordinary thing for a Sinhalese boy to have the Governor as his godfather, but young Solomon came from no ordinary family. Thirteen years before his birth, his father had succeeded to the office of Maha Mudaliyar which *his* father had occupied before him. The person who held this post was considered the 'first Sinhalese gentleman', the principal Ceylonese aide to the British Governor.[2] The Maha Mudaliyar presided over the network of 'native headmen' which assisted in the colonial administration, operating parallel to and in concert with the British government's formal bureaucratic machinery which was manned by civil servants. Unlike the colonial bureaucracy, the headman system

---

[1] He was not knighted until 1907, but he will be described here as 'Sir Solomon' to distinguish him from 'young Solomon', his son.

[2] S. D. Bandaranaike, *Remembered Yesterdays* (London, 1929), pp. 18–19 and 109. This post was kept in the family. When Sir Solomon retired in 1927, he was succeeded by his brother-in-law.

Between the seventeenth and early nineteenth centuries (especially between 1796 and 1833) the Bandaranaikes strengthened their positions by forging marriage alliances with several other leading *Goyigama* caste families whose prominence derived from their links to the island's colonial rulers. Y. Gooneratne, *Relative Motives: A Personal Memoir of the Bandaranaike Family of Sri Lanka* (London, 1986), p. 6, and P. Peebles, 'The Ritual Status of the Sinhalese Mudaliyars', forthcoming, p. 10.

After the British conquest, they gained further power and wealth which enabled them to extend the lands under their control by securing contracts from the colonial rulers. (I am grateful to Patrick Peebles for confirming this.) They also performed very valuable services for the British in that early period, as when an ancestor of Sir Solomon, one William Adrian Dias Bandaranaike, acted as translator and arch-collaborator with the British at the time of the conquest of the previously autonomous Kandyan kingdom in central Ceylon in 1815 (Goooneratne, *Relative Merits*, pp. 10–11).

14

penetrated all the way down to the village level. By the time young Solomon was born, the formal administration had grown to the point where men in the upper echelons of the mudaliyar system had comparatively little to do. But someone in Sir Solomon's position atop the system was often asked by the British to provide information on the doings and opinions of the Ceylonese. This enabled him to exercise substantial influence over the distribution of certain kinds of official patronage, especially the twice-yearly bestowal of imperial honours among the indigenous population, an elaborate array of 'swords, medals, titles and privileges'. These symbols of status had come increasingly to serve as substitutes among the mudaliyars for power as the headman system had yielded influence to the modern colonial bureaucracy.[3]

This reinforced in the minds of the mudaliyars an already intense preoccupation with status, and no one was more acutely preoccupied or more lavishly rewarded with trappings that bespoke supreme status than Sir Solomon. He was the recipient of an early knighthood and eventually gained admission to the Order of St Michael and St George – an exceedingly rare thing in those days (or in more recent times) for a non-Western and non-white subject in the Empire. He was an occasional guest at Buckingham Palace when in London and he took a prominent part in ceremonials during royal visits to Ceylon. In 1902, for example, when the future King George V and Queen Mary toured the island, he rode in the royal coach with them on their initial progress through the capital.[4] Those who remember Sir Solomon with sympathy speak of him as an imposing, virile figure, a stickler for protocol in the late Victorian mode, a man who always dressed for dinner when dining alone at his estate on the chance that a British visitor might drop in unexpectedly. He maintained an impressive menagerie of exotic animals for the entertainment of foreign guests. His memoirs and diaries give the impression both of a man who was bluff and jolly in a rather stuffy way, and of an enormously puffed-up ego which made him appear both ridiculous and faintly sinister.[5] Lady Daphne Moore, the wife of Ceylon's last Governor, considered him 'one of the biggest snobs I ever met'.[6]

Young Solomon's mother, whose name was Daisy, was the eldest

---

[3] The quotation and these points are from Peebles, 'The Ritual Status', p. 10. See also his *The Transformation of a Colonial Elite: The Mudaliyars of Nineteenth-Century Ceylon*, University of Chicago doctoral thesis, 1973.

[4] Bandaranaike, *Remembered Yesterdays*, pp. 89, 93 and 116.

[5] This was, for example, the impression formed by a perceptive British Foreign Office official during the late 1930s. Interview with Lord Garner, London, 28 October 1979.

[6] Lady Moore to Jan Smuts, 10 April 1947, private correspondence, Jan Smuts papers, University Library, Cambridge. I am grateful to Hugh Tinker for alerting me to this source.

daughter of another member of the small super-elite at the apex of Sinhalese society. Her father, S. C. Obeyesekere (who was himself later knighted), was Sir Solomon's first cousin, but that understates the closeness of their relationship. When the cousin's father had died, Sir Solomon's father had taken him in and raised him like an elder brother to his own son. Throughout their married life, Lady Bandaranaike always began letters to her husband with the greeting, 'Dear Uncle Sol'.[7] If this suggests a certain distance between husband and wife, it is once again an understatement. Their marriage was marked by considerable mutual hostility. Lady Bandaranaike was a formidable and highly intelligent woman with an explosive temper, much given to brilliant displays of verbal abuse. She was impatient with Sir Solomon's more sluggish intellect and with his relative lack of learning. He had not even finished secondary school,[8] whereas both her father and her real uncle, J. P. Obeyesekere, were lawyers who had served in the Ceylon Legislative Council. The Obeyesekeres also possessed more lands and wealth than Sir Solomon and when, as often happened, he faced financial difficulties, he usually turned to his sister – who had married the immensely wealthy J. P. Obeyesekere – to bail him out.[9] All of this led Lady Bandaranaike to the view that her Obeyesekeres were clearly the superior side of the family. She was not timid in pointing this out to her husband and, in return, his treatment of her was cool to the point of callousness.[10] Their time together at Horagolla was filled with bitter strife. Lady Bandaranaike had little hesitation in pouring scorn upon Sir Solomon even before guests and often in coarse terms.[11] This was deeply embarrassing to him both by the standards of the highly anglicized, Edwardian atmosphere which he had created at Horagolla and by the standards of Sinhalese society in which the wife is expected to be wholly subordinate to her husband. Indeed, Lady Bandaranaike flagrantly behaved as the very opposite of the ideal wife in a great many respects.[12] The extreme and frequent conflict that ensued between his parents appears at times to have driven young Solomon into emotional isolation for his own protection.

[7] See the letters in file 12 of BP (Bandaranaike Papers).
[8] Bandaranaike, *Remembered Yesterdays*, pp. 5–6.
[9] This is well-known in the island. Interview with a close relative, Frederick Obeyesekere, Hulftsdorp, 5 September 1978.
[10] See, for example, from their later years, Sir Solomon Dias Bandaranaike Diaries, 4–8 July and 29–30 October 1939, NASL.
[11] These comments are based on interviews with numerous relatives and friends of the family in Colombo, August–September 1977.
[12] S. J. Tambiah and B. Ryan, 'Secularization of Family Values in Ceylon', *American Sociological Review*, xxii, 3 (June 1957), p. 294; M. A. Straus, 'Childhood Experience and Emotional Security in . . . Sinhalese Social Organization', *Social Forces*, xxxiii (1954–55), pp. 155–56.

The estrangement between father and mother ran deep and after Lady Bandaranaike bore the second of their two daughters, she was forced – almost certainly at Sir Solomon's insistence – to take the girls and leave the estate. Thereafter she divided her time between Colombo and their homes in the cool hill country in the island's interior, while young Solomon remained with his father at Horagolla. The break, which occurred somewhere between his eighth and eleventh years, was arguably the most brutal shock that a boy of that age could experience.[13] After it occurred he had only sporadic contact with his mother and sisters. They accompanied the menfolk to England in 1910, but father and son stayed in a separate hotel from the daughters and Lady Bandaranaike.[14] The boy would see his mother on her occasional visits to Horagolla, but these were 'mostly to slang the old man and then go away again'.[15] The pain and trauma which young Solomon surely felt over her departure was reinforced by the anguish of his mother, whose letters to her son nearly always contained long, highly charged and unmistakably genuine passages expressing affection in almost desperate terms. The correspondence with mother and sisters indicates that when they were together they delighted in their pets and jolly pranks and games, which surely made the separation harder on all of them. Sir Solomon sometimes failed to communicate with his wife for months at a time, causing her to miss weddings and other events. And although she was widely known as a big spender, he appears to have been consistently tight-fisted so that she frequently found herself and her daughters short of funds. As a result, Lady Bandaranaike was sometimes forced to appeal through young Solomon to his father, which would have placed the boy squarely in the midst of family tensions and would have reminded him how very difficult his father was to deal with.[16]

Sir Solomon's insensitivity reached proportions that almost certainly alarmed both mother and son in 1912 when Lady Bandaranaike had to ask the thirteen-year-old boy to plead with his father to arrange treatment for young Solomon's sister who was suffering severe headaches and eye trouble at a convent school.[17] The family separation became excruciating later that year when Sir Solomon announced that the boy could not join his mother and sisters for his usual Christmas visit because he wanted his

[13] This was particularly true given the idealisation of the mother which occurs in Sinhalese society. See Ryan and Tambiah, 'Secularization', pp. 293–94. For one indication of the trauma that Bandaranaike experienced as a result, see the discussion of his reaction to Poe's poem *Lenore* in chapter 2 of this book.

[14] Bandaranaike, *Remembered Yesterdays*, p. 141.

[15] Interview with a close relative of Bandaranaike, Colombo, 28 September 1977.

[16] See the family correspondence in file 7, BP.

[17] Lady Bandaranaike to S. W. R. D. Bandaranaike, 21 September 1913, file 7, BP.

son 'to see and learn how to receive the numerous people who come to pay their respects to him during Christmas . . .' Lady Bandaranaike advised young Solomon to 'tell him you don't care a bit about the old cronies . . . you must come to us straight . . . my whole heart craves for you my son'.[18] But permission to leave was not given, nor apparently was he able to join them for the New Year holiday as his mother had hoped. It appears that the result, revealed in a letter from his sister Alix on his birthday a week into January, was that 'Mother is bringing up a baby.'[19] For the rest of her life, Lady Bandaranaike took in infant orphans, mostly boys, and raised them as surrogates for her absent son. It became a tradition which Bandaranaike's sister Alix maintained until her death in 1977. The mother was deeply wounded by the separation and it left deep scars on the boy as well. It was a palpable realization of the fear of desertion which all children experience,[20] and instilled in him a profound aversion to the risks which relationships of trust and commitment entail.

Young Solomon spent much of his youth in a state of near isolation, largely cut off from sustained, intimate relationships. After banishing Lady Bandaranaike from the estate, Sir Solomon did not provide his son with the warmth and emotional sustenance which the boy needed. His official doings took him away frequently and for extended periods. Even when he was present, he was too distant and (as we shall see) ambiguous in his treatment of his son to compensate for his long absences. To make matters worse, he insisted that the boy not mix with children from the nearby villages or indeed with children of elite families from elsewhere in the island, either at school or through any other form of regular contact. This was in part a result of Sir Solomon's concern over various illnesses – some of which were serious – which troubled the boy repeatedly. But more important was the father's conviction that a son of the supreme Ceylonese family was too good to mix with others, even children of the elite. The boy had the occasional company of his cousin Charlie, who lived close at hand. But from an early age, Charlie was away most of the time at school or elsewhere with his family.[21]

It was intended that young Solomon have the companionship of a tutor, but misfortune – or, more probably, Sir Solomon's carelessness in recruiting – led to difficulties on this front. A man of dubious qualifications from the Channel Islands named Henry Young was hired to fill this role. He apparently taught the boy to read, a task that cannot

[18] Lady Bandaranaike to S. W. R. D. Bandaranaike, 7 December 1913, file 7, BP.
[19] Alix Bandaranaike to S. W. R. D. Bandaranaike, 8 January 1914, file 7, BP.
[20] See, for example, B. Bettelheim, *The Uses of Enchantment: The Meaning and Importance of Fairy Tales* (Harmondsworth, 1978), pp. 10–11, 15 and 19.
[21] Interview with Charles Seneviratne, Veyangoda, 23 September 1977.

have been difficult with so bright a pupil, although he left it until young Solomon was eight. But his main teaching skills lay in the fields of boxing and fencing, for which his student was far too small. Young's supervision of the boy was at best erratic, owing in part to his 'fondness for the bottle'. He also indulged in some bizarre pastimes. Among other things, he made 'quite a performance' of killing and butchering pigs on the kitchen table. Such doings taxed Sir Solomon's sense of propriety and Young was eventually passed on to cousin Charlie as a tutor.[22]

The isolation extended beyond the personal level to the realm of thought and belief. The boy was deprived not only of companionship and warmth but of any sustained acquaintance with a code of ideas or principles. Sir Solomon appears to have possessed little more than the rudiments of a system of beliefs, partly because his education had been cut short. He certainly lacked the imagination and the inclination to transmit such a system to his son. What he passed on to the boy – more by statuesque example than by explanation – was a code of etiquette which consisted mainly of an imitation of the manners of the Edwardian colonial service. The ideas which formed the basis for this code were undergoing serious erosion during the boy's youth, but this was probably irrelevant at this stage of his life. These ideas were set forth with so little competence that he never seems to have imbibed them.

His encounters with people outside the family in his first ten years offered no escape from this desiccated intellectual environment. The English women who served as his sisters' nannies may have given him a rudimentary introduction to Anglicanism. But his contact with them, even when they lived on the estate, was so intermittent and their departure with his mother came so soon that he can have gained little from this quarter. The boy regularly accompanied Sir Solomon to the parish church near the estate for Sunday service. But the father's insistence that his son not mix with boys of inferior status prevented him from attending Sunday school where he might have been taught in terms that a child could understand. His first tutor, Henry Young, clearly did little to enrich his intellectual life. Young had no discernible 'philosophy' and a subsequent student 'didn't even know what religion Mr. Young was'.[23]

Of course, many children spend their early years without encountering a system of beliefs, and it is unfair to expect a boy of this age to commit himself to a creed. But it is worth noting that young Solomon emerged from his first ten years thoroughly unfamiliar with the experience of being won over – however tentatively – by a coherent body of ideas. And

[22] *Ibid.*   [23] *Ibid.*

when his second tutor, who was competent to explain such things, came
on the scene in the boy's eleventh year, their relationship was too hostile
to permit such a delicate process to occur.

Young Solomon was provided with but one barren, invidious notion
which had to serve as the central 'teaching' of his youth. In his own
words, 'I was brought up with the idea of greatness and superiority to
others surrounding me and imbued with the notion of my greatness to
come.' This was summed up for him by the Latin motto, *Primus Aut
Nullus*.[24] In Sir Solomon's preoccupation with striking proper Edwardian attitudes, in his doting comments to his son, in his insistence that the
boy remain isolated from companions of lesser rank, in the constant
presence of fawning servants, in young Solomon's opulent, lonely
pastimes – shooting champagne bottles off the verandah with his English
shotgun was a favourite[25] – in all of these things the same message was
given to the boy. You are superior. Greatness awaits you. It is hardly
surprising that he came to accept so omnipresent a notion – or that part of
him did. And it occupied such a central place in his life that in adulthood
he was never able to let it go. He might modify and temper it, but it was
never far from the crux of things.

A moral and intellectual environment in which this notion could stand
unrivalled was plainly desolate. Since it offered little to engage so quick a
mind, young Solomon turned in upon himself, as he had already learned
to do in the face of solitude and parental strife. But he had too keen an
intelligence and too creative an imagination to wilt in that arid
environment. Even without an adequate tutor, he became a keen reader
with an acute sensibility for words, taking great delight in the study of a
dictionary. He turned to the romanticism of boy's adventure yarns, fairy
tales and poetry and became, in his own words, 'something of a dreamer
and had the sensitive imaginative nature of an artist'.[26] In the absence of
steady companionship, he developed the habit of concentrating upon
imaginings, melodramas in which he was the protagonist which he played
out within his own mind to the exclusion of things external – a habit that
he never fully abandoned. This is not to say that he was introspective. He
showed few signs of self-examination at any time in his life. Rather, these
daydreams offered an escape from self and from loneliness. His principal

---

[24] S. W. R. D. Bandaranaike, 'Confessions of a Schoolboy', handwritten manuscript, lot
23.25, serial 41, BP (no page numbers exist).

[25] Interviews with two relatives of Bandaranaike, Colombo, 27 August and 14 September
1977.

[26] This is from one of his short stories and refers to a character who is a thinly disguised
version of himself. S. W. R. D. Bandaranaike, 'The Mystery of the Missing Candidate',
Speeches and Writings (Colombo, 1963), p. 486.

boyhood companion's most vivid memory of those early years has young
Solomon trudging along, struggling grimly under the weight of a heavy
cushion held at arm's length over his head and reciting with great feeling
a favourite verse from a poem.[27]

> I am monarch of all I survey,
>   My right there is none to dispute,
> From the centre all round to the sea,
>   I am lord of the fowl and the brute.
> O solitude! Where are the charms
>   That sages have seen in thy face?
> Better dwell in the midst of alarms,
>   Than reign in this horrible place.[28]

In his companion's memory, the verse ends with young Solomon
collapsing in a heap, unable to stand up under the weight of the cushion.

His choice of this poem, like his unsuccessful struggle with the
cushion, had to do with strength and power. Neither this nor the ironic
character of this lyric on authority were accidental. He had become and
would remain intensely preoccupied with the element of power in human
relationships. This is hardly surprising in a boy growing up in a society so
hyper-sensitive to gradations of status and in a family in which parents
waged an open and clamourous power struggle. But his perceptions of
power and authority were distinctly ambiguous. We have seen how part
of him believed in and craved superiority and future greatness – the sort
of greatness that implied supreme status and power over others. And
after several years marked by long periods on the estate when he
encountered nothing but obliging servants, he was able to feel comfortable only when others were clearly subordinate to him, when he had
to make only minimal personal commitments to others.

And yet, as the poem suggests, he also felt uneasy about authority. He
probably sensed that the authority to which he aspired implied a certain
forfeiture of close human contact. He also knew that he did not actually
reign in that horrible place. In his relationship with his father, he held a
position of great weakness. That relationship would have been central to
his life under any circumstances, but in the absence of the rest of the
family it became even more profoundly important. Young Solomon's
authority over servants and peasants – with whom he dealt quite

---

[27] This memory was recalled repeatedly. Interview with Charles Seneviratne, Veyangoda,
23 September 1977.
[28] This is the first stanza of William Cowper's *Verses, supposed to be written by Alexander
Selkirk, during his solitary abode in the Island of Juan Fernandez*, in N. Nicholson (ed.), *A Choice
of Cowper's Verse* (London, 1975), p. 57.

haughtily[29] – was derived from and dependent upon his father's power. Sir Solomon's treatment of his son was marked by ambiguities which were reflected in the boy's equivocal attitudes to power. While doting upon his son and surrounding him with abundant material comforts, he maintained a clear distance from the boy. He offered him few gestures of personal warmth and rather brusquely 'laid down the law' to him.[30] The boy appears also to have acquired some of his mother's contempt for the ceremonials in which Sir Solomon engaged with his 'cronies', and this inclined him to look with a certain scorn upon the symbols of the colonial regime's authority which were displayed on these occasions. Young Solomon's bad manners were openly applauded and encouraged by his mother who delighted in the cheeky doings of 'my naughty darling'.[31]

The boy had seen his father use his power to harsh, destructive ends. He was almost certainly aware that villagers' cows straying onto the estate were summarily shot and that peasants – including youths – caught stealing coconuts were flogged.[32] He knew also that it was at Sir Solomon's behest that Lady Bandaranaike had been exiled from their home. The boy was not just uneasy over his father's use (or abuse) of authority, he was clearly afraid of it. There is abundant evidence in his writings, both in youth and in adulthood, that he was preoccupied with fear and indeed with terror.[33] An indication of the fear that marked his relationship to his father emerges from a curious source. The boy was an avid reader of fairy tales, and they continued to fascinate him well beyond early manhood. During a spell in hospital at Oxford in 1923, he re-read the fairy tales of his youth. Recalling this later, he wrote

There are such gorgeous fairy books, the Red, the Blue, the Crimson, and so on . . . that I had gloated over in the long past. I experienced the same thrill as before,

[29] It must be emphasized that such treatment of peasants contrasts sharply with Bandaranaike's behaviour as an adult. But two incidents from his boyhood will illustrate this point. He had taken to firearms at an early age and, on one occasion, 'as a joke' he fired an air gun at a village boy, wounding him in the throat. On another, his shotgun discharged accidentally, narrowly missing a passing villager. Both incidents left his companion (not to mention the villagers) severely shaken. But young Solomon remained unruffled by these events. Interview with the companion in question, Colombo, 12 September 1977.

[30] Interviews with two relatives of Bandaranaike, Colombo, 27 August and 14 September 1977.

[31] Letter, Lady Bandaranaike to S. W. R. D. Bandaranaike, 1 March (no year), file 7, BP.

[32] See, for example, letter, Wambeek to Sir Solomon Dias Bandaranaike, February 1920, file 16, BP.

[33] From his adult writings, see for example two short stories, 'The Horror of Mahahena' and 'The Adventure of the Soulless Man', in his *Speeches and Writings*, pp. 491–528. From his school-days, see for example this description of a visit to the ruins of Pompeii: 'I especially remember the body of a dog; it affords a study of such abject fear as one can ever hope to see in a living creature. The starting eyeballs, the hair standing on end, the ghastly snarl of intense fear, still haunt me.' (Lot 25.23, serial 14, BP.)

when the youth kissed the Fairy of the Dawn or Ball-Carrier circumvented the Bad One. And then, what cunning illustrations by Henry Ford, so satisfying to the imagination.

I often wonder what is the magic of the undying attraction of these stories . . .[34]

As Bruno Bettelheim has shown, fairy tales have a unique appeal to children because 'in a much deeper sense than any other reading material, [they] start where the child really is in his psychological and emotional being. They speak about his severe inner pressures in a way that the child unconsciously understands . . .'[35] One fairy-tale motif that appears to have had a special significance for young Solomon was that in which an ordinary person comes into conflict with a giant. 'This theme is common to all cultures in some form, since children everywhere fear and chafe under the power which adults hold over them.'[36] The tales which are cast in this motif allow the child to ease his anxiety about the threat of adults' authority because they show the person outwitting the giant and winning through to a happy ending.[37]

At the age of sixteen, young Solomon wrote an essay at school recalling 'A Day at Naples' which he had spent in the company of his father on a trip to Europe. Most of it is a well-written but largely predictable travelogue. At the close of the essay, however, he abruptly shifts into the fairy-tale motif and produces a startling image.

The last I saw of Naples was a mass of twinkling lights, having as a background, dark Vesuvius, which appeared to scowl down on the quiet city beneath, as a fierce giant might have looked, in the days of the fairies, at a child playing merrily at his feet, and quite unconscious of his mighty enemy, till a blow from the giant's iron club crushes him forever.[38]

The child in this image does not win through in the end. He is not given an opportunity to exercise his guile to outwit the giant. He does not even see his adversary, but sits innocently at his feet while 'his mighty enemy' savagely murders him. It is difficult to escape the conclusion that this is a reflection of the extremity of young Solomon's unconscious fear of his father.[39]

The boy reacted to his father and the barrenness of his early life not only with fear, but with anger. At a very early age he developed an aggressiveness which allowed him to vent his frustration. He tended, in

[34] S. W. R. D. Bandaranaike, 'Memories of Oxford' in his *Speeches and Writings*, pp. 52–53.
[35] Bettelheim, *The Uses of Enchantment*, p. 6.   [36] *Ibid.*, p. 28.
[37] *Ibid.*, pp. 29–34, 183–93 and 311–13.   [38] Lot 23.25, serial 13, BP.
[39] For another less vivid example in the same vein from his boyhood writings, see the poem 'In the Grip of the Grizzly' at the Bandaranaike Museum, Colombo. See also his aversion to 'God the Father' in the discussion of his change of religion in chapter 4.

his own words, 'to contradict my elders – which, bye-the-way, was not seldom' and he developed an 'off-hand supercilious treatment of people'.[40] In behaving in this way, he was defying the ways of his father who – despite his snobbery – usually treated guests in an accommodating, good-humoured manner. The boy was imitating the abrasive, intolerant actions of his mother. In so doing, it is likely that he was identifying with her hostility towards his father and accepting her belief that Sir Solomon was to blame for her cruel separation from her son and home.

And yet young Solomon's aggressive behaviour was seldom aimed directly at his father, but rather at other adults – guests, or peasants from near the estate. There are rather complex and contradictory explanations for this which strongly suggest that the son's response to the father possessed deep ambiguities. Young Solomon responded dutifully in his face-to-face dealings with his father. One reason for this is that part of him acknowledged and depended upon Sir Solomon, both because the father's authority enabled the boy to get away with offensive behaviour and because the son genuinely craved warmth from his father,[41] so that he could not allow a clear break to occur between them. But another part of him rejected the legitimacy of the father's power for him. He felt compelled to kick against it and yet shrank from overt resistance out of fear of Sir Solomon. The expulsion of Lady Bandaranaike from the estate had graphically demonstrated the dangers that open defiance might entail. His reactions in later years to every authority figure that he encountered were marked by remarkably similar ambiguities.

On the estate, the boy restrained himself until he was out of his father's immediate presence and then mocked his father's authority and resisted surrogates to whom Sir Solomon had delegated authority. Among the characters who figured prominently in the dramas that the boy played out in his imagination, 'father' did not appear *per se*. Instead, Sir Solomon was transformed into a foppish character called 'Finton'. The name itself has a faintly comic ring to it and we may be sure that this was no accident, coming as it did from a mind with an exceptional gift for the use of language. In his occasional encounters with playmates, young Solomon used only this name to refer to his father.[42] The precise sense in which Finton was a figure of fun is important. The humour arose from his failure to justify his rather pompous pretentions to authority. This was probably derived in the first instance from his mother's open disbelief in

[40] Bandaranaike, 'Confessions of a Schoolboy'.
[41] This is clear from Bandaranaike's daydreams about his father's care for him while he was ill during his Oxford days (Bandaranaike, 'Memories') and from his consistent refusal in later years to allow a break to occur between them.
[42] Interview with a sometime youthful companion of Bandaranaike, Colombo, 17 September 1977.

Bandaranaike dressed to be received by the Governor of Ceylon.

Sir Solomon's personal authority, but it gained credence as the boy's extraordinary facility with English – the language used within the family – developed. Sir Solomon lacked both the ideas and the nimble wit to hold his own in quick repartee and he had difficulty writing.[43] The father's authority was brought further into question when young Solomon learned, at some point in his youth, that many members of the island's elite believed that the Bandaranaikes made their way in life through good connections rather than merit. When he arrived at boarding school at the age of fifteen, he announced to the head boy that he intended 'to show that I am the one Bandarranaike who has brains'.[44]

When young Solomon came to understand his father's role in the power structure of British Ceylon, which was more thoroughly collaborationist than that played by the parents of any other member of Bandaranaike's generation of Afro-Asian leaders, he quite naturally translated his inability to accept Sir Solomon's authority into a suspicion of the colonial political order. His mother's scorn for the ceremonials in which Sir Solomon engaged had already inclined the boy in that direction. Sir Solomon was fond of dressing his son in an approximation of court dress: cutaway coat, knee breeches, stockings and pumps, sporting a ceremonial sword and admiral's full dress hat. If notes scribbled by Bandaranaike several decades later are to be believed, one occasion on which he was fitted out in this fashion proved embarrassing for Sir Solomon:

When about ten years old, my father took me one day to lunch with the Governor, Sir Robert Chalmers. At lunch, the Governor (half jokingly) suggested making me a Gate Mudaliyar [a high post in the headman system]. I immediately said I did not want such a position but wished to do public work. When we returned home my father scolded me for retorting to the Governor.[45]

This may overstate things somewhat, but the recollections of two boyhood acquaintances suggest that it is not a vast exaggeration of his youthful outlook.[46] It was but a modest step from this to outright opposition to colonialism and to revulsion at his father's willingness to pander to Europeans, as when he laughingly called himself a 'muddy liar', a faintly racist and clearly insulting parody of his title as supreme 'mudaliyar'.

[43] Letter, Sir Solomon to S. W. R. D. Bandaranaike, 17 June 1908, file 7, BP.
[44] Fragment of a printed document by 'Mr Sara' (probably Saravanamuttu), the head boy, lot 23.25, serial 41, BP.
[45] Bandaranaike's own biographical notes, written for an election campaign leaflet, 9 January 1956, Bandaranaike Museum.
[46] Interviews in Colombo with Sir Senerat Gunawardena, 3 September 1978, and with another schoolmate, 19 August 1978.

Far from rendering him timid, young Solomon's fear of his father impelled him to seek to wriggle free of Sir Solomon's authority, not by outright rebellion which might have caused a clear break between them, but by indirection, by attempts to evade his father and his authority. His success at this had major implications for both his personal development and his later political career, in that it made it unnecessary for him to adopt direct rebellion as a strategy.[47] It was not pleasant for the boy to engage even in indirect resistance to his father's authority in order to evade it, but, in his own words; *'at the cost of my happiness, I preserved my personality'* (italics his).[48] The child in the fairy-tale image suffers disaster at the giant's hands. But part of young Solomon, the keen reader of fairy tales, had also comprehended what Bettelheim has described as

the message that fairy tales get across to the child in manifold form: that a struggle against severe difficulties in life is unavoidable, is an intrinsic part of human existence – but if one does not shy away, but steadfastly meets unexpected and often unjust hardships, one masters all obstacles and at the end emerges victorious.[49]

The main obstacle against which the boy mounted his campaign of resistance was his second tutor and companion, one A. C. Radford, a recent graduate of Cambridge whom Sir Solomon hired in his son's eleventh year. Their acquaintance was to last for four years.

The story can largely be told in S. W. R. D. Bandaranaike's own words, written when he was eighteen.[50] He explains first that he was raised differently from 'other, ordinary, normal boys', inasmuch as he was more accustomed to the company of adults and believed in his 'superiority to others . . . [and] my greatness to come'. Radford was

an ordinary, sane, beef-eating young Englishman. He could not or would not ever try to understand my unique case, but endeavoured to turn me into the ordinary English schoolboy of my age, which was his ideal for me. Thus he felt shocked whenever I happened to contradict my elders . . . He laughed at my dreams of greatness – 'Silly little boy' he called me – he was angered by my offhand supercilious treatment of people.[51]

Sir Solomon had delegated considerable authority to Radford, including powers to decide when the boy was 'worthy of reward'[52] and to administer discipline: 'I was often punished for these misdeeds by

---

[47] By contrast, Erik Erikson has shown that Luther's inability 'to evade his father' left him imprisoned so that he was forced to make 'rebellion the very centre of [his] self-justification', *Young Man Luther: A Study in Psychoanalysis and History* (London, 1972), p. 62. [48] Bandaranaike, 'Confessions of a Schoolboy'.

[49] Bettelheim, *The Uses of Enchantment*, p. 8.

[50] Bandaranaike, 'Confessions of a Schoolboy'. [51] *Ibid.*

[52] Radford's report on the Lent term, 1911, lot 23.24, serial 41, BP.

canings, standings-in-the-corner, impositions, etc. . . . I was asked to call Mr. Radford "Sir." The discomfort, shall I say, that it gave me at first to do so was great. For failing to say "Sir" I have received many imposts [? semi-legible] . . .'[53] Radford called him an 'Absurd, obstinate little boy' for his reluctance to call him 'Sir'. But the boy's attitude is hardly surprising since the only person whom he had ever so addressed before was the Governor of Ceylon.[54]

There ensued a long, acrimonious struggle between tutor and pupil in which the boy missed no opportunity to be rude. Even when Radford got him through the Cambridge Junior Examination – his most important achievement – young Solomon showed little appreciation. Lady Banda-ranaike had to instruct the boy to express his thanks to the tutor with a gift which she had had to buy.[55] The conflict is reflected in Radford's report to Sir Solomon at the end of the Lent term, 1912:

the work of the term has been very unsatisfactory all round . . .

it is one long struggle to get him to do as he is told . . . much valuable time wasted . . .

instead of seeing the 'why + wherefore' of his mistakes his one idea is that he is right + that books, tutors + everyone else are wrong, the result being that the same mistakes are made . . .

he knows everything before it is explained + therefore pays no attention to an explanation . . .

I hoped with time + patience things might improve, however this term they have been almost unbearable and I am beginning to think perhaps it would be better for him if you were to get someone else to teach him . . .[56]

The tutor, by acting in the role of surrogate for Sir Solomon, embodied the threat which the father posed to the boy's identity. But because he was only a surrogate, young Solomon – who by this time had become quite a tough lad – found it possible and indeed necessary to resist, in order, as he saw it, to survive as himself.

Mr Radford never realized my peculiar position and the necessity to use suitable methods in dealing with me. . . . [He] spent his time in an attempt to destroy my

---

[53] The 'mental and corporeal terror' which young Solomon experienced – the former mainly at the hands of his father, the latter mainly at the hands of Radford – was not 'associated with collective and ritual observances . . . [which] contain some inner corrective which keeps the child from facing life all by himself . . .' (Erikson, *Young Man Luther*, pp. 65–66). In other words, the manner in which these terrors were visited upon the boy conveyed to him quite vividly the message that life *was* to be faced in isolation. Such experiences intensified his difficulties in developing close, trusting personal or political relationships.   [54] Bandaranaike, 'Confessions of a Schoolboy'.

[55] Lady Bandaranaike to S. W. R. D. Bandaranaike, 5 October 1913, file 7, BP. See also, Warden Stone to S. W. R. D. Bandaranaike, 28 October 1918, file 5, BP.

[56] A. C. Radford to Sir Solomon Dias Bandaranaike, 28 March 1912, file 9, BP.

ideals, and hoist his own upon me, while I spent my time stubbornly, little boy
that I was. . . .

if I had given in then, my personality would have been lost forever. But O! the
misery I passed through! And the stamp of it remains on me yet, for it is not good
for a boy of that age to be unhappy . . . *at the cost of my happiness, I preserved my
personality.* . . .

But enough! The release came, and as I hope, it did not come too late. The War
broke out, my tutor had to offer his services to his country, I was sent to St.
Thomas' College.[57]

This experience was important to the boy's development in several
ways. Radford got his education back on the rails when it might have
suffered irreparably from further neglect. Despite the antagonism
between them, he provided companionship during four important years
in which young Solomon's difficulties in dealing with other people might
have intensified dangerously. It was also important for the boy to see
an Englishman serve as his father's employee and subordinate. In a sense,
Radford was just another of the servants, although he occupied a rather
exalted position. This enabled the boy to adopt a slightly snobbish view
of this Englishman. This helped him to smother at an early stage any
sense of racial inferiority that he might have felt and prepared him well for
his years as an Oxford student and as a politician in British-ruled Ceylon.
His time with Radford was his first sustained campaign of resistance to
what he saw as illegitimate authority. It was crucial for young Solomon's
– and Ceylon's – later development that the boy regarded this campaign
as a success. Had he succumbed, he would have looked on authority and
on himself quite differently. Victory here gave him confidence that he
could win through and it prepared him for a whole series of campaigns
later in life against what he saw as illegitimate authority. Most notable
among these were his protracted encounters with Ceylon's British rulers
and with D. S. Senanayake (the man who led the island to independence)
and his successors. In these subsequent struggles, Bandaranaike displayed
the same ambiguities which were on view in his dealings with Radford
and Sir Solomon: a dogged unwillingness to surrender coupled with a
tenacious refusal to break completely with the authority on which he was
partially dependent.

The successful encounter with Radford also whetted his competitive
appetite for life, at Ceylon's finest private secondary school. St Thomas'
College offered an escape from the banality and loneliness of life on the
estate and he looked forward to it. But his arrival at the school was not
entirely free of exasperation. Sir Solomon insisted that he live not in the

[57] Bandaranaike, 'Confessions of a Schoolboy'.

dormitory with the ordinary sons of the elite, but on his own in the house of Warden Stone. The Maha Mudaliyar's status was such that the Warden agreed, against his wishes, to this unprecedented arrangement.

Well, at the beginning of the first term, 1915, I was taken by my father to the Warden's house, luggage and all. The Warden and Mrs. Stone spoke to me very kindly, and when my father rose to go away, and was saying good-bye to me, I noticed the Warden deep in contemplation of the ceiling! I wonder whether he expected me to burst into tears or make some such disgusting exhibition of myself? On the contrary, I never felt happier in my life than at that moment, when I realised that at last I was at school and it was no dream.

When I was shown my room by Mrs. Stone, she said something to me which set me thinking. 'You must not expect' she told me, 'to be called Master Solomon or anything here by us.' 'Good Lord!' I thought to myself, 'what a prig she must be supposing me to be.'[58]

His absence from the dormitory earned him taunts from some of the boys.[59] The Warden asked the head boy to prevent others from bullying the newcomer and as a result, young Solomon was seated next to the head boy at table.[60] This discouraged overt incidents, but it intensified ill feeling against him. He would in any case have had difficulties fitting in since he was, by his own account, 'entirely unused to the ways and pursuits of other boys'.[61] His isolated and poorly supervised life on the estate had left him with some eccentric traits, among which was an aversion to frequent baths. He was soon broken of this, presumably by the Warden or his wife, but not before other boys had dubbed him 'won't-bathe-Banda'.[62] Quirks such as these and his family's status inspired most members of his form to impose a social 'boycott' upon him for several months.[63] He chafed at the isolation which his father's pretensions and poor judgement imposed upon him. 'Try as I may,' he wrote, 'there was always something that marked me out as different – and superior to those about me.'[64] He soon made another unhappy discovery. The highest prestige at St Thomas' went to those who excelled at team sports – especially cricket. Because he had grown up in isolation, he could not play it, and he was mocked for what schoolmates chose to see as

[58] *Ibid.*
[59] Interviews with two of his classmates, Colombo, 4 September 1977, and Kandy, 7 September 1977. Bandaranaike himself remarked on 'the slightly hostile feeling it aroused' (*ibid.*).
[60] Excerpt from an unnamed article by 'Mr Sara', lot 23.25, serial 41, BP.
[61] Bandaranaike, 'Confessions of a Schoolboy'.
[62] Interview with a former schoolmate, Colombo, 23 September 1978.
[63] Interview with one of the ringleaders, who later became a friend after much effort by young Solomon, Sir Senerat Gunawardena, Colombo, 16 September 1978.
[64] Bandaranaike, 'Confessions of a Schoolboy'.

cowardice because of his 'inability to face a cricket ball'.[65] All of the success which his fierce competitive determination gained him in individual endeavours – tennis, marksmanship, debate, the high jump[66] – failed to compensate in the eyes of St Thomas' society for his ineptitude at team sports. It is likely that his resentment over this fell once again upon his father.

And yet, despite young Solomon's unhappiness at his personal isolation and at his father's visions of his superiority, he could not bring himself to let go of these things. The ambiguity in his feelings towards his father – fearing his authority while depending upon it – generated a similar ambiguity in his view of his own superiority. This is apparent in his two stated ambitions upon entering the school. One side of him could look critically upon his sense of superiority and say 'Obviously I was anything but a healthy-minded boy at this stage.'[67] It was this side of him which expressed his first ambition 'to associate with the other boys, unhampered by any feeling of being different to them in any way . . . to be just one of them, bursting at last the bonds of "superiority" . . .'[68]

But the other side of him expressed 'the other ambition . . . to excel in intellect – to do greater things than anyone else had done before me . . .', to establish, in other words, his superiority. He also continued to cling to the belief in his own high destiny: 'I believed in myself; I knew I would eventually vindicate my "greatness", I knew that I had the ability to do so'.[69] The two ambitions were clearly contradictory and, although neither was abandoned, the latter prevailed over the former. He plunged fiercely into his school work, literally burning the midnight oil and throwing a tantrum in the classroom when another boy's essay was judged the best in the class.[70] His need to assert his superiority and – after the harsh experiences of youth – his inability to take the risks which close friendships entailed impaired his ability to develop the comradeship which one side of him desired. He found it impossible to form a friendship of equals with any other boy. He retreated behind an aggressive manner which was partly a superficial device to ward off others and partly a genuine manifestation of his drive for supremacy. He made cutting jokes about other students, especially those who were his intellectual rivals, offering for example, a cruel imitation of the stutter of one of his most distinguished classmates.[71] He thus never broke out of the

[65] *CDN*, 19 September 1958 and interviews with two of his schoolmates, Colombo, 4 September 1977, and Kandy, 7 September 1977.   [66] Lot 23.25, serials 7–12, BP.

[67] Bandaranaike, 'Confessions of a Schoolboy'.   [68] *Ibid*.   [69] *Ibid*.

[70] Interviews with two of his schoolmates, including the person in question, Colombo, 4 September 1977 and Kandy, 7 September 1977.

[71] Interview with the person in question, Kandy, 7 September 1977 and Colombo, 26 August 1977.

personal isolation which had always dogged him and would always do so.[72]

His notebooks from St Thomas' are those of an articulate and spirited writer with impressive analytical skills for a boy of his age. He was given to extreme, dismissive comments – a characteristic that marked his oratory in later years. In an essay on *Cymbeline*, for example, he described one character as 'an unmitigated fool' and spoke of 'the inane expression' on the face of another. But most of the time his exuberance expressed itself in good, vivid writing – sometimes too vivid for the tender sensibilities of his tutors. He was informed that references to Iachimo's attempts to seduce Imogen were 'not to be used here'.[73] He succeeded brilliantly in his work and within just over a year of his arrival his achievements had earned him a place among the leaders of the school. He remained somewhat aloof even from his friends,[74] but he had added another chapter to the success story which began with the struggle against Radford.

Three things contributed to the relentless energy with which he attacked his studies. First, after emerging unbowed from the long siege with Radford, he had confidence in the strength of his will and felt 'far maturer in mind' than the other boys. Second, he felt driven to live up to his notion of his superiority. Finally, by attaining superiority through his own labours, he was beginning to pull himself clear of the shadow of his father, and in this endeavour he had his beloved mother's strong encouragement.[75] His scholastic distinction was *achieved* superiority. It was not *ascribed* to him because he was the son of the Maha Mudaliyar. And he found this new kind of superiority all the more satisfying because it had eluded his father in *his* student days. By showing 'that I am the one Bandaranaike who has brains', he had begun to change the rules upon which his subordination to his father had been based.

He appears to have had one other important experience at St Thomas'. The evidence is not wholly conclusive, but he seems to have found it possible to accept as legitimate the authority of a superior. In the lives of most boys, this would not be a remarkable event. But for Bandaranaike it was possibly the only time in his life that he did not feel compelled to rebel against authority. (He may have had a similar experience at Oxford, but the evidence is even more incomplete.) The man who exercised this authority was Warden Stone. By all accounts he was somewhat stern but

---

[72] Interview with two of his schoolmates, Kandy, 7 September 1977 and Colombo, 26 August 1977.   [73] Quotations are from his English notebook, file 17, BP.
[74] Letter from (name illegible) to S. W. R. D. Bandaranaike, 12 January 1916, file 5, BP; and interviews with three schoolmates, Colombo, August 1977.
[75] Letter, Lady Bandaranaike to S. W. R. D. Bandaranaike, 14 July (no year) and 7 May (no year), file 7, BP.

gentle, a reserved man, a fine teacher of Greek who was quite perceptive in dealing with boys. As young Solomon wrote, one advantage of living with the Warden was that:

> I was unhampered by the rules to which boarders had to adhere and was free to work whenever I pleased. The Warden, however, told me not to work later than 10.30 P.M. I used to sit up later when I had much work to do, but one day I fell asleep in my chair and woke up about 12 P.M. . . .
>
> . . . This happened during my first term, and being fresh from the Radford regime, I expected harsh treatment. Next day Warden casually mentioned to me, 'Bye the way, Bandaranaike, your light was up very late last night.' 'I tried to get through some work, Sir', I replied, 'but fell asleep in my chair.'
>
> 'Now you see for yourself', he said, 'that you really cannot keep up later than 10.30. Even if you can, you are too sleepy to do good work.' I was agreeably surprised at this kind of treatment. It made a far greater impression on me than harshness would have done. Needless to say, never after that did I attempt to work later than 10.30.
>
> . . . Warden Stone is able to appreciate a boy's point of view. He never tries to force his ideas on a boy against his wish. He has often told me 'Stick to your own opinion.' There is no doubt that the Warden is the most respected Master in the College. I do not mean that he is a popular hero, dominating the imagination of the boys . . . The Warden is tolerant and he is human; and the boys know it and like him for it.[76]

Stone apparently saw through young Solomon's 'sharp severity', the aggressive and occasionally snobbish manner which made him appear to be an adult while still a child. He probably realized that some of it was genuine early maturity and toughness developed amid the adversity of life on the estate. But he appears to have seen that much of it was bravado to conceal wounds and emotional disabilities. He soon learned that the boy possessed a gentler sensibility, a keen 'instinct for literature' and he tried, delicately, to foster it. When the boy unburdened himself in an essay on his childhood experiences, Stone encouraged him. 'Part 1 is, if it serves its purpose, a means of relieving your mind of the close & confining influences of your boyhood. To express them vividly is the best way of escaping from them.'[77]

Stone's gentle, magnanimous and tolerant ways appear not only to have led the boy to accept the Warden's authority, but to have fixed in his mind a notion of what constituted the legitimate exercise of authority. Stone's humane manner seems to have become an ideal which Bandaranaike unconsciously carried through life. This was important both for

---

[76] Bandaranaike, 'Confessions of a Schoolboy'.
[77] Quotations are drawn from a letter, Warden Stone to S. W. R. D. Bandaranaike, 28 October 1918, file 5, BP; and *CI*, 28 February 1925.

his own career and for Ceylon's political development, in two ways. First, the authority of any superior who fell short of the ideal was resisted indirectly or evaded as Sir Solomon's authority had been. And, since every superior fell short of the ideal, attempts at such resistance and evasion were more or less constant. As we shall see, this made him an exasperating subordinate and hampered his contribution to collective efforts in which he was a junior partner. But it also made it almost inevitable that he would one day go it alone in politics. Second, Bandaranaike's conception of what constituted legitimate authority set too high a standard to be successfully applied in politics. It was unrealistic – indeed it was utopian – to expect a ruler, a Prime Minister, to govern in the gentle magnanimous manner of a headmaster. A developing polity facing social and economic stress was rather different from the sixth form at St Thomas'. And yet when Bandaranaike himself achieved supreme power in Ceylon, it is likely that one of the models that he sought, unconsciously, to emulate was Warden Stone. This made him an excessively generous premier and led him to political and personal disaster.[78]

However, young Solomon does not seem to have come away from his encounter with Stone with even a rudimentary commitment to any set of beliefs. The Warden was an Anglican clergyman who sought to impart no secular values other than self-reliance and a certain tolerance and, as we shall see in chapter 4, Bandaranaike was uninspired by Christianity. Thus, he seems to have emerged from his schooldays with an unimpaired capacity for turning inward and allowing the free play of his imagination to carry him wherever it might lead. Commitments to fundamental beliefs do not seem to have restrained him unduly in these internalized journeys. In later years he therefore often altered his stated views radically to gain short-term advantages. His command of language and his delight in lyricism, about which we shall hear more in chapter 2, enabled him to clothe these frequent changes in eloquent expressions of well-nigh utopian idealism. But it left many onlookers with the impression that he was basically an opportunist with a utopian turn of mind.

As early as 1916, Warden Stone thought it best for young Solomon to get away from Ceylon and the burdens of family and status. The boy was tough enough and bright enough to cope with university studies after a further six months' preparation at a school in England.[79] But the dangers

[78] It should be said that it is possible to place a different interpretation on the document 'Confessions of a Schoolboy' in which Bandaranaike expresses his admiration for Stone. He wrote it knowing that Stone would read it and it is possible that he is less than sincere in what he says and is seeking to curry favour. But, on balance, I am inclined to accept most of the sentiments there as genuine.

[79] Letter, Warden Stone to S. W. R. D. Bandaranaike, 15 May 1916, file 5, BP.

of wartime travel and the severe shortage of berths on ships forced him to remain in Ceylon for three more years. He completed his studies at St Thomas' and spent a further year living with his mother in Colombo and reading classics under Stone's tutelage. Then in the autumn of 1919, he was finally able to travel to England to take his place at Oxford. There he would once again face intense loneliness in his private life and would seek escape and compensation in a strenuous struggle for public achievement and for a renewal of his belief in – as he himself put it – his superiority and destiny.

2

SCHOLAR, 1919–1925

In 1919, the number of students who went from Ceylon to Britain's ancient universities was still quite small. Simply to have been at Oxford or Cambridge conferred enormous status on young Ceylonese so that, for most of them, glittering successes there were unnecessary. Bandaranaike, however, was not just any young Ceylonese. He did not, for example, attend just any Oxford college. Sir Solomon's intense preoccupation with status had surfaced a full decade before his son arrived to begin his studies, when he had entered the boy's name at Christ Church, one of the more venerable of Oxford's colleges. The son had acquired his father's acute concern with status, but he sought it more by achievement than by family background or by association with a posh college. He approached Oxford, as he approached everything in his life, with a powerful need to establish his own supremacy. Simply being there was not nearly enough. For his reputation among the folks back home and – more crucially – for his own satisfaction, Oxford had to provide some sort of triumph. In a memoir of his Oxford years, written in the early 1930s, Bandaranaike recalled his childhood reading of adventure books like *Tom Brown at Oxford*, which 'made a profound impression on my boyish imagination'.

I still smile when I think of all the wonderful things I decided I was going to do at the 'Varsity: the heroic leadership of the undergrads in a 'town and gown' fight, the winning of a first in classics and the easy achievement of a 'blue', the endurance with a courageous smile of the dark rites which caused such terror to Verdant Green, and, lastly, the dazzling of the Union by the brilliance of my oratory. Beautifully tinted bubbles in the air![1]

For an Asian student in the Oxford of 1919 – facing racial prejudice and the superior preparation of his fellow students – the achievement of any sort of triumph was a very tall order. It was to be testing time for him.

Bandaranaike reached England in the early autumn of 1919. On October 8, a 'damp and dreary' day, he took the train to Oxford and called

[1] S. W. R. D. Bandaranaike, 'Memories of Oxford' in his *Speeches and Writings* (Colombo, 1963), pp. 3–4.

upon one of the senior dons at Christ Church. When the latter heard that Bandaranaike intended to study classics, he tried to dissuade him since students who did not have English public school preparation usually fared badly in this field. Bandaranaike was determined, however, and his choice was provisionally accepted.[2] He then 'marched gallantly into Hall (though very nervous) and took my seat with the other Freshers. The unfortunate officials had a deal of trouble over my name . . .'[3]

Bandaranaike was disappointed to learn that the shortage of rooms at Christ Church had forced the college to find him lodgings in a private home two miles away. The family with which he stayed soon showed him that not all English people were 'strong, silent . . . cold and reserved . . . It may be true of the public school man, but the working classes possess . . . what may be called the "cockney" temperament, which is not restricted to London.'[4] His landlord was 'equable, good-natured and essentially sane' and his landlady 'kind hearted – though fussy'. She brought him delicious breakfasts and stood by as he ate them, talking incoherently, often about her 'floating kidney'. If the people were pleasant, the room was not. It was a 'horror . . . Drab, dreary and smug . . . [with a] dingy curtain – it nearly drove me mad'.[5] He quickly wrote to his father asking for a painting of Horagolla, a deer head and deer, leopard and python skins to spruce it up.[6]

I had to escape from it that first lonely evening, and I thought I would go to our College J.C.R. [Junior Common Room] for tea. I opened the door rather diffidently and walked in. A cheerful fire was blazing in the grate, and a crowd of young men were talking and laughing loudly in a fog of tobacco smoke. I hastily picked up an illustrated paper, crept into a corner seat, and ordered tea. Suddenly there burst into the room a thin tall youth with a pale aristocratic face, in light grey flannel trousers and a salmon pink tie. They all mobbed him, shaking him by the hand and patting him on the back, amid a shower of greetings and banter. How I envied him as I timidly peeped at the scene over the edge of my illustrated paper! How sadly I wondered, in the already dissolving dreams of my boyhood, whether I would ever be greeted like that myself![7]

It was the beginning of a long siege that would test him more severely than his encounter with his tutor, Radford. Bandaranaike's own account of it is worth quoting at length.

[2] Letters, S. W. R. D. Bandaranaike to Sir Solomon Dias Bandaranaike, 11 October 1919 to 3 August 1920, private correspondence file, BP; and Bandaranaike, 'Memories', p. 5.
[3] Letter, S. W. R. D. Bandaranaike to Sir Solomon Dias Bandaranaike, 10 October 1919, private correspondence file, BP.   [4] *CI*, 8 July 1925.
[5] Bandaranaike, 'Memories', pp. 6–7.
[6] Letter, S. W. R. D. Bandaranaike to Sir Solomon Dias Bandaranaike, 10 October 1919, private correspondence file, BP.   [7] Bandaranaike, 'Memories', pp. 7–8.

My first year at Oxford, once the novelty of things had worn off and I had settled
down to College routine, I recollect as a period of disappointment and frustration.
In all directions I found myself opposed by barriers, which, though invisible and
impalpable, were none the less very real. I wrote a story for our College magazine,
the 'Cardinal's Hat', which was politely returned. To get even a trial for one of the
Christ Church tennis teams was apparently an impossibility; a few half-hearted
efforts to catch the President's eye at Union debates proved futile. But the most
humiliating disappointments were reserved for the social sphere. With positive
rudeness and brutal frankness one might be able to deal more or less effectively;
bounders and snobs can be suitably handled. But the tragedy of it was that the vast
majority of my fellow undergraduates did not behave in the former manner and
were certainly not the latter. The trouble was far more subtle and deepseated: in a
variety of ways one was always being shown, politely but unmistakably, that one
was simply not wanted. It is terribly wounding, after laboriously patching up an
acquaintanceship with one's neighbour at dinner in Hall or at lectures, to be
passed by him in the street as though he had never seen one, or, still worse, to see
him hurry off with a hasty nod through fear that he might have to walk with one
along the street, or again to notice the embarrassed manner in which an urgent
engagement is pleaded whenever an invitation to lunch or tea is extended . . .[8]

This ordeal was partly the result of racial prejudice which was stronger
in Christ Church – one of Oxford's 'snootiest' colleges – than elsewhere,[9]
and partly of the natural reserve of his fellow students. But whatever its
cause, it seemed – like the earlier spell with Radford – to be a struggle 'to
survive' as himself, to keep his faith in his destiny intact. He responded to
this trial as he had to Radford.[10]

I must honestly confess that what chiefly saved me . . . was my conceit! Although
at the Union I never seemed able to catch the eye of the President, I knew that I
could make a much better speech than most of those who were given preference
over me; I knew that there were many members of the tennis team I could beat if I
were only given the chance; I knew I could write better Greek prose than many of
the scholars, with their long, rustling gowns, who looked so superciliously at the
'darkie' who had the temerity to read for the Honour School of Classics. I felt that
I had only to be patient, and keep on trying, and sooner or later I would succeed.
I also realised that within the cold, outer Oxford of mere routine there was a
wonderful inner Oxford, into which it was well worth travailing to win an entry.
But how?[11]

The answer did not readily present itself and in the months that
followed, the battering that Bandaranaike's ego took gave rise to at least
one rather striking occurrence. Listen carefully to the tone in which the
story is told.

[8] *Ibid.*, p. 9.   [9] Interview with Malcolm MacDonald, London, 9 April 1977.
[10] Bandaranaike, 'Memories', p. 10.   [11] *Ibid.*, p. 10.

While returning to my lodgings one evening, more than usually bitter at some disappointment, I passed a beggar on the pavement; he was not an unusual type, old, with a sickly-white face, thread-bare, patched clothes and gaping boots. He held a few boxes of matches in his hand for sale. In the usual, whining voice he begged for a penny; he said that he was very hungry. There was nothing strange in all this, and ordinarily I would have tossed him a penny and walked on, but I was in a black mood that day. This old man now, he was probably a humbug like the rest of them, trying to gain my sympathy by a pretence of hunger when what he really wanted was probably to go to the nearest pub. I stood and contemplated him for a moment, and then as the whim entered my mind, 'I won't give you money', I said. 'If you are hungry, come with me and I shall give you something to eat.' . . . Reluctantly he came. I seated him before a roaring fire in my room and, quelling with a stern eye any incipient desire to raise questions on the part of a bewildered landlady, ordered tea and bread and butter and crumpets – lots of them.

He was obviously hungry; he consumed enormous quantities with a grim concentration. The sight fascinated me: I had never seen such stark hunger in a human being before. Gradually, with the warmth of the fire and the warmth inside him, he relaxed and became loquacious. Probably a good deal of what he said was false, but there was clearly a thread of truth that ran through his tale – the unceasing struggle from his youngest days against hunger, against cold, against illness and despair; never had fate given him anything like a chance, and yet he was cheery enough. My petty worries faded before this elemental fight for existence. Finally, hat in hand, the old man shambled off, leaving in my room a dank and musty smell, but in my heart a new strength and a new hope.[12]

There was little warmth or compassion in this action, or for that matter in the telling of the tale. There is an aloofness, a crisp clinical quality in Bandaranaike's description of the man and of his own actions that is slightly chilling. He acts on a 'whim', as a result of his own bitterness rather than of the beggar's need, and his offer of food is less a gesture of generosity than a manipulative act. Even when the man turns out to be genuinely ravenous, Bandaranaike sat 'fascinated', rather like a laboratory technician observing an experiment. This 'stark hunger in a human being' engages his interest more than his sympathy, his intellect more than his heart. He appears to gain new strength from this experience partly because his own sufferings seem small by comparison, but mainly because he has managed to put himself in a position of superiority, as benefactor to a white man. It is not clear whether he particularly enjoyed the act of giving. His main purpose in offering food was to assuage his own need rather than the old man's. Bandaranaike was not always like this in those days. His university acquaintances tend to remember him as 'lively, stressing his own ego, perhaps defensively, self-centred but most kind', with 'a loneliness of spirit'.[13] And there is no doubting the deep wounds that he suffered from fellow-students. But this incident suggests that when his ego was bruised, Bandaranaike could be aggressively, even dangerously self-indulgent.

Vacations during the first year at Oxford brought him little respite from his depressing situation. His father had travelled to England at about the same time he had, and Sir Solomon remained in London for nearly a year. Bandaranaike spent Christmas with his father, but this appears not to have been a happy experience since on several later occasions he sought to avoid Sir Solomon.[14] In part, this was surely because he felt uncomfortable and bored with his father. But this was aggravated by the presence in London of his sister Anna. She was presented as a debutante at Buckingham Palace in 1920, but was being treated for an eye ailment that was probably the result of the severe emotional illness which later overtook her completely.[15] Bandaranaike tended therefore to spend his vacations alone, mainly studying classics, either in Oxford or at seaside hotels.[16] He was at least fortunate in never being short of funds to move about.

Near the end of his first academic year at Oxford, his father and a few other relatives visiting England came up for the day from London. He arranged a lunch for them to which he invited three student acquaintances. They were all young men of impeccable social background – one was heir to an earldom – which surely impressed Sir Solomon.[17] Indeed, impressing him seems to have been the main purpose of the occasion. One of those present clearly recollects Bandaranaike 'showing off during the lunch, talking "clever" so to speak, and at the end saying words to the effect that that was an example of Oxford talk'.[18] Now Sir Solomon had on many famous occasions entertained British guests, including aristocrats. But talking 'clever' was never his strong suit, and Oxford talk was quite beyond him. So although Bandaranaike intended this lunch to please his father – and it no doubt did – he was also sending him a clear signal that he could operate with apparent aplomb in the idiom of

[13] These phrases, from a letter to the author by Sir Godfrey Nicholson, 1 April 1977, are typical of remarks by over a dozen of Bandaranaike's Oxford contemporaries which were made in conversation with the author.

[14] Letters, S. W. R. D. Bandaranaike to Sir Solomon Dias Bandaranaike, 28 November 1919, 2 and 27 March, 18 May and 10 July 1920, private correspondence file, BP.

[15] Letters, Lady Bandaranaike to Sir Solomon Dias Bandaranaike, 23 February 1920, file 12, BP; and S. D. Bandaranaike, *Remembered Yesterdays* (London, 1929), p. 203.

[16] Letters, S. W. R. D. Bandaranaike to Sir Solomon Dias Bandaranaike, 27 March, 7 April, 5 and 10 June and 3 August 1920, private correspondence file, BP.

[17] Letter, S. W. R. D. Bandaranaike to Sir Solomon Dias Bandaranaike, 18 May 1929, private correspondence file, BP; and Bandaranaike, *Remembered Yesterdays*, p. 238.

[18] Letter, Sir Godfrey Nicholson to the author, 1 April 1977.

Ceylon's (and, ultimately, Sir Solomon's) masters. To Bandaranaike's student guests at the lunch, his display of the Oxford manner seemed artificial and embarrassing. Some of Bandaranaike's Ceylonese contemporaries at Oxford recall similar behaviour. One has said that he was 'the only Sinhalese to wear a bowler hat'.[19] But as we shall see, this tended to be truer of his earlier than of his later years there. He became more restrained as he found ways to establish himself.

At about this time a well-intentioned English student in Christ Church organized a tea party for him and several Indian students to help to ease what Bandaranaike himself described as their 'pathetic and lonely state'.[20] He later recalled:

> Of easy conversation there was none . . . The whole thing was ghastly. I found myself gradually becoming more and more angry with my fellow-guests as well as our host. I saved myself from doing something desperate by making a hasty excuse and running away . . . I went for a long walk, down the High, over Magdalen Bridge and looked at the typically English scene, touched by the mellow light of the evening sun, the river winding into the distance through soft meadows, carpeted with a velvety green, the rich splashes of colour of Magdalen gardens . . . suddenly the solution of my problem flashed into my mind: 'Before I am their equal I must first be their superior.'[21]

This 'new-found philosophy', this 'fundamental truth'[22] – in which Bandaranaike's acute preoccupation with status and power in personal relationships is again evident – was an accurate, understandable assessment of the Oxford of 1920. Achieving it was more difficult.

Before long, his circumstances improved somewhat. He was allotted a spacious set of rooms in Christ Church, on which 'an up-to-date firm of furnishers soon worked wonders'. His near neighbour, a certain Captain Anthony Eden, was soon a passing acquaintance and two fellow classics students were on the same staircase. As he began his second year, it was to the classics examinations, five months away, that he turned his attention. He had found his tutor's warning about the superior preparation of English public school boys to be true, so that he had to work extremely hard to hold his own among them.[23] But now that he was no longer assailed by the extremes of loneliness, he 'thoroughly enjoyed' the grind. This was the first step in his campaign to establish his superiority and he was 'determined to make a desperate bid for a first class'. His tutor was encouraging, thinking him the Christ Church classicist most likely to get a first. In the event 'I obtained a good second, but was not too

[19] Interview, Colombo, 2 August 1977.   [20] Bandaranaike, 'Memories', p. 14.
[21] *Ibid.*, pp. 16–17.   [22] *Ibid.*, p. 18.
[23] Interview with R. St. L. P. Deraniyagala, Colombo, 25 August 1977.

disappointed . . .'[24] Nor should he have been. For a student from Asia, even with Warden Stone's tutoring, it was a very strong showing.

Bandaranaike's tutor wanted him to continue with a strenuous academic load, but he demurred. 'I had had enough of working hard . . . and was determined, for the rest of my Oxford career, to do just enough to get through the remaining exams, and no more. I wished to sample other sides of Oxford life.'[25]

He decided to study law 'which I felt, without any disparagement of that noble branch of learning, was not likely to cause too great a strain on my time or energy'.[26] He may also have been attracted by the reputation of the Christ Church law tutor who, in the words of a colleague, was 'a supremely idle man'. In greeting new students, he would 'vehemently recommend that they should read some other school; those who persisted were sent away and told to "browse generally in the field of law"'.[27] As Bandaranaike put it, he 'liked to take things easy; so, for a time, did I. We got on together fairly smoothly.'[28]

With a small circle of friends established in Christ Church, Bandaranaike now found life enjoyable. His account of an average day in this period is interesting both for the moment of characteristic grandiloquence that it contains and because it shows how serious he was about taking things easy. It began with a breakfast of heroic proportions, to which guests often came:

porridge, followed by fish of some kind, an omelette, liver and bacon or devilled kidneys, which with plenty of toast and Oxford marmalade, washed down by well brewed coffee, would launch us for the day. Then I might saunter in for a lecture or two . . . That over, some refreshment was needed before lunch, and a few of us would wander off to the Cadena Cafe and nibble a piece of chocolate, and sip some coffee, while lazily admiring the pretty waitresses. A light lunch – something cold – in my rooms, and then a change into flannels, and off for tennis. Christ Church meadow, where we played, is situated about a quarter of a mile from College, and is reached by crossing a ferry over the river. It was a pleasant place, carpeted with soft grass and sprinkled with little white and yellow flowers. As I lay stretched on the grass, in between my matches, my muscles relaxed, and drowzily watched a few whisps of fleecy cloud chasing each other in the blue sky, the while a gentle breeze fanned me, I thought, with an idle wonder, of the life I had been leading only a few months earlier, sitting cramped at my table in a stuffy room for many hours every day, poring over my books. Healthily bronzed by the sun, my chest broadened and the slight stoop I had acquired gone, my starved muscles rippling under the soft skin, I left, in the place of the austere exaltation of the student, the pleasant sensuous contentment and physical well-being of a young faun stretched

[24] Bandaranaike, 'Memories', pp. 18–21.   [25] *Ibid*., p. 22.   [26] *Ibid*., p. 22.
[27] J. C. Masterman, *On the Chariot Wheel* (London, 1975), p. 119.
[28] Bandaranaike, 'Memories', p. 22.

in some Grecian glade. Then an enormous tea in our pavilion, some more tennis, and back to College for a shower-bath and dinner. After dinner, an hour or so smoking a pipe and chatting in the J.C.R., and then to bed. This programme might be varied, on a slack day, by drowsing on the river in a punt or a canoe, or reading a novel or playing billiards at the Union.[29]

He had come to Oxford with three ambitions: to obtain first class marks in classics, to play tennis for his college team and to be President of the Union.[30] He had come close enough to the first to be satisfied, but even though he had been tennis champion of his school, the second turned out to be beyond him. Thus in the autumn of 1921, his third year, he turned his attention to the university debating society, the Oxford Union. He had previously attended a few of the weekly debates, but had found it impossible to gain the floor. On 17 November, the motion for discussion was 'That the parliamentary system does not answer the needs of democracy.'[31] Bandaranaike was determined to have his say.

I tried many times to catch the President's eye, but without success, until, in desperation, I sent up a note to him, asking whether he would give me a chance of speaking. After a few minutes he sent it back with the words 'print your name'. This I did, and returned it. Late in the night, shortly before the debate closed, he nodded to me, and I walked up to the despatch box tremblingly. I spoke for about fifteen minutes.[32]

It was nothing less than the best speech of the night and was reported as such in *Isis*, a student magazine. Bandaranaike was stunned at this turn of events, worthy of the boy's adventure books of his youth. 'The inner portals of Oxford, at which I had been fumbling so long, were at last open to me.'[33]

The portals opened slowly, but steadily. A fortnight after his first speech, he was asked by the Union's President to act as a teller in a debate in which he once again spoke impressively. The following week he was invited to give one of the four main speeches on the government's Egyptian policy, which as he rightly says, 'was well received'.[34] He appeared twice more as a featured speaker in February 1922. On the second of those occasions, he defended liberal policies towards India against a hard-line conservative attack in 'One of the finest debates since the war' and again he shone. The opening conservative speaker performed badly. The resulting gloom that 'weighed as a pall over the

[29] *Ibid.*, p. 24.
[30] From a speech to the boys at St Thomas's College, *CI*, 8 July 1925.
[31] Bandaranaike, 'Memories', pp. 25 and 27; and Oxford Union Society, 'Rough Minute Book, 1919–1925' (hereafter 'Rough Minute Book'), 17 November 1921.
[32] Bandaranaike, 'Memories', p. 27.
[34] *Ibid.*, pp. 31 and 33; and 'Rough Minute Book', 1 December 1921.

House was ruthlessly swept away' by Bandaranaike in a speech that was 'extremely fluent, able, and moving'.[35] He was gradually becoming an established figure in the Union and he continued to impress with 'his vigorous thinking and his animated, insistent delivery' during the remainder of the academic year.[36]

It was not just his oratorical skill that his audience found remarkable. Before him, Asian students in the Union had spoken only in debates on India. Bandaranaike happily tackled issues such as the League of Nations, the Russo-German treaty, parliamentary democracy and Victorianism. He did so with enough good humour to become 'popular among the members' and to reassure conservative members that he did not take the vaguely liberal views which he usually expressed with undue seriousness. One of his contemporaries has even claimed that Bandaranaike began his Union career as something of a rightist.[37] The accounts of the debates do not support this recollection, but it is true that he did not hold rigorously to any particular viewpoint. If by the end of his career in the Union, he tended call himself a liberal who believed 'that Socialism is at present impossible to practise'[38] it had less to do with political conviction than the fact that a majority of Union members – from whom he sought election to office – were liberals.[39] As Bandaranaike himself wrote: 'I steadfastly refused to join any party at Oxford; I was not concerned with any particular English party, I simply called myself a Nationalist.'[40] Whatever the setting, being simply a 'Nationalist' always leaves a great many questions unanswered. Being a Ceylonese or – since Ceylon never arose in Union debates – an Indian or Asian nationalist left every question unanswered except on those rare occasions when the eastern Empire was discussed. Bandaranaike was apparently quite untroubled by the vague, incomplete nature of his thinking at a stage in life when many students are busy erecting codes and ideologies for themselves. His aversion to entanglements with systems of ideas, which first surfaced here, was to survive more than three decades in public life, despite much talk of fierce commitment.

Bandaranaike's successes at the Union, which continued during the autumn of 1922, were 'partly due to the great trouble I took' in preparing

[35] 'Rough Minute Book', 8 February 1922; *Oxford Magazine*, 2 March 1922; and *Isis*, 1 March 1922.

[36] *Oxford Magazine*, 4 May 1922; and 'Rough Minute Book', 4 and 18 May 1922.

[37] C. Hollis, *The Oxford Union* (London, 1965), pp. 168–69.

[38] *The Cherwell*, 14 June 1924. See also, *Morning Post*, 10 June 1924 and *Isis*, 11 June 1924.

[39] Interview with Lord Gardiner, London, 12 February 1979; and E. Waugh, *A Little Learning* (London, 1983), pp. 182–83. See also, on Bandaranaike's positions in Union debates, 'Rough Minute Book', 17 November 1921, 8 February, 4 and 18 May 1922; Hollis, *The Oxford Union*, pp. 168–69; and C. Hollis, *Oxford in the Twenties: Recollections of Five Friends* (London, 1976), p. 49. [40] Bandaranaike, 'Memories', p. 29.

speeches, now that he was free of a heavy load in his formal studies: 'many other speakers were, no doubt, quite as good or better than myself. But it did not mean to them quite all that it meant to me, and they probably did not care to take the infinite pains that I took.'[41] This soon brought him the status that he so keenly craved.

a new world had opened to me. Gone were the days when I wandered with shame about the dark and dingy outer halls of Oxford. I had gained entrance to the richest inner chambers of 'Varsity life . . . It was a new and not altogether displeasing experience for me to walk about the streets, while undergrads nudged each other and pointed me out, 'That is so-and-so.' Young men no longer hesitated to greet me and walk along with me, who would have avoided me furtively before. What snobs the majority of Englishmen really are! In an extremely gentlemanly way, of course.[42]

November brought a debate on the proposition 'The indefinite continuance of British sovereignty in India is a violation of British political ideals,' and in supporting this, Bandaranaike made 'the best speech I ever delivered at Oxford'. This was not easy since many present were opposed to the motion or were apathetic.

My first task, therefore, was to kindle a real interest in the subject. I started by cracking a few jokes, making a few biting remarks at the expense of the opposition. Members began to sit up in their seats and take notice. Now that I held their attention, it was time to give them some more solid food. I proceeded to develop my argument. Soon the House hung breathless on my words; there was dead silence among the audience, which was too absorbed even to applaud. I was conscious of such power over my fellow-men as I had never known before. For a few moments I was master of the bodies and souls of the majority of my listeners. I unrolled the scroll of British history, tracing the trend of British political ideals, as they appeared to me, mounting steadily to the crest of my peroration, in which, with a lingering memory of Walter Pater, I compared the British love of freedom to the pictures of the Italian Renaissance 'where you find a thread of golden light pervading the whole work; it is in the air, it dances in the eyes of men and women, it flickers in their hair, and is woven into the very texture of their flesh. And the thread of golden light which illumines for ever the life of this people is their love of freedom and free institutions . . .'. Not a sound was heard in that vast hall as I ceased, picked up my notes, and walked back to my seat. Then a storm of applause broke out, which refused to be quelled for many minutes.[43]

The student magazines shared Bandaranaike's delight with the speech. One described it as 'a passionate appeal for freedom, tempered with wit and rhetorical skill. Its brilliance dazzled the House, which gave him a magnificent reception, which he fully merited.'[44] The supreme accolade came from the Union President, Edward Majoribanks, the pale aristocrat

[41] *Ibid.*, p. 31.   [42] *Ibid.*, p. 41.   [43] *Ibid.*, pp. 43–44.   [44] *Isis*, 8 November 1922.

whom Bandaranaike had so admired that first evening at Christ Church. In reviewing his time as President, Majoribanks told the Union that his speech 'was a *tour de force* of eloquence, and in my opinion Mr Bandaranaike is the most eloquent speaker at the Union'.[45]

This was heady stuff indeed, and it gave Bandaranaike the confidence to stand as one of three candidates for the post of Junior Librarian in December 1922. He came a poor second but was one of five men elected to the Standing Committee which managed day-to-day Union affairs. Three months later he narrowly lost the election for Junior Treasurer – 216 votes to 213 – to Gerald Gardiner, a future British Lord Chancellor, but topped the poll for the Standing Committee.[46] During these months, he improved noticeably in his ability 'to unfold a large and ramified argument frequently developed in terms of high metaphor' and 'celebrated literary perorations'.[47] Even the young Evelyn Waugh – then a member of the Union and, where non-whites were concerned, the opposite of a flatterer – conceded that Bandaranaike was 'really good'.[48] In June 1923, Bandaranaike finally broke through to win the election for Union Secretary by a handsome margin from a field of six including, as a distant sixth, one E. A. St J. Waugh.[49]

This might have been the start of still greater achievements in the Union, possibly culminating in the presidency. But soon after the election, Bandaranaike was struck down with paratyphoid that kept him in bed for many weeks and prevented him from appearing at the Union during the autumn term in which he held his office. It was of course bitterly disappointing. Later, he managed to regard it as a learning experience, in which he discovered 'the vanity of all things'.

The first fortnight was miserable enough. The low fever in the morning, rising sharply towards noon, to reach its highest at day-fall; the hot pain in the stomach, the dry, parched lips, and the throbbing, aching head; the darkened room, the smell of disinfectants, the hushed voices of the nurses – all helped to weave a pall of black depression about me that made me feel very near the banks of the dark stream. I wondered, in my clearer moments, what my attitude to death really was. I decided that it had no fears for me, though for my parents, for my friends, for the work I would have to leave undone, I felt a regret. But deep within myself, for myself, I had no grief; nor had I joy, only a profound, impersonal tranquillity.[50]

45 Bandaranaike, 'Memories', p. 44.
46 'Rough Minute Book', 7 December 1922 and 15 March 1923.
47 *Oxford Magazine*, 15 February 1923 and *Isis*, 30 May 1923.
48 M. Davie (ed.), *The Diaries of Evelyn Waugh* (London, 1976), p. 151.
49 'Rough Minute Book', 14 June 1923. Bandaranaike regarded Waugh 'as an undersized, red-faced, rather irresponsible youth'. Their principal encounter appears to have been a skirmish over Waugh's unpaid Union dues which Bandaranaike was charged to collect. The dues were paid. Bandaranaike, 'Memories', pp. 50–51.
50 Bandaranaike, 'Memories', p. 51.

There also emerged during this illness a tendency which Bandaranaike had displayed during earlier encounters with depression and stress and which arose again in later years. He came very near to a state of melancholia, dwelling with fascination on images of horror, terror and death. Recall the story of the murderous giant in his account of that boyhood visit to Naples in the company of his father, just before facing surgery in London. The theme also emerged in his discussion of the wretched first year at Oxford which he described as 'a bad time', a 'nightmare struggle' in which he suffered from a 'mental malaise'.

I fell into a deep depression. I remember reading Edgar Alan [sic] Poe with a morbid delight; that strange mingling of melancholia, horror and beauty seemed to suit both my mood and my surroundings: for surely there was a touch of the House of Usher about that sitting room of mine . . .[51]

He was particularly gripped by Poe's 'Lenore', a poem saturated with extravagant images of death. It is 'an anthem for the queenliest dead that ever died so young' and strongly suggests that the wound the young Bandaranaike had suffered, when separated from his mother, had not yet fully healed.[52] The bout with paratyphoid provoked similar thoughts.

what strange shadows the flickering lights threw on the walls, peopling them with the giants, demons, and sprites of the fairy tales of long ago, terrible shapes, grotesque and menacing, that swayed rhythmically to the throbbing of a fevered brain.[53]

A good deal of this can be put down to Bandaranaike's cavalier way with narrative. But it also betrayed a fascination for the morbid and grotesque which ran throughout his life as an undercurrent beneath his air of aloof rationality, a fascination which – amid great stress in the last months of his life – came to the surface again.

In November 1923, still too weak to take part in Union proceedings, he stood *in absentia* for the post of Junior Treasurer. Not surprisingly after a five-month silence, he lost. By February of 1924 he was back, giving the kind of splendid performances that his audience had come to expect. In March he tried again for Junior Treasurer and this time won easily.[54] His next term was one of high visibility and impressive speaking at the end of which, in June, he sought the presidency.

Bandaranaike did not expect to win. He realized that his illness had broken the moment of his steady rise through the offices of the Union which might otherwise have left him well placed for this election. He

[51] *Ibid.*, pp. 10 and 16.
[52] C. W. Kent (ed.), *The Poems of Edgar Allen Poe* (New York, 1965), p. 53.
[53] Bandaranaike, 'Memories', p. 51.
[54] *Isis*, 27 February 1924; 'Rough Minute Book', 21 and 28 February and 13 March 1924.

knew that his main opponent, H. J. S. Wedderburn, enjoyed high social
standing – he was heir to the Earldom of Dundee – and that he was a solid
if unspectacular member of the Union who had much sympathy after an
unsuccessful attempt at the presidency. To his credit, Bandaranaike
graciously makes no mention of a further factor in the election, racial
prejudice. But one of his contemporaries has recalled that:

> there was reason to think that the word had gone out among the old life-members
> who lived around in Oxford that it would be undesirable that the Union should
> have a President who was not white, and it was rumoured that they turned up in
> some numbers and recorded against him in sufficient numbers to ensure his
> defeat.[55]

This comment probably overstates the impact of prejudiced voting
because when the ballots were counted Bandaranaike came a poor third.
Had he finished second, it might be possible to claim that racial motives
had been decisive, but they were not. Nonetheless, there was no escaping
the substantial presence of bigotry in this election. It was also true that
'Bandaranaike believed that there was such a bloc against him' and that he
was deeply hurt by this.[56] It left him sceptical, throughout his political
career, of the motives of many (though certainly not all) Britishers,
particularly of Conservatives who held office during most of the
subsequent colonial period.

He was also acutely aware that of the three candidates for the Union
presidency, he was clearly the most accomplished speaker – a fact which
the man who came second freely acknowledged.[57] Mere ability and
achievement were not enough. Although he had shown hmself their
superior, he could still not be their equal. Ascriptive attributes – those
gained by reason of birth, family, caste, race, etc. – which had so often
yielded advantages for Bandaranaike and would continue to do so, here
worked against him. This was galling and it is worth noting that it was
not the last time that it happened to him. Between 1948 and 1951,
opponents within Ceylon's ruling party thwarted his desire to be
successor-designate to the first premier, despite the poor quality of his
rivals. Once again an accident of birth – the fact that he was a
Bandaranaike – counted against him. In that period, when it seemed that
he had lost the chance to lead his country, the unhappy memory of the
Union presidency must have come readily to mind.

---

[55] Hollis, *The Oxford Union*, p. 169.
[56] For the quotation, see *ibid.*, p. 170. Interview with Malcolm MacDonald, London, 9
April 1977; and Waugh, *A Little Learning*, p. 184.
[57] Bandaranaike, 'Memories', p. 57.

There is something else in Bandaranaike's account of his Oxford years that deserves our attention. At first glance, a discussion of his aesthetic sensibility may seem irrelevant in a political biography, but there is plenty to learn here. Consider this sample of his writing:

It is strange, when one begins to grope in the past, to discover how certain incidents, considered important at the time, have faded from one's mind, while comparatively trivial happenings remain etched clearly and in detail. Perhaps the mind adopts an instinctive selection, and what it retains and rejects is guided by what is fundamentally important, although it may not appear so to the reason. For instance, of my voyage to England, on my way to Oxford, I remember only one little incident distinctly. After nearly two weeks on board, with the sound of the sea ever in my ears and the brine in my eyes, my nostrils, and my mouth, I landed at Port Said with some friends. As I loitered on the road while the others carried on an intensive campaign of bargaining for curios, a street-hawker thrust a bunch of fresh flowers into my hands. I took them up and buried my face in them. Oh! the softness of the petals against my cheek, and the delicate fragrance in my nostrils, the essence of Mother Earth herself. For a fleeting moment I glimpsed eternal beauty in the beauty of a flower. I saw and smelled and felt those flowers with a clarity of understanding I had never experienced before.[58]

Even before reaching Oxford, Bandaranaike had developed a keen awareness of the beauty of things – not only things in nature but in art as well, particularly in literature. This is hardly surprising given his boyhood isolation on the family estate where he was forced in upon his own lively imagination, to batten on poetry and adventure stories. At Oxford, he found ample opportunities to cultivate this side of his life and, as this passage suggests, he adopted a particular view of moments of aesthetic appreciation. This incident in Port Said seemed, years later, to be 'fundamentally important, although it may not appear so to reason'. In this moment, he obtained 'a clarity of understanding I had never experienced before' – greater clarity from the senses than when he had relied on reason. These and other remarks on his Oxford years betray quite specifically the influence of Walter Pater, the nineteenth-century critic and Oxford don whose writings Bandaranaike revered and actually read aloud in later years as entertainment.[59]

For Pater, education had less to do with honing the powers of reason or cultivating the intellect than with developing 'a certain kind of temperament, the power of being deeply moved by the presence of beautiful objects'.[60] In his view, a person felt the impact of beauty not

---

[58] *Ibid.*, p. 13. [59] Interview with J. Vijayatunga, London, 6 November 1979.
[60] W. Pater, *The Renaissance: Studies in Art and Poetry*, 6th edn (London, 1904), p. x.

when he exercised his intellect, but when he ceased to do so. Art and
literature were most fully appreciated in the way that music was
experienced, through feeling rather than thinking. Pater thus preached a
kind of elevated hedonism, urging upon his reader a life of intensity,
seeking after the experience of beauty:

A counted number of pulses only is given to us of a variegated, dramatic life. How
may we see in them all that is to be seen in them by the finest senses? How shall we
pass most swiftly from point to point, and be present always at the focus where the
greatest number of vital forces unite in their purest energy?

To burn always with this hard, gemlike flame, to maintain this ecstasy is success
in life.

. . . we may well catch at any exquisite passion, or any contribution to
knowledge that seems by a lifted horizon to set the spirit free for a moment, or any
stirring of the senses, strange dyes, strange colours, and curious odours, or work
of the artist's hands, or the face of one's friend. Not to discriminate every moment
some passionate attitude in those about us, and in the brilliancy of their gifts some
tragic dividing of forces on their ways, is, on this short day of frost and sun, to
sleep before evening. With this sense of the splendour of our experience and its
awful brevity, gathering all we are into one desperate effort to see and touch, we
shall hardly have time to make theories about the things we see and touch.[61]

These sentiments clearly touched several chords in Bandaranaike.
Pater's writing helped him to understand the moments of aesthetic
appreciation that he had experienced before coming to Oxford and they
whetted his appetite for more of the same. Pater also provided a lofty
rationale for the intense seriousness with which Bandaranaike took
himself and his feelings. He seemed to justify the self-indulgent, inward-
looking, narcissistic streak in Bandaranaike which was such an important
element in a young life that had been and would always remain lonely,
incapable of friendships on the basis of equality. Pater's aversion to
theorizing also appealed to Bandaranaike who often argued political
points in the Union not by proceeding from first philosophical principles
to his conclusion, but rather by means of 'celebrated literary perorations'
– as when he 'quoted Diodorus to prove that Socialism is at present
impossible to practice' or 'delighted the House' by depicting the League
of Nations 'as a beautiful angel beating her wings in a luminous void'.[62]

Pater also had an 'acute sense of mortality, of death as the mother of
beauty',[63] and this appealed to Bandaranaike who evoked images of death
not only in his Oxford memoir but in his schoolboy essay on Naples, long
before he had encountered Pater's work. As we have seen, Bandaranaike

---

[61] *Ibid.*, pp. 236–37.
[62] *Oxford Magazine*, 25 May 1922; *Isis*, 30 May 1923; and *The Cherwell*, 14 June 1924.
[63] D. Donoghue, *The New York Review of Books*, 14 May 1981, p. 40.

also shared Pater's sensitivity to what the latter described in his essay on Leonardo da Vinci (a Bandaranaike favourite) as 'the interfusion of the extremes of beauty and terror'.[64]

Bandaranaike took up the quest for moments of intensity. In Gilbert Murray's Greek recitations, 'one could hear the clash of the armies of heroes'. Sculpture had a similar effect. Bandaranaike found

The Aphrodite of Melos, an immortalisation in marble of a moment of exquisite beauty, and the Bacchante of Scopos, the very spirit of paganism itself. . . .

I was transported by Homer to the age of the chivalry, the loyalty, the wrath, and the love of the epic figures of the dawn of Hellenic civilisation, and by the lyrical choruses of Europides to the moonlit meadows of happy Athens; or in listening to the greatest orator of all time, Demosthenes, pleading with an undying eloquence for his life and honour, and to the rolling grandeur of Cicero's periods – these days brought a tranquil and serene happiness to me that I had never known before.[65]

For Bandaranaike, moments such as these were doubly valuable. They were intensely pleasant when they occurred, but when recounted in print or in speeches they had an impact on others and, not incidentally, cast Bandaranaike in the role of the man of refinement and lofty vision. This was useful both at Oxford and after his return to Ceylon. It was so appealing to him that he allowed lyrical imagery to intrude into areas where it did not belong. We have already noted how he sometimes used it as a substitute for argument in political debate. It went a good deal further than that. In his account of the less happy times at Oxford, he quotes from Shelley: 'Life, like a dome of many coloured glass stains the white radiance of Eternity . . .' He then tells us that the poet has hit upon 'an eternal truth', and offers this comment: 'The dome of life would never be perfect unless the grey and dark tints mingled with the bright and gay, and happy is he who has not overmuch of either. This moralizing the reader must pardon . . .'[66] The thing to notice here is neither his pedestrian use of Shelley's metaphor nor the banality of his observation, but his choice of the word 'moralizing' to describe his comment. We search in vain here for any reference to questions of right and wrong, for signs that his conscience has been consulted. Here and later in life, Bandaranaike tended to equate moralizing with grand, lyrical images or phrases which vaguely implied generalizations about life. They have little or no substance as comments on ethics. This is not to say that he never

---

[64] Pater, *The Renaissance*, p. 104. Bandaranaike's romantic fascination with the likes of Pater and Poe was probably closely linked to his excitement when performing before the Oxford Union. For a discussion of this general trend, see R. Sennett, *The Fall of Public Man* (New York, 1977), chapter 9.
[65] Bandaranaike, 'Memories', p. 19. [66] *Ibid.*, p. 9.

addressed himself to questions of right and wrong. As a politician, he was constantly called upon to denounce evils and commend the good, and his patriotism and sympathy for the disadvantaged were genuinely felt. But that is just the point. They were *felt* but not rigorously thought through. When we examine his loftiest sentiments which should have revealed the basic principles which underpinned his actions, we usually find little but lyric and rhetoric. These things generate feeling but little meaning. Bandaranaike soars away towards a utopian vision which is poetic in character and which therefore cannot provide guidance in the making of specific, day-to-day political decisions. His reference to the Garden of Hesperides, with which this book begins, was an oft-repeated example. His lyrical notions of 'moralizing' rendered his political career a journey without detailed maps.

After the initial hurt at failing to win the Union presidency had worn off, disappointment did not taint Bandaranaike's memory of his Oxford years. His accomplishments had, after all, been substantial. A strong second class mark in classics and a tolerable third class in law on the basis of very little work were admirable.[67] His reputation as arguably the best speaker of his day at the Union[68] was remarkable when we consider that his preparation consisted of precocious patter before indulgent parents at Horagolla and a brief spell as a debater at St Thomas'. His success at mastering, quickly and effectively, the alien idiom of Union debate was nothing short of extraordinary. (His inclination and talent for adapting new idioms to his own purposes formed another major theme in his political career.) Bandaranaike could therefore justifiably claim that his 'lonely struggle' at Oxford had led to 'final triumph'. He had learned once again that he could rely on his 'conceit' to bring him through adversity, a lesson grimly cherished in years to come.

He also felt confident enough to restrain his earlier tendency to adopt the trappings and style of Oxford. In a comment which again suggested that for him, relationships could entail only the positions of a superior and an inferior, he wrote that he was saved, 'from being more submissive to, and receptive of, the influence of the University; for acquiring, for instance, an Oxford manner and accent. My feeling towards Oxford was more that of a conqueror than a submissive and grateful son.'[69] This is slightly misleading. In later years, he revived the gestures and phrases of

---

[67] One examination was passed on the strength of an all-night cramming session (*ibid.*, p. 39). Also, a letter to the author from J. F. A. Mason, Librarian of Christ Church, 21 February 1977.

[68] Bandaranaike, 'Memories', p. 57 and *Oxford Magazine*, 31 May 1923.

[69] Bandaranaike, 'Memories', p. 42.

Oxford when the occasion seemed to demand it. But it is also true that having been a success at a great British university, having proven himself in some respects 'their superior', he felt far freer in later years to pick and choose among things British than did Ceylonese educated at home – including D. S. Senanayake, the most important pre-independence politician.

He hints at this in his characteristically florid description of his final day at Oxford, in which his belief that he had a (rather vague) mission in life also comes through.

I had nothing to do that last afternoon, and the spirit moved me to go out for a long walk. Down the High, past Magdalen Bridge, out into the country. Bitter-sweet memories thronged my mind as I took the self-same way that I had once treaded at a crisis that proved to be the real beginning of my Oxford career. All the details of that lonely struggle and the final triumph passed before my mind's eye. On my return, I lingered on Magdalen Bridge. The typically English scene, subdued and mellow in the evening light, faded from my eyes, and the glare and dust of my own country took its place: blue skies and dancing sunlight, with a white road winding amidst coconut groves and green paddy fields; dark, cool nights, with star bejewelled skies, alive with the cries of innumerable crickets; the pathetic, huddled village huts, the dirt, the poverty, the disease. My country, my people. Aye, it was there that my work lay, and Oxford had revealed to me my life's mission. As I thought of Oxford, there was a strange dryness in my throat, and in humbleness of heart I realised the truth that, for all the fine airs I liked to give myself about her, I too loved Oxford passing well, and was proud to acclaim myself one of her grateful sons. And Oxford was the dearer to me because she had taught me to love my own country the better.[70]

The reader might well ask how Bandaranaike could emerge with this rosy outlook from an Oxford heavily populated by veterans of the trenches. Paul Fussell has brilliantly set out the sense of disillusionment, ambiguity and bitter irony which the First World War bequeathed to modern memory.[71] Was Bandaranaike blithely drifting, in a Tom-Brown-at-Oxford daydream, through a world rendered cynical by the horrors of the western front? No, he was not. More than two dozen interviews with Oxford undergraduates of the day – both veterans and non-veterans – consistently indicate that returning soldiers were reluctant to talk or even to think about the war. Instead, there was a surge of what for many must have been a rather forced optimism, a burst of enthusiasm to build a better world.[72] Few students had yet come to terms with the tragedy that

[70] *Ibid.*, p. 59.
[71] P. Fussell, *The Great War and Modern Memory* (New York and London, 1975).
[72] In addition to interviews, see for example Hollis, *The Oxford Union*, pp. 154–55; and interview with General Sir John Glubb, BBC Radio 4, 14 March 1978.

had befallen their generation. Many sought to recapture the lost innocence of the pre-war years. The disillusionment and ironic sensibility, which Paul Fussell has depicted, crystallized – at Oxford at least – only later, after war literature had been published for some time, and had been widely read.

Bandaranaike's Oxford, then, was not a place where sneers greeted his flights of idealistic rhetoric. Nor was he the only student who arrived with boy's-adventure-book expectations. The air was thick with largely accurate anticipation that this body of young men would rule the world, or a very substantial portion of it. Bandaranaike's successes – all of which were *achieved*, in an environment where for once the attributes of birth weighed against him – confirmed his extravagant view of his future. As he wrote in the early 1930s:

I suppose, in my own small way, I am one of those unfortunate beings who are driven by destiny. In passing, I may say that I have a deep sympathy for the much harassed, but pious, Aeneas. Not for such is a life of quiet or happiness or the enjoyment of the ordinary pleasures of men. As a boy at school, as an undergraduate at Oxford, and now in the wider arena of life, I have ever been conscious of some task I had to perform, of the need for striving and effort that appears to have no end, but rather to increase in the widening circle of a ripple on the surface of a pool. But there is also a part of me that longs for ease and quiet. Sometimes I yearn with a fierce yearning for the calm content of a priest, sheltered in his cloistered temple, or the care-free happiness of some jungle-dweller with the singing of the birds about him and the blue sky above him, or even the humdrum life of the average man with its small delights and small troubles. But, alas! it cannot be.[73]

It is revealing and not at all surprising that Bandaranaike responded to the story of Aeneas, since there were several striking parallels between the classical hero and his view of himself, then and later. Aeneas' father was Priam, King of Troy at the time of the city's destruction. In other words, his father had presided over an old order which time had overtaken while the son was still a young man. Bandaranaike's exposure at Oxford to Asian nationalism[74] had strengthened his boyhood view that his father's political support for the British in Ceylon and the headman system over which he presided were anachronisms. Aeneas' mother was a goddess and

[73] Bandaranaike, 'Memories', p. 31. His use of the word 'pious' here should not be taken to imply religious piety. It is borrowed here from the frequent use in *The Aeneid* of the Latin word *pius* to describe Aeneas. This word implies devotion to one's duty, one's mission.
   Bandaranaike identified strongly with Aeneas despite his view that Virgil's Latin epic was very much 'an imitation of the Homeric tradition' and inferior to it. For him, there was 'a unique beauty in the Aeneid' that made it more compelling than Homer's great works ('Memories', p. 19).

[74] He was for a time President of the Indian students' society, the Majlis.

throughout his life he idolized her and looked to her for solace and aid. Bandaranaike's relationship to his mother was quite similar. After escaping with a band of followers from the wreckage of Troy, Aeneas faced trials and adventures for many years until he fulfilled the destiny which had been foretold and of which he had long been acutely aware. He did so by establishing a new order, a new civilization, a new Troy, by founding the city of Rome. In this Bandaranaike could see further parallels. He too would leave behind him his father's bankrupt politics and strike out with a band of followers in an effort to establish a mode of politics which was quite new but which he also saw as a revival of Lanka's ancient greatness.

When he read the story of Aeneas, he found that 'every page is touched with the tears of things, every line melodious with sadness'.[75] This is not to say, however, that he had developed an understanding of tragedy or irony. *The Aeneid* is no tragedy. It has a happy, indeed a glorious ending and it was precisely that which so appealed to Bandaranaike. He left Oxford with expectations of epic proportions, with a view of his time there and of his future that was downright melodramatic. He lacked both an awareness of the dangers of *hubris* which classical tragedy teaches and an understanding of man's capacity for destructive folly which was apparent in that more recent tragedy in the fields of France and Belgium. He left England more confident and resilient than when he had arrived, but decidedly – even dangerously – uncritical of himself.

[75] He is quoting George Gissing, 'Memories', p. 19.

3

NOVICE, 1925–1931

When Bandaranaike returned to Colombo in February 1925, he was met at the jetty by a large family throng and taken to All Saints Church for a service of thanksgiving for his safe return. A few days later he was driven to the estate at Horagolla, the last three miles in procession 'headed by a number of caparisoned elephants and attended by dancers and music'. At the boundaries of the estate, he was met by 'a mammoth crowd' gathered round 'gorgeous pandals' where he 'was received with respectful obeisances' and presented with florid and obsequious addresses by local villagers. Then, on the lawn before the great house, there followed performances by beasts from Sir Solomon's private menagerie, a school sports meet, devil dances and fireworks.[1]

All of this bespoke the father's expectation that his son would fit happily and conventionally into the most highly anglicized non-Western elite (the elephants and devil dances notwithstanding) in the British Empire. The only departure from his own career that he desired was that Bandaranaike serve within the regular departments of government rather than in the traditional headmen's hierarchy which had waned in importance. An appointment to the Attorney-General's staff had been arranged and the son was also expected to step into the quasi-feudal role of squire-to-be on the family lands.[2]

Bandaranaike soon made it plain, however, that he would accept neither these roles nor his father's authority. The first sign of this came in his response to the speeches of welcome at Horagolla. He abandoned the customary aristocratic aloofness by apologizing for not being able to address them in Sinhala and then said 'if fate has decreed for me a prominent place among you, it is not that I may be your master but that I may be your servant'.[3] Sir Solomon stiffened visibly at this remark.[4] Other surprises soon followed. Bandaranaike showed a disinclination for

[1] S. D. Bandaranaike, *Remembered Yesterdays* (London, 1929), pp. 254–55; *CI*, 24–28 February 1925; and *CDN*, 5 March 1925.
[2] Interview with R. St. L. P. Deraniyagala, Colombo, 18 September 1977.
[3] S. W. R. D. Bandaranaike, *Speeches and Writings* (Colombo, 1963), p. 83.
[4] Interview with Sir John Kotelawala, Kandawela, 9 September 1978.

Anglican worship, refused to call at Queen's House to pay his respects to the Governor and set about learning Sinhala. He declined his father's offer of a comfortable monthly allowance and supported himself from his earnings at the Bar. He settled into the family's town house in Colombo and was often seen driving the old Citroen which he had brought back from England to district courts near the capital where he nearly always appeared for the defence. He was a gifted and successful trial lawyer, but litigation was not his main interest. His real passion, on which he spent most of his spare time, was politics.

Politics? To Sir Solomon 'politics' was something that occurred in the drawing rooms and garden parties of British officialdom where patronage powers were bestowed in exchange for one's cooperation. 'Politics' to his son had another meaning or, more precisely, several different meanings, all of which were alien to Sir Solomon. As a long-term vision and ideal, 'politics' meant assisting the people of the island toward self-government. But for the present, in the tightly circumscribed world of non-official politics in Ceylon, 'politics' meant three other things. It meant making speeches in order to gain a reputation as a dynamic man on the move. It meant acquiring a modest network of followers to support a claim to an organizational base. And finally, it meant winning admission to the small circle of leaders who had been wrongfully imprisoned by the British during the riots of 1915 and had risen to pre-eminence in non-official politics during the early 1920s. The first two goals were means to this last end.

Bandaranaike's accomplishments as an orator at Oxford were well known in Ceylon before his return, indeed the Governor himself had remarked on them.[5] This generated numerous invitations for public addresses and he was happy to oblige. We find him in those early months discoursing upon such topics as 'The Choice of the Civilisation', 'Where East Meets West', 'Ceylon as a Mandate of the League of Nations' and 'Our Place in the British Empire'.[6] These talks contained occasional jibes at British imperialism, but such sentiments won little applause from the prosperous anglicized Ceylonese who came to hear him. Since he believed above all that 'One had to suit his speech to his audience,'[7] he seldom adopted this tone. Indeed, it is difficult to find any thematic consistency in these speeches. The influence of British liberalism and Indian nationalism, a guarded empathy with and criticism of Fabian socialism, and a vague, idealistic attachment to the internationalism of Woodrow Wilson – all of these crop up now and again.

[5] See, for example, *CI*, 6 December 1926.
[6] *CI*, 4 April, 1, 4 and 8 July, 25 August and 7 September 1925; *CML*, 3 July 1925; and newspaper cuttings in lot 23.25, serial 41, BP.   [7] *CI*, 8 July 1925.

But his main concern was to see that he 'held his audience spellbound'[8] and this led him into some questionable doings. On one occasion, he dragooned a friend who owed him a favour into arguing the proposition that 'Mahatma Gandhi is a menace to India' in a public debate in which Bandaranaike was to argue the case against – even though the friend was an ardent admirer of the Mahatma. Whatever their reservations about resisting British rule, the people of Colombo regarded Gandhi with enormous affection and Bandaranaike's demolition of his opponent was greeted with thunderous cheers. But to his poor friend (and a few discerning observers) 'it was too easy, almost vulgar . . . he might as well have defended motherhood'.[9] Another astute friend and aide of Bandaranaike watched these performances – which were by turns lyrical, bombastic, humorous and indignant – with mounting unease. Of his brilliance there was no doubt, but a perceptive eye could detect in his unrestrained manipulation of his hearers the suggestion of something approaching contempt for his audience.[10] This was an impression that he conveyed to shrewd onlookers throughout his life, but it was at its most extreme here, during his political noviciate.

To Sir Solomon, the annoying thing about this speechmaking was not what his son said or how he said it, but *that* he said it. In his view, it was permissible and even necessary to *appear* publicly, but to *perform* publicly implied too great a concession to ordinary folk. His distaste for this was probably intensified by the discovery that Lady Bandaranaike approved of it and was slipping quietly into the back of public meetings to hear these speeches. The son's involvement with popular politics had also intruded upon the father's comfortable personal routine. Bandaranaike's occupation, in happy bachelor frugality, of the family's Colombo house had littered the place with legal briefs, his contingent of dogs and – in Sir Solomon's view – some political associates of very dubious family and caste backgrounds. This last consideration seemed such an indignity to the old knight that he ceased overnight visits to the house. This forced him into an inconvenient hour's drive from the capital to the estate.[11]

Bandaranaike's decisions to live off his own comparatively modest income and to mix freely with men and varied castes deserve scrutiny, since they arose from attitudes which were important both in his own life and in the political and economic history of modern Ceylon. His attitude towards money and material comforts had the double-edged quality which was characteristic of so much in his life. On the one hand, he was

[8] *CML.*, 3 July 1925.
[9] Interview with the friend in question, Colombo, 22 September 1980.
[10] Interview with J. Vijayatunga, London, 10 November 1981.
[11] Interview with R. St. L. P. Deraniyagala, Colombo, 2 September 1977.

exceedingly careful about money. Examples abound, but two will suffice to illustrate the point. He was brusque and unbending in demanding payment of the full (and, for ordinary people, quite hefty) legal fees before undertaking cases – regardless of clients' circumstances. And his vigilance over his purse went to such extremes that he sometimes offended people close to him. In 1926, an aide asked if he might have a lift in Bandaranaike's car over a distance of a mile and a half. He readily agreed, but on the condition that his aide reimburse him for the fuel consumed on the journey.[12] Such behaviour is partly explained by the young man's awareness of the chronic financial problems which his father faced. Sir Solomon had a sizeable income from his lands, but this was inadequate to sustain his lavish lifestyle. He was compelled on many occasions to seek the aid of his sister, Mrs J. P. Obeyesekere, whose husband (his cousin) owned large estates near Horagolla. Sir Solomon also borrowed heavily from money-lenders in Colombo and it is possible that young Bandaranaike had to make good some of those debts.[13] In any case, his father's troubles left him with a certain meanness of spirit in matters of personal finance which at times narrowed his vision – although it did not restrain him from large, even rash, expenditure on political campaigns or from generous hand-outs to constituents once he achieved elective office.

Yet this same trait had a broadening, liberating effect upon him as well. The desolate opulence in which he had grown up had left him with an aversion to materialism. We might expect a young barrister from Christ Church to have expensive tastes, but as a matter of choice he led an almost Spartan existence. He spent so little on clothes that friends were sometimes embarrassed to see the same outfits reappearing and he ate so little that they worried about his health. He took the occasional glass of wine and spent money on books from Britain. But pipe tobacco and English sausages were the only luxuries – if that is the word for the latter – in which he regularly indulged. This lifestyle did not arise out of an effort to conquer his appetites, he was simply bored by most consumer goods and by avid consumers. Most prosperous Ceylonese fell within that category. With Bandaranaike, boredom turned easily to contempt and it was with something close to contempt that he viewed the conspicuous consumption of the *haute bourgeois* society from which he had come.

He was similarly contemptuous of the Ceylon elite's preoccupation with social status in general and caste in particular. Despite their devotion

[12] Interview with J. Vijayatunga, London, 10 November 1981.
[13] Interviews with Frederick Obeyesekere, Hulftsdorp, 27 August 1978 and R. St. L. P. Deraniyagala, Colombo, 9 September 1978.

to Buddhism, the institution of caste flourished among the Sinhalese. They did not possess a single, coherent caste hierarchy into which all major social groups were well integrated, as was found among Hindus in most regions of India. Several important caste groups in the coastal strip running north and south of Colombo appear to be late immigrants from South India who stand somewhat apart from the caste system which prevails among most Sinhalese. At least one of these, the *Karavas*, refused to acknowledge the claims to supremacy within the Sinhalese system of the *Goyigamas*. Nonetheless the *Goyigamas'* traditional status, wealth, landholdings, educational advancement and numerical strength – they represented roughly one-half of all Sinhalese[14] – ensured that their claim to pre-eminence was accepted by most Sinhalese. Among *Goyigamas* there existed marked status distinctions. A broad network of families who were linked at least distantly to one another by marriage were seen by many as the 'first-class' *Goyigamas*. Within this category, the Bandaranaike–Obeyesekere family alliance was seen by its members and by many others to stand at the pinnacle.

When in boyhood Bandaranaike had been taught that he was superior to all others, it was intended that he absorb his parents' strong sense of superiority to non-*Goyigamas*. But the isolation in which he was raised – which was itself the result of family snobbery – prevented him from developing a keen caste prejudice. His dealings were almost exclusively with Europeans and 'first-class' *Goyigamas*. Members of other castes were so seldom seen that the boy did not acquire the familiarity with distinctions of dress, diet, occupations, etc., which was essential to the cultivation of a young bigot. The main social distinction which he learned in boyhood came through contact not with other castes but with others of his own caste. It was the notion that no matter how exalted the status of other *Goyigamas*, he – the heir to the pre-eminent Ceylonese gentleman – was superior. (From this notion arose much of the subsequent conflict between Bandaranaike and other *Goyigama* politicians like D. S. Senanayake.) In the absence of knowledge of non-*Goyigamas*, this extreme snobbery became a curious kind of egalitarianism. Lower castes might not have much to recommend them, but neither did fellow-*Goyigamas*.

At St Thomas', caste was systematically de-emphasized. At meals, when caste prejudice might be expected to surface, the only distinction was between boys whose parents had paid for two courses and those who had signed on for three. At least one of young Solomon's friends was a classmate of humble caste status. The friendship developed despite the

[14] B. Ryan, *Caste in Ceylon* (New Brunswick, 1953); J. Jiggins, *Caste and Family in the Politics of the Sinhalese, 1947–1976* (Cambridge, 1979); and M. Roberts, *Caste Conflict and Elite Formation: The Rise of the Karava Elite in Sri Lanka, 1500–1931* (Cambridge, 1982).

objections of Sir Solomon and the initial suspicions of the boy in question.[15] The amusement gained from defying his father and finding a friend helped him to include in his sense of personal superiority the notion that caste prejudice should be viewed with scorn. This impartiality in the matter of caste – born of an extreme but curiously humane conceit – was one of the few ideas from which he never wavered.

Those who would brand Bandaranaike as an agent of his class or as a prisoner of his social milieu should take note of this. Not only did he fail to share the appetites for wealth and consumer goods and the caste prejudices of other prosperous Ceylonese, he viewed these attitudes as pathetic and detestable. This increased his isolation from other members of the elite – including many fellow-politicians – who did not take kindly to his lofty attitude. But it also freed him to sympathize with progressive alternatives to the conservative political, social and economic policies of contemporaries. His monumentally secure social position, his unshakable confidence in the superiority of his intellect and education and the delight which he took in weighing up ideas (the commodity that most interested him), all made it possible for him to think the unthinkable. As we shall see, the explanation for his later evolution into a cautious man of the centre-left rather than a radical lies not in the fetters of class or caste but in an irresolute, frequently timid way with supreme power and in an eccentric conception of what constituted legitimate authority.

Bandaranaike spent his initial six months back in Ceylon gathering round him the elements of his first political organization. He had little difficulty in doing so. He offered young men of ambition and idealism a remarkable range of attractions – an impeccable social pedigree, an Oxford education, the appearance of wealth, a reputation for spectacular oratorical skill and an acquaintance with the most advanced political ideas coming out of Europe and India. A small number of men – Sinhalese of different castes and at least two Tamils – including several students from the Colombo Law College, a few lawyers, a school teacher, a journalist and a struggling printer, attached themselves to him and in October 1925, formed the Progressive National Party.

It cannot be said that this organization achieved great things. Its membership never exceeded fifteen to twenty, and although its meetings were held once or twice a month at Bandaranaike's home or a law office, it accomplished little in its first eleven months. Soon after its establishment, it was affiliated to the Ceylon National Congress, the island's principal

---

[15] Interviews in Colombo with H. A. J. Hulugalle, 29 August 1978, Sir Senarat Gunawardena, 12 September 1978, and another schoolmate, 6 September 1977.

(and distinctly ineffectual) political association, and this enabled Banda-ranaike to gain a place on the large Executive Committee of the Congress in December 1925. The Party spent time discussing Bandaranaike's then rather fanciful plan for a federal system for Ceylon.[16] For him, this was little more than an intellectual trifle, which he soon abandoned when he realized that it contravened the desire of most Sinhalese – especially chauvinists – for a unitary state. But Tamils who have sought greater autonomy from the island's central authorities have never forgotten it, and have consistently exaggerated its importance. It was not until September 1926 that the Progressive National Party attempted a major public initiative. It was a fiasco.

The Party had resolved to sponsor celebration of a 'Ceylon National Week' in early September. It had done so on the assumption that a Ceylonese nationalism akin to that which had developed in India was smouldering beneath the surface of the island's public life. These festivities were intended to fan it into flames, but the initial response was so lukewarm that it was hastily decided to scale the week down to a single National Day. Leaders of various communities were invited to share the stage on Sunday, 4 September, at a public meeting where Bandaranaike would deliver an address to open a discussion of Ceylonese nationalism. The large Colombo Public Hall was hired for the purpose, but at the appointed hour 'hardly fifty' people had arrived, 'mostly young men, some students perhaps, being grouped in the front seats'. After a delay of half an hour, only a few more had trickled in, leaving the body of the hall yawning emptily.

What had been planned as an occasion for heroics had become, inescapably, a farce. Intensely embarrassed, Bandaranaike attacked the island's vaunted political leaders as 'people who arrogated to themselves the position of leaders, who met in their own bedchambers and evolved schemes which they considered would meet the needs of the country . . .' Their arrogance, he said, was apparent from the number of refusals he had had to invitations to speak at this meeting. These politicians only wanted to increase the number of seats for themselves on government councils. In Ceylon, self-government 'meant a few individuals wanting to get the government into their own hand . . .' He then extended his assault to the populace as a whole. Several schemes for political reform had been published in the press, but 'nobody had taken the slightest interest . . .' The people of Ceylon were like a caged animal at the zoo that was unaware of its captivity. As bitterness welled up within him, he resorted to increasingly charged rhetoric, most of which – perhaps

---

[16] Interviews with James Rutnam, Colombo, 3 and 7 September 1977.

fortunately – his audience could probably not understand. There existed 'an extraordinarily putrescent atmosphere . . . What they called quiet contentment was nothing more then the quiet of the charnel house.' He then changed the mood, soothing them with lyricism before delivering the sting in the tail.

He remembered once visiting the buried cities of Ceylon, looking at the country round from the hill at Sigiriya and from the hill at Mihintale, as far as the eye could reach. It was all one vast forest, relics of a bygone glory. It was not right that a servile race should inhabit the same locality which their ancestors inhabited in power and glory.

His despairing tone clearly reflected the Progressive National Party's disastrous showing on its first major occasion. That evening an open air rally and torchlight parade attracted a far better turnout, but the credit for that went to Colombo labour organizations with which Bandaranaike and his Party had no connection.[17] Indeed, the use of the word 'party' to describe this association overstates its substance. It was so totally dominated by Bandaranaike that it was little more than an extension of his own ego. On the single occasion when a member disagreed with him at a Party meeting, the leader ruled the man out of order without protest from others present.[18] The relationship between leader and led is illustrated by the surprise and delight of the members when Bandaranaike condescended to ride in the second-class carriage with them on the train to Galle for the Ceylon National Congress session in late December 1926. It was their first and last ride together. When he was elected Joint Secretary of the Congress at Galle, the purpose for which the Party was created had been fulfilled. He lost interest in it and it soon expired. As one of its members has said, 'When he was able to climb a little higher, he dropped us. He had used us but we weren't bitter. We had tried to use him too. Only he succeeded.'[19] In itself, the Progressive National Party has little significance. But the loose manner in which it was organized and the lofty manner in which it was led were apparent in each of the political associations which Bandaranaike subsequently founded. This recurring pattern yielded him a few advantages and a great many problems.

Bandaranaike was mightily criticized after the embarrassments of the National Day. He was described as 'a discredited "politician" whose activities add to the gaiety of our otherwise humdrum public life' and a man 'more to be pitied than blamed'. Others were less savage,[20] but he

[17] *CI*, 6 September 1926.
[18] *CML*, 22 and 25 June, 18 July 1926 and interview with James Rutnam, Colombo, 9 September 1978.   [19] Interview with James Rutnam, Colombo, 28 September 1978.
[20] *CI*, 17 and 21 September 1926.

could not have been elected an officer in the Congress just three months later had he not partially redeemed himself. The opportunity to do so arose at the Colombo Municipal Council election in early December 1926. The Municipal Council was one of the few elective bodies in Ceylon that offered its members substantive influence and patronage powers. A keen struggle developed over the seat for Maradana, the largest ward, which in those days was a mixture of working-class and lower-middle-class areas. Limitations on the franchise enabled middle-class voters to predominate, although a substantial number of better paid workers could vote.

In October, it became known that the incumbent at Maradana, A. E. (later Sir Ernest) de Silva – an extremely wealthy Colombo patrician and a leader of the *Salagama* caste group – was to be challenged by one A. E. Goonesinha. A one-time law student, Goonesinha had worked for more than a decade as a small-time journalist and campaigner among the poor of Colombo. Between 1919 and 1922, he had led a spectacular and successful protest against a municipal poll tax. In 1922 he founded the Ceylon Labour Union which quickly became the most powerful force for workers' rights in the island.[21] His aims were hardly very radical by comparison with later organizers, but he was a frightening and even a loathesome figure to many members of the middle class.

There were several reasons for this. First, he represented the spectre of an assertive working class. To middle-class people who had had to make few concessions to labouring interests – they had yet to pay income tax – this was very disquieting. Goonesinha, who came from the *Hinna* caste which was numerically weak and low in status, faced prejudice on that account as well. Finally, his abrasive manner had earned him a host of enemies. His blistering condemnations of leading figures of polite society and, ironically, his attempt to gain admission to that society further angered many middle-class people. They were also alarmed by the raucous behaviour of some members of his entourage who appeared to many to be mere thugs – an opinion based mostly on fear but partly on fact.

Many of Goonesinha's working-class supporters resided in Maradana and it appears that at least a sizable minority of them had the vote. He was thus a formidable candidate, and the incumbent de Silva did not relish a contest with him. It required energetic, full-time campaigning which was not an attractive prospect to a patrician businessman who enjoyed dabbling in politics for the prestige which it offered. Indeed that prestige would probably suffer amid mud-slinging and it would be necessary to organize 'some muscle', as one activist put it, to meet the force of

---

[21] A. E. Goonesinha Memoirs, typescript, pp. 1–2 and 9–11.

Goonesinha's 'more robust associates'.[22] Bandaranaike, who viewed the election as a chance to establish himself politically, was quick to see the incumbent's distaste for the struggle. He also had close at hand one of the few men who could approach a man of A. E. de Silva's eminence with the suggestion that he step aside – Sir Solomon.

This, however, posed difficulties. Bandaranaike's desire to enter electoral politics was painful to Sir Solomon, in both public and private life. He was less than a year from retirement as Maha Mudaliyar and he rightly saw elections as a threat to the status which he had enjoyed in that role. His status was derived in part from ascription (family, caste, etc.) and in part from assiduous cultivation of Ceylon's British rulers – that is, from above. This entailed alienation from the island's people. The status and authority which the son now sought to acquire were derived – at least in theory (the Bandaranaike name always counted in his favour) – from achievement, from his ability to earn the confidence of the electorate, which is to say from below. Implicit in this were a challenge to British rule in Ceylon and an effort to develop solidarity with the island's people.[23] Bandaranaike's rejection of government service for a legal practice and a career in the new politics had also eroded Sir Solomon's authority within his family. Several of Lady Bandaranaike's relatives had taken to the law or to non-official posts on representative councils or to both, including her father and uncle. She lost no opportunity to remind her husband and son of the impression which had developed by the late nineteenth century that the brightest members of the elite mudaliyar families took to the law while the dullards entered the headman service.[24] She thus rejected Sir Solomon's claims to pre-eminence in the family, which were based largely upon ascriptive criteria, out of regard for her relatives' achievements. Young Bandaranaike's decision to enter electoral politics seemed an endorsement of her view.

Yet despite all of this, Sir Solomon agreed to ask the incumbent councillor to stand aside. It is likely that he did so for several reasons. First and most obviously, he loved his son, depended on his relationship with him and wanted him to become a success, in spite of his distaste for the career that the young man had chosen. Second, he was pleased to feel needed, to find that his son had still to depend upon his patronage in some way. Finally, he had a deep loathing for his son's opponent, Goonesinha.

---

[22] Interview with J. Vijayatunga, London, 10 November 1981.

[23] Sir Solomon's position was not based exclusively upon ascription. While he had inherited a great deal of land, he had substantially extended his holdings through his own purchases, although he was able to do so partly as a result of his political position which was based largely upon ascription.

[24] P. Peebles, The Transformation of a Colonial Elite: The Mudaliyars of Nineteenth-Century Ceylon, University of Chicago doctoral thesis, 1973, pp. 255–56.

This arose out of an incident in June 1925, when Sir Solomon had become the first Ceylonese to receive the KCMG in the king's birthday honours. A public meeting was organized by prominent citizens to decide how to commemorate the event. But what was intended as an occasion for acclaim went badly wrong when Goonesinha packed the meeting with noisy supporters and shouted from the floor that Sir Solomon was unworthy of this or any honour. Speeches of praise were drowned by 'jazz music' from rowdies in the audience and two motions to salute the old knight were put and lost.[25] The memory of this rankled with both father and son.

Legend has it that Sir Solomon even appeared on the public platform with Bandaranaike during the campaign, but this is untrue. He did, however, take one further step of vital importance. Maradana ward contained a very large number of Muslims. A leading figure among them was W. M. Abdul Rahiman who had represented them in the Legislative Council. Sir Solomon and Abdul Rahiman were close friends, partly because the Maha Mudaliyar had supported the British government's extreme actions against Sinhalese nationalist leaders during the 1915 riots between Muslims and Sinhalese.[26] Sir Solomon used his influence to persuade Abdul Rahiman to support his son in Maradana. He did so in a slightly churlish mood which betrayed his doubts about electoral politics, telling his friend that young Bandaranaike 'is *your* son', as if he were temporarily disowning him.

Abdul Rahiman, 'spent a few thousand rupees' on Bandaranaike's campaign[27] and chaired a public meeting of Muslims as the canvassing neared its close. It filled a large hall to overflowing. On the platform were leading Muslims including 'High Priests' of two major mosques and three legislative councillors. Abdul Rahiman opened the meeting with direct appeals to voters' fears of Goonesinha as leader of the working class. Bandaranaike deserved their support, he said, because he possessed three essentials: wealth, education and social status. A second speaker echoed this view, saying that Goonesinha's 'work had been for a certain class . . . His work had been directed against the Government . . . what they wanted were men who could work in cooperation with the Government . . .' Bandaranaike was the better man because he was 'a gentleman . . . a man of education and wealth'. Others continued in this vein.

[25] *TC*, 30 June 1925 and *CI*, 30 June and 1 July 1925.
[26] Sir Solomon may have even assisted the Muslims after the riots by intriguing within the government against the Sinhalese leaders.
[27] Interview with Sir Razik Fareed, son of Abdul Rahiman, Colombo, 1 September 1978. Bandaranaike's opponent saw Abdul Rahiman's efforts as vitally important (Goonesinha Memoirs, p. 25).

Some may have expected these words to embarrass Bandaranaike, the angry young 'Progressive' who coveted the roles of 'servant' to the common man and advocate of 'Workers' interests.[28] But he showed no sign of it as he rose to reply. After reminding the audience that Abdul Rahiman was the 'friend of his father and his grand-father' and that Islam was a great civilization, he took up the potentially embarrassing theme as his own.

He offered them as security all the education he possessed, whatever means he possessed, all the time he had . . . [Goonesinha would] fight for the labourer against every other class . . . [but Bandaranaike] did not come as the representative of any section or class or community.[29]

In making these remarks, he was clearly mindful of his dictum that 'To impress an audience was the be-all and end of public speaking.'[30]

The contest for the Maradana seat was more keenly fought than any previous municipal election. It received wide coverage in the press and was followed with 'intense excitement' by residents of Colombo. Both candidates and their supporters worked far harder than was customary, as there was genuine anxiety on both sides. Bandaranaike had better connections among the elite, but it was thought that his opponent's years of work in the city might still carry him through. Goonesinha, who was facing suits for insolvency, had little money to spend.[31] Bandaranaike, with help from his mother's family, was able to spend much more, mainly on 'huge fleets' of cars driven by election entrepreneurs, which plied the streets of Maradana with loudspeakers.[32]

As polling day neared, the campaign was marked by violence. Much of it came from Goonesinha's side, to be sure, but his opponent must share some of the responsibility. One of Bandaranaike's lieutenants recalls persuading 'gang leaders' in Maradana 'to intimidate people to vote for him'.[33] An anti-Goonesinha paper reported that on the eve of the poll three men called at a house, asked the owner if he was working for Goonesinha and when he said yes, knocked him to the ground and struck him. When his wife 'worshipped' them and asked them to stop, they hit her as well.[34]

---

[28] Bandaranaike had been elected to office in the Ceylon Workers Federation, an association which was less a trade union than a circle of patricians with patronizing attitudes towards workers. Federation leaders lobbied for members' interests, but labourers had to behave in a subservient manner. See Goonesinha Memoirs, p. 10.

[29] *CI*, 6 December 1926.   [30] *CI*, 8 July 1925.

[31] *CI*, 7–8 July 1925 and Goonesinha Memoirs, p. 25.

[32] One man did propaganda work for Goonesinha free of charge for several days in order to squeeze a higher fee from Bandaranaike in the long run. Goonesinha Memoirs, p. 25; newspaper cuttings for 15 December 1926 in lot 23.25, serial 41, BP.

[33] Interview with J. Vijayatunga, London, 10 November 1901.

[34] *CI*, 14 December 1926.

On election day, 14 December, votes for all wards were cast in the park opposite Colombo Town Hall. This meant that many voters from Maradana had to travel a mile or more and it put Bandaranaike, with greater resources, at an advantage. As the day progressed, a 'record' crowd gathered in the park to see Maradana produce by far the heaviest poll in the city, with the 'infirm and decrep[i]t . . . the lame and the halt . . . tottering to the polling booth'. That evening, as 'excitement was raging' with rival crowds exchanging 'wild cries and hooting', it was announced that Bandaranaike had won, 1,801 votes to 1,186.[35]

The ambiguities in Bandaranaike's relationship with Sir Solomon are apparent in the Maradana episode. It was in one sense a victory for the son over the father. Sir Solomon had agreed to act as servant to the interests of his son by promoting his career in a mode of politics which he found distasteful. Success on polling day had given the son further leverage in his effort to become independent of the father. But in another sense, this episode yielded clear gains for the father. After rejecting Sir Solomon's financial assistance and plans for a career in government service, Bandaranaike had been forced to turn to him for help which may have been decisive in the election. And if the father thus seemed the servant of the son, those who recalled Goonesinha's insulting treatment of Sir Solomon could regard Bandaranaike as the servant of his father in the campaign against Goonesinha. As always, both father and son were too emotionally dependent upon one another to allow the bond between them to break, but neither found it a comfortable relationship.

This election ended Bandaranaike's political dependence upon his father and with this and Sir Solomon's retirement a few months later, relations between father and son move to the periphery of our story. The election also brought to public notice a relationship which later acquired many of the characteristics of the young man's ties to Sir Solomon. For the first time, Bandaranaike's name was widely linked to that of D. S. Senanayake, a key figure in the Sinhalese political elite and the man who led Ceylon to independence two decades later. At the Muslims' election rally it was he who proposed the vote of thanks and his name appears among those who acted as Bandaranaike's patrons on polling day.[36] Both of these things seemed quite surprising at the time. Senanayake and the Muslims were thought to belong to opposite camps politically. He had been among the Sinhalese leaders imprisoned during the Sin-halese/Muslim riots of 1915. He had been in the same cell block with Goonesinha on the hair-raising occasion when the British summarily

---

[35] *CI*, 15 December 1926; and newspaper cuttings for that date in lot 23.25, serial 41, BP.
[36] *CI*, 6 December 1926; and lot 23.25, serial 41, BP.

executed one of their cellmates and then washed the blood of the death-chair in the prisoners' washroom.[37] Senanayake had no special affection for the Bandaranaike clan. He had been deeply offended just after the troubles of 1915 when Bandaranaike's maternal grandfather, Sir Christoffel Obeyesekere, blamed the riots upon Senanayake and his friends whom he described as 'half a dozen designing villains who had been trying to pose as leaders of the Buddhists . . . nobodies . . . [hoping] to make somebodies of themselves'.[38] Sir Solomon and his Anglican relatives shared his opinion and viewed with distaste the Senanayakes' Buddhism, their recent (late nineteenth century) rise to wealth and social prominence and their refusal to show deference to British officialdom.

And yet here was Senanayake supporting young Bandaranaike. He did so for two reasons. First, Bandaranaike's political ideas were far more advanced than those of his forebears and he had shown himself eager to ally himself to the nationalist elite in general and the Senanayakes in particular. This was apparent from Bandaranaike's efforts, soon after his return, to join associations in which leading nationalists were active.[39] He had also taken special pains to obtain the patronage of F. R. Senanayake, the leading nationalist of the day and the elder brother of D.S., before his untimely death in mid-1925, and had paid public tribute to his memory.[40] Second, D. S. Senanayake needed Bandaranaike to check the rise of A. E. Goonesinha. Despite their time in jail together, Senanayake regarded Goonesinha as an unreliable egotist whose energetic denunciations of the nationalist elite appeared genuinely threatening because of the popular support he could command. This support came not only from urban workers – whom Senanayake was probably prepared to concede to him – but also from youthful idealists, mainly at the Law College, whom Senanayake wished either to win over or to neutralize. Bandaranaike's willingness to cooperate and his youthful dynamism made him an ideal foil for Goonesinha.

Bandaranaike emerged onto the balcony of the Town Hall to a 'tumultuous uproar from the thousands gathered below'. He spoke in Sinhala:

I did not come forward as the representative of the rich . . . but as a friend of the poor of Maradana. It is true that Mr Goonesinha works for the labour classes [sic]. I have been returned today by those labouring classes . . . I have not been

[37] Goonesinha Memoirs, pp. 3–5.
[38] As quoted from *Ceylon Hansard*, 11 August 1915, p. 406, by K. M. de Silva in K. M. de Silva (ed.), *University of Ceylon History of Ceylon*, vol. iii (Peradeniya, 1973), p. 392.
[39] These included – in addition to the Ceylon National Congress – the Low Country Products Association, the All-Ceylon Village Committees Conference and the Lanka Maha Jana Sabha. *CI*, 4 April, 30 June, 7 and 9 September 1925.
[40] *CI*, 21 September 1926.

elected because I bear a name which was honoured nor because I am a rich man. I
have been returned because you wished me to be your representative . . .[41]

This speech is not merely inconsistent with that made at the Muslims'
election meeting, it is its diametrical opposite. Such inconsistencies and
self-contradictions appear in rich and chronic profusion throughout
Bandaranaike's career, and it is important to understand from the outset
that there is no simple explanation for them. His inconsistencies often
arise out of attempts to gain some short-run advantage and it is tempting
to view them – flatly and simply – as cynical, hypocritical acts. To take
that view, however, would be unfair to Bandaranaike. He is more
complex than that.

Consider that a very large number of his self-contradictions first see the
light of day in speeches to large crowds. Astute observers of his
speechmaking over the years consistently recall that he seemed to have a
palpable *need* to sweep crowds off their feet. The same insecurity which
made it impossible for him to tolerate a single friendship of equals
throughout his adult life drove him to dominate any audience that he
addressed. Aides who in later years accompanied him on speaking tours
where roadside crowds responded warmly, had to tear him away from
them so that he would not exhaust himself. He seemed intoxicated with
their response, so that 'at times it seemed that he couldn't help himself'.[42]
To produce the response, he tended, largely unconsciously it appears, to
tell his audiences what they wanted to hear. This tendency was reinforced
by the habit which he had acquired, in the Oxford Union and in litigation,
of assuming whatever posture was required of him by the occasion and of
making the best and most single-minded case possible. In full oratorical
cry, Bandaranaike was like a method actor who loses himself in the role
that he must play. But before a different audience a short time later he
might easily lose himself in a contradictory role, without fully realizing
what he was doing. This was particularly common in his early years in
politics, but he never fully lost the habit. It makes him a less malevolent
figure than he might have been had he been simply a wilful liar, but no
less dangerous a man.

Many of Bandaranaike's self-contradictions were, however, conscious
acts, but even some of these fell short of being out-and-out lies. Like any
good debater or lawyer, he had trained himself not only to argue his own
case, but to understand fully the other point of view, in order to anticipate
his opponent's every move. This was more than just an exercise required

[41] *CI*, 15 December 1926; and newspaper cuttings for that date in lot 23.25, serial 41, BP.
[42] Interviews with two former aides to Bandaranaike, Colombo, 21 August 1977 and 5 and
12 September 1978.

of him by his profession. He regarded the ability to understand another's viewpoint as the first mark of an educated man. Throughout his life, he took special delight in weighing up choices by empathizing with alternative views – in the role of a presiding (and hence superior) arbiter, a latter day Solomon, as it were. This made him something of a free thinker, a role that came easily to someone so relatively free of entanglements with interest groups. And yet, when he faced a crowd, in response to the demands of advocacy, Bandaranaike sometimes consciously adopted unambiguous positions despite genuinely ambiguous feelings. The ambiguity showed itself later, but not in the form of a candid admission of indecision, for such a display of irresolution would have violated the rules of advocacy. It showed itself in the form of a flat contradiction of the previous position on that issue. Grey areas which were resolved into white on one occasion were on another resolved into black. Thus, some of his conscious inconsistencies were not so much lies as overzealous concessions by an extremely flexible man to what he took to be a public expectation. He was not above intentional deception based upon crass calculations of self-interest, but that is only part of a complex story.

After his victory at Maradana and – a week later – his election as Joint Secretary of the Ceylon National Congress, Bandaranaike must have felt very close to winning the acceptance among leading nationalists which was the main goal of the first phase of his career. He still had some way to go, however. His friend, former schoolmate and Congress Secretary, R. S. S. Gunawardena, had had to 'fight and threaten and bully' to persuade leading Congressmen to allow Bandaranaike to become Joint Secretary with him.[43] Bandaranaike's youth, which had made him such an attractive opponent to Goonesinha, now counted against him. Senanayake and his elite nationalist colleagues had not forgotten the smug arrogance of the Bandaranaike clan, and the young man's theatrical speeches – particularly his attack on Ceylon's 'putrescent' politics – had given the impression that he shared the wayward egotism and truculence which had turned them against Goonesinha.

There thus developed an uneasy relationship between Bandaranaike on one side and D. B. Jayatilaka, Senanayake and the leading Congressmen on the other. Bandaranaike, as ever, found it impossible to accept the authority of any superior, and yet, as in the relationship with his father, he felt exceedingly reluctant to allow a complete break to occur between them. This was mainly because he felt politically dependent upon them,

---

[43] Interview with Sir Senarat Gunawardena, Colombo, 12 September 1978.

but it went deeper than that to an emotional dependence as well. However much he might kick against their authority and however much they might provoke him over the years ahead, he was unable to sever the tie until all political justification for it had long since vanished. Despite their refusal to accept him fully, they found within a few years that it was politically unwise to cut him loose. He became too formidable and audacious a figure to be trusted in opposition. In Bandaranaike's failure to win the acceptance of Senanayake and his associates lay the central dilemma and driving force of most of his career. In time, this stormy relationship came to represent far more than an encounter of individuals. In the things which they held in common and the things on which they diverged, we can find nearly every important element of the political history of modern Ceylon.

The next phase of Bandaranaike's encounter with Senanayake and company occurred within the Ceylon National Congress, a body which requires explanation. Its name, which echoed that of India's great organization, is rather misleading. For although it was Ceylon's most important political association up to 1946, the Congress was a loosely structured, undisciplined, unrepresentative, undemocratic and insubstantial thing. It had been founded, rather reluctantly, in late 1919, by a group consisting mainly of patricians. They had come belatedly to realize that their appeal for a greater voice in the island's affairs was scarcely credible in the absence of an association which claimed to represent the people of Ceylon. They were led by a Tamil of vision and brilliance, Sir Ponnambalam Arunachalam, who sought to build the Congress into a major force on the basis of communal cooperation and at least occasional extra-constitutional agitation. On both counts, he was soon disappointed. Within two years, contention between Sinhalese and Tamils (and between Kandyan and Low Country Sinhalese), which was more the result of petty private quarrels and the Governor's divide-and-rule tactics than of communal antagonism, had shattered whatever cohesion Congress had possessed. This and the fear of extra-constitutional action among the men whom Arunachalam called 'our own Tories' caused him to break with the Congress in 1921. Its heyday had passed less than two years after its birth.[44]

Thereafter, Congress leaders claimed that their organization was broadly representative of the people of Ceylon, that it had well-developed nationalist principles and policies which had emerged democratically out

[44] K. M. de Silva, 'The Formation and Character of the Ceylon National Congress, 1917–1919', *Ceylon Journal of Historical and Social Studies*, x, 1967 pp. 70–102; 'The Ceylon National Congress in Disarray', *Ceylon Journal of Historical and Social Studies*, new series, ii, 2, 1972, pp. 79–117 and iii, 1, 1973, pp. 16–39; and de Silva (ed.), *University of Ceylon*, vol. iii, pp. 381–407.

of the party structure and to which members were committed. Reality was different. The Congress President himself conceded in his annual report in 1926 that Tamils, Muslims, Burghers and Kandyan Sinhalese had shunned the organization. That left only the Low Country Sinhalese and few of them outside the small westernized elite had any involvement with Congress.[45] Its proceedings were highly undemocratic. Real decision-making power lay not in the large annual conference of the Congress, but in the theoretically subordinate Executive Committee which met each month. The Executive, which re-elected itself each year and chose the Congress President, also drew up the resolutions that were put to the annual conference where they were nearly always rubber stamped. Some of the rare cases when the conference rejected the Executive resolutions were actually inspired by the Executive in response to changing political circumstance.[46] When the leading figures on the Executive found their dominance challenged, they were not above concealing information from the conference, preventing even eminent members from speaking, packing the conference with their supporters and selectively applying discipline which in normal times was never used.[47]

The Congress was an umbrella organization composed of representatives from a wide range of associations which were not local Congress branches but bodies with separate identities. As a result, the Congress amounted to a great deal less than the sum of its parts. The connection between many of these affiliated associations and the Congress was very tenuous. Its leaders wanted to maintain links with as many affiliates as possible, to give the appearance of strength. So associations which drifted away, collapsed or even turned into adversaries were kept on the books as participating groups. The same was often true of individuals. Once a nominal tie was forged with Congress, it was extremely difficult to break free of it.[48] It is also difficult to take the nationalist rhetoric of Congress leaders when they did not even ask the British for independence until 1942, and when one of the least conservative of Congress Presidents placed his daughter among the debutantes at Buckingham Palace in 1930.[49]

[45] *CI*, 18 December 1926. See also *CI*, 1 June, 1 September 1928 and 21 December 1929.
[46] *CI*, 16 and 19 November 1928 and 21 December 1929.
[47] *CI*, 2 and 17 September, 22 and 30 October 1928, 11 September and 21 December 1929. See also S. W. R. D. Bandaranaike (ed.), *Handbook of the Ceylon National Congress, 1919–1928* (Colombo, 1928).
[48] *CI*, 14 May, 4 June and 20 November 1928, 28 October 1929; and *CDN*, 8 December 1930. There were a very few exceptions: for example, *CI*, 27 February, 17 and 22 October 1928.
[49] *CI*, 19 July 1930. See also, M. Roberts (ed.), *Documents of the Ceylon National Congress and Nationalist Politics in Ceylon, 1929–1950*, vol. i (Colombo, 1977), pp. 5–48.

When Bandaranaike joined R. S. S. Gunawardena as Joint Secretary in 1926 they worked with others who wanted to forge it into a cohesive political force. They pressed for a new party constitution that would create a small central executive, elected by the broad Congress membership and possessing the authority to discipline wayward members and provide authoritative day-to-day leadership. Loosely affiliated associations would lose their separate identities and become subordinate branches of the Congress and funds would be systematically collected to provide a firm financial base. The chequered history of this scheme is revealing. When it was first presented to the Congress Executive Committee in June 1927, it had a 'heated' reception from members who preferred an organization that made few demands upon them. Nevertheless a committee was appointed to consider the idea. This tactic was adopted in the confident hope that the scheme would die amid the committee's inactivity, and die it did. As a result, we find Bandaranaike a year later requesting that another committee be established to consider the same problem. This time he and his allies were more persistent and over a year later, in July 1929, it was agreed to place a scheme, closely modelled on Gandhi's 1920 constitution for India's Congress, before the annual conference which accepted it in December 1929. This did not produce immediate results however, for the following month leaders met to 'consider', not to implement, the changes. In fact, they were only very imperfectly implemented because in 1931 the Congress adopted such a constitution yet again which in turn was unimplemented so that similar reorganizations were adopted without practical effect in 1934, and so it went.[50]

One cause of this bizarre cycle of decision and inaction was the unwillingness of the most powerful figures in the Congress to accept these changes. These men, most especially D. S. Senanayake and D. B. Jayatilaka, derived their power from several sources: imprisonment in 1915, seniority in politics, membership in the legislature, links to the colonial authorities and to interest groups and associations, professional eminence, caste and family connections, landed wealth and ties to one another. Their membership in Congress was of comparatively minor importance to them alongside these things. If Congress operated democratically on a broad membership base, less eminent men like Bandaranaike might ram through unpalatable policies. If Congress were

[50] *CI*, 30 May 1927, 10 May and 1 June 1928, 1 July 1929, 10 January 1930, 16 March, 19, 27 and 30 November and 19 December 1931, 17 and 27 December 1934, 16 February 1935; and *CDN*, 18 July 1931 and 26 March 1935. No serious attempt at fundraising was made before 1935 (*CI*, 16 January 1935). The operations of Congress were not tightened up until 1941. For more on this, see Roberts (ed.), *Documents*, vol. i, pp. 5–49.

able to impose discipline, these eminent men might lose their near-total freedom to manoeuvre. So when the Congress began to move in a direction they disliked, they resisted such trends and, when necessary, temporarily detached themselves from the organization.[51] Since they were far more powerful than the insubstantial Congress, the Congress caved in and thereby remained insubstantial.

Whatever reputation Bandaranaike may have had for good judgement and a willingness to subordinate personal interest to a larger cause suffered a blow within a few weeks of his election as Congress Secretary. On 9 February 1927, 4,000–5,000 labourers in Colombo harbour went on strike for higher wages. This was carefully organized by Goonesinha's Labour Union so that the men had at least limited funds to maintain them and the support of other workers to whom the port managers might turn for blacklegs. Bandaranaike spent nearly the first fortnight of the strike on holiday and returned to Colombo as the confrontation was approaching a climax. A handful of workers came to him to say that they were desperate and ready to return on the management's terms. Although he held office in a labourers' association, implying that he was an advocate of the working class, Bandaranaike went on his own initiative to the managers of the port in the guise of a mediator. He told them that the strikers' resolve was weakening, that Goonesinha's ulterior motives lay behind the strike and then granted an interview to the newspaper most hostile to the workers' cause.[52] He stated that the real aim of the strike was to raise the income of 2,000–3,000 manual workers to a level where they could qualify as electors in the Colombo North constituency of the Ceylon Legislative Council. Bandaranaike was eyeing that seat for himself and clearly anticipated a rematch with Goonesinha. He described the strike as 'nothing short of a crime against the state' and against the workers,[53] without specifying how enfranchisement and higher wages would harm workers' interests.

His intervention proved irrelevant to the settlement of the strike which followed soon after, but it provoked a stormy reaction. One hundred copies of the paper containing his interview were burned at a union rally and workers attempted to burn his effigy in a park. The following month, Bandaranaike was listed as a patron and speaker at a meeting to form a

---

[51] The classic instance of this came later, in 1943, when D. S. Senanayake resigned from Congress and – standing alone – maintained and even enhanced his political pre-eminence. For earlier examples, see *CDN*, 11 March 1930; and *CI*, 4–5 January 1928 and 17 December 1934.

[52] For the interview, see *TC*, 24 February 1927. See also *TC*, 10–22 February 1927.

[53] The quotation is from *TC*, 24 February 1927. See also *TC*, 25 February 1927 and *CI*, 1 and 3 March 1927.

rival union. When it was learned that trouble was brewing, he stayed away, but the mention of his name at the meeting brought howls of derision. A 'seething crowd' raised 'shouts, shrieks, catcalls, booing, hoots and a variety of other pleasant and unpleasant noises' and hurled brickbats, stones, eggs and pieces of wood at the platform. The hall emptied when police arrived with bayonets fixed and one of Bandaranaike's co-patrons was chased up the road by the crowd.[54]

In a letter to the press aimed at self-justification, Bandaranaike revealed the problems of perception which led him into this tangle. First, he had no clear notion of his role in the dispute. Almost within the same breath, he described himself a neutral intermediary and the workers' advocate, but then presented a view of the workers which was compatible with neither role. The strike weapon, he said, should only be used in extreme cases:

especially in a country like this where the labourers or at least a majority of them are not in a position to form an opinion for themselves by seeing every aspect of the matter either by reading the newspapers or otherwise and are solely dependent on whatever their 'soi-disant' leaders choose to tell them . . .[55]

Bandaranaike at this time had not moved far beyond the condescending, patronizing outlook of Horagolla or Christ Church. This was apparent from his decision to accept office in the Ceylon Workers' Federation, a 'union' which Goonesinha had refused to join because at meetings patrician officers sat in armchairs while workers squatted on the floor.[56] It was also apparent from Bandaranaike's imperious manner with his legal clients and from his positive enjoyment of their obeisances[57] – things of which D. S. Senanayake, a down-to-earth, unpretentious, straight-talking politician, could never be accused. Yet at the same time, Bandaranaike genuinely felt a romantic attachment to the downtrodden – especially to the *rural* poor who were less assertive, but to labourers as well. In later years, he shed much of this patronizing attitude, but in the 1920s it was there, unmistakably, and it figured prominently in his handling of the main problem which confronted him and Ceylon's political leaders in those years – constitutional reform.

Since 1924 Ceylon had been governed under a constitution which had pleased neither the British authorities nor Sinhalese politicians. There existed an Executive Council, on which colonial officials enjoyed heavy predominance, that was responsible for governing Ceylon. These officials

[54] *TC*, 25–26 February 1927; and *CI*, 19 March 1927.
[55] *CI*, 2 April 1927.   [56] Goonesinha Memoirs, p. 10.
[57] Interview with J. Vijayatunga who served Bandaranaike as a translator with clients who spoke only Sinhala, London, 10 November 1981. Bandaranaike's manner towards ordinary folk changed markedly in later years.

were also represented as a minority of twelve out of forty-nine within the Legislative Council, the island's principal law-making body which had considerable authority over the public purse. The thirty-seven non-official legislators included three appointees of the Governor, eleven members representing communal electorates and twenty-three chosen from territorial constituencies. Officials disliked the constitution because those with executive responsibilities were only a minority within the legislature and because legislators could use their investigative powers to embarrass civil servants. Sinhalese leaders disliked it because it excluded them from executive authority and because of an over-representation of non-Sinhalese.[58] The unhappiness which the constitution engendered led to the announcement in April 1927, that a Special Commission would be appointed to prepare reforms.[59]

One of the main concerns of the Commission, which was headed by Lord Donoughmore, was the possible extension of the franchise beyond the all-male 4 per cent or so of the population then able to vote.[60] This issue brought Bandaranaike squarely up against the contradiction between what we might call his formal political 'theories' – which were vaguely those of an English 'radical liberal'[61] – and his elitist political prejudices. The former dictated support for the broadest possible extension of suffrage which he had advocated to members of the Progressive Nationalist Party and in private conversation.[62] But his elitism, which was reinforced by his misadventure with the harbour workers, inclined him toward a more cautious approach. His inability to commit himself firmly to principle left him, here as so often, without fixity or ballast and he allowed his course to be determined by the winds of opportunity. In 1927 they were blowing a stiff breeze in the direction of caution. All of the leaders of the National Congress desired a grant of full responsible government to the greatest possible number of elected representatives – among whom they expected to find themselves. But

[58] Seven of the twenty-three territorial members were Tamils, and communal electorates sent three Europeans, two Burghers (Eurasians, often claiming Dutch descent), three Muslims, two Indians and one Tamil into the Council. The Governor could avoid deadlocks between the legislature and the executive by manipulating non-Sinhalese and some wayward Sinhalese members. So although he had the power to override Legislative Council decisions, he found this necessary on only one occasion between 1924 and 1931. See, in this regard, K. M. de Silva's discussion in de Silva (ed.), *University of Ceylon*, vol. iii, pp. 365–72. Also, C. T. Blackton, 'The Empire at Bay: British Attitudes and the Growth of Nationalism in the Early Twentieth Century', in M. Roberts (ed.), *Collective Identities, Nationalisms and Protest in Modern Sri Lanka* (Colombo, 1979), pp. 370–74.

[59] *CI*, 11–12 April 1927.

[60] *CI*, 5 September 1929 and de Silva (ed.), *University of Ceylon*, vol. iii, p. 371.

[61] Lot 25.23, serial 41, BP.

[62] Interviews in Colombo with James Rutman, 9 September 1978 and Sir Senerat Gunawardena, 12 September 1978.

none of the more prominent Congressmen wanted an extension of suffrage. At this point, Bandaranaike was still struggling to gain favour among these leaders, so he sided with them against a few young progressives in the debate over Congress policy.[63]

The only people who advocated universal suffrage in the Donough-more Commission hearings were A. E. Goonesinha and two British residents of Ceylon.[64] When the Congress delegation which included Bandaranaike presented their testimony in November 1927, the Commissioners expressed surprise that they desired powers akin to a sovereign British government without any extension of popular participation. The Congress leaders who described themselves as 'old fashioned [believers in] . . . Gladstonian Liberalism'[65] replied that the present requirement of an income of Rs 50 per month allowed in 'the competent adult population who were fitted to the franchise'. They claimed that 'In another five years Rs 50 would bring in about 90% of the people',[66] an estimate which they surely knew to be wildly erroneous.

The Donoughmore Commissioners were unimpressed with these views, and in 1928, they astonished Ceylon's politicians and British officials throughout the Empire by recommending the vote for all men over twenty-one and all women over thirty (later amended to admit women over twenty-one). They also proposed the merger of executive and legislative roles within a single State Council of sixty-one members, to last for a term of five years. Fifty members were to be elected from territorial electorates – a major gain for the previously under-represented Sinhalese – while eight were nominated by the Governor to give adequate representation to minorities. A further three members were to be the Officers of State in charge of executive portfolios which were excluded from non-official control: Finance, Justice, and the Public Services, Defence and External Affairs. Under a scheme borrowed from the London County Council, each member of the State Council was to serve on one of seven Executive Committees: Home Affairs; Agriculture and Lands; Local Administration; Health; Education; Labour, Industry and Commerce; and Communications and Works. Each Executive Committee would elect a Chairman who, with the Governor's approval, became a Minister and sat on a Board of Ministers which did not operate on the principle of collective responsibility. This division of the Council into seven distinct committees was intended to ensure that minority rep-

[63] Interview with Sir Senerat Gunawardena, Colombo, 12 September 1978.
[64] *CI*, 18 January 1928.
[65] *TC*, 22 November 1927. This statement was edited out of Bandaranaike's record of the testimony. See Bandaranaike, *Handbook*, p. 834.
[66] Bandaranaike, *Handbook*, pp. 829–30 and 835–36; and *TC*, 22 November 1927. The latter quotes these percentages as 12 and 90.

resentatives would have an influence over policy and to discourage the formation of political parties which, it was feared, could develop along communal lines. Each Executive Committee had to win the approval of the Council for its expenditure and broad policy. The Governor's powers were increased to balance those of the State Council. His right to reserve legislation for the royal assent was extended to cover several new types of bills. He was also empowered to suspend decisions of Executive Committees in these same areas and he retained control of matters concerning civil servants.[67]

Despite the adoption of the principle of territorial representation which increased Sinhalese strength in the legislature and embittered minorities, the leaders of the Ceylon National Congress were deeply disappointed by the Commission Report. Their *naïveté*, about both the impression that they had made upon the Commission and the political realities of their time, is apparent from the fact that they 'had envisaged the grant of full-fledged parliamentary institutions – the orthodox cabinet form of government . . .'[68] with something approaching sovereign powers. The division of the State Council into Executive Committees annoyed Congress leaders who aspired to ministerial posts, because it would prevent ministers from developing both collective strength and – since a minister was only first among equals on his committee – independence from their fellow legislators. The strengthening of the Governor's position also came as a rude shock to their expectations, although a cursory survey of imperial policy would have shown that the Donoughmore scheme was decidedly generous. The grant of universal franchise was acutely embarrassing. Congressmen could hardly claim to be the island's political vanguard when the imperial power itself was more radical than they on this vital issue.

Their reactions to the reforms, both initially and over the months that followed, were marked by confusion and inconsistency. The first response of the Congress Executive Committee was to condemn the report because it bestowed inadequate powers. On reflection, however, Congress leaders realized that the scheme offered considerable opportunities and that there was little prospect of their flimsy organization forcing major revisions. When Congress met in special session in September 1928 the new mood prevailed. Speakers stressed that they were 'more than delighted' with the scheme and claimed that the Congress position on the franchise 'had been misunderstood'. Bandaranaike agreed, explaining that the Congress had always wanted an extension of the franchise. The meeting then endorsed the reforms. The

[67] De Silva (ed.), *University of Ceylon*, vol. iii, pp. 373–77; and *The Donoughmore Report* (London, 1928). [68] De Silva (ed.), *University of Ceylon,* vol. iii, pp. 494–5.

occasion would have passed smoothly had not one leader, who wore a monocle, reminded delegates of the underlying attitudes of most Congress leaders by objecting to 'ordinary people . . . presuming' to speak on so exalted a matter as constitutional reform which 'was a scientific question which could not be dealt with by everybody. It must be dealt with by gentlemen who had the ability to understand it. (Hear, hear.)'[69]

The one issue on which Congressmen were not prepared to accept the reforms was the enfranchisement of Indian workers in Ceylon with five years domicile and six months continual residence in the eighteen months before registration. They feared that Indian voters might elect European planters or Indian Tamil representatives. Either would reduce Sinhalese influence in the State Council, and Indian Tamils might forge an alliance with indigenous Ceylon Tamils – groups which had remained distinct until then. Congress leaders also saw this issue as a means to an alliance with Kandyan Sinhalese who felt especially threatened because Indian estate workers were concentrated in their constituencies.[70] Congressmen mounted a vigorous campaign which played upon anti-Indian prejudice and in which Bandaranaike's voice could be heard warning of 'the Indian menace'. This led to yet another change in their stand on the franchise. After first opposing universal suffrage and then accepting it, Congress leaders in November 1928 sought to use the opposition to Indian voters to introduce a literacy test which would have cut the electorate by 1.5 million.[71] The British eventually compromised on the franchise for Indians – though not for Ceylonese – but this owed far less to Congress objections than to the breadth of the opposition beyond Congress, including that of the Governor.

Throughout this period, Bandaranaike continued to use stinging rhetoric and, at times, this proved an embarrassment. When the Congress met in mid-1929 during a dispute with the Governor, Bandaranaike denounced the reforms as 'a complete sham . . . [a] cruel joke . . . playing to the vanity of people, giving them toys such as ministries to play with, with large salaries and taking away every tittle of power . . .' He described the Secretary of State for the Colonies as 'a bull in a china shop', called a prominent Ceylonese conservative 'an unscrupulous traitor' and recommended a 'dose of Kruschen salts' (a strong laxative) to the Governor who was 'suffering from a mental aberration'. The press deplored this 'comic entertainment', with Bandaranaike 'raising his voice and brandishing his arms after the fashion of a cheap Swedish acrobat'.[72] At a public

[69] *CI*, 2 September and 30 October 1928.
[70] *CI*, 2 and 18 September, 1 October and 2 November 1928.
[71] *CI*, 16 November 1928, 4 February and 4 April 1929.   [72] *CI*, 19 August 1929.

meeting a few days later, he attempted a dramatic response to this criticism. He stood holding a pencil in one hand and said: 'I am a peaceful man who does not wish to enter into any quarrel but if there be any who comes in my way and shows fight let him be very chary for I shall break him in twain.' At that moment, 'amidst tense silence', he tried to snap the pencil in two for effect. To his mortification, it would not break.[73]

His comments on the Donoughmore Constitution flatly contradicted Congress policy. A few weeks later, when a despatch from the Colonial Office rejected nearly every Congress amendment to the scheme, Bandaranaike hastily proposed that they 'turn down this scheme and go back to the country on this issue'. This notion, which characteristically was suited to politics in Britain or India rather than Ceylon, was hatched without consultation with Congress leaders. Less than three weeks later, as Congress accepted the reforms, he reversed his position and 'publicly recanted his heresy . . . burning with the ardour of a new convert . . .'[74] In charting his inconsistent path on this and other issues, it is necessary to stress that he was not unique. The Congress leadership also changed course on the reforms at various times and the most eminent Congressmen sought to justify their acceptance of less than responsible government by falsely claiming that they had always preferred that.[75] Nor was this uniquely a feature of the 1920s. Such inconsistency – and the prima donna-ism and lone-wolfery among individual politicians which causes them to break free of the discipline of political organizations and to make frequent shifts in their stated views to gain short-term advantages – have survived as prominent features of the island's politics to the present day.[76] A fuller discussion of this must be left until chapter 5, but it is worth noting here that the problem has both personal and systemic dimensions and adequate analyses must deal with both.

The period between 1928 and mid-1931, when the election to the first State Council occurred, was a busy but reasonably peaceful time for Bandaranaike. He continued to build up his legal practice,[77] and his intelligence and legal training served him well on the Colombo Municipal Council where he was a creative, sensible member. There was time for the pedigree greyhounds that he raised with great care for Kennel Club shows, and for occasional breaks away from the city. One man, then a

[73] *CI*, 24 August 1929. See also the mockery of this event, *CI*, 2 September 1929.
[74] *CI*, 19 and 21 November 1929.
[75] *CI*, 9 and 11 September, 19 November and 21 December 1929.
[76] See, for example, J. Jupp, 'Five Sinhalese Nationalist Politicians', in W. H. Morris-Jones (ed.), *The Making of Politicians: Studies from Africa and Asia* (London, 1976), pp. 183–94.
[77] See, for example, *CI*, 14 February and 20 November 1928, 19 January 1929; and *CDN*, 29 January and 15 September 1930.

promising young writer with whom he briefly co-edited a literary magazine, recalls a few weekends at rural rest houses where Bandaranaike sat in his dressing gown sipping white wine and reading aloud from the works of Walter Pater. But those who knew him best echo the view of one of his Oxford acquaintances that 'although he gave an outward impression of self-assurance, he was basically shy'. They see him as a man who was quite lonely at the best of times and who would have been something of a recluse had it not been for his political activities.[78]

He put an enormous amount of work into establishing himself in various political associations. As Joint Secretary of the National Congress, he edited (together with R. S. S. Gunawardena whose name does not appear with Bandaranaike's on the title page) a massive *Handbook* in 1928 which is still the principal documentary source on the early years of that body. He was a member of the Political Study Circle, a small discussion group which was to fulfil D. S. Senanayake's voracious appetite for learned advice on key policy issues.[79] To make himself widely known in the outstations, Bandaranaike travelled constantly to speak to local citizens' associations, until he was seen to have 'more personal knowledge of [them] . . . than any man in this country . . .'[80] He managed to gain the presidency of two associations which, though rather insubstantial, enabled him to claim a link with urban labour (through the Ceylon Workers Federation) and with village leaders (through the All-Ceylon Village Committees Conference). And it appears that he also became the Chairman of one Village Committee and expanded its activities beyond mere road repair by starting a medical dispensary.

The election to the State Council in June 1931, was not a strenuous test for Bandaranaike. The increase in the number of elected seats enabled him to turn away from Colombo, where competition was fierce, and stand in the new constituency of Veyangoda which embraced both the family estate at Horagolla and the lands of his mother's family nearby. The prestige of Sir Solomon and – perhaps more crucially – the reputation for philanthropy of Sir Solomon's sister, Mrs J. P. Obeyesekere, made Bandaranaike a cast-iron certainty there. A quixotic Buddhist monk talked vaguely of standing against him, but in the event Bandaranaike was one of nine candidates returned unopposed.[81]

This first election by universal adult suffrage among the non-western

[78] Interviews with J. Vijayatunga, London, 10 November 1981, and R. St. L. P. Deraniyagala, Colombo, 4 September 1977 and 19 August 1980.
[79] *CI*, 2 February, 8 March and 18 October 1928 and 21 and 23 March 1929. Also, interviews with James Rutnam, 17 September 1977 and 9 September 1978.
[80] *CI*, 12 September 1928.
[81] Five of the nine, including D. S. Senanayake and D. B. Jayatilaka, were members of the old Legislative Council. *CI*, 5 August 1930 and *CDN*, 5 May 1931.

peoples of the British Empire was regarded by many as an inspiring event, but on close examination it loses much of its lustre. The total number of eligible voters fell far short of universality. In order to vote, it was necessary to register by completing official forms and submitting them – by post or through headmen – to the government. These forms were supposedly available in rural areas from major and minor headmen, but many headmen were disinclined to distribute forms either out of laziness or out of antagonism towards the electoral process which threatened their influence. Their reluctance was reinforced by an initial indication from the government that it was not their duty to assist in registration – a policy which was eventually but rather tardily reversed. Some headmen never received registration forms, as a result either of inefficiency or a desire by some superior (and mainly *Goyigama*) headmen to prevent registration in areas where their adversaries' supporters or certain non-elite castes lived in great numbers. Registration forms were rather complicated and villagers were naturally reluctant – after encounters with money-lenders and land-grabbers – to put their signatures on documents. A campaign to explain the election and the new legislature might have eased villagers' suspicions, but too little time was allowed for this. Most registrations were done by candidates or their agents, including – illegally – headmen working for candidates. This appears to have occurred most often in constituencies where a candidate was from a local patrician family or was linked to local headmen.[82] In these circumstances, it is perhaps surprising that as many as 1,582,942 or 63 per cent of those entitled to vote actually managed to register.[83] But this figure is still low enough to dampen our euphoria about 'universal' suffrage.

Even more regrettably, in most Sinhalese areas, those who were unable to vote came mainly from caste groups of lesser status and power. They were prevented from voting mainly by their own apathy and suspicion, and by efforts to thwart their registration. But some of those who registered faced physical intimidation which sometimes was quite effective. This requires explanation. These disadvantaged castes were rather unevenly distributed across the rural landscape, so that they were often concentrated in particular areas of a constituency. If constituencies

[82] *CI*, 21 July and 16 August 1930 and 21 November 1931 (concerning a later by-election); and *CDN*, 15 May 1931. Also, interviews with Sir Senerat Gunawardena, Colombo, 4 October 1978.
[83] This is based upon a necessarily rough estimate of the adult population in 1931 of 2,500,000. Extrapolated from H. E. Peries, *Census of Ceylon, 1953*, vol. i (Colombo, 1957), p. 6 and vol. ii (Colombo, 1959), p. 1. There were 706,723 votes cast. This was a 57.6 per cent turnout in constituencies where contests occurred. But it represents only 28.3 per cent of the estimated adult population.

had contained a large number of polling stations, it would have been difficult to deny these people access to the ballot box. But in 1931, as in every election before 1960, the number of polling stations was quite small. This meant that in rural areas where the terrain was often difficult, voters frequently had to traverse great distances to reach the polling place.[84] If an unscrupulous candidate knew that a group hostile to him was concentrated in a particular area and that they had to travel along a particular route to reach the polling station, he could prevent them from voting by destroying a bridge or blocking the route with rocks, fallen trees or gangs of toughs.

It must be emphasized that much less of this occurred in 1931 than in subsequent elections. Evidence of such doings is difficult to come by since the victims were usually unable or too frightened to report them and to testify at election petition hearings, but obstructive tactics probably had a significant influence on the final tallies in five to ten constituencies. Sadly, the main reason for the comparatively low incidence of intimidation and sabotage was the woeful inadequacy of the 1931 voting registers. It was unnecessary to obstruct people who had no vote.

The very small number of polling stations also forced candidates to depend heavily upon motor transport to carry voters to the polls. This made things very difficult for candidates without substantial funds. To stand for election required a deposit of Rs 1,000 – a large sum in those days – and to pay for cars and buses could severely strain resources. It was in these circumstances that there first appeared on the political stage a figure who lent a distinctive, though not particularly salubrious, air to Ceylon's politics over the next three decades – the bus owner. He played a relatively minor role in 1931. Politicians had not yet fully realized his potential usefulness, and he had not yet fully realized theirs. But he was at work nonetheless in three roles which were to grow to such importance in the elections of 1936, 1947 and 1952 that, by the early 1950s, bus magnates could plausibly claim to have the island's most formidable politicians at their beck and call.[85]

Their first role was simply to carry voters from remote villages to the polls. In Ceylon at that time, this was entirely legal. In 1931, the as yet naïve voters often felt obliged to support a candidate who had registered and transported them. Bus owners' second contribution was to the systematic impersonation of voters. Bus loads of lackeys were ferried from polling station to polling station, constituency to constituency, following the injunction from American machine politics to vote

---

[84] *CDN*, 13 and 25 June 1931. The figure of 2,000 polling stations which the government issued three months before the election (*CI*, 16 April 1931) is ridiculously high.
[85] See, for example, *TC*, 12 February 1951.

early and often. In 1931 impersonation appears to have occurred mainly in urban areas, where changes of clothes were sometimes provided to outwit poll watchers moving from station to station. It should be emphasized that I do not believe that impersonation changed many electoral results.[86] It was far less effective than intimidation and interdiction. But in 1931 it was plausibly alleged that at least one rural seat was won on support from deceased voters,[87] and impersonation certainly occurred in many other rural areas. The participation of dead and fictitious voters was the principal form of impersonation to occur in 1931 and it should be noted that they represent a certain *restraint* on the part of politicians. In subsequent elections, competition grew so keen that living voters turned up to find that their votes had already been cast. Few such complaints were heard in 1931.

The bus owners' third role was the provision of thugs on wheels. This came naturally to them since it was their practice to seek monopolies on lucrative routes by sending gangs of thugs to attack rivals' buses and personnel along roads and at bus stands. For three decades from the mid-1920s grievous assaults on bus drivers were routine, murder was not unusual and attempts to destroy rivals' buses with passengers still inside occurred occasionally – and sometimes successfully. When toughs were needed for intimidation in 1931, and more especially thereafter, bus owners readily obliged.[88] (The other main sources of such men were the employees of candidates who owned lands, mines or industrial undertakings and – when trade union organizers contested seats – unionized labourers.)

One final abuse which marred this election was the harassment of canvassers. This tended to occur when a candidate who was from outside the constituency or from a less powerful social group (or both) challenged a patrician candidate who was well connected with the landed families and headmen of the area. When such a contest developed, headmen at both the local and supra-local levels often conspired not only to register the names of fictitious voters and to prevent the registration of less powerful groups, but also to frighten people campaigning against the patrician. Vivid accounts of this emerge from a 1931 by-election which was more exhaustively covered by the press than general election contests

---

[86] I am grateful to W. Howard Wriggins for stressing this point to me.

[87] *CDN*, 25 June and 5 July 1931.

[88] There are hundreds of reports of violence on the bus lines between 1925 and 1956. For a selection from this period, see for example, *CI*, 5 June and 9 October 1928, 14 August 1929, 14–15 November 1931; *CDN*, 7 and 20 November 1930, 18–19 August 1931. It is ironic that intimidation and sabotage in rural constituencies obviated somewhat the need to bribe voters. The use of 'filthy lucre and liquor' (*CDN*, 27 November and 11 December 1930) was mainly a feature of *urban* elections until 1947.

because it occurred in isolation. In the by-election, the daughter of a leading headman sought to succeed her father after his death. The superior headman in the area organized resistance to her opponents through village headmen. One canvasser for an opponent who represented depressed caste interests was waylaid by a local headman who 'abused him . . . called him a pariah dog . . . and threatened to assault him . . . would get others to assault him and strip him of his trousers and smash his motor cycle . . .' The frightened canvasser escaped injury by promising to support the patrician candidate. The local headman openly stated that the district's leading headman, a relative of that candidate, was overseeing her campaign. Witnesses to this incident were too terrified to accompany the canvasser to the police station. Constables there told him not to file a complaint and agreed to escort him home. The canvasser was then attacked by thugs in the presence of three policemen, but even then the local police superintendent refused to investigate the matter.[89]

It is impossible to say whether the police here were frightened into playing a neutral role or were conniving with the headman. But in many cases locally powerful groups – led by headmen who were supposed to represent the colonial government's authority in the hinterland, and including policemen who were supposed to enforce it – succeeded in undermining that authority and the much-heralded electoral process.[90] Further discussion of electoral abuses can be left until later. But it is worth noting in passing that the man who ultimately took action against the three main sources of abuse – the small number of polling stations, the bus owners and the headmen – was S. W. R. D. Bandaranaike.

The election was reported as if it had been fought along party lines, but this was very misleading. The most important 'party' was the Ceylon National Congress which, as we have seen, was an insubstantial body. Congress candidates stood in only twenty-eight of fifty constituencies and won only seventeen seats. The 'party' had forbidden its members to stand or campaign against one another, but Congressman faced Congressman in four cases, including one which involved two former Presidents of the Congress. In many places Congressmen canvassed for anti-Congress candidates. Goonesinha's Labour Party put up six candidates, of whom three were successful. The only other 'party' to nominate more than one person, called itself the Liberal League and got eleven of its eighteen candidates elected. The League, however, had a far more tenuous existence than even the Congress. Indeed, it was little more than a convenient label beneath which those not enamoured of Congress could

[89] *CI*, 21 November 1931.
[90] Interviews with Sir Senerat Gunawardena, Colombo, 1 and 4 October 1978, and with two others active in that campaign, Colombo, 12 September 1977 and Kandy, 16 September 1977.

gather. They included radicals to the left of Congress who claimed that they sought election only to defy colonial authority by resigning from the Council and – in greater numbers – some of Ceylon's most eminent reactionaries who opposed Congress because it supported an income tax. The press, which used party labels, admitted that it was often difficult to determine candidates' party leanings. In reality, individual candidates stood or fell on their own resources.

A boycott of the election was organized by Tamils in the Northern Province, where they predominated, in protest against the increase in the number of Sinhalese seats. Unsuccessful attempts were made to extend it into Sinhalese areas to show opposition to the reforms. The boycott left unfilled four of the nine seats which would normally have gone to Tamils.[91]

The election brought only modest changes in the type of men – no women stood – who populated Ceylon's legislature. Nineteen members of the old Legislative Council had stood and fifteen were returned. *Goyigamas* still predominated – they comprised almost two-thirds of the Sinhalese victors – despite the extension of the franchise. In terms of education, the new Councillors were, with only a handful of exceptions, members of a rather exalted elite. The large number of lawyers, fifteen out of thirty-eight Sinhalese, is not surprising, but it is significant that ten of them were Ceylon-trained proctors rather than London-trained barristers. All of the proctors practised at courts in or very near their constituencies rather than at Colombo and two of the five barristers (including Bandaranaike) practised mainly in lower courts in or near their constituencies. This strongly suggests that the main reason so many lawyers found their way into the Council was not that they understood constitutional issues better than others, but that their practices helped them to understand the power structures in their base areas and to cultivate powerful local allies. This view is reinforced by the fact that the vast majority of Councillors were quite closely identified with their constituencies.

Christians in 1931 probably numbered no more than 8 per cent of all Sinhalese and 10 per cent of the island's population. Over 90 per cent of Sinhalese were Buddhists. The large number of Christians elected (fifteen, including Bandaranaike and ten other Sinhalese) indicates that religion played a minor role. Many Christian candidates took the precaution of having Buddhist monks appear with them to extol their generosity to Buddhist institutions.[92]

Many had expected the enlargement of the electorate to bring radicals

[91] J. Russell, The Ceylon Tamils under the Donoughmore Constitution, University of Peradeniya doctoral thesis, 1976. Also, *CDN*, 8–30 May and 22 June 1931.
[92] *CDN*, 25 June 1931.

like A. E. Goonesinha, with contacts among poorer voters, into the
Council. But apart from Goonesinha himself and S. A. Wickremasinghe,
who would develop into a Marxist leader, none was elected. This was not
because many such men had been defeated, but because only three or four
had stood. Ceylon in 1931 had few radicals who possessed the
organizational skills, the financial and political resources and the
sophistication in English (a prerequisite for candidates) to stand for
election. The institutional infrastructure required to produce such men
did not exist in Ceylon (as it did in India) at that time. The island's post-
secondary colleges turned out a small number of graduates each year. The
small circle of elite secondary schools developed conservative attitudes
among their students, and the products of such institutions had little
difficulty, even in the early depression years, in finding useful employment. They were taken into the system while still in their teens, before
they could develop iconoclastic views. The members of the westernized
elite who later established leftist organizations were still overseas in 1931,
in British (and, in one case, American) universities, imbibing Marxist
attitudes which were so popular there. The limits which the faulty system
of registration placed upon the electorate and the machinations of bus
owners, headmen and thugs also weighed in favour of moderate and
reactionary candidates. Indeed, members of the emerging generation of
political leaders who had previously expressed anti-headmen sentiments
now found headmen useful, even essential, in winning elections.

Nonetheless, this election sounded a clear note of warning to the old
order in rural Ceylon. Candidates who came from elite headmen's families
encountered difficulty if they relied primarily upon family status to win
them votes. Four of them were beaten – indeed, two were thrashed – a
fifth scraped through and a sixth might have lost had officials not assured
him victory by a late change in the polling day to wreck his opponent's
plans for borrowed transport.[93] To be at all secure in politics, candidates
from such backgrounds had to have access to people with organizational
skills to muster supporters, motor transport and money. Those who
relied too heavily upon what they themselves called 'the feudal pull',
upon the bonds of obligation between subordinate and superior, those
who were too complacent about their constituents' affections and too
unused to flexing economic muscle – such people had little future in the
new politics. Elite candidates in the Kandyan highlands at the centre of
the island were especially vulnerable, unlike the low-country elites who

[93] The first four constituencies were Katugampola, Hambantota, Puttalam and Ratnapura
(*CDN*, 25 June 1931). The fifth was Galagadera and the sixth, Gampola. Interview with
Sir Senerat Gunawardena, Colombo, 3 September 1978. He lost Gampola in 1931, but
won it against the candidate from a leading headman's family in 1936.

were far more familiar with the need to wheel and deal. Men who opposed elite Kandyans found that the mere act of addressing voters as equals was a radical departure for poor people, to which they responded avidly.[94]

Bandaranaike gained a rather artificial impression of the 1931 election. As an unopposed candidate, he stood at one remove from its unseemly side – from the tawdry conspiracies to deny voters their rights, the courting of wealthy backers and the thugs' barbarities. (Nor had he known, during his 1926 campaign in Maradana, that toughs had been mobilized by certain of his aides who felt that a gentleman should not be taxed with such information.)[95] He was not wholly ignorant of these things in 1931, but they did not intrude too much upon a young man's naturally optimistic view of a process which had brought him – rather earlier than he might have hoped – to a position of considerable responsibility and promise. For him the election campaign consisted of brief visits to others' constituencies for impassioned speeches, for the giving and receiving of flattery, for the warmth of the crowds' applause.

After the election, Bandaranaike could look back on the six and a half years since his return from Oxford with a certain chastened satisfaction. There had been disappointments. He had only begun to learn, through repeated embarrassment, that hasty action and slashing rhetoric could lead to trouble. His tendency to strike rather extreme postures on public platforms in response to the demands of advocacy, and to change those postures when confronted with a different audience had earned him a reputation for inconsistency. Nor did a few instances of wilful dishonesty go unnoticed. His confidence in his abilities, education and social position gave him a useful resilience, but he still felt frustrated by the coolness shown to him by leading politicians who were suspicious of his background, his abilities and his occasionally devious ways. There were other reasons to feel depressed. In late 1929, he publicly confessed to feeling 'despondent' at allowing himself to be caught up in the pettiness of the political game. At Oxford, he said, he had dreamed of doing great things for the people of Ceylon, 'for the poor and ignorant, the industrial workers and the peasants'. He conceded that he had failed in this.[96] A year later, he admitted to 'feeling rather bitter':

So many hours of his time, the expenditure of so much trouble and energy, and what was it all worth? Nothing. Where would it all lead to? Nowhere . . . nothing ever came of it; there did not appear to be any movement in Ceylon which led to any lasting good . . .[97]

[94] Interview with Sir Razik Fareed, Colombo, 1 September 1978.
[95] Interview with J. Vijayatunga, London, 10 November 1981.
[96] *CI*, 16 December 1929.   [97] Bandaranaike, *Speeches and Writings*, p. 576.

Nonetheless, much that had happened in this period need not have depressed him. His victory in 1926 against the feared Goonesinha gave him an ideal start in politics. It helped him to establish – both privately and publicly – a substantial degree of independence from his father and the things that his father represented. It helped him to show, in his work on the Municipal Council, that he could be a first-rate legislator, and to gain grudging admission to the second rank of the emerging political elite. His work in various public associations, his endless speechmaking and no doubt his eminent name had earned him widespread recognition as a man of promise. The delimitation of constituency boundaries under the new Constitution provided him with a legislative seat that would remain safe for the rest of his life. The opening of seven ministries to elected legislators in 1931 created the opportunity for him eventually to entrench himself very near the apex of power.

Even in some of his misadventures – the short-lived Progressive National Party, his ill-considered intervention in the harbour strike, and his outburst against the island's 'putrescent' politics – there were signs that he was prepared to look beyond the narrow political conventions of the day. The Sinhalese chauvinism which tainted and ultimately undermined his career in later years was not yet a major preoccupation in this early period. He had shown himself to be free of caste prejudice which was enough to mark him out as a more progressive figure than most of the island's prominent politicians. And although he was still too timid to differ with them over class-based issues, the first indications that he would do so were discernible in some of his speeches. Membership in the new State Council would bring this more sharply into focus, since it would confront Bandaranaike and Ceylon's political elite with the major issues of the day: the needs of ordinary people for land, education, other services and a sense of cultural identity.

4

COUNCILLOR, 1931–1936

Bandaranaike had looked forward with great expectancy to the opening of the State Council in July 1931, but events soon dampened his euphoria. He had rather naïvely hoped that the Ceylon National Congress would function as a coherent force in the Council, but a meeting of Congress legislators a week before the opening provided several ill omens. Even before the meeting, they were badly divided by quarrels which had arisen during the election and by jockeying for the seven ministerial posts. They were asked to commit themselves to the principles on which Congress had fought the election, but then could not agree on what these principles were. Since Congressmen numbered only seventeen in a house of fifty-seven members, a proposal to empower D. B. Jayatilaka to negotiate over ministries with other elements in the Council required unanimous support to be fully effective, but it failed to receive it. Jayatilaka then forged an agreement with nominated European Councillors, but the price that he paid – a promise not to seek constitutional revision or an extension of the Council's power over the public service and finance – astonished younger Congressmen by violating the pledge to seek constitution reform on which at least they had campaigned.[1]

The system for allotting legislators to the seven Executive Committees, which was less predictable than expected, further confused matters by causing unforeseen contests between Congressmen for ministries. One such occurred within the Executive Committee for Local Administration, on which Bandaranaike sat (by preference). He, the youngest member, rather blithely aspired to the chair, but found that two other Congressmen harboured similar ambitions. He discreetly withdrew, unlike the others who divided four votes between them and let in a non-Congressman, Charles Batuwantudawe. He was a barrister, son of a famous Sinhalese scholar, a supporter of Buddhist schools and youth groups, and was to be one of the most ineffectual ministers in the first State Council. Only three ministries went to Congressmen: Agriculture

[1] *CDN*, 1 and 3 July 1931.

and Lands to D. S. Senanayake, Education to C. W. W. Kannangara and Home Affairs to Jayatilaka. The last won by a single vote, cast by a European. Five of the seven ministers were Sinhalese and Buddhist, the four already named plus T. B. Panabokke, a proctor and the leading Kandyan in the headman's hierarchy, at Health. An Indian Tamil barrister and representative of estate workers, Peri Sunderam, reassured minorities by winning Labour, Commerce and Industry. And the wealthy Muslim merchant, H. M. Macan Markar, emerged at Communications and Works. Jayatilaka was chosen Leader of the House.[2]

However unlikely Bandaranaike may have seemed as a ministerial candidate, he appears to have felt aggrieved at his exclusion and to have blamed Congress ministers for it. He was not a man to bottle up a grievance for long. His first utterance in the chamber where he was to serve until his death was an ill-considered challenge to Jayatilaka which was promptly ruled out of order. His maiden speech a few days later contained reference to Cicero and Disraeli, passages in Latin and Greek and a quotation from Milton. It was generally regarded as 'overdressed'. Bandaranaike's main theme was that councillors and ministers should reduce their pay and emoluments in light of the poverty of the masses. His main target was the minister from his own Executive Committee, under whose leadership he chafed bitterly. In an entirely honest and accurate comment, which was nonetheless self-righteous, he implied that for his modest lifestyle he needed no large salary. He 'enjoyed no special advantages but lived off his income at the Bar . . .'. If ministers were more concerned with salaries than with the poor, an army of hungry peasants might pull down the Council chamber.[3]

This was more than Jayatilaka could abide. He and other Buddhist nationalists had been snubbed by rich conspicuous consumers of the Bandaranaike clan for decades and now he was being lectured on austerity by the latest in the line. He leapt to his feet to protest:

The mob that will march up from the other end of Veyangoda may have to pass a magnificent residence with a menagerie which they will have to pull down (loud laughter). And perhaps the mob will wait there to question the laird as to why there should be a magnificent residence with all those menageries and every amenity of civilised life while the people in that district are starving. (Uproarious applause.)[4]

Onlookers were astonished at this encounter because, until then, it had been assumed that Bandaranaike was a protégé of Jayatilaka. A few days earlier they had been jointly feted by a labour association and they had worked closely during the election campaign.[5] Indeed, this clash probably

---

[2] *CDN*, 3, 7–10 July 1931.   [3] *CDN*, 11 and 29 July 1931.
[4] *CDN*, 29 July 1931.   [5] *CDN*, 27 July 1931.

surprised Bandaranaike himself. He responded with an attempt to explain himself which only made things worse. His tone in doing so suggested disbelief that Jayatilaka should take offence at his remarks. There emerges here an insensitivity, a tendency towards self-indulgence, an un-selfconsciousness in Bandaranaike. At such moments, there was about him an air of the precocious youth whose verbal excesses were tolerated, even enjoyed by early audiences, and not taken at face value. He noticed not the content of his words so much as the flair with which they tripped off the tongue and he was taken aback when others heeded their literal meaning. In time he learned greater caution in public statements, but his inability to foresee or accept the full consequences of his rhetoric, which was as naïve as it was malign, was always there. And that, together with conscious irresponsibility in public statements – as is evident in the second of the quotations which precede the preface to this book – in later years took a grievous toll.

Bandaranaike's quarrel with the ministers did not end there. It was fuelled not only by his thwarted ambition but by more widely shared grievances over the ministers' dealing with British officials who – in contravention of the spirit of the Donoughmore reforms – were determined to minimize the State Council's power. On the Council's second full day, members rejected a supplement of Rs 50,000 for civil servants' sea passages despite ministers' support for it. The Governor immediately used his special powers to declare it passed. Since expenditure on civil servants consumed almost half of Ceylon's budget, this reminded legislators of their limited authority and heated protests followed. Bandaranaike helped to lead them, claiming that ministers had shown 'miserable weakness'[6] in supporting the motion. This was no isolated clash[7] and ministers were soon forced to make concessions to councillors' desire for firmness in their dealings with the Governor. A few weeks later, when Bandaranaike's name was proposed for the Ceylon National Congress presidency, Congress ministers may have seen this as an opportunity to soothe his vanity and did not oppose him.

Neither of these things did much to ease the ministers' lot in Council debates. The Governor's powers were sufficient to overwhelm or outmanoeuvre them in almost any situation. They were thus forced to seek accommodations with him which provoked further conflict with councillors. And Bandaranaike's elevation to the Congress presidency only whetted his appetite for contention. Thus in January 1932 we find him attacking the Board of Ministers as 'an extraordinary spineless body who could swallow anything that they were given . . . That any good

[6] *CDN*, 8 August 1931. See also, 30 July and 3 August 1931.
[7] *CI*, 6 November and 19 and 21 December 1931.

thing could come out of the Board of Ministers was a matter of grave doubt.'⁸ In making these attacks, he claimed to speak as the 'Leader of the Congress Party in the Council.'⁹ This was pretentious and misleading since Congress legislators were not a coherent group and since their real leaders were still Jayatilaka and Senanayake, but it made things doubly embarrassing for ministers.

A climax was reached, in March 1932, when Bandaranaike introduced a motion protesting against the 'grave invasion' of the Council's rights by the Governor, who had rammed through numerous measures against the legislative will. He spoke as if the Congress held a majority rather than 30 per cent of the seats and asked that Congress members take no further part in Council proceedings until they could 'obtain the mandate of his party' and then return to demand constitutional reform. D. S. Senanayake rose and authoritatively squashed this scheme by demonstrating that it could accomplish nothing. He did not have to explain the most pertinent fact, that Bandaranaike was engaging in a fantasy in his references to 'his party'. Instead, he expressed his own bitter regret that the Council lacked adequate powers. Their only sensible choices were 'to clear out . . . to go out and suffer to the bitter end' or to make the best of the unhappy situation. Empty protests such as Bandaranaike's only emphasized their weakness. The young man had been bested and indeed humiliated, for he was assailed in the press for this 'farce', his 'mock heroics' and the 'orgy of talk' of 'prating patriots'.¹⁰

His response to this was curious and revealing. Within a month, he was publicly hailing the 'tremendous amount of good work' done in the State Council. The Constitution had 'not been a curse but a blessing in disguise' and of Jayatilaka, he said 'there is no more devoted and sincere worker for the welfare of the people'. The newspapers were 'like a pack of dogs . . . howling and jumping and barking', criticizing the Council without constructive comments.¹¹ Bandaranaike had kicked against authority – in this case against Senanayake, Jayatilaka, and other ministers – but even as he rebelled, he was unable to sever his ties to them. His political position was heavily dependent upon them and he could not bring himself to go it alone. So, having been humiliated at their hands, he undertook a complete reversal of view, apparently quite cheerfully, and resumed for a time the role of the helpful subordinate. This pattern recurred repeatedly in his later dealings with authority – with that of the British and with D. S. Senanayake after independence. Not surprisingly, it made him seem inconsistent, irrational and cowardly. It intensified suspicions of him and

⁸ The quotation is from *CI*, 27 January 1932. See also, *CI*, 18 and 22 January and 6 and 10 February 1932.   ⁹ See, for example, 13 and 18 February 1932.
¹⁰ *CI*, 17–18 March 1932.   ¹¹ *CI*, 11 April 1932.

ensured that he could never achieve political pre-eminence until many
years later when he ended his reliance on others and set out to build an
independent force.

The echoes of Indian nationalism in Bandaranaike's more defiant
speeches were not just coincidental. The period between late 1930 and
early 1933 can be seen as something of a Gandhian phase in his career. His
extensive, albeit selective, borrowing from the Gandhian canon began at
the December 1930 conference of the Ceylon National Congress where he
offered a 'spirited advocacy' for the spinning of *khadi* (homespun cotton
cloth).[12] It was no accident that this occurred amid one of the major
agitational phases of the Indian struggle, but it was rather belated. On the
day – nine months earlier – when a few Ceylonese had met to protest
Gandhi's arrest after the famous salt march, Bandaranaike had been
warning his countrymen of the 'Indian menace'.[13] Nevertheless by May
1931, he had occasionally taken to embracing that most visible element of
the Gandhian idiom, the wearing of *khadi*. Our first glimpse of him as a
State Councillor is a press photograph taken on the threshold of the
Council building, just before its ceremonial opening. He is standing next
to his father and the image they present suggests not just two generations
but two world views, two modes of politics – one which time has
overtaken and another struggling to find its way. Sir Solomon is dressed
in a grey cutaway coat and striped trousers with grey kid gloves, a fedora
and spats. His son wears a white homespun *dhoti*, *banian*, shawl and
sandals.

Several things about Bandaranaike's approach to the wearing of *khadi*
and to this occasion were distinctly odd. First, he was not content (as were
some other councillors) merely to appear in what he called the 'national
dress'. He also felt it necessary to announce his intention in advance in a
letter to the press. He began with a pretentious suggestion, which was
almost certainly untrue, that 'there is apparently some curiosity regarding
the dress in which I shall be attending the dinner at Queens House [and
the State Council] . . .'. He would wear: 'national dress . . . of cloth spun
and woven at my centre at Urapola . . . for footwear I shall wear a pair of
sandals made of Ceylon leather by a poor Ceylonese cobbler living in my
Ward of Maradana. I have also secured some very nice Ceylon made
buttons, manufactured, I believe, at Wellawatte.'[14] There are clear echoes
here of Gandhi's call for simple, indigenous dress and support for local

---

[12] *CDN*, 13 and 15 December 1930 and S. W. R. D. Bandaranaike, *Speeches and Writings*
(Colombo, 1963), p. 577. Bandaranaike had had a fleeting encounter with Gandhi
previously, during the latter's tour of Ceylon when he addressed the Colombo
Municipal Council of which Bandaranaike was a member.
[13] *CDN*, 26 March 1930.   [14] *CDN*, 8 and 13 July 1931.

Bandaranaike in 'native dress' after his initial election to the Ceylon
legislature, alongside his father who is turned out in the Edwardian manner.
(Courtesy of the British Library Newspaper Library.)

cottage industry. But they clash with the patrician tone: '*my* centre at
Urapola . . . *my* Ward of Maradana . . .' And the Gandhian mood is
shattered completely by the unintended comedy of his next comment, a
recommendation of other *khadi* garments for other occasions: 'for riding,
a pair of riding breeches, a suitable pair of trousers for tennis, a loin cloth
for working in the field, etc.'[15] If Gandhi was unlikely to don riding
breeches or trousers for tennis, we may be sure that Bandaranaike stopped
well short of both the loin cloth and work in the field.

Bandaranaike was not entirely at home in this new attire. It was
reported that he wore socks in his sandals – a breach of custom – and that
they were held up by suspenders of foreign origin. And a day later, he had
reverted to the European suit and high stiff collar in which he eventually
sat for his official photograph.[16] His much talked of commitment to a

---

[15] *CDN*, 4 and 8 July 1931. See also, *CDN*, 25 May 1931.
[16] *CDN*, 8–9 July 1931 and the picture gallery in the old Parliament building, Galle Face,
    Colombo. A correspondent wrote to the press (*CDN*, 10 July 1931):

        I wish to make a simple plea
        Against the inconsistency
        Of those who hastily divest
        Them of the garments of the West . . .

'revival' of the 'national dress' was throughout his life called into question by his habit of appearing, often and unexpectedly, in European clothes. Collette, the brilliant cartoonist of the 1950s, captured this perfectly when he depicted Bandaranaike clad on his left side in 'national dress' and on his right in a European suit.

There is also considerable doubt about whether there was a national dress to revive. None of the alternatives in use by the Sinhalese seemed appropriate. The ceremonial Kandyan costume required the wearer to swathe himself laboriously in fourteen yards of cloth and was far too complex for everyday use. The usual dress of a male villager was a sarong which seemed unsuitable for sittings of the State Council. And for many low country Sinhalese – even those who were but slightly westernized – European trousers and shirt were common to an extent unknown in India. Bandaranaike obliquely acknowledged the difficulty by conceding that 'there may be some divergence of opinion as to the exact form of national dress we should adopt . . .' In fact, the form which was adopted was largely derived from South Indian dress, although a Sinhalese nationalist could hardly admit it. When Bandaranaike wore the 'national dress' to his bride's Kandyan village on his wedding day years later, some of the local peasants mistook the bridegroom for a Tamil.[17]

In addition to his concern for dress reform, Bandaranaike drew occasionally upon other elements of Gandhian canon, but he soon found that many of the Mahatma's tenets did not suit his purposes and Ceylon's political environment. An austere lifestyle, which Bandaranaike welcomed, would never be popular among the Ceylonese elite. Concern for the uplift of untouchables was largely irrelevant to the Sinhalese caste system. Anti-casteism was relevant and commanded Bandaranaike's support, but caste has generally been a forbidden topic in public discourse. Gandhi's campaigns for the Hindi language sought (even if it partly failed) to unify Indians who spoke a multiplicity of languages, whereas an emphasis on Sinhala and Tamil (the only two vernacular languages) tended to divide Ceylonese. The political use of religious symbols, which he might also have borrowed from Gandhi, was in the early 1930s impossible for the still nominally Anglican Bandaranaike. Finally and most crucially, unlawful or even lawful acts of defiance towards the imperial power received only the most minimal support at the best of times.

Bandaranaike learned this by experience. In late 1931, he spoke of 'the

---

[17] I am grateful to Jane Russell for this information. See also, *CDN*, 4, 7–8 and 23–24 July 1931 and J. Russell, The Ceylon Tamils under the Donoughmore Constitution, University of Peradeniya doctoral thesis, 1976, pp. 217–18. This thesis was eventually published as *Communal Politics under the Donoughmore Constitution, 1931–1957* (Dehiwala, 1982).

suffering and sacrifice which the struggle will inevitably involve', but it is impossible to find even the faintest beginnings of a 'struggle' in Ceylon. In January 1932, he demonstrated his unwillingness to accept the legitimacy of British rule when he spoke at a rally in Colombo to protest at the arrest of Gandhi (although it was ten months late and he had been freed by then), where a decision was taken to boycott British goods. But nothing came of this or of his talk of a 'coming countrywide struggle',[18] partly because the basis for such struggles had not been developed and mainly because he made no attempt to translate his words into action. Although his earlier articles on spinning were not published as a pamphlet until May 1933, his Gandhian phase was ebbing rapidly to a close by late 1932. Attempts in January of 1933 to mount demonstrations in Ceylon in sympathy with renewed Congress civil disobedience in India fell quite flat without any assistance from Bandaranaike or other prominent politicians. Gandhi was sentenced to a year in prison in August without a tremor of protest from the island's elite. Although Bandaranaike talked occasionally of encouragement for indigenous industry and even tried to launch a further unsuccessful boycott of British goods,[19] he had largely abandoned the Gandhian way by early 1933. He maintained his calls for dress reform and the revival of indigenous language and religion but, as we shall see, his manner of doing so was distinctly un-Gandhian.

This raises a much larger question. It is remarkable that on an island only a few miles from mainland India, no serious attempt at civil disobedience was made during the Gandhian heyday. However superficial and irresolute Bandaranaike's flirtation with Gandhian politics may seem, he went much further than most Ceylonese politicians in identifying with this mode of resistance to British rule. As he said, 'The factors which militate against its successful use, particularly in a country like ours, are many.'[20]

What were they? First there were the habits of mind of the Sinhalese elite. Throughout the elite, there was a marked prejudice against India and Indians. This was based not upon unhappy encounters with India but rather upon a *lack* of encounters, upon great ignorance of India. It was vastly more common – then as now – for members of the Sinhalese elite to travel to Britain rather than to India for study or the serious exchange of ideas. And very few extended stopovers in India were made *en route*. Many

[18] The quotations are from *CI*, 19 December 1931 and 17 August 1932. See also, *CDN*, 25 July 1931 and *CI*, 21 December 1931 and 11 January 1932.
[19] *CI*, 4 and 18 January, 6–13 August and 10 November 1933, and 14–17 September 1934. See also, 'The Spinning Wheel and the Paddy Field', in Bandaranaike, *Speeches and Writings*. [20] *CDN*, 25 April 1935.

who had been to Britain, repeatedly and for long periods, had never been to Bombay or even Madras. Ceylon newspapers had far more in them about Britain and the west than about their near neighbours. Even Sinhalese intellectuals – then as now – were rather poorly informed on conditions in India and on the subcontinent's vibrant intellectual life. Many prosperous Sinhalese, whose main contact with Indians was with labourers in Ceylon, tended to generalize from that experience. A matron of the Bandaranaike–Obeyesekere clan once refused to entertain Jawaharlal Nehru to tea on the grounds that she did not sup with coolies, until it was explained that – like Ceylon – India had its patricians too.[21] Those who liken the Sinhalese view of India to an Afrikaaner mentality are guilty of some overstatement. But there was and is a great deal of suspicion that Tamils in Ceylon have over their shoulder in India tens of millions of Tamils and hundreds of millions of Indians who differ from Sinhalese in customs, religion and – it is erroneously but repeatedly said – race.

Members of the Sinhalese elite generally saw themselves as more sophisticated than their Indian counterparts, by which they usually meant more westernized. It is true that western influences were more prevalent among them. Western manners, food, drink, clothing, music, language, literature, sport, modes of entertainment, Christianity, Christian education, modes of thought and political precedents – all of these things loomed larger in the life of the Sinhalese elite than among their counterparts in any region of India. But to say this is not to endorse the claims of would-be Sinhalese sophisticates. Western influences could penetrate more deeply into their lives because there was less to stand in their way than in India. This is not intended as a slur against the Sinhalese, but as a reminder that the low-country areas of Ceylon where the most westernized Sinhalese lived had experienced almost four centuries of domination by Portuguese, Dutch and British regimes, all of which were more uncompromising than were the British in India,[22] partly because these areas were so much smaller and easier to control than the regions of India. Inevitably this western domination, and the process of urbanization which touched the lives of a larger proportion of Sinhalese than was true of any Indian regional group, had eroded indigenous customs and habits of mind. It had sapped the strength of traditional power centres and cultural, educational, religious and social institutions of the kind

---

[21] Interview with Frederick Obeyesekere, Colombo, 9 September 1978.
[22] Compare P. Peebles, The Transformation of a Colonial Elite: The Mudaliyars of Nineteenth-Century Ceylon, University of Chicago doctoral thesis, 1973, with D. A. Washbrook, *The Emergence of Provincial Politics: The Madras Presidency, 1870–1920* (Cambridge, 1976).

which proved so formidable in shaping Indian responses to British rule. It had left a larger proportion of the Ceylonese elite with an inadequate grasp of indigenous languages and a lack of sympathy with indigenous culture and religion than was true in the regions of India. The regional responses in India to British cultural imperialism were earlier in developing, borrowed less from alien models and were more amenable to elite–mass integration than was true in Ceylon. Bandaranaike himself implicitly lamented the results of de-culturation in low-country Ceylon and linked a Buddhist cultural revival to his dream of 'a people, who do not cringe, whine and beg, who are jealous of their rights and privileges . . .'.[23]

The indigenous traditions of India's regions also tended to be more fully and richly integrated with western ideas than in Ceylon. In painstakingly assimilating European life styles, many (perhaps most) westernized Ceylonese sought the indispensable marks of elite member-ship rather than substantive acculturation through western learning.[24] It was secondary schools rather than universities which most westernized Ceylonese attended and by which people have always tended to be judged, whether or not they attended a university. Ceylon's leading secondary schools were valued more for the provision of gentlemanly attributes than for the education that they offered. Biographical sketches of important Ceylonese nearly always stress achievements at cricket and rugby before academic honours. This was far less common among westernized Indians. In most (though not all) regions of India, western-style universities had been established in the mid-nineteenth century and had developed more quickly and far more extensively than in Ceylon where a University College was not founded until 1921. Medical and legal colleges had been founded earlier, but there were in 1930 only 891 post-secondary students in the island.[25] A great many Indians studied in universities in or near their own regions, often in institutions run by Indian religious groups. Higher study in India was thus more closely linked to indigenous ideas and language than in Ceylon. A far larger proportion of Ceylonese than Indian graduates before 1940 had attended British universities. Not surprisingly, graduates of India's regional universities were less alienated from the masses of their regions than were Ceylonese who had been to Oxbridge and London.

[23] Bandaranaike, *Speeches and Writings*, p. 293. This will emerge from a close reading of 'Buddhism and National Progress', written in 1934, in *Speeches and Writings*, pp. 292–94. It is also implicit in much of his later political rhetoric, especially from 1955–56.
[24] Peebles, The Transformation, p. 231. His comments on the nineteenth century remain largely appropriate, in this regard at least, to Bandaranaike's lifetime.
[25] There were 360 in law, 193 in medicine and 338 in arts and sciences. K. M. de Silva (ed.), *University of Ceylon History of Ceylon* (Peradeniya, 1973), vol. iii, pp. 272–73 and 470–71.

Another element which seldom arises in discussions of Ceylon's political history is important to an understanding of it. There existed among Ceylonese, and most especially among elite Sinhalese, what might be termed a habit of deference to those of superior status and power. This extended with diminishing strength beyond the island's westernized elites to elites in the villages, and survived through Bandaranaike's lifetime and beyond. The patience of subordinates in the face of autocratic and wayward behaviour by party leaders, including Bandaranaike, can only be explained in terms of an unconscious but strong deferential bent.

Its origins can be traced in part to pre-colonial Sinhalese society in which 'Proximity to the ruler was a criterion of status . . .', and to Sinhalese kings' demands for great deference from subjects.[26] The strong inclination among Sinhalese to seek the ruler's patronage was used and developed by the island's European rulers who inherited the high status of traditional rulers. The Portuguese, who held low-country Ceylon from the 1590s, ruled quite uncompromisingly but nonetheless used Sinhalese officials as intermediaries between themselves and the people. The Dutch, who had replaced them by 1658, maintained most Sinhalese officials in their posts and governed through them, using them as translators. Sinhalese mudaliyars (superior headmen) were forced to profess Christianity, which usually meant a change from Roman Catholicism to the Dutch Reformed faith[27] since most had accommodated themselves to Portuguese preferences in this and other matters. The Dutch system, which cultivated and institutionalized the deference of people at several levels by creating titles and symbols of office in response to a desire for visible demonstrations of status, was inherited by the British when they replaced the Dutch in 1796. In establishing their rule across southern Asia, the British usually accepted and developed pre-existing patterns of governance, and so it was in Ceylon. Like the Dutch, they found that 'the mudaleyars sought the tangible signs of legitimacy from the colonial powers *more than direct material rewards* . . . The mudaleyars competed hungrily for the symbols of status – medals, titles, retainers, and privileges that could be used to enhance one's claim to rank.'[28] In the nineteenth and early twentieth centuries, Sinhalese sought land grants from the British less as sources of wealth than 'as symbols of government patronage'.[29] The florid sycophancy of the memorials which senior Sinhalese mudaliyars – including Sir Solomon Dias Bandaranaike[30] –

---

[26] Peebles, *The Transformation*, p. 69. He notes that when members of the Karava, Salagama and Durava castes told stories of their groups' founders – traditionally an occasion for emphasizing the exalted status of forbears – they spoke, respectively, of Sinhalese kings' mercenaries, their weavers of gold tassels and officials at their weddings.　[27] *Ibid.*, p. 49.　[28] *Ibid.*, p. 65.

[29] *Ibid.*, p. 222.　[30] See the material in file 4, BP.

addressed to British officials were paralleled by the servile tone of petitions which the mudaliyars themselves received from below.

D. S. Senanayake and many of his associates, including young Bandaranaike, loathed this cringing tone. But they realized that this attitude towards the island's rulers permeated the various Sinhalese elites. (Indeed, some of them shared elements of it themselves.) They also realized, perhaps instinctively rather than consciously, that civil disobedience was an unpromising alternative in such an atmosphere. It may also have crossed their minds that, as likely heirs to the British and to the deference which the British enjoyed, they had good reasons for not changing the deferential ways of their countrymen.

The non-occurrence of civil disobedience is explained not only by habits of mind but by more tangible impediments as well. The small number of post-secondary students in Ceylon left politicians without an important source of footsoldiers and key lieutenants for agitations. The needs of Ceylon's economy generally exceeded the supply of graduates so that the existing order seemed far less alienating to educated young people than in India with its large numbers of educated underemployed. Similarly, Ceylon's politicians were unable to proceed, as so many of India's regional leaders did, on the reassuring assumption that they had behind them an indigenous population of massive numerical strength. In Ceylon, the numbers simply were not there. The island's population – just over 6 million in 1931, of whom less than 3 million were Sinhalese of the comparatively modernized low-country on whom disobedience had to be based – was not vastly greater than that of the largest British Indian districts.

There also existed in Ceylon political, social and economic structures which impeded the adoption of Gandhian modes of resistance. Civil disobedience required a degree of solidarity among leaders, but the political structures created under the Donoughmore Constitution – particularly the Executive Committees – systematically fragmented the island's political leadership. If disobedience *required* political cohesion, it also *produced* it. Gandhi's great agitations strengthened his organization by forcing members to decide between opting out and submitting to discipline. They emerged from their shared adversity with shared values that added to the solidarity of the movement.[31] In the absence of such struggles in Ceylon, political organizations remained flaccid and insubstantial.

---

[31] See, for example, D. A. Low (ed.), *Congress and the Raj: Facets of the Indian Struggle* (London, 1976) and J. Manor, *Political Change in an Indian State: Mysore, 1917–1955* (Canberra and New Delhi, 1977).

This fact and the absence of penetrative political structures, such as good local government institutions, made it impossible for politicians to begin to bridge the social gulf which separated the small political elite in Colombo from the mass of rural dwellers. The social cleavage which separated Sinhalese and Tamils also added to Sinhalese leaders' aversion to civil disobedience. It was difficult to conceive of an issue that would unite both groups sufficiently for struggle against the government, and the Tamil boycott at the 1931 election had associated defiant techniques with Tamil sectarianism in Sinhalese minds.

Finally, the structure of the economy weighed against civil disobedience. Ceylon was far more heavily dependent upon exports, mainly to Britain and almost exclusively through expatriate trading firms, than was any region of India. British planters were a far more formidable force – in the economy as a whole and in the control of land – than in Indian regions and Sinhalese had generated little in the way of their own banking and credit institutions. Nearly two-thirds of private capital invested in Ceylon in the 1930s was in non-Ceylonese hands. Ceylon had not developed major industrial houses of the type which sometimes lent aid to nationalists in India because nineteenth-century entrepreneurs had preferred to invest in sectors protected by (and hence dependent upon) the government – mainly country liquor and toll rents.[32] Thus, Ceylon possessed no 'national bourgeoisie'. In the absence of more than minimal economic self-sufficiency, political defiance was an exceedingly difficult choice. Nearly all of the politicians who might have initiated disobedience were linked to British economic interests, usually through investments in planting or extractive industries which depended on export or through landholdings which had been acquired – often a generation earlier – by manipulating colonial officials and ordinances. It is likely that they not only *were* linked to British interests, but they *felt* linked to them. They also recognized that many of the landholders and entrepreneurs who were their key supporters also felt dependent upon British interests. Bandaranaike was for the most part an exception to this, but in the first State Council, exceptions were in short supply.

The most immediate and compelling reasons for this reluctance to adopt civil disobedience were, however, political. If leading politicians were doing reasonably well out of the colonial economy, they were doing extremely well out of the new political order. Those who became ministers in 1931 had an opportunity shared by few of the world's colonial subjects to establish themselves as pre-eminent leaders in the short term and, ultimately, as heirs to sovereign power. Those who failed

[32] Peebles, The Transformation, p. 175.

to gain ministries could take comfort in their ambitions. The Donoughmore system was too promising to warrant serious disruption.

These men were elitists. Their testimony before the Donoughmore Commission had demonstrated this. So did their refusal to allow the Ceylon National Congress to become democratic or to acquire organizational substance.[33] So did their reluctance as ministers to use patronage powers to forge transactional alliances with followers who might curtail their freedom of manoeuvre. So did their refusal to carry out the Donoughmore mandate to build a strong, penetrative system of local boards. Civil disobedience meant popular mobilization through a strong, extensive organization, and when the suffering was over, the footsoldiers and middlemen in the organization would feel that they had earned the right to a greater voice in public affairs. The island's leading politicians had been reluctant enough to grant them the vote, and they were hardly prepared to risk their freedom of action by drawing them into greater political involvement. Finally, the senior leaders had been to prison once, involuntarily, in 1915. It had been a harrowing experience and it was unlikely that they wished to repeat it. Nor did they care to launch a movement which would end their monopoly on jail-going, from which they had had plenty of political mileage.

After his humiliating defeat in the Council by the ministers in March 1932, which had cowed him into submission, Bandaranaike served for a time as a helpful supporter of the ministers. During 1932 he assisted them in, among other things, a campaign for constitutional reforms to limit the Governor's power and make ministers responsible to the whole Council.[34] His change of heart and the growing realization in the Council that there was little hope of early concessions from the British helped to mute conflict between councillors and ministers. Attention now focused on the principal conflict of the time, that between the Council led by its ministers and the Governor backed by the Secretary of State for the Colonies. This conflict became sharper as the depression forced painful decisions about retrenchment.[35] (It is both sad and revealing that it was mainly in this manner, and not in terms of mass deprivation, that the depression arose for debate in the first State Council.) The comparatively generous recommendations of the Donoughmore Report were fulfilled neither by its supposed embodiment, the Order in Council, which violated the letter of the Report,[36] nor by the actions of Governor Sir Graeme Thomson

[33] For more on this see M. Roberts' extended introduction in vol. i of his *Documents of the Ceylon National Congress and Nationalist Politics in Ceylon, 1929–1950* (Colombo, 1977).
[34] *CI*, 25 April, 22 June and 21 July 1932.
[35] See, for example, *CI*, 2 and 8 January, 23 February and 2, 3 and 25 March 1933.
[36] See, for example, *CI*, 4 July 1932.

who violated its spirit. When Thomson suffered a mental breakdown and was replaced by Sir Edward Stubbs in December 1935, Ceylon's politicians hoped for some improvement, but it soon became apparent that Stubbs was another old-fashioned colonial administrator who took the same hard line.[37]

Bandaranaike was unable to accept the authority of any superior with any comfort and, within seven months of his submission to the ministers' authority, he was again crossing swords with D. S. Senanayake.[38] Such incidents cropped up now and again throughout the life of the first State Council, but they happened less often than before 1931, and when they happened, the results were less embarrassing for Bandaranaike. This was because his criticisms of ministers and the British were now presented more shrewdly, with less reliance on rhetoric and more evidence, carefully marshalled. There was still plenty of the old presumptuous self-advertisement in these forays, but it was leavened with sensible suggestions and telling insights. His criticism of a land bill in 1933 revealed that the measure unwittingly strengthened the hands of village headmen to the detriment of the peasants it was intended to help. His resignation from a Select Committee in 1934 dramatized its ill-treatment by ministers and their timid motives for appointing it in the first place.[39] His sheer nerve which had often landed him in trouble now sometimes brought him credit, as when he stated – accurately – that some councillors were taking money for favours. As a letter to the press put it, 'he waggles his tongue like a village drunkard might brandish the rice pounder. And sometimes, he hits his man.'[40] These successes reassured him, and helped to calm and relax him. His speeches grew less shrill and he tended far less often to lose himself amid the careening momentum of his own invective. This growing assurance, the product of success, brought further success.

The clearest signs of this change in him emerged from his motion of no confidence in the Board of Ministers in June 1933. It was defeated 35–7, but Bandaranaike's long speech of indictment was an impressive and positive contribution. It contained almost none of the bursts of emotion or misplaced lyricism of earlier speeches but enumerated, soberly and comprehensively, widely held concerns that ministers were too secretive in dealing with the Council and too timid in dealing with the Governor. Despite the discomfiture and heated response of some, it helped to clear the air by giving ministers a chance to vindicate themselves and earned

[37] *CDN*, 27 December 1933; *CI*, 14 February and 31 July 1934.
[38] *CI*, 6 October 1932.
[39] *CI*, 7 September 1932; 19 October 1933; *CDN*, 3–4 November 1932, 15 February 1934. See also, *CI*, 13 September 1934; *CDN*, 1 March and 3 April 1935. For an earlier example, see his success in repealing a draconian provision for punitive police action. *CI*, 7 March 1932. [40] *CDN*, 4 January 1934.

Bandaranaike praise for his thoroughness, 'audacious eloquence' and 'moral earnestness'. He could be well 'satisfied that he had succeeded in his effort to invigorate the board'.[41]

The mention of Bandaranaike's involvement with land legislation raises an issue which he and most other leading politicians of the day addressed only intermittently, but which nevertheless had immense importance for the ordinary people of Ceylon. It is impossible here to provide more than a brief outline of some of the most important elements of this very complex topic.[42] In 1840, the British had passed what became known as the Waste Lands Ordinance which declared that all lands that were not permanently cultivated or in certifiable ownership were the property of the Crown. This had the effect of denying many rural dwellers access to lands that they had long used for grazing and – crucially – for shifting cultivation, a very widespread practice. This rendered the state both the main landowner and the main source of new land. It also made the colonial state in Ceylon a hugely important force in the island's economic life. The main purpose of the Ordinance was to make it easier to sell large blocks of land for plantations, and not only Europeans but Ceylonese with wealth and connections in the colonial establishment – including, very prominently, the Bandaranaike–Obeyesekere clan – made major acquisitions as a result.[43]

By the 1920s and 1930s, it had become apparent that under the Ordinance a serious shortage of land for ordinary peasants had developed. The main cause of this was population growth,[44] but two other processes were important. First, plantations for the production of tea, rubber and coconut had grown – as a result of legitimate sales under the Ordinance – to the point where only modest lands were available for peasant cultivation in many parts of the island.[45] Second, land-grabbers, unscrupulous men with an understanding of the nuances of land law – often underemployed proctors (small-time lawyers) or money-lenders – had cheated a very large number of peasants out of land which was

[41] Quotations are from *CI*, 16 June 1933. See also, *CI*, 14–16 June 1933.

[42] There is a large literature on this extremely complex topic. See *inter alia*, M. Moore, *The State and Peasant Politics in Sri Lanka* (Cambridge, 1985); E. Meyer, *Depression et malaria à Sri Lanka, 1925–1939: l'impact de la crise économique des années 1930 sur une société dépendante*, Ecole des Hautes Etudes en Sciences Sociales, Paris doctoral thesis, 1980; V. Samaraweera, 'Land, Labour, Capital and Sectional Interests in the National Politics of Sri Lanka', *Modern Asian Studies*, xv (1981), pp. 127–62; and B. H. Farmer. *Pioneer Peasant Colonization in Ceylon: A Study in Asian Agrarian Problems* (London, 1957).

[43] This is based on conversations with Eric Meyer and Mick Moore.

[44] I am grateful to Mick Moore for this point.

[45] Tea plantations were a near-monopoly of Europeans, coconut plantations were 'totally dominated' by Ceylonese (overwhelmingly Sinhalese) and rubber plantations were roughly equally divided between the two. Samaraweera, 'Land, Labour', p. 136.

rightfully theirs.[46] When they were not foreclosed upon or defrauded
outright, peasants facing a dispute with the Crown over their legal
entitlement to a plot of land were often persuaded to sell cheaply to land-
grabbers out of fear that they would lose their case. Sheer poverty forced
many others to sell.[47] It is impossible to quantify the shortages of land
which peasants faced in various parts of Ceylon, since the infrequent
investigations of the problem failed to probe deeply and systematically
into it. Indeed it is remarkable that in the British period neither the
colonial authorities, nor leading figures like Senanayake and Bandaranaike, nor even the Marxist politicians who emerged in 1936 were
sufficiently interested in the plight of the peasantry to undertake the kind
of systematic surveys of agrarian society that were commonplace in
British India. And when somewhat more serious enquiries were made
after independence in 1948 such as the Kandyan Peasantry Commission
Report, they suffered from the desire among nationalist politicians to
blame plantations – especially British plantations – for the sufferings of
ordinary rural folk.[48]

This was a major theme among Ceylonese politicians from the 1920s
onward and it became particularly important after 1931 when an elected
politician – D. S. Senanayake – served as Minister of Agriculture and
Lands. He more than anyone was responsible for a fundamental shift in
official land policy: from serving the interests of plantation owners, to
providing Crown lands as plots for landless and land-poor rural
dwellers.[49] During the 1930s, this was done by making available large
tracts (particularly in the North Central Province) for colonization as
small family farms by peasants from the densely populated southwest and
from areas (especially in the Central Province) where plantations left little
land for peasant cultivation. Senanayake's main initiative in this vein was
the Land Development Ordinance of 1935, but he had mounted a major
effort as early as 1932 to aid people hit by the depression.[50]

[46] This is based on conversations with Eric Meyer about his research on land-grabbers,
most of which is still unpublished. See, however, Meyer, Depression et malaria . . .;
CDN, 2 November 1933 and H. Clifford, 'Some Reflections on the Ceylon Land
Question', *Tropical Agriculturist*, lxviii (1927), pp. 240–92.
[47] Samaraweera, 'Land, Labour', p. 134.
[48] I am grateful to Eric Meyer for explaining the biases in that report. See, *Report of the
Kandyan Peasantry Commission, Sessional Paper XVIII – 1951* (Colombo, 1951).
[49] It should be emphasized that this change had been occurring for some years before
Senanayake became a minister. For example, curbs on the alienation of Crown land to
estates had been imposed in 1925. And certain British civil servants in Ceylon – notably
C. V. Brayne – had helped to develop the ideas which Senanayake now set out to
implement.
[50] See, for example, *CI*, 18 and 24 June 1932. Bandaranaike himself said when the Land
Development Ordinance of 1935 was being debated in the State Council that the policy
set out in the Ordinance 'has already been adopted . . .'. It was 'a policy which this
House has already endorsed'. *Towards a New Era* (Colombo, 1961), p. 903.

This policy was politically useful in several ways. It enabled Senanayake and his colleagues to present themselves as nationalists and progressives – men who had ended the colonial regime's preferential treatment of planters to aid the poor peasant – without reducing the holdings of landowning Ceylonese. In other words, the policy was distributive rather than redistributive. By emphasizing the iniquity of foreign planters, they gained the sympathy of many Kandyan Sinhalese in whose area most of the European plantations could be found. At the same time, this deflected attention from the doings of Sinhalese land-grabbers who provided much-needed electoral support for numerous state councillors. Indeed, some councillors had themselves amassed fortunes partly through land-grabbing. This could not be said of D. S. Senanayake, but some of his distant relatives and more than a few of his political allies fell into this category. One effect of some of Senanayake's policies as minister after 1931 was to secure greater freedom for land-grabbers from the British Settlement Officer, for which they had been pressing since the late 1920s. It is possible that this was unintentional, but with a man as immensely adroit as Senanayake, this is unlikely.

Bandaranaike came from a family which had acquired its lands at public auction several decades before the Senanayakes came to prominence and long before the Ceylonese land-grabbers' heyday in the late nineteenth and early twentieth centuries. If some of those auctions were carefully arranged so that they would succeed (thanks to the Bandaranaike–Obeyesekeres' connections with the British), they still had the appearance of far greater legitimacy than the doings of land-grabbers.[51] Bandaranaike had no need to rely on land-grabbers for election to the State Council and was therefore free to hold them in contempt on two counts. He shared his relatives' haughty distaste for them as pretentious newcomers to the social scene who had amassed wealth by unsavoury means. And as a young reformist whose somewhat vague desire to uplift the peasant was matched by his scorn for most westernized Ceylonese, he detested them as exploiters of the poor. Senanayake and company tended to see this purely as Bandaranaike family snobbery, and to regard his reformist rhetoric as a mere pose. This placed one further impediment in the way of an easy working relationship between Bandaranaike and more senior councillors.

That uneasiness intensified in 1932 when Bandaranaike presented to the State Council his own plan to assist the peasantry. His proposal both anticipated and embellished the scheme which Senanayake and his Executive Committee for Agriculture and Lands were preparing for formal enactment. It called for the colonization of uncultivated areas of

[51] These comments are based on discussions of his research with Eric Meyer.

the dry zone and an extension of wet zone farming onto Crown lands, both of which the Executive Committee had in mind. To support farmers moving onto these new lands, it sought to create government agencies that were not radically different from those foreseen by the Committee. His main innovation was to propose that 'the Government should control production, distribution, and the price of rice throughout the country'.[52]

By presenting this plan, Bandaranaike caused intense irritation among members of Senanayake's Executive Committee. He appeared to them to be usurping their ideas to win publicity in what was clearly an empty gesture, since the Minister of Agriculture and Lands would not allow a youthful member of the Local Administration Committee to design his policy for him. Indeed, J. L. Kotelawala advised Bandaranaike in the debate, 'that he should not try to teach his grandmother the art of ovisuction (Laughter)'.[53] By offering this scheme publicly rather than privately to the Executive Committee concerned, Bandaranaike was circumventing normal procedures and channels, which caused further annoyance. So did the extravagant claims that he made for his proposal, which was 'going to solve . . . the problem of the adverse balance of trade, the problem of poverty, the problem of underemployment'.[54] The most exasperating thing about this was that Senanayake and company felt unable to put him in his place by engineering the defeat of his motion, since that would mean voting against many of their own plans. The Council passed it and thereafter it was studiously ignored.

When Senanayake's Land Ordinance – probably the most important enactment of the first State Council – was debated at its second reading in 1933, Bandaranaike's speech emphasized points on which he dissented from the bill, but this was misleading. His 'socialist' viewpoint, on which he placed some stress, did not actually entail much disagreement with the bill since both he and it proposed that the state should retain ownership of lands made available to peasants. It appears that both his and Senanayake's preference for this arrangement sprang not from any enthusiasm for state ownership but, as M. P. Moore has noted, from an elitist distrust of the peasant's ability to manage his land rationally.[55] This was not the last time in Bandaranaike's career that the problem of land and the needs of the peasantry arose. We shall see, for example, how colonization schemes raised both of the dominant themes of his later years: Sinhalese parochialism and reformism. But at this early stage, it is

[52] Bandaranaike, *Towards a New Era*, p. 887. See also his relatively progressive views on land in *CI*, 26 June 1935.
[53] *CDN*, 4 November 1932.   [54] Bandaranaike, *Towards a New Era*, p. 888.
[55] For Bandaranaike's views, see *ibid.*, pp. 901–4. For Moore's, see his *The State*, p. 87

enough to say that Bandaranaike's sympathy for the poor peasant and his disdain for the landed *nouveau riche* who had allied themselves with D. S. Senanayake had not inspired the younger man to chart a markedly different course of his own.

No event in Bandaranaike's life has provoked more ecstatic or cynical comment than his decision to declare himself a Buddhist. The ecstatics see this as a case of a young man seeing the light and returning to the great cultural well-spring of Lanka. The cynics recall that Bandaranaike's clan changed its religion each time Ceylon changed rulers: Roman Catholics under the Portuguese, Dutch Reformed under the Dutch, Anglican under the British. In their view Bandaranaike was simply responding to the change to universal suffrage in a predominantly Buddhist island – he was a 'Donoughmore Buddhist'. What are we to make of this? It is impossible to probe the man's mind for a definitive answer, but a relatively plausible explanation is at hand.

It is beyond dispute that Bandaranaike showed few public signs of this impending change before mid-1933. In 1929, he voiced a grievance of some Buddhist monks in the Colombo Municipal Council, but this signifies little since they were his constituents. In 1930, he wrote a letter to the press supporting the chief custodian of the Temple of the Tooth in Kandy who was quarrelling with the Government Agent there. But the custodian was incidental to the main aim of the letter which was to lampoon Ceylonese who did not stand up to British officials. As Congress President, he addressed several Buddhist associations, but this was wholly in the line of duty. This is the sum total of his public involvement with Buddhist interests in that period and none of its suggests that he was becoming one of them. Those who view his Buddhism as a political gimmick might seize upon his agreement in September 1930, to preside at the annual meeting and sale of the Colombo Church Missionary Society. But this should not be taken too seriously since it is the single occasion on which he is known to have engaged in church activities and it is very likely that he was pressured into it by his mother, a CMS enthusiast.[56]

Indeed, it is next to certain that on his return from Oxford, Bandaranaike was no Christian. He has claimed – and Buddhist and Christian schoolmates agree – that when he left St Thomas', he was quite diffident towards the rather flimsy version of Christianity he had been taught at Horagolla.[57] He says that he 'gave up going to church' and

[56] *CI*, 7 November 1929 and 15 October 1932; *CDN*, 22 January and 29 September 1930; and interview with Frederick Obeyesekere, Colombo, 9 September 1978.

[57] S. W. R. D. Bandaranaike, 'Why I Became a Buddhist' (probably written in early 1934) in *Speeches and Writings* (Colombo, 1963), p. 287, and interview with Sir Senerat Gunawardena, Colombo, 1 September 1978.

'Desultory reading at Oxford tended to confirm, rather than dissipate my doubts.' His Ceylonese Christian contemporaries in England have no evidence to the contrary. Indeed his cousin (an astute observer) who was at Cambridge at the time recalls a conversation in which Bandaranaike set forth what seemed a genuine disillusionment with Christianity on rationalist grounds and indicated his growing conviction that Buddhism, as presented in books, was refreshingly compatible with his outlook. This witness was and is a committed Christian and Bandaranaike, who was on cordial terms with him, had no incentive to tell him this.[58]

There is also remarkable coherence and consistency in his explanations of his inability to accept Christianity. The basic difficulty was the notion of a personal God who was Father to all men. Bandaranaike's comments on this offer such clear and – to add to their credibility – unintended echoes of his relationship with his father that they strongly suggest a connection between these two things. Referring to his boyhood, he wrote:

even at this early age I suffered from a peculiar disability. While acquiring for Christ a sort of personal affection as towards an elder brother, to whom one could pour out one's troubles, I was never able to attain a conception of God the Father. My prayers were all really addressed to Christ: God had no real meaning for me.

[When he left school] I now realised that the foundation of Christ's teaching was the love of and complete surrender of oneself to a personal God. . . . I was able to love Christ as a man, but I found myself utterly unable to accept or surrender myself to this God . . .[59]

He returns to the theme repeatedly in his essay explaining his change of religion. 'I could not believe in a personal God . . .', 'I could not love a God . . .' Buddhism was attractive because 'there is no need for a man to be dependent on the will of God, whose favour he had to seek and whose wrath he had to fear; that man must work out his salvation for himself, appealed irresistibly to my own mentality'.[60] The parallel between Bandaranaike's fear and rejection of his father's authority and his distaste for the Christian concept of God the Father is well nigh irresistible. As he wrote in another essay from this period: 'The man, who has been freed from the need to beg even from God, who realizes that there is no Being to whom he can go crying like a child to escape the consequences of his own acts . . . is surely the man who should have attained the very apotheosis of manhood.'[61] This point is the principal reason given for his disenchantment with Christianity. The extent to which it echoes,

[58] *Ibid.*, pp. 287–88 and interviews with R. S. de Saram, Kandy, 6 September 1977, E. B. Wickramanayake, Colombo, 8 September 1977 and R. St. L. P. Deraniyagala, Colombo, 23 August 1978.   [59] Bandaranaike, *Speeches and Writings*, p. 287.
[60] *Ibid.*, pp. 287 and 290.   [61] *Ibid.*, pp. 292–93.

unconsciously, his relationship with Sir Solomon and his subsequent inability to accept the authority of superiors indicates that that disenchantment was genuine.

His adoption of Buddhism is another, more complicated matter. First, it is difficult to put a precise date upon it. Certainly by February 1934, when he offered public lectures on 'Why I Embraced Buddhism', the change had occurred. But a lecture on religion the previous August to the Young Men's Buddhist Association suggests an earlier decision, as does his involvement in October 1933, in a memorial meeting for an eminent *bhikku* (Buddhist monk), a *very* Buddhist occasion.[62] How genuine was his commitment to Buddhism? It could not have escaped a man as preoccupied with politics as Bandaranaike that the change made good political sense. There can be no doubt that this influenced his decision and that some of his explanations for the change are rationalizations. But these explanations also contain enough substance and coherence to suggest that this was, to a very considerable extent, an honest decision.

After his return from Oxford, he came into contact with at least two sources of sophisticated explanations of Buddhism. The first of these was his Buddhist schoolmate, R. S. S. Gunawardena, who became a close colleague both in the legal profession and in politics and who was intelligent enough and close enough to Bandaranaike to be able to discuss personal belief with him. Bandaranaike told him soon after his return from Oxford that he was something of a rationalist, that he believed in 'cause and effect'. Gunawardena replied that he sounded like a Buddhist and he (and, no doubt, others) raised the themes which had attracted Bandaranaike to Buddhism at Oxford and which he later accepted[63] and outlined thus:

Although I could not believe in a personal God, I did believe in some kind of continuance, a struggle, evolution towards a final goal. Just as higher bodily powers have evolved from lower ones through millions of years, there surely is a similar evolution of the spirit or life-essence, or whatever one likes to call it . . . while disbelieving what is the foundation of theistic religion, the existence of God, I believed a vital ingredient of all religions, the fact of some continuance . . . the continuance and evolution contemplated in the (Buddhist) Dhamma exactly coincided with my own views.[64]

Gunawardena was also able to urge Buddhist principles upon Bandaranaike at moments when the latter was annoyed with his own overexuberance. On the most important such occasion, a badly shaken

[62] *CI*, 23 August, 21 and 31 October 1933; *CDN*, 12 February 1934.
[63] Interviews with Sir Senerat Gunawardena, Colombo, 1 and 9 September 1977.
[64] Bandaranaike, *Speeches and Writings*, p. 290.

Bandaranaike accepted Gunawardena's opposition to hunting after he had accidentally wounded a villager on a shooting trip in the jungle.[65]

The study of Sinhala brought him into contact with a second source of sophisticated interpretations of Buddhism, *bhikkhus* of the *Amarapura Nikāya*, a cluster of low-country orders. It had been developed mainly by non-*Goyigama* Sinhalese as an alternative to the *Siyam Nikāya*, the wealthy and exclusively *Goyigama* order based in the great Kandyan temples. Bandaranaike was attracted by their opposition to caste exclusiveness and by their apparent dislike for the elements of magic which often attended the doings of the *Siyam Nikāya*. He lamented

the admixture of other, and often antagonistic, elements, with the pure current of Buddhist doctrine . . . The survival of caste distinctions, and their invasion of even the Sangha [clergy] . . . [and] various deep-rooted superstitions, beliefs and practices – survivals perhaps of an earlier aboriginal faith – still flourish darkly, obscuring the sun-rays of the Buddha's teaching.[66]

He was attracted to 'the pure current of Buddhist doctrine' because it was intellectually demanding, presenting a certain 'subtle difficulty' without easily accessible rituals or personifications of the deity. He argued that this 'religion of reason, as opposed to blind faith' seemed a more satisfactorily modern answer to his needs.[67] To this reader at least, his explanations seem largely genuine. This is not to say that his change of religion had nothing to do with considerations of political advantage. But his public explanation is sufficiently consistent both with his unguarded comments to relatives and friends and, with his view of paternal authority to make it substantially credible.

Bandaranaike was also genuinely attracted to Buddhism at an aesthetic level and, as his fascination with lyrical imagery suggests, this probably provided a potent reinforcement to his conscious decision to become a Buddhist. Throughout his life, he was haunted by the silent elegance of the ancient ruins at Anuradhapura and elsewhere, and his description in a short story of what might almost have been a scene from his youth suggests another sort of aesthetic resonance that may have influenced him. He describes a journey which a rich, westernized Sinhalese youth makes to Kandy to watch the Esala Perahera, the extraordinary religious procession in which the sacred tooth relic is carried out of the Temple of the Tooth and through the streets of that beautiful old hill capital. He describes the scene thus:

That night, John stood on the verandah of the Queen's Hotel, watching the procession go by, the temple officials in their gorgeous robes, walking in front,

while rolls of white cloth were placed along the road, that they might not defile
their feet, the long row of elephants bright with their gaudy trappings, with the
finest of them all in the centre, bearing the sacred relic – all moving slowly, with a
tantalizing slowness and swaying from side to side as they went; the dancers with
their grotesque masks and still more grotesque movements; the weird, unearthly
music, the pipes, the drums – all combined to create in John's mind a feeling of
unreality; it all seemed to him a dream, the figment of a disordered mind. He
looked on, and, as he looked, the barriers of time seemed to roll away, and he
seemed to be transported to an age long past, to a time of his country's glory and
its power, when that same procession passed along those same streets. And then
his eyes wandered to the lake beyond, its waters silvered by the rays of the moon.
He saw the forest-clad hills in the distance rising darkly to a star-bespangled sky.
He looked nearer, and saw the crowds along the lake-bund – the older men and
women tired and worn, the young men and girls watching with parted lips and
shining eyes, while, occasionally, the crying of a child mingled with the music of
the pipes and then something seemed to snap in John: a wild, throbbing love
surged through him. 'My country, my people', he murmured, 'how wonderful it
all is, and I never knew it till today.' His fingers fumbled at his stiff shirt front and
collar; in an instant he would have torn away those highly respectable garments of
civilisation and mingled with that surging mass – his people. Just then he heard
the voice of one of his friends, ' John, you fat-head, come and make up a four at
bridge.' The reaction made him stagger and reel like a drunken man for an instant:
then, he steadied himself and went. 'Good gracious!' said someone, 'What have
you done to your shirt, John? It is all crumpled up.' 'My dear fellow', said John, 'I
never could bear a starched shirt front. Don't you think a crumpled one looks
jollier somehow? Like a face creased in smiles. Two no trumps is my call!'[68]

Finally, it is important to notice the *kind* of Buddhist Bandaranaike had
become by 1934, because this changed many years later. The assumptions
and themes that emerge from his comments are characteristic of what
Gananath Obeyesekere has called 'Protestant' Buddhism,[69] which had
been gaining currency among the Sinhalese middle classes since the late
nineteenth century. He believed that Buddhism should be brought into
the centre both of everyday life and of the political arena. He believed that
'the chief and most portentous message of the Buddha is surely this: that
man alone is responsible for his own salvation . . .'. Bandaranaike, like
other members of the rising Sinhalese middle classes (and like members of
Europe's rising middle classes when Protestant Christianity had taken
hold in the west), was not prepared to leave religion to specialist priests.

[68] *Ibid.*, pp. 465–66. This initially appeared in *The Island Review*, September, 1926 which he
       edited with J. Vijayatunga.
[69] G. Obeyesekere, 'Religious Symbolism and Political Change in Ceylon', *Modern Ceylon
       Studies*, i (1970), pp. 43–63; and 'Theodicy, Sin and Salvation in a Sociology of
       Buddhism', in E. R. Leach (ed.), *Dialectic in Practical Religion* (Cambridge, 1968),
       pp. 7–40.

He therefore emphasized the equal role of the laity with the clergy in purifying Buddhism and preventing its decline into 'an established Church' bound by 'ritual and dogma'.[70] Much of his highly intellectualized Buddhism was self-taught, learned from books, and in that he was similar to the leading figure in the rise of 'Protestant' Buddhism, Anagarika Dharmapala. Bandaranaike had read many of his writings and, on at least one occasion, had met him during the 1920s. Thereafter he was influenced by a follower of Dharmapala, H. Sri Nissanka, a learned and respected legal and political colleague.

The point to remember about all of this is that for Bandaranaike, as for so many other westernized Sinhalese, 'Protestant Buddhism' was rationalistic and individualistic in the extreme. One of its fundamental claims is that Buddhism is something for the individual. As a matter of dogma it throws the believer onto his own resources. His own will and reason are everything, and his appetites and even his emotions are to be quelled. This has the effect of isolating believers by for example making it difficult for them to enjoy the company of others in regular temple worship. It can even undermine warm emotional relationships with members of their families. It tends to leave people with inadequate resources when they face emotional trauma, so that when personal crises arise, many Protestant Buddhists break down and/or turn to the forms of magic which are available in many Buddhist temples in Ceylon. Bandaranaike's Buddhism reinforced his already considerable isolation. And given both his capacity for fulsome responses to things that moved him such as the Kandy Perahera, and his fascination – evident once again in his account of the Perahera – with things 'weird' and 'unearthly', his 'Protestant' Buddhism was unlikely to provide fulfilment. Indeed, as we shall see in chapter 8, it proved inadequate when he came under great stress in the last months of his life, so that he too turned to supernatural solutions to his difficulties.

Bandaranaike's Buddhism has always been regarded by many with scepticism, whereas his claim – in later years – to be a socialist has been broadly accepted even among some Marxists. And yet a careful study of the evidence suggests that things should perhaps have been the other way round. The real tests of this arose much later, but the straws in the wind from this early period are worth a glance. Bandaranaike's Oxford contemporaries recall him as an Asquithian liberal 'like all of us'.[71] His early speeches show him at times to be vaguely sympathetic to socialism,

[70] R. Gombrich, 'From Monastery to Meditation Centre: Meditation in Modern Sri Lanka', paper presented at the University of London, 1979, typescript, p. 8.
[71] Interview with Lord Gardiner, London, 6 February 1978.

but then he was vaguely sympathetic to a great many other, un-socialist, things as well. His acceptance of the Congress leaders' opposition to a broader franchise before the Donoughmore Commission hardly marked him as a radical. Nor did his presidency of the Workers' Federation at whose meetings middle-class leaders sat in chairs while the labourers sat round them on the floor.[72] Yet by 1933, others were saying that 'Mr Bandaranaike is a socialist in thought, though a Congressman' and he was describing himself as 'essentially a socialist'.[73]

It is impossible to find much in his record in the Municipal Council or the first State Council to lend credence to this claim. He supported measures for taxation and modest spending on the public good, but this proves nothing. Outside the State Council, he did little – apart from the speech quoted above – to generate a socialist movement. His suggestion that Ceylon should have a five-year plan for agriculture led a reactionary newspaper to 'suspect' that he had 'a Bolshevik bias',[74] but even this paranoid editor could not be sure. When Ceylonese students returning from the west in 1935 began a genuine socialist movement, Bandaranaike made sympathetic noises but stayed at a distance. When challenged, he explained his diffidence thus: 'As a Socialist, I wish I could believe that things are moving rapidly towards a "purposive eruption of social revolution". The signs of this are distressingly absent.'[75]

As an adult, he always had a vague romantic sympathy for the common man in his unhappy plight.[76] And during his time in the first State Council he certainly proved himself to be a *reformist*, as when he persuaded the Council to ban the quartering of punitive police forces in an area – at local residents' expense – in the hope of uncovering 'possible' crimes by persons unknown.[77] In 1932, he pressed for debt relief to aid those badly affected by the depression,[78] and in 1935 for action to support the peasantry during the devastating malaria epidemic.[79] And as we have seen, his views on land policy were also mildly reformist, but his desire that the state retain ownership of land made available to peasants was based on an elitist suspicion that peasants might mismanage the land. A reformist is not the same thing as a socialist. His inclination after 1932 to make occasional references to socialism is best explained by the growing popularity of socialism in Europe and among young Indian nationalists

[72] A. E. Goonesinha Memoirs, Colombo.
[73] *CI*, 15 March and 2 May 1933. See also, *CI*, 22 November 1935.
[74] *CI*, 13 June 1933. [75] *CDN*, 25 April 1935.
[76] See, for example, his complaints during the 1931 election campaign about how police, mudaliyars and lesser headmen were prone to bribes, often did the bidding of rich men and harassed labourers. *CDN*, 28 May 1931.
[77] See, for example, *CDN*, 11 April 1935. [78] *CI*, 16 March 1932.
[79] See, for example, *CDN*, 14 March and 3 April 1935.

like Jawaharlal Nehru. He had lost little of his tendency to borrow from alien idioms and models.

Another alien idiom was also gaining currency in Europe at that time. As Bandaranaike put it, 'European Bourgeois democracy . . . was breaking up . . .' and Soviet communism and ultra-nationalism in Italy and Germany were moving in to replace it. The emergence of this last movement had an influence upon many Asian politicians who watched trends in Europe, and Bandaranaike was among them. This is a delicate subject, so let it be plainly stated that he never had any enthusiasm for Europe's fascists. He understood from the start that they represented 'dictatorship', and 'hysterical nationalism', and he had a clear distaste for both.[80] Nonetheless he believed that their ultra-nationalism represented an important trend in modern history. In Germany it appeared to him to be, very substantially, the result of the vengeful treatment imposed upon the German people by the peace of Versailles.[81] Despite his extremism, Hitler seemed in part to represent the reaction of a people to unjust treatment, so that Bandaranaike found it possible in 1934 to mention him in the same breath with Mazzini and Garibaldi.[82] He never lost his strong aversion to the fascists' vicious and dictatorial ways, but as a historical phenomenon, they suggested that nationalism of a more parochial and chauvinistic kind than that which Gandhi offered might be effective among Asian peoples who had been unjustly treated by alien powers. (Others, such as Subhas Chandra Bose in Bengal, also formed this view.) Bandaranaike was probably influenced by a vague sense that this was the trend of the times when he decided to experiment with parochial nationalism.

This experiment eventually culminated in the formation of a communal political organization called the Sinhala Maha Sabha, but those who date its foundation in 1934 are probably three years too early.[83] However, during the life of the first State Council, there were signs that Bandaranaike was adopting parochial postures. When the depression caused unemployment among Sinhalese to rise, Bandaranaike campaigned vigorously for restrictions on Indian immigrants in order to maximize jobs for Sinhalese, particularly in the Colombo port.[84] His heated exchanges with Tamil state councillors increasingly marked him out as a Sinhalese nationalist. By March 1935, his frequent clashes with one Tamil, G. G. Ponnambalam, were established as one of the liveliest aspects of Council debates, warranting front page attention by lobby

[80] See, for example, *CDN*, 11 April 1935.
[81] *CI*, 2 May 1933; *CDN*, 11 April 1935.   [82] *CI*, 9 August 1934.
[83] This is discussed more fully in note 13, chapter 5.
[84] *CI*, 1 September 1933, 12 December 1934; *CDN*, 17–18 November 1933.

correspondents. Ponnambalam, an uncompromising advocate of Tamil interests, was in some ways very like Bandaranaike – a barrister and a rather grandiose, combative and brilliant orator – and one of the few who could hold their own with the maturing Bandaranaike in debate. Bandaranaike became known for his tendency in Council 'to serve out fire and brimstone mostly to his pet aversion from Point Pedro (Ponnambalam)', and the pet aversion reciprocated lustily.[85] Bandaranaike also found, as he toured the island between 1934 and 1936, that appeals on behalf of Sinhalese language, religion, culture and interests caught the imagination of people who had previously been politically apathetic. This was particularly true of certain sections of society – Sinhala-medium school teachers, ayurvedic physicians, Village Committee members – whose response was modest but not insignificant.[86] Nonetheless, in this same period he was clearly hesitant at times to use communalism which he described in mid-1935 as 'reactionary' and 'a dangerous thing'.[87] It remained a relatively minor theme until after the 1936 election, but it was there in the mid-1930s, quietly germinating.

Those years also saw a change in Bandaranaike's stance on the role of political organizations in public life which brought him into line with Senanayake and other leading politicians. Until the end of 1933 his position had been ambiguous. On the one hand, he was prepared to assume the chair in political associations which deferred to him, which were often more nominal than real, which existed to provide a platform for his views and an instrument for his advancement.[88] On the other, he laboured manfully to transform the Ceylon National Congress into a disciplined organization of corporate substance in which prominent individuals might subordinate their interests to those of the party. But by December 1932, when he ended his year as Congress President, he had realized that it was next to impossible to remake the Congress without the cooperation of unwilling leaders like Senanayake and Jayatilaka. He therefore abandoned serious organization building and accepted that associations should exist mainly as extensions of prominent leaders' ambitions. He did so partly out of necessity, but also because by then he had begun to achieve real prominence in politics. His interests would suffer if he were subject to discipline within a strong organization. This

---

[85] *CDN*, 27 March 1935. See also, *CI*, 9 August 1934 and 15 August 1935; and his 'bellicose' defence of the Ceylonese from British disparagement, *CDN*, 1–2 March 1935.

[86] Interview with two co-workers who campaigned round the island on these themes with him in that period, Colombo, 18 August 1980.

[87] He was giving a public lecture to the Young Men's Buddhist Association in Colombo. *CI*, 15 June 1935.

[88] Among these were the Progressive National Party, the All-Ceylon Village Committee Conference and the Ceylon Workers Federation.

change became clear in December 1934, when he surprised everyone by
joining Senanayake and Jayatilaka in opposing the scheme for organizational reform which he himself had authored.[89]

At the State Council election in February and March 1936, Bandaranaike
was again unopposed. This freed him to campaign for others and he
appears to have concentrated his efforts in a handful of constituencies
where his allies and clients (the two categories usually overlapped) were
standing. He backed them not out of 'party' solidarity – indeed some of
them appear not to have been members of the Congress – but because he
wanted to develop a pool of personal supporters in the second State
Council. At least three of them managed to defeat incumbents and, when
they later manoeuvred themselves onto the Executive Committee for
Local Administration in the new Council, they helped to secure that
ministerial post for Bandaranaike.[90]

Other prominent politicians also backed candidates on personal
grounds, at the expense of 'party' solidarity which was even less
important in 1936 than it had been in 1931. D. S. Senanayake and J. L.
Kotelawala, both of whom were also unopposed (as were a total of seven
incumbents), concentrated their efforts in Dedigama constituency where
Senanayake's son Dudley was standing. This left many candidates who
were Congress members without support from Senanayake which they
urgently needed. The newly knighted Sir Baron Jayatilaka (also unopposed), the Leader of the State Council and supposedly 'the big chief' of
the Congress, openly flouted his 'party' responsibilities first by refusing
to support one ex-President of Congress because his opponent was a
Jayatilaka relative, and then by opposing a former Congress Joint
Secretary in favour of a non-Congressman whose caste and patrician
background were more to his liking.[91]

Indeed neither Congress nor any other so-called 'party' made any
collective impact this election. One newspaper editor had foreseen this
more than a year earlier at a time when Senanayake, and other notables
had opposed a proposal that Congress nominate candidates and when

[89] *CI*, 27 December 1934.
[90] The three were R. S. S. Gunawardena in Gampola, A. P. Jayasuriya in Horana and
Jayaweera Kuruppu in Ratnapura. A few other candidates, probably including
C. W. W. Kannangara, received financial aid from Bandaranaike, which came from his
mother's side of the family. *CDN*, 19 February and 19 March 1936, interviews in
Colombo with a member of the Bandaranaike family, 4 September 1977; A. P.
Jayasuriya, 9 September 1977 and Sir Senerat (R. S. S.) Gunawardena, 1 September
1978.
[91] The ex-President of Congress was G. K. W. Perera, and the Joint Secretary was
R. S. S. Gunawardena. Congress leaders also failed to support T. G. Jayewardena in
Balangoda and he lost. *CDN*, 4 and 19 February 1936.

both Senanayake and Bandaranaike had agreed that the time was not right for Ceylon to develop a party system.[92] Candidates' personalities, personal backgrounds and personal resources were usually the dominant factors in deciding the results.[93] It is little wonder, then, that election profiles of constituencies in the press almost never mentioned parties and that the main source book on elections gives candidates' parties in 1931 but not 1936.[94] In this election, 'The Congress was no more a party than it was an omnibus.'[95]

The 1936 election was held on a much wider franchise than that of 1931. The total registered electorate had risen by 81 per cent, from 1,319,830 to 2,385,774, thanks mainly to more energetic efforts by the colonial bureaucracy to register voters.[96] This still fell well short of the total of potential voters which was probably just under 3 million.[97] The increase in votes cast between 1931 and 1936 was a less dramatic but still impressive 59.8 per cent.[98] This broader participation altered the tone and character of numerous electoral contests. People from numerically powerful but disadvantaged castes almost certainly made up a large proportion of not-yet-registered voters (as did Tamils living in Sinhalese areas),[99] given the prejudices against them of high caste headmen who still had a major role in registration. But enough had become eligible to make the two most depressed groups – the *Bathgamas* and *Wahumpuras* – an important if not yet a decisive force in several constituencies. This was a major cause of the sharp increases in violence and intimidation[100] and in personal and caste-based vituperation[101] which marked this election.

[92] *CI*, 2 November and 17 December 1934.
[93] See, for example, *CDN*, 1, 3 and 5 February 1936. See also the comments in mid-1935 of two Congress leaders on Congress as 'a sinking body' and so forth in *CI*, 8 July 1935.
[94] *CDN*, 2–15 February 1936.
[95] Comment by the political correspondent, *CDN*, 2 March 1936.
[96] G. P. S. H. de Silva (ed.), *A Statistical Survey of Elections to the Legislatures of Sri Lanka, 1911–1977* (Colombo, 1979), pp. 91–107 and *CDN*, 11 June 1935. For insight into the colonial authorities' perception of all of this, see correspondence, Officer Administering the Government to Secretary of State, 29 June 1935, and Governor to Secretary of State, 25 November 1935, in CO 54/926/1, PRO.
[97] This is necessarily a rough estimate extrapolated from growth rates between decennial censuses and taking into account the high death rate in 1935 due to the malaria epidemic. Source: H. E. Peries, *Census of Ceylon, 1953*, vol. i (Colombo, 1957), p. 6 and vol. ii, 2 (Colombo, 1959), p. 1.
[98] Of the registered electorate, 47.37 per cent (1,130,190 voters) voted, as against 53.58 per cent (707,204) in 1931. De Silva, *A Statistical Survey*, pp. 91–107.
[99] See, for example, Bernard Aluwihare Diaries, 3 June 1940, University of Peradeniya Library. As a candidate in a constituency with a large Tamil minority, he was in a position to know.   [100] *CDN*, 5, 14–15, 19, 21, 24–25, 27–29 February 1936.
[101] *CDN*, 3 and 5 February 1936. These reports were corroborated in numerous interviews with political activists who took part in this election, interviewed in 1978 and 1980. A strike of bus company employees just before the election threatened to deprive rich candidates of transport, but this was settled at the last moment. *CDN*, 21–22 February 1936.

Table 4.1. *Sinhalese castes in the first
two State Councils*

Caste	1931	1936
Goyigama	26	28
Karava	4	3
Salagama	2	1
Hinna	1	1
Dhobi	1	1
Potter	1	0
Chunam	0	1
Durava	0	1
Uncertain	3	3
Total	38	39

In some ways, the composition of the new State Council differed little from that of the old.[102] In another sense, however, this is misleading since there was a very considerable turnover. No fewer than fifteen Members of the first State Council were defeated, eight of them by large margins. Eleven others chose not to seek re-election, so that just over half of the councillors elected in 1936 – twenty-six of fifty – were fresh faces. Over 40 per cent of the incumbents who defended their seats were beaten.[103] Intensely elitist councillors who were seen to be unresponsive were soundly beaten,[104] as were the three candidates backed by European planting interests.[105] Incumbents who relied too heavily on exalted status in the traditional headman system also usually lost. The most startling example of this was the narrow defeat in his own bailiwick of T. B. Panabokke, who stood at the very pinnacle of the Kandyan hierarchy and who was a minister in the first Council, by Bandaranaike's associate R. S. S. Gunawardena who came from a humble caste and from a distant part of the island.[106]

The depression and the malaria epidemic which devastated much of the island in the months before the election had made the electorate impatient with unhelpful councillors. Those who organized relief for their

---

[102] This is based on discussions of the list of the State Councillors with several Sinhalese informants in Kandy and Colombo, August, 1980.
[103] These figures are based on de Silva, *A Statistical Survey*, pp. 91–107 and *CDN*, 5 February – 7 March 1936.
[104] See, for example, the cases of E. W. Perera and F. A. Obeyesekere, both of whom were embarrassed (*CDN*, 6 February 1936). [105] *CDN*, 10 and 13 February 1936.
[106] See also the defeat of Mrs Adeline Molamure at Ruwanwella.

constituents reaped their reward at the election, but several who did not were ousted in favour of newcomers who had done so.[107] Among these were Philip Gunawardena and N. M. Perera, young Marxists (indeed, they thought of themselves as Trotskyists, although they did not advertise this during the election) who had recently returned from overseas and who would figure prominently in the island's politics for another three to four decades. The new State Council retained for the most part the conservative character of the old one, partly because underpopulated rural areas which tended to be conservative were systematically over-represented, as they were at every election in Bandaranaike's lifetime. But the outcome of 1936 indicated that the electorate was already far from docile and that, as more disadvantaged voters came onto the rolls in later years, the island's political elite would need to find new ways of responding.

During this first five years as a state councillor, Bandaranaike had achieved considerable prominence by travelling tirelessly to address public meetings and local associations of various sorts. This gained him wide recognition, at least in low-country Sinhalese areas, but the public that he sought most to impress was not so much the mass as the national political elite. It was helpful that he was known in market towns in the provinces, but it was more important that he be *seen* to be known there by State Council members and press barons in Colombo. His increasingly positive contributions to the work of the Council and his immense if sometimes misspent gifts as an orator also added to his reputation among the elite, although his relations with Senanayake and other senior leaders remained troubled.

Bandaranaike did not seek to reinforce his increasing public recognition by developing the kind of transactional ties to clients in the hinterland that politicians in Indian's regions were forging in this period. He shied away from organization-building, not only for the Congress but for himself as well – indeed, this remained his practice throughout his career. His pockets may frequently have been empty because he responded to constituents' pleas for hand-outs,[108] but they were distributed randomly, as and when appeals arose. The result was a *neo-durbari* mode of operation (to use an Indian analogy)[109] resembling the customs of Ceylon's traditional landed aristocrats, a highly personalized,

---

[107] See Meyer, Depression et malaria, and *CDN*, 1–2 and 6–7 February 1936.
[108] Interview with R. St. L. P. Deraniyagala, Colombo, 18 September 1978.
[109] See D. A. Low's introduction to his *Congress and the Raj*. He refers thus to a type of politics in which modern politicians granted crowds or groups audiences, *durbars*, and remained haughtily aloof from them.

unsystematic bestowal of largesse to supplicants who called at the *walaūwa* (country mansion).[110] This made Bandaranaike the kind of politician – the patrician, speechmaking constitutionalist without a solid organizational base – that was being swept aside in India in that period. But in Ceylon all major politicians were patrician constitutionalists, so he was at no disadvantage. Despite universal suffrage, the national-level political arena remained rather cut off from pressures from below. Hence the importance of a man's reputation among fellow councillors.

The relative isolation of the national level from lower levels in the political system suited leading politicians since it left them with great freedom for manoeuvre. They took advantage of this to develop their double-sided relationship with the colonial authorities: close cooperation as ministers of the Crown on the one hand, and on the other, frequent forceful (but always lawful) protests about the inadequacy of the existing dyarchy that left finance, law, defence, external affairs and massive reserve powers in the hands of colonial officials. The isolation of the national level left most leading politicians less alert than they might have been to the possibility of new social forces emerging in a system which was open enough to invite this. When most of these leaders considered the possibility that numerically powerful low caste groups might seek to become an important factor in elections, they thought that they could cope by coopting low caste leaders and – more especially – by intimidating low caste voters. Indeed, this occurred in many places in 1936, not least at Dedigama under J. L. Kotelawala's direction on behalf of Dudley Senanayake's candidacy.[111]

One politician who was not so insensitive to the potential emergence of new social forces and who was more inclined to respond positively to them was Bandaranaike. His experiments during the early 1930s with various political styles or models – whether Gandhian, socialist or parochialist – may appear embarrassing at times. But they bespoke an awareness that new modes had to be and ought to be developed to accommodate and even to encourage the growing participation of ordinary and indeed disadvantaged folk. His experiments with various political styles suggested that his response to these new social forces would be that of a patrician populist who used emotive issues as a substitute for a decentralization of power and genuine participation through a strong party organization. But this still made him a far more

---

[110] I am grateful to S. J. Tambiah for raising this point.

[111] See in this regard, J. Jiggins, *Caste and Family in the Politics of the Sinhalese, 1947–1976* (Cambridge, 1979), p. 72 and *Ceylon Observer*, 17 March 1974, cited by Jiggins. Sir John Kotelawala confirmed this version of events in an interview, Kandawela, 16 September 1978.

forward-looking leader than most of his contemporaries. And it was possible for a discerning eye to perceive in the results of the 1936 election clear signs – the growth of the electorate, the defeat of so many incumbents, the victory of a few leftists and candidates of humble origins, the need to intimidate disadvantaged groups – that new forces were beginning to stir.

5

MINISTER, 1936–1946

Throughout his first term in the State Council, Bandaranaike had hankered impatiently after ministerial office. There was more than raw ambition in this, since several ministers had performed poorly, while in his better moments Bandaranaike had shown analytical skills to match his great oratorical gifts. This stood in especially sharp contrast to the head of his own Executive Committee, the Minister of Local Administration, Charles Batuwantudawe, who had acquired such a reputation for corruption and ineptitude that he had no hope of a second term.[1] It was widely expected that Bandaranaike would succeed him and on 19 March 1936, he did so with the unanimous support of his Executive Committee.

The selection of the new ministers has usually been viewed as a triumph for Sir Baron Jayatilaka and, above all, for D. S. Senanayake. He is seen to have distributed Sinhalese followers and the four nominated Europeans, who were inveigled into an alliance, among the seven Executive Committees in such a way as to ensure the election of a Board of Ministers composed entirely of low-country Sinhalese allied to him.[2] There is some substance in this interpretation, but Bandaranaike had two good reasons for believing that he would have been elected even without their support. First, a caucus of Tamils, Marxists and others opposed to Senanayake and Jayatilaka had indicated that they were prepared to back him for the post at Local Administration, probably on the strength of his attacks on ministers in the previous State Council. Bandaranaike even attended a meeting of this group and, although he left with several other Sinhalese when a motion for the defeat of the two senior leaders was passed,[3] he could still have expected some votes from that quarter. Second and more crucially, he managed to pack his Executive Committee

---

[1] *CDN*, 8 February 1936. He conceded this himself when he sought the speakership before the ministerial elections. He came a poor third in a field of three. *CDN*, 18 March 1936.

[2] The best account of this is J. Russell, The Ceylon Tamils under the Donoughmore Constitution, University of Peradeniya doctoral thesis, 1975, pp. 329–37, 340 and 348.

[3] *CDN*, 16 March 1936 and S. W. R. D. Bandaranaike, *Towards a New Era* (Colombo, 1961), pp. 65–66.

with allies, including at least two who were opposed to the Senanayake–Jayatilaka caucus.[4] He also backed Senanayake's effort to elect an all-Sinhalese Board of Ministers and, as a result, gained support in his own quest for office. But, as he well knew, he did not owe his ministerial status to this.

The creation of an all-Sinhalese Board was intended to hasten the day when Ceylon would be permitted Cabinet government, and in some respects it was successful. It undermined confidence in the Executive Committee system by showing the British, and Ceylon's minorities – especially the Tamils – that the system offered no firm protection to minority interests. It also served as an occasion for the new ministers – who agreed on the need for a Cabinet system as an advance towards full self-rule – to revive discussion of constitutional reform.[5] At the same time, however, the formation of the Board sowed doubts in some British minds about Ceylon's fitness for greater self-government because it frightened minorities with the prospect of Sinhalese solidarity and dominance, and it contributed to the polarization of communal relations.

D. S. Senanayake and Sir Baron Jayatilaka were cautiously optimistic that the new Board could operate as a reasonably cohesive force in order to produce something approaching *de facto* Cabinet government. They tentatively welcomed the inclusion of Bandaranaike – one of their most incisive critics in the first State Council – in the hope that his talents might now serve the interests of the ministerial team and of its two leaders. A sceptical press was amused to see the erstwhile firebrand seated next to Jayatilaka so that the Leader of the House might 'have the opportunity of plucking Mr Bandaranaike's sleeve if perchance he forgets and by force of habit attacks the Board of Ministers'.[6] But within only three weeks Bandaranaike had grown restive, complaining about the reluctance of some legislators – including, we may be sure, some fellow-ministers – to increase the powers of local boards now under his supervision.[7] As early as the first budget debate he ostentatiously broke ranks with his colleagues by revealing confidential ministerial discussions and rejecting what he called the 'grandmotherly advice' of the Minister of Labour. Loyalty to his constituents and to the House, he said, took precedence over loyalty to the Board of Ministers.[8]

This breakdown in ministerial unity, which thereafter existed only intermittently, was inevitable. The Constitution alone made it so by giving each minister a separate power base within the Council, in the

[4] These were Sir Senerat Gunawardena and A. Ratnayake, interviews in Colombo with each of them on, respectively, 6 September 1978 and 26 August 1977.
[5] This is convincingly set out in Russell, The Ceylon Tamils, pp. 334–37, 340 and 348.
[6] *CDN*, 1 April 1936. [7] *CDN*, 22 April 1936. [8] *CDN*, 12 September 1936.

form of an Executive Committee. The London government's reluctance to allow a Cabinet system to develop, despite support for the idea in June 1938 by the progressive new Governor, Sir Andrew Caldecott, gave ministers little incentive to cohere. The breakdown was not solely Bandaranaike's doing. The determination of Jayatilaka and Senanayake – who had not forgotten the haughty ways of the Bandaranaike–Obeyesekere clan – to keep their young colleague in a secondary role contributed greatly to the split. Bandaranaike was no more willing to accept the authority of a superior in 1936 than at any other time in his life, so he quite naturally began to seek an issue, a constituency, an organization of his own.

He did not have far to look. The depression had thrown large numbers of urban labourers out of work.[9] Bandaranaike's main response was not to seek a remedy for unemployment but to affix the blame for it, which led him not to economic prescriptions but to communalist accusations. Since a substantial minority of urban labourers still in work – especially in Colombo – consisted of Indians originally hired to do jobs that Sinhalese preferred to avoid, it was easy to attribute joblessness among the majority to them. This had lately become a major theme in the speeches of A. E. Goonesinha, whom Bandaranaike had defeated in the municipal election ten years earlier. He had once championed the cause of Indian labourers but now, with his base among the Sinhalese working class threatened by Marxist union organizers, Goonesinha had turned to parochialism.[10]

For several months after its formation, the Board of Ministers attempted to maintain an ambiguous collective stand on the communal issue. Sir Baron Jayatilaka presided over one of Goonesinha's municipal election rallies and spoke darkly of the 'Indian invaders' of ancient Lanka. But before Indian audiences he also condemned Goonesinha's 'wild utterances' and stressed his desire to promote national unity.[11] Bandaranaike's position during 1936 was similarly equivocal. In October, he supported the more pro-Indian candidate in a State Council by-election and then spoke publicly of his ambition to make speeches in Tamil.[12] But as we saw in chapter 4, he had long dabbled in Sinhalese chauvinism and by late 1936 or early 1937, he appears to have decided that it should be a central – and possibly *the* central – theme in his career.

[9] The colonial government's inadequacies at information-gathering make it impossible to know the precise scale of the problem, but it was clearly very serious. *CI*, 18 December 1936 and *CDN*, 20 January 1937.

[10] See, for example, *CDN*, 7 April 1936. Further material is available in the A. E. Goonesinha Memoirs, typescript and V. K. Jayawardena, *The Rise of the Labour Movement in Ceylon* (Durham, 1972).

[11] *CDN*, 21 September and 2 November 1936. For the ministers' collective stand, see *CDN*, 11 January 1937.   [12] *CDN*, 9 October and 27 November 1936.

The organization that he was to build into a communalist vehicle – the Sinhala Maha Sabha (Great Sinhalese Union or League) – was born amid confusion. At some point in 1936[13] after preparatory meetings at his home, Bandaranaike invited numerous, mainly younger members of the new State Council and a small number of prominent citizens to a meeting to establish a new political association. Many of those who attended did so in the expectation that some sort of centre-left Fabian organization with nationalist overtones would emerge. One model in their minds was India's Congress Socialist Party, a leftist caucus within the Indian National Congress. When the public meeting to found the organization was convened, however, pressure by Sinhalese cultural revivalists from the literary world forced the adoption of a largely communalist set of aims. The name of the new association echoed the title of India's Hindu Mahasabha which stood on the parochialist right, far removed from the Congress Socialists. This caused surprise and dismay among several of the younger state councillors present and small number of them left the meeting and the Sabha. It may even have surprised and disconcerted Bandaranaike who was sympathetic both to parochialism and to social and economic reform,[14] and who regarded the Sabha thereafter as an agency of communal resurgence first, but of vaguely Fabian reform as well.[15] He certainly saw less contradiction between these two purposes than did many of his contemporaries in the State Council and the press.

The relative emphases which he placed on communalism and reform over the next two decades were, as we shall see, largely dictated by short-term tactical considerations rather than by any underlying set of priorities. From the founding of the Sabha until 1942 when the impact of the Pacific War began to be fully felt in Ceylon, communalism served his immediate interests best. During 1937, Bandaranaike moved rather tentatively towards a hard-line communalist stand. At first, he merely offered rather fanciful, utopian visions of the harmony which he claimed had prevailed in village Ceylon before individualism had broken it down. He called for attempts to revive this amiable atmosphere by building

[13] There is considerable confusion about the date of its founding. Jane Russell, who is quite scrupulous, places it in 1934 (Russell, The Ceylon Tamils, p. 223). K. M. de Silva, who is very authoritative, prefers 1937 in his *University of Ceylon History of Ceylon*, vol. iii (Peradeniya, 1973), p. 520. Bandaranaike certainly campaigned on communalist themes as early as 1934, but there is no documentary evidence to show that the Sabha existed that early. Three sources indicate that 1936 is correct. Sir Senerat Gunawardena is quite insistent that the initial meeting, which he attended, occurred when he was a state councillor (interview, Colombo, 6 September 1978) and he was elected in 1936. Bandaranaike himself said in 1938 that the Sabha was two years old (*TC*, 5 September 1938). Finally, in 1939 it held its third annual session (*CDN*, 3 June 1939).
[14] Interview with Sir Senerat Gunawardena, Colombo, 6 September 1936 and Russell, The Ceylon Tamils, pp. 223–24. [15] See, for example, *CDN*, 13 October 1937.

inexpensive club houses in villages where peasants could learn team spirit and cleanliness and develop their muscles on parallel bars, in order to defend themselves against the village bully.[16] By year's end, however, he had taken to decrying the 'economic stranglehold that Indians are gaining in Ceylon', claiming (with only limited validity) that trade in town and village alike was controlled by Indians, as was much of the money-lending that had ensnared so many Sinhalese villagers. He had reluctantly concluded that *Ceylonese* nationalism 'is scarcely possible'. Genuine nationalism could only emerge from common language, culture, customs, history and 'Race'. These things united Sinhalese, but they tended to divide the majority from the Tamil and Muslim minorities.[17] He reminded audiences that it was he who had first suggested in Council the restriction of Indian immigration[18] and he called for action to protect 'all the Sacred places' of Buddhism and to punish those who had desecrated them.[19]

There were certain incongruities in these statements that tended to undercut Bandaranaike's authority in making them. In speaking of the Sinhalese as a distinct 'Race' he laid himself open to the charge that he was one of 'those who professed to be Sinhalese but were descendants of Temple servants' – a reference to his family's acknowledgement of a Tamil Brahmin immigrant as a distant but prominent ancestor.[20] Some may also have recalled occasions in the late 1920s when he argued that the 'first thing' Ceylonese must do was to 'cooperate with those who are akin to us in race and culture, i.e., Indians'.[21] His speeches in the 1930s in defence of Buddhism also encountered intense suspicion – at this time and throughout his life – from Buddhists who regarded his conversion as an act of political expediency.[22] He contributed to these doubts by displaying a cavalier disregard for consistency in role-playing. In mid-1938 for example, he appeared in 'native dress' at a Sinhala Maha Sabha rally to say that if the Sinhalese 'adopted English [language] and English customs there would be no Sinhalese in the future'. Yet within a fortnight, he could be seen in a press photograph wearing a western suit

[16] *CDN*, 20 March 1937.
[17] *CDN*, 18 November 1937, 23 and 25 May 1938.   [18] *CDN*, 3 June 1937.
[19] The immediate reference here was to a European woman who had recently been photographed in an objectionable pose by a statue of the Buddha, but its implications for Tamils living in ancient Buddhist centres like Anuradhapura was not lost on his Sinhalese audience. *CDN*, 23 May 1938.
[20] For the accusation, see *CDN* 10 December 1937. For evidence on his ancestry, see R. L. Dias Bandaranayaka, *Genealogy of the Family of Dias Bandaranayaka of Ceylon* (Colombo, n.d.), pp. 1–2; A. Wright, *Twentieth-Century Impressions of Ceylon* (London, 1907), pp. 522–23 and 525; and J. T. Rutnam in *Tribune* (Colombo), 19 July and 30 August 1957.
[21] Undated clipping from the *Ceylon Morning Leader* in lot 23.25, serial 41, BP.
[22] See, for example, *TC*, 23 October 1938.

alongside his greyhound Billy Micawber, winner of six prizes at the Kennel Club dog show.[23]

Despite these problems with credibility, or perhaps because of them, Bandaranaike's rhetoric grew increasingly shrill and extreme as the months passed. This does not appear to have earned him a broad popular following – his organization was, as we shall see, too insubstantial for that. But the motions that it generated at public meetings gave him – not for the last time – the impression that he was developing a solid power base. On one occasion, while inveighing against Indians of both the mercantile and labouring classes, he produced a statement which many regard as his most extreme utterance:

I will say here frankly. I will say plainly that nothing will please me more than to see the last Indian leaving the shores of Ceylon. I say that deliberately. When the last Indian leaves these shores I shall be a happy man because I know what is going on in this country.[24]

By 1938, there was (not surprisingly) concern at his 'racial ebullitions' and 'communal poison'.[25] In January 1939, he was reported to have told a public meeting that 'I am prepared to sacrifice my life for the sake of my community, the Sinhalese. If anybody were to try to hinder our progress, I am determined to see that he is taught a lesson he will never forget.' After the speech, a woman in the audience reportedly likened Bandaranaike to Hitler and asked Sinhalese to give him their support.[26]

He would not have relished the comparison and it certainly exaggerates his extremism. His remarks here and all others like them must be taken with a sizable helping of salt. They are of a piece both with earlier empty threats (as on the occasion when the pencil would not break) and of incessant calls over the years for struggle and sacrifice – none of which possessed any substance.[27] The comments quoted above and such breathtaking claims as his assertion in 1940 that the Sinhala Maha Sabha had helped to create better understanding 'in every part of the island'[28] obviously contributed to a devaluation of language. But it should also be

[23] *CDN*, 21 July 1938 and *TC*, 4 August 1938.
[24] The precise date of the statement is, curiously, uncertain. This quotation is from much later, *CDN*, 11 September 1943.
[25] *TC*, 7–8 and 26 September and 21 October 1938. In the last of these, one of Bandaranaike's own relatives, an eminent member of the Obeyesekere family, expressed concern.
[26] From the Tamil-owned newspaper, *The Hindu Organ*, cited by Russell, The Ceylon Tamils, pp. 248–49.
[27] For a sampling, see *CDN*, 13 December 1937, 2 and 5 March 1938, 4 March 1940, 21 and 31 March and 28 July 1941.
[28] *CDN*, 5 August 1940. For other remarks in this vein, see *CDN*, 30 March 1938, 4 and 23 March 1939.

understood that he uttered threats from the public platform with only half a thought and without the slightest intention of translating them into action. His colleagues in the State Council and others in the island's political elite knew this all too well. They had already begun to recognize – what became fully apparent during his years as Prime Minister – that however much he might slash and fulminate as an orator, Bandaranaike as a political *actor* away from the public platform was largely lacking in the aggression and wholly lacking in the personal vindictiveness which were so common among Ceylon's politicians. Partly for this reason, there was less disquiet among Ceylon's moderates over his communalist speeches than their criticisms of him suggest. Few of them felt that Bandaranaike – who, his rhetoric apart, had always shown an instinctive if vague attachment to liberal institutions and reformist notions – fully believed what he was saying. His 'quick-change-artist temperament' which led him to borrow temporarily from the political styles of others (as in his Gandhian phase), his tendency to couch any argument from the public platform in the strongest possible terms and his inconsistency as a communalist even in this period[29] made this seem little more than his 'latest political dance' or 'fancy dress'.[30]

This sense of artificiality was reinforced when observers considered Bandaranaike's relationship with the Tamil minority's arch-communalist, G. G. Ponnambalam. This 'pocket Demosthenes' was one of a tiny handful of legislators who could hold their own with Bandaranaike in Council debates and the sparkling verbal duels between them became more frequent and vitriolic as Bandaranaike turned increasingly to communalism after 1936. At a personal level, however, the two men were known to have reasonably cordial relations.[31] Since in this period neither had achieved pre-eminence in his own community and both saw communal polarization as a means to that end, each found it advantageous to exaggerate the threat which the other posed.[32] So although the two men taunted one another mercilessly – in one exchange Bandaranaike associated Ponnambalam's ancestry 'with a simian prelude', as Governor Caldecott put it[33] – they were in some ways covert allies. At times they joined forces overtly and this, like their amiable

[29] He wavered, for example, on his original communalist decision to exclude Indian estate workers from voting in Village Committee elections, until accusations of inconsistency forced him to retreat (*CDN*, 3 June and 18 November 1937 and *TC*, 3 September 1938). See also, *CDN*, 4 and 23 March, 25 May 1939 and 11 and 14 January 1941.

[30] *TC*, 20, 26 September 1938. [31] *TC*, 20 and 26 September 1938.

[32] Interviews with numerous people who were close to one or both men, Colombo, September 1980. Bandaranaike publicly acknowledged this cordiality. See Russell, The Ceylon Tamils, p. 300.

[33] Secret Report, 'Things Ceylonese', 7 September 1939, in CO 54/971/11, PRO.

personal relations, raised doubts about their devotion to the communalist cause. In 1932, for example, both had been members of the ephemeral Liberal League.[34] In 1942, they united in a call for a national government containing all communities, and the following year in a bizarre episode, Ponnambalam urged Tamil estate labourers to vote for the Sinhala Maha Sabha candidate in a State Council by-election.[35] These things indicated to many that for Bandaranaike, Sinhalese chauvinism was more a tactical ploy than a matter of conviction. They were essentially correct, but his chauvinism was no less dangerous for that.

Bandaranaike did not invent Sinhalese communalism. Throughout his career, he tended to adapt existing political and cultural models to his needs, as did most politicians from the Sinhalese low country, an area which had suffered considerable de-culturation in more than three centuries of European rule. The elites in the low country made far greater use of borrowed modes of thought and behaviour than did, for example, their counterparts in the provinces of British India. In earlier times, this had mainly entailed the copying of the ways and manners of the island's European rulers, but by the 1930s, low-country politicians had begun to take up Fabian, Gandhian, Marxist and indigenous parochialist idioms. Bandaranaike was a more sophisticated and intelligent borrower than most, but he went about it avidly nonetheless, as his earlier Gandhian prase and his Nehruvian postures during the 1950s indicated.

Central to the communalist world view was the belief that the Buddha had designated the island as a sacred redoubt where the purity of the faith would be defended from alien influences.[36] Sinhalese Buddhists tended to see themselves as a 'lion race', charged with this protective mission. The term *jati*, which throughout south Asia means one's own 'type', 'kind' or 'ilk' and which in most Indian languages refers to small caste groups, is usually used by Sinhalese to refer to the linguistic group which is perceived as a 'race'. It is also used to signify 'nation', and this makes it difficult for many Sinhalese to conceive of Ceylon or Sri Lanka as a nation–state embracing both Sinhalese and others.[37]

The notion that the Sinhalese constitute a 'race' is inaccurate. They are neither a racially homogeneous group nor racially distinct from their Tamil neighbours. For example, the large *Karava*, *Durava* and *Salagama*

[34] J. Russell, 'The Dance of the Turkey Cock – The Jaffna Boycott of 1931', *Ceylon Journal of Historical and Social Studies*, viii, 1 (January–June, 1978), pp. 58–59.

[35] *CDN*, 15 August 1942 and 11 September 1943. The Sabha candidate in the by-election at Balangoda was Bandaranaike's father-in-law, a Kandyan aristocrat and prominent headman. He was badly trounced.

[36] M. Roberts, 'Foundations of Sinhalese and Tamil Nationalism and Some Implications', *Ceylon Studies Seminar* (1973).

[37] I am grateful to Gananath Obeyesekere and C. R. de Silva for assistance on this point.

caste groups who form a sizable minority of the Sinhalese are clearly quite late immigrants from south India. Many Sinhalese families – including the Bandaranaikes and the Jayewardenes – have Tamil, Muslim or European ancestors.[38] And in the mid twentieth century, as Sinhalese settlers moved into north-eastern and north-central parts of the island, some residents of those areas who had spoken Tamil two generations earlier took up Sinhala as their first language and duly gained admission to the 'race'.[39] But despite this, the fiction was and is widely affirmed as fact among the Sinhalese. Their concern with the defence of Buddhism has become bound up with their unease at the presence of a predominantly Hindu Tamil population in the northern and eastern areas of the island, with tens of millions of Tamils and hundreds of millions of Indians standing behind them, across the narrow Palk Straits. These anxieties have led to celebrations of Sinhalese heroes of old such as Dutugemunu (Dutthagamani) who is said – erroneously[40] – to have reconquered portions of the island from Tamil invaders.

Bandaranaike took up this body of ideas more energetically than most politicians of his day, but nearly every other Sinhalese leader often operated within it as well. These included not only the State Council Leader Sir Baron Jayatilaka, but also D. S. Senanayake, J. L. Kotelawala and the young J. R. Jayewardene. Their sentiments were made especially plain in the Council's 1939 endorsement of repatriation for Indians.[41] Senanayake, who was clearly emerging as the island's pre-eminent leader as senility overtook Jayatilaka, was a particularly energetic champion of communal interests. He warned of the need for solidarity to protect the 'race' and the Buddhist faith. He sometimes equated the 'nation' with the Sinhalese population, speaking of them as 'one blood, and one nation . . . a chosen people'.[42] He favoured a ban on the sale of land to non-Ceylonese, spoke of the Indians' 'treacherous' love of their own land and endorsed the disenfranchisement of Indian workers with comments such as this: 'I do not think a greater blow to the national life of a country has been dealt, even by the Germans in Poland than what has been done Up-country by the enfranchisement of so many Indian labourers.'[43]

[38] See note 20. Also, interview with J. R. Jayewardene, Colombo, 11 September 1978.
[39] R. L. Stirrat has, for example, encountered such groups in western coastal areas near Chilaw.
[40] R. A. L. H. Gunawardena provides a very useful summary of the historical origins of the Sinhalese chauvinist idiom in 'The People of the Lion', *Sri Lanka Journal of the Humanities*, v (1979), pp. 1–36.
[41] See, for example, *CDN*, 29 March 1937, 10 January, 29 March, 19 May and 25 June 1940, and 3 April 1940. Jayewardene was not elected to the State Council until 1943.
[42] *CDN*, 15 April 1939. See also, 2 May 1938 and 10 January 1939.
[43] Quotations are from *CDN*, 23 February and 26 December 1940. See also, 15 June and 29 July 1940.

Senanayake's main initiative to assist Sinhalese lay in his ministry's huge land colonization schemes. He claimed, without gross exaggeration, that of 3.5 million acres of cultivable land in Ceylon, 2 million was owned by foreigners (mainly British planters) and a further million was mortgaged to non-Ceylonese, leaving only half a million firmly in the hands of the island's people.[44] By colonizing uncultivated areas in north-central Ceylon, he sought to reduce this imbalance. He saw to it that the benefits of this programme went not to Ceylonese in general but to Sinhalese. (Indeed, most of the beneficiaries were members of the *Goyigama* and *Salagama* castes. Senanayake did not regard Sinhalese from disadvantaged castes or from the urban working class as part of his constituency.)[45] On the large Minneriya scheme, for example, the colonists included a mere seven Tamils and three Muslims.[46] By populating these lands with Sinhalese, Senanayake also succeeded in converting many areas which had had either a Tamil majority or a rough balance of linguistic groups into areas of Sinhalese predominance. This contributed enormously to Senanayake's popularity among Sinhalese since it made him seem a modern successor to earlier heroes who were said to have reconquered northern and eastern parts of the island from the Tamils. Sinhalese chauvinists naturally regarded the whole of the island as 'sacred space'. And since the north-central areas which took the main thrust of the colonization effort contained the ruins of great Buddhist centres such as Polonnaruwa and, most especially, Anuradhapura which was commonly called 'the sacred city',[47] Senanayake's programmes had potent appeal.

Nowhere was that more apparent than in Bandaranaike's attempt to carve out a prominent role for himself in what one scholar has called the 'reconquest'.[48] His opportunities at the Ministry of Local Administration were far more limited than Senanayake's at Agriculture and Lands. Indeed, he remained effectively cut off from land policy until he became Prime Minister in 1956, which is thus when the issue will next arise in this discussion. But in the late 1930s and early 1940s he cleverly took up a pre-existing scheme to preserve and restore the ruins of Anuradhapura, a capital of ancient Sinhalese kings and a modern centre of Buddhist

[44] *CDN*, 17 September 1941. Statistics on control of land at that time were rather unreliable.

[45] In pursuing this policy, Senanayake was ignoring an official proposal to allot land to the urban poor who had been badly hit by the depression. See *Sessional Paper XXIV of 1931*.

[46] *CDN*, 18 October 1939.

[47] E. Nissan, The Sacred City of Anuradhapura: Aspects of Sinhalese Buddhism and Nationhood, University of London doctoral thesis, 1985.

[48] D. E. Smith, 'Religion, Politics and the Myth of Reconquest', in R. N. Kearney and T. Fernando (eds.), *Modern Sri Lanka* (Syracuse, 1979), pp. 83–99.

pilgrimage. This entailed moving homes, the city administration and business district – with its mosques, churches, slaughter-house and its non-Sinhalese majority, all of which offended Sinhalese Buddhist chauvinists[49] – away from the ancient religious quarters to a distant resettlement area. It cause great hardship to the up-rooted, but it appealed to many Sinhalese as a forceful reclamation of sacred precincts.[50] Bandaranaike made much of this programme. The Sinhala Maha Sabha held numerous rallies in Anuradhapura, often on Buddhist holy days with large processions in which religious symbols and ritual figured prominently, and he addressed at least one such meeting from within the Sacred Bo Tree Temple.[51] For him the restoration of Anuradhapura was more than an exercise in political manipulation. He was genuinely haunted by the aesthetic beauty of the ruins and hoped to retire there to write an epic novel,[52] but the political uses of the scheme were also considerable.

This ambiguous mixture of unfeigned delight in the grandeur of the ruins and considerations of political advantage was typical of this exceedingly complex man. From the mid-1930s onwards, Bandaranaike was genuinely attracted to two notions of how politics in Ceylon should develop. The first was the need for a political and cultural revival among the Sinhalese, but he was also keen to promote reform, to provide social justice for all of the island's disadvantaged. By the end of the war, this would lead him to advocate 'socialism', although he usually avoided that word during the late 1930s and early 1940s.[53] To Bandaranaike, 'socialism' almost always meant liberal reform and stopped well short of the common ownership of the means production (although he was more aggressive on the means of exchange and on essential services). But it nonetheless meant genuine and often far-reaching changes which were intended to benefit not just Sinhalese but the disadvantaged of every community.

---

[49] This had been a source of dispute long before a Buddhist memorial on the subject in 1894. J. D. Rogers, 'The Social Context of Riots in Sri Lanka', typescript, pp. 41–46. I am grateful to Elizabeth Nissan for clarifying this point.

[50] *CDN*, 26 August, 5 September, 17 December 1940, 8 February, 5 March, 10 June, 11 October and 14 November 1941, 25 March 1943, 18 September 1944, 21 and 23 March and 1 May 1946. Bandaranaike clearly intended to give this impression (interviews with two Sabha lieutenants, Colombo, 16 and 21 August 1980). See also the Colonial Office view in CO 54/985/9, PRO.

[51] *CDN*, 8 February 1941. See also, 7 May 1941 and 26 June 1944.

[52] Interviews with one relative and several political aides of Bandaranaike, Colombo, September 1977 and September 1980.

[53] This was the agreed view of those cited in note 52. See also, however, his advocacy in 1942 of socialism as a means to achieve postwar reconstruction (*CDN*, 11 December 1942).

116 The expedient utopian

Bandaranaike, then, was at once a Sinhalese chauvinist and a cosmopolitan reformer.[54] At no time after 1936 did he ever cease to be both of these things. (Some analysts would with some justice call him a patrician populist, but the term 'populist' has come to be used so loosely and variously that its utility in political analysis has been largely destroyed.) Here was a situation and a man replete with incongruities which were apparent not only in the tension between these two notions, but also in the way that he arrived at them. His enthusiasm for reform was born of an overweening elitism. This was clear for example in 1938 when he expressed surprise during a tour of Australia that his group's driver was 'included quite naturally in the party at lunch' and 'engaged him in so lively a discussion of politics'.[55] This was a novel experience for someone who had dwelt among the upper crust at Oxford and in Ceylon, but far from being repelled by it, he was delighted. It confirmed his (rather theoretical) belief in the worth of the common man, a belief which in part grew out of his snobbish contempt for the petty pretensions of the Ceylonese elite. A few weeks later, he resumed his efforts to force unwilling urban councils to accept a broadened franchise because 'I cannot accept . . . that intelligence, honesty or integrity in private life are to be measured in terms of the passing of an examination or the possession of some property.'[56]

Bandaranaike would have claimed that there was no contradiction between being a cosmopolitan reformer and an advocate of Sinhalese interests. He would have pointed, with some justice, to the sufferings of ordinary Sinhalese under colonialism. No matter how often he stressed the anti-colonial rather than the anti-Tamil elements of Sinhalese chauvinism, there was no escaping its anti-Tamil implications. There was always more tension than harmony behind his reformism and his Sinhalese chauvinism – the two great themes in his political career.

These themes are best seen as two poles on a broad spectrum of postures that he adopted at various times throughout the remainder of his life. His oscillations between these two poles followed a rational pattern. He turned towards Sinhalese chauvinism when, loosely speaking, he was

---

[54] It might also be stressed that in addition to his enthusiasm for a Sinhalese revival and for cosmopolitan reform, Bandaranaike was thoroughly convinced of the value of the rule of law, of civil liberties and of elections on the basis of universal suffrage as the ultimate source of political authority. In his attachment to reform, he differed markedly from D. S. Senanayake and many of the others with whom he joined to form the first post-independence government in Ceylon. And in his liberal constitutionalism and his attachment to democracy, he differed from some of those who succeeded to power after Senanayake's death in 1952, most especially Bandaranaike's predecessor as Prime Minister, Sir John Kotelawala. [55] *CDN*, 10 February 1938.
[56] *CDN*, 25 February 1938. See also 21 November 1936, 21 and 24 October 1938 and 3 February 1940.

'in opposition', when those at the apex of the political system refused to accept him as a full partner. There were two such periods during his career: the one under discussion between 1936 and 1942 or so, when both the British and the Senanayake–Jayatilaka clique held him in suspicion, and later between 1951 and 1956 when he was literally in opposition after resigning from Senanayake's post-independence ruling party. He turned towards the opposite, reformist pole during phases in which he achieved at least a substantial share of power at the apex of the system. There were again two such periods: between 1942 and 1951 when the exigencies first of war and then of domestic politics impelled others to draw him into a unified leadership, and between 1956 and 1959 when he was Prime Minister.

This oscillation between communalism and a more cosmopolitan, reformist stance was not peculiar to his career alone. It became a main theme in the politics of Ceylon. This owes something to the power of Bandaranaike's example, but it owes more to the logic of the political situation. Politicians have tended to whip up Sinhalese chauvinism when in opposition, only to veer towards a statesmanlike, liberal reformism in the interests of all communities when, after achieving power, they found themselves the custodians of the unity of the entire island.

In the years between 1936 and 1942, he found it increasingly difficult to maintain credibility as a reformer. That role had been easy to cultivate in the first State Council where conservative and indeed reactionary defenders of the socio-economic status quo had predominated, but the election of 1936 had brought a small number of genuine radicals into the Council. They made Bandaranaike's occasional reformist rhetoric seem distinctly tame and they pounced gleefully upon his inconsistencies, branding him a 'Renegade Socialist Coward' to his intense annoyance.[57] More importantly, however, Bandaranaike's Sinhalese chauvinism increasingly crowded his reformist tendencies to one side. A striking example of this occurred in 1941, when the need to maintain a hard communalist line against Indian immigration and all things Indian led him even to criticise Ceylonese leaders for attending meetings to honour Jawaharlal Nehru,[58] the man on whom he would later model himself during his reformist phases.

Despite statements to the contrary by Bandaranaike and at least one historian, the main vehicle for his communalism, the Sinhala Maha

---

[57] *Ceylon Hansard* (1936), p. 881 and *CDN*, 25 July and 6 September 1936. It should be emphasized that in 1938, when the press stated that Bandaranaike had advocated socialism, he vehemently denied this (*CDN*, 25 June 1938).

[58] *CDN*, 6 and 28 January 1941.

Sabha, possessed only very modest organizational substance.[59] It operated at two levels: in the island at large through branches in Colombo and
provincial towns, and within the State Council. Bandaranaike claimed to
have formed nineteen branches by November 1937 and – with a
vagueness that raises suspicions about the transient nature of some of
them – '25 to 30' by August 1938.[60] Membership was said to stand at 1,500
the following month.[61] A great many of these local units of the Sabha
were very hastily arranged, often just before local council elections, and
few remained strong for very long. Of the sixty-seven branches that had
supposedly been formed by January 1940, it was said – in what was
almost certainly an understatement – that 'many . . . were not very
active'.[62] In part, this was because branch committees were so huge –
usually about fifty members – as to be unwieldy. The usual practice was to
cram as many local notables as possible onto these committees in order to
persuade people that the local establishment backed the Sabha.[63] But
many people merely lent their names without enthusiasm so that, for
example, the president of the Mariakadde branch resigned within a month
of his election. An eminent 'member' of the committee at Anuradhapura
stated that he had been named without being consulted and that in truth
he opposed the Sabha. Rallies to establish branches were frequently held
immediately after public meetings of existing associations (often in the
same room) to ensure a sizable, if semi-captive audience.[64] Some branches
suffered serious internal dissension and even open strife.[65] Many met only
a few times and, when they found that they could make virtually no
impact upon a national leadership consisting almost entirely of State
Councillors, quickly withered away. At both national and local levels, the
Sabha's organizational weakness was compounded by severe under-
funding.

Most members of Sabha branch committees came from the pre-
eminent *Goyigama* caste, but other castes of middling-to-high status were

59   Jane Russell has written that 'unlike the Ceylon National Congress' the Sabha 'had a
     strong grass-roots organisation' (The Ceylon Tamils, p. 367). If our yardstick is the
     insubstantial Congress, there is some truth in this. But by any objective criteria, the
     Sabha's organization was distinctly unimpressive.
60   *CDN*, 18 November 1937 and 9 August 1938.
61   *CDN*, 5 September 1938.   62   *CDN*, 1 January 1940.
63   *TC*, 6 and 13 September 1938 and *CDN*, 23 January 1939. On organization-building,
     see also *CDN*, 13 October 1937, 21 July and 5–6 August 1938, and *TC*, 9 and 12 August
     1938.
64   See, for example, *CDN*, 23 January 1939 and 24 September 1941. Also, interview with a
     Sabha activist, Colombo, 27 September 1980.
65   For example, a meeting over which Bandaranaike presided to establish a branch at
     Maradana erupted into pandemonium over the choice of the local patron and president.
     Several people 'nearly came to blows – some even went to the extent of threatening
     murder'. *CDN*, 5 September 1938. See also, *TC*, 1 November 1938.

well-represented in many areas as well. More depressed groups figured only rarely. Membership was drawn overwhelmingly from the urban middle classes, with merchants and (often rather impecunious) professional men playing a prominent part. A small number of branches responded to Bandaranaike's appeal for 'social service' which, he insisted, was to be given to all castes and to Buddhist and Christian Sinhalese alike. In most cases, however, this consisted mainly of lectures on the need for solidarity among Sinhalese and (more occasionally) modest handouts of money to members of groups being proselytized.[66]

The influence of the Sinhala Maha Sabha only very rarely penetrated into rural areas to any degree or for sustained periods. The issues of Indian influence and immigration, on which it tended to concentrate, evoked a response mainly in urban centres and in some rural Kandyan areas near tea estates worked by Indian labourers.[67] Weak Sabha branches composed overwhelmingly of westernized urban people were not equipped to reach out to Sinhalese villagers. A very few people from the groups that in 1956 carried Bandaranaike's communalist message to the rural masses – *bhikkhus* (Buddhist clergy), ayurvedic physicians and Sinhala-medium teachers – had passing associations with the Sabha. In the later 1930s and early 1940s, these interest groups had not yet crystallized, these people were poorly politicized and they tended to distrust Bandaranaike as a Buddhist and Sinhalese chauvinist by convenience rather then by conviction.

Within the State Council, the strength of the Sinhala Maha Sabha was also more apparent than real. Bandaranaike liked to give the impression that it operated in Council as a closely-knit political *party*, but it was a far more amorphous body than he implied. Several of its more prominent members including two future Prime Ministers – the Minister of Communications and Works, J. L. (later Sir John) Kotelawala, and Dudley Senanayake – joined 'for the fun of it' and took an inconstant interest in it.[68] Councillors drifted in and out of the Sabha's loose caucus, the membership of which hovered around fifteen to seventeen in a House of fifty.[69] Its membership in the State Council was, more often than not,

---

[66] In 1941, a newspaper called *The Nation*, owned by Bandaranaike and aimed at boosting him and the Sabha, was founded. But he appears to have lost interest in it before long, and it never made much impact. See in this connection, bound volumes of *The Nation*, NASL.

[67] Eric Meyer's research on the period up to and including the mid-1930s found *no* evidence of anti-Tamil feeling in *rural* areas. There was a virtual absence of Sinhalese–Tamil violence in rural or urban areas until 1956. For that, see J. D. Rogers, *Crime, Justice and Society in Colonial Sri Lanka* (London, 1987).

[68] The quotation is from a minor Sabha enthusiast (interview, Colombo, 6 September 1980), confirmed by Sir John (interview, Kandawela, 9 September 1980).

[69] See, for example, *TC*, 8 December 1938 and Russell, The Ceylon Tamils, p. 202.

divided on important issues and on several occasions very serious splits developed within it. The most sustained and spiteful of these arose when one faction sought to drum Bandaranaike's boyhood friend, R. S. S. Gunawardena, out of the caucus. This was inspired by prejudice against his humble caste background, by his sympathies for his Indian estate-worker constituents and by rivalry over the post of acting minister during Bandaranaike's absence on a foreign tour.[70]

Such squabbles, which undercut Bandaranaike's authority within the caucus,[71] appear to have moved him to curtail councillors' opportunities for participation. That led in turn to an erosion of the Sabha's already modest corporate strength so that it tended, over time, to degenerate into 'yet another of Mr S. W. R. D. Bandaranaike's protean political manifestations', which was little more than 'an annexe to the personal ambitions of its President'.[72] The Sabha – like every other party or association Bandaranaike led and, it should be stressed, like every other major party that has ever existed in Ceylon[73] – suffered from an excessive concentration of power in the hands of its leader. If at times it seemed a force to be reckoned with, this impression owed more to the tireless touring and speechmaking of its leader and to the emotional responses which his rhetoric evoked than to its organizational substance.

The development of the Sinhala Maha Sabha inevitably led to an estrangement between Bandaranaike and the Sabha on the one hand and, on the other, most of his fellow ministers and the Ceylon National Congress to which they were at least tenuously attached. We saw in chapter 4 that the Congress had long been an insubstantial force and in the late 1930s its fortunes, if anything, declined still further. The creation of the pan-Sinhalese Board of Ministers in 1936 was hailed as a victory for the Congress,[74] but this claim was of a piece with other exaggerations of its importance. All of the new ministers were nominal members of Congress, but their elections both to the Council and to the Board had far more to do with their influence as individuals.

Only a few weeks after the ministers were chosen, Bandaranaike's initial efforts to develop a circle of followers in the Council had led some to see him as an opponent of the Ceylon National Congress.[75] Before long, this impression gained general acceptance as he attacked other

[70] *CDN*, 15 November 1937 and *TC*, 13 September 1938.
[71] See, for example, *CDN*, 15 November 1937, and *TC*, 14 December 1938.
[72] *CDN*, 15 November 1937 and *TC*, 26 September 1938.
[73] J. Manor, 'The Failure of Political Integration in Sri Lanka', *Journal of Commonwealth and Comparative Politics*, xvii, 1 (March, 1979), pp. 21–46.
[74] *CDN*, 21 September 1936.   [75] *CI*, 10 December 1936.

leading politicians for their lack of zeal in the Sinhalese revivalist cause. His criticisms were sometimes accompanied by ritual assurances that the Sabha was not opposed to the Congress, but his main thrust was so patently hostile to Congress and its most eminent members that these remarks could not be taken seriously. By early 1939, Congress leaders were so worried by the response evoked by Bandaranaike's communalist speeches that they hit back with claims that he was impeding further political reform by making the Ceylonese seem more divided than they were.[76] The accusation had little substance since the British were disinclined to grant a constitutional advance, but it signalled a clear breach between Bandaranaike and his ministerial colleagues. This went further at the end of 1939 when he told the annual conference of the Sinhala Maha Sabha that he viewed with 'cynical amusement' the 'small clique, the "Old Gang"' who used the Congress 'merely to lend a semblance of public opinion to their opinions and wishes'. They were guilty of 'butchering all that was valuable in the Congress'.[77]

Many people were, not surprisingly, taken aback a few days after that salvo when it was revealed that Bandaranaike had never ceased to be a member of the Congress and that his name had been included in the Congress Executive Committee 'at his particular request'.[78] There followed a spate of letters to the press demanding an explanation from Bandaranaike and a 'straight answer' on whether he had advocated communal representation in the State Council which both the Congress and Board of Ministers opposed. He wrote to say that he saw no contradiction between membership in the two bodies and, after dodging the issue of communal representation, falsely accused the Congress President of advocating it.[79] Bandaranaike was at his least edifying at such moments, devaluing language and unwittingly demeaning himself in a deperate bid to have things both ways. It did not end there. The Congress Executive soon met to consider his expulsion. He attended for the first time in more than five years (and for the last)[80] and stated that his recent speech 'was not in any spirit of disloyalty to Congress . . . While continuing as an Executive Committee member of the Congress I would not have attacked the Congress as a body.' After that scarcely credible climb down, the motion to expel him was withdrawn.[81]

Why did he subject himself, here as on several other occasions, to such

[76] See, for example, *CDN*, 6 and 14 March 1939.
[77] *CDN*, 1 January 1940.   [78] *CDN*, 3 January 1940.
[79] Bandaranaike's letter is in *CDN*, 15 January 1940. See also, 6, 10 and 12 January 1940.
[80] M. Roberts (ed.), *Documents of the Ceylon National Congress*, vol. i (Colombo, 1977), pp. 470–78. In the same period, he had also failed to take part in any national conferences of the Congress (vol. ii, pp. 1237–366).   [81] *CDN*, 18 January 1940.

embarrassment – which a largely hostile press was happy to emphasize[82] –
when he had had nothing to do with Congress for years, and when an early
break with it (which came, quietly twelve months later) was virtually
inevitable?[83] He did so for three main reasons, each of which reveals
something important about his perceptions of himself and of politics.

It was first of all nearly impossible to embarrass Bandaranaike. Others
often felt embarrassment for him when he back-tracked or contradicted
himself. But on few if any of these occasions did he himself appear to feel
that way. His monumental self-confidence about his place in Ceylon
society made him heartily complacent and exceedingly thick-skinned
about these things. He held the island's westernized elite in such
contempt that he did not much care what they thought of him, and he felt
reasonably sure that the masses would neither fully recognize nor
remember his inconsistencies. After a youth in which his precocious,
often outrageous, comments and doings were indulged and applauded he
was hardly likely to be a model of restraint in adulthood.[84] (Indeed, many
people believed, with some justice, that he had acquired his brashness
from his mother.)[85] Yet alongside his serene self-confidence in such
matters, personal insecurities acquired during a painful childhood drove
him to seize avidly, at times even brazenly, upon anything that seemed to
offer some tangible or potential advantage in the power game. In early
1940, it still seemed possible that his nominal link to Congress might at
some point yield dividends and he was loath to let it go.

The second reason has already been hinted at. It is at first glance

[82] The *Ceylon Daily News* and the vernacular papers owned by the Lake House group, which
were owned by Ceylonese who supported D. S. Senanayake and his close allies, opposed
Bandaranaike as an individual. The *Times of Ceylon* group spoke for British planting and
commercial interests and would emphasize anything that would embarrass Ceylonese
politicians. This did.

[83] The break, which occurred in January 1941, was revealed in *CDN*, 9 January 1942.

[84] See the material in file 7, BP.

[85] Lady Bandaranaike was well known for offensive behaviour and for caustic, sometimes
vulgar language. (This was consistently affirmed in a large number of interviews in
Colombo in 1977, 1978 and 1980.) Governor Caldecott suspected that Bandaranaike's
thick skin and penchant for aggressive language had been acquired from his mother who
'was generally regarded as volatile and irresponsible'. (Secret Report, 'Things
Ceylonese', No. 14, CO 54/982/2, PRO.) One instance of her insensitive behaviour
occurred at the All-Asia Women's Conference in Lahore in 1931 when she called upon
the Maharani of Gwalior who was wearing an impressive set of pearls. Lady
Bandaranaike herself described the scene: 'whilst talking to her, I exclaimed "Are these
pearls real". My attention was drawn to them because they looked unreal. They were like
uneven lumps of mother-of-pearl, as large as an olive, and of peculiar blackish
whiteness . . .'

She responded to accusations of a breach of etiquette by writing: 'If it is English
etiquette, I have never made a study of it and never mean to . . . The art of running after
everything English is not one of my accomplishments . . . Sinhalese etiquette does not
bar one Eastern[er] from making such a remark to another.' But she then rather spoiled
the effect by recalling her numerous encounters with British royalty. (*CI*, 25 March
1931. See also, *CI*, 23, 26 and 28 March 1931.)

remarkable how much illogical, contradictory behaviour Bandaranaike thought that he could get away with. (Many of those in the front rank of Ceylon politics thought along similar lines, though few carried their inconsistencies as far as he did.) A moment's reflection on the structure of politics in modern Ceylon, however, makes this seem less surprising. The Donoughmore Constitution provided opportunities for a small number of ministers to develop limited but significant networks of clients and popular support through the distribution of patronage. Far more crucially, since patronage powers were quite modest, it enabled them to achieve widespread popular recognition which gave them huge advantages in their dealings with aspiring political rivals and with their subordinates. In the case of a few ministers – most notably in the British period, D. S. Senanayake and Bandaranaike – public exposure and the already lofty status of their families in the island's social hierarchy reinforced one another. This made them daunting figures who expected and received an immense amount of deference not only from ordinary folk but also from members of various elites. Had they created political parties or associations of genuine substance, based on democratic decision-making (such as, for example, the Congress in India after 1919), this deference would have gradually dissipated. But no such organizations have ever been allowed to develop in Ceylon,[86] so that deference to leading figures in pre-eminent political families persisted through Bandaranaike's lifetime and even to the present day. Because he expected and received such deference, he felt that he would not be called to account by subordinates for inconsistent behaviour.

The third reason that Bandaranaike sought to remain within the Congress in 1940 was that he could not bring himself to make a clean break with the leading politicians in Congress, especially D. S. Senanayake who by 1939 had achieved *de facto* pre-eminence among the island's politicians.[87] In part, this was because his links to them yielded political advantages, and because he was always timid about confrontational action, his abrasive words notwithstanding. But he also had an inner need for relationships with figures of authority against whom he chafed so bitterly. Had he broken off two or three such relationships during his life it might be possible to dispute this, but he refused to do so.

There were also several reasons for Bandaranaike and Senanayake to make common cause. Both wanted the British to increase the powers of elected politicians and introduce a Cabinet system, and by working smoothly together, they could demonstrate how well that system might work. Both resented the hauteur and racism of many British residents of

---

[86] Manor, 'The Failure of Political Integration'.
[87] His pre-eminence was formally confirmed with his election as Leader of the State Council after the long-overdue resignation of Sir Baron Jayatilaka in late 1942.

Ceylon, some of whom were second-rate people who had gone to the colonies in search of the success which would have eluded them at home. Both shared an awareness of the handicaps which many Sinhalese (and, both would have added, Ceylonese) had suffered as a result of colonialism, a desire to right those wrongs and an anxiety over the size of the immigrant labour force from India.[88] Both believed in the rule of law and – with some reservations, mainly on Senanayake's side – in representative government, universal franchise and a liberal conception of civil rights. They also shared a preference for elite domination of politics and a high degree of centralization in party organizations and the political system, on the assumption that they – individually or collectively – would stand at the apex.

The two men were also united by a grudging, limited respect which each felt for the ability and the political strength of the other. Bandaranaike saw Senanayake as his only thoroughly ministerial colleague whom he had long acknowledged as 'the best of the ministers',[89] whose effectiveness at the key Ministry of Agriculture and Lands, and seniority had earned him a very powerful following. He also admired Senanayake's capacity for forceful, combative action (which Bandaranaike himself lacked),[90] his ability to recognize his own limitations and what appeared – at least in the period covered by this chapter – to be his reliability as a political bargainer. Senanayake had less respect for Bandaranaike, whose inconsistencies and appetite for the main chance compounded the older man's distaste for the social stratum from which the young man came. But if Bandaranaike seemed to lack backbone and the kind of virile stubbornness in holding to one viewpoint for which Senanayake was famous, he was also both clever and ready to mobilize social groups – both disadvantaged castes and communal extremists – whom Senanayake preferred to keep on the margins of the power game. He had therefore to be treated warily, with a certain reluctant respect.

Bandaranaike was an immense improvement over his sorry predecessor as Minister of Local Administration. He brought to his new office intellectual gifts, ambition and solid support from his Executive Committee – all of which had been lacking before. He began to show signs of a certain laziness and inattention to detail[91] which became more

---

[88] *CDN*, 12 February 1940.   [89] Roberts (ed.), *Documents*, vol. ii, pp. 1190–91.

[90] See, for example, Senanayake's resignation in February 1940. Bandaranaike threatened such action quite routinely, but he very seldom translated this into action.

[91] The perceptive if somewhat biased Governor Caldecott noted that 'If he were not indolent, he could . . . exercise a considerable mental capacity; but he finds it easier to peddle words than to deal in facts with the result that he never considers it worth his while to learn his brief or to match sound with sense.' Secret Report, 'Things Ceylonese', No. 14, CO 54/982/2, PRO.

noticeable a decade later, but he could still be immensely energetic when
it came to speaking tours, skirmishes with opponents and legislation that
he cared about. Within a relatively short time, he had pushed through
improvements in electoral procedure and measures to rationalize the
system of local councils and increase their powers modestly.

His main aim, however, was to create regional councils of elected
Ceylonese. In this he failed and this failure, which was repeated during his
time as Prime Minister, has had a major impact on the island's politics,
even to the present day. In proposing regional councils, he was taking up
and developing a recommendation of the Donoughmore Commission
which both the British authorities and leading politicians in Ceylon had
studiously ignored. The British had done so because they preferred to
minimize opportunities for elected politicians and because such councils
would have drained power away from colonial bureaucrats at whatever
level – provincial or district – they operated. The politicians had ignored
it partly because they had other things on their mind and partly because
Bandaranaike's wretched predecessor at the ministry did not press the
idea. But they also preferred to maintain the high degree of centralization
at the national level where they operated.

Bandaranaike proposed to create regional councils which would be
indirectly elected by existing local councils (that is, in villages, towns and
cities). There would be one in each of the island's twenty districts, a
departure from the Donoughmore scheme which suggested one for each
of the nine provinces. The councils would have three main roles. They
would replace the various, largely moribund advisory committees which
most ministries appointed in each district and would coordinate the
disparate roles played by those committees. They would provide a crucial
link between the scattered and isolated local councils and the island's
power centre in Colombo, making possible a rational integration of the
apex and base of the political system which was sorely lacking. And
finally, the elected members of the councils would take over many –
Bandaranaike sometimes said all – of the functions of those still quite
autocratic bureaucrats who administered the districts.[92]

He sometimes claimed that this scheme and his plans to strengthen
local councils constituted a programme of decentralization, to put greater
power in the hands of ordinary people. There was some truth in this, but
since it makes him seem a dissenter from the pattern of over-
centralization and elite dominance which has always prevailed in Ceylon's
politics, it needs careful examination. He certainly wanted to enlarge the
powers and the purses of *local* councils, which made good sense since they
were grossly under-funded. He had some rather minor successes in doing

[92] Interviews with two close associates of Bandaranaike in this effort, Colombo, 18 August
and 4 September 1977.

so and – since local councils took over a small number of functions previously performed by bureaucrats at the supra-local level – this qualified as a very modest dose of decentralization.[93] It must be stressed, however, that Bandaranaike was even more determined to maintain his ministry's *control* over local councils,[94] and this placed him firmly among the guardians of Ceylon's over-centralized political system. So did his lifelong preference for over-centralization in the parties that he led, and so did his plan for regional councils. Regional councils were to gain power not at the expense of the State Council or of any person or institution at the national level, but at the expense of bureaucrats at the regional level. Power was to shift horizontally, not from the apex of the system downward. This plan can be viewed as an example of democratization – and as a much-needed measure to integrate national, intermediate and local levels – but not of decentralization.[95]

Why did his attempts to create regional councils fail? Part of the explanation lies in poor political manoeuvring on his part. He very sensibly sought to introduce the scheme on an experimental basis in only one district, but he unwisely allowed his first four years as minister to pass before proposing it to the State Council.[96] He might also have won more support for the plan had he not attacked fellow ministers and councillors so sharply and so often, and had his open displays of ambition not alerted others to the plan's potential advantages for him. It was certainly unlucky that a world war occurred when it did, an event that increased British reluctance to introduce innovations that might disrupt the workings of government. But all of these factors were less important than the overriding fact that the regional councils scheme threatened the vital interests of both the British authorities and Bandaranaike's ministerial colleagues.

British influence outside Colombo depended very substantially upon the control exercised by the chief civil servants who ran the *kachcheries* or headquarters offices in the provincial and district capitals. Before the introduction of the Donoughmore Constitution in 1931, these civil servants had been wholly dominant at the provincial and district levels, thanks to their control of all employees of various government departments working within their bailiwicks. After 1931, their power had been diluted somewhat as various Ceylonese ministers sent more and

---

[93] Bandaranaike would have preferred greater, though still limited, decentralization to local boards, but he faced opposition from other ministers and Councillors. *CDN*, 22 April and 25 September 1936, 25 January, 8 May and 28 June 1937.

[94] See, for example, *CDN*, 25 September 1936, 10–11 and 17 July and 22 August 1941.

[95] His eagerness during the 1920s to promote genuine decentralization through federalism in Ceylon must be seen as a piece of youthful enthusiasm and not a guide to his basic attitudes in later years.   [96] *CDN*, 11 July 1940.

more specialist employees – health and education inspectors, agricultural advisors, local government and public works officers and the like – into the hinterland. These employees had to work with and through the chief civil servants in their districts, but their first loyalties were usually to the departments for which they worked and to the ministers who supervised them.[97] The British did not want to see the authority of their chief civil servants in the districts decline further.[98]

Bandaranaike's regional councils plan also threatened the newly acquired powers of other Ceylonese ministers over their networks of specialist employees. His councils were intended, ultimately, not only to displace chief civil servants but also to exercise close supervision of the specialist employees of various ministries. Since the councils would fall under the purview, if not the tight control, of the Minister of Local Administration (Bandaranaike), they would in effect have given him greater powers than those of any other minister. It is hardly surprising then that the scheme was never enacted into law, despite unanimous but meaningless State Council votes in favour of the plan in principle.[99] This had profound implications for the island's subsequent political development, for this was probably the last time that a proposal to create regional councils did not alarm Sinhalese chauvinists who, a few years later, came to see it as a capitulation to Tamil demands for autonomy and eventually separatism. This and later rejections of the plan left Ceylon without adequate integrating structures between the national and local levels and, ultimately, between elite and mass, both of which have contributed abundantly to the island's subsequent woes.[100]

It had not gone unremarked during the 1930s that Bandaranaike had yet to take a wife. In 1937 for example during a visit to Jaffna, he had paid a visit to a local 'mystic' (more out of curiosity than any belief in the supernatural) and the press reported that 'the Swamy advised him to link his destiny with a fair partner after his own heart'. Over a meal of 'rusks and water', the holy man – who was by the way a Tamil Hindu – told him that if he remained 'in single-blessedness' he should abandon politics and become a Buddhist monk in order to reach Nirvana.[101] He needed no reminding that a shrewd marriage could strengthen his political position (though that is probably not what the mystic had in mind). Elite families, and none more than his own, had been forging judicious alliances since

---

[97] This conclusion is based on numerous interviews with such officials in the island in 1977, 1978 and 1980.
[98] See, for example, Secret Report, 'Things Ceylonese', 28 December 1939, CO 54/971/11, PRO.   [99] See, for example, *CDN*, 22 June 1939 and 11 July 1940.
[100] This theme will be developed further in chapters 7 and 8.
[101] *CDN*, 26 January 1937.

well before the British era in Ceylon.[102] So when he set out in 1939 and 1940 to arrange such a union himself,[103] he was conforming to the traditions of his clan, although his situation and therefore his criteria were somewhat different from those of his forbears in the old mudaliyar elite. Their concern was to align themselves with partners from very prominent families among the 'first-class *Goyigamas*' of the low country which was, as it were, their 'constituency' in the bygone days before elections became crucial. This necessarily implied Anglican rites, to which all pre-eminent low-country mudaliyars were committed. The landed wealth of the prospective spouse – which in the low country usually meant coconut and sometimes rubber plantations – was an important consideration.

The arena in which Bandaranaike operated was much larger, embracing the entire island or at least the portion of it inhabited by the Sinhalese majority. A marriage across caste lines might in one way have broadened his social force, but it would have scandalized so many *Goyigamas* that it was unthinkable. The obvious step, then, was to find a bride from among the Kandyan elite as no less a man than D. S. Senanayake (among others) had done before him.[104] That implied a Buddhist marriage since most eminent Kandyans had not converted to Christianity. It was in this context that Bandaranaike became engaged in 1940 to Sirimavo Ratwatte. Her family had risen to prominence as owners of paddy (rice) lands in the Kandyan hill country in the nineteenth century[105] and her father held a very high position in the Kandyan headmen's system and in Buddhist lay circles. Her brother had been involved in the Sinhala Maha Sabha since 1938.[106] This clearly had greater private than public importance for Bandaranaike but Governor Caldecott only exaggerated modestly in reporting to London that: 'This marriage is of great sociological and political importance . . . This union between a first-rank family of the lowlands and a first-rank family of the Kandyan highlands represents an accretion of political influence to the Sinhala Maha Sabha.'[107]

[102] See, for example, P. Peebles, The Transformation of a Colonial Elite: The Mudaliyars of Nineteenth-Century Ceylon, University of Chicago doctoral thesis, 1973, pp. 58–59.
[103] That he made such an arrangement is confirmed by members of both the Bandaranaike–Obeyesekere and Ratwatte families in interviews at Colombo and Kandy, August 1978.   [104] Russell, The Ceylon Tamils, p. 266.
[105] This is based on Eric Meyer's findings on the landed elite of the nineteenth century, relayed to me in conversation.   [106] *TC*, 12 and 19 August and 11 November 1938.
[107] Secret Report, 'Things Ceylonese', 18 October 1940 in CO 54/977/7, PRO. He added this: 'Whatever opinion one may hold of young Bandaranaike as Minister of Local Administration, or as founder and leader of the Sinhala Maha Sabha, or as a pervert [Caldecott's slip] for political purposes from Christianity to Buddhism . . . one is bound to admit that he has taken to himself a wife who appears thoroughly nice, placid and sensible . . . a good wife and the discipline of married life may help to provide young Banda with the ballast that he sadly lacked.'

On the day of the wedding members of Bandaranaike's family, no strangers to pomp, were immensely impressed by the 'decorations and enormous crowds all along the route' which covered many miles to the Ratwatte home.[108] Those who attended recall both an elegant marriage ceremony followed by a splendid reception, and a day marked by incidents that bespoke a certain tension between the ways and values of the bridegroom and those of the waning colonial order in which his father had been such a pivotal figure. When the Governor arrived, Bandaranaike subtly snubbed him by turning away to greet the child of a peasant standing near at hand.[109] Later, when the Governor proposed a toast to the bride and groom, he spoke at greater length of his joy for Sir Solomon than of the couple. And although Bandaranaike was by now a teetotaller who had asked – in conformity with conservative Buddhist sentiments – that no alcohol be served, one guest noted that the fruit cup consisted mainly of champagne, though no one would admit it.[110] After a week's honeymoon, the couple were given an even more lavish homecoming on the Bandaranaike estate. The arrival of the Governor on this occasion appears to have been given greater prominence than that of the newlyweds, and it was followed by an elaborate ceremony in which local headmen of the area paid their respects to Sir Solomon and the couple – apparently in that order.[111] This was somewhat counterbalanced, however, when Ceylon's Minister of Education read out a greeting – partly in verse – from the Sinhala Maha Sabha 'to their leader' and Bandaranaike responded with an unexpectedly vehement appeal to all Sinhalese to be ready to fight for the community.[112]

He could nevertheless move with ease into the anglicized idiom when the occasion demanded it. A fortnight later, the couple went on a trip to India, where Bandaranaike was part of a three-man delegation that also included D. S. Senanayake, for talks with Indian leaders. Bombay was 'lots of fun – tennis, riding, bridge and parties' and in Delhi they were given lunch by the Viceroy, Lord Linlithgow. Mrs Bandaranaike sat next

In a later report ('Things Ceylonese', No. 14, CO 54/982/2, PRO), however, he expressed disappointment. 'On the domestic side an unpleasant altercation, in the course of which he denied his wife both board and bed, was overheard by fellow guests in a Government Resthouse' and his public behaviour raised doubts about 'his retention of ministerial office'.

108 Entry for 3 October 1940, Sir Solomon Dias Bandaranaike diaries, NASL.
109 These comments are based on interviews with three guests at the wedding, Colombo, August 1980.
110 Entry for 3 October 1940, Bernard Aluwihare Diaries, University of Peradeniya Library.
111 Entries for 9–10 October 1940, Sir Solomon Dias Bandaranaike Diaries, NASL, and interview with two witnesses, 16 August, 1978, Colombo.
112 Undated press cutting in *ibid.*, 10 October 1940.

to His Excellency playing the role of the reticent wife which was to be hers throughout her husband's life. Bandaranaike broke the ice with the Viceroy by telling him that Sir Solomon had been a guest of Lord Linlithgow's father at Hopetoun House, his ancestral home, in 1895.[113] There is no record of the reaction of Senanayake who was present at table, but it cannot have been sympathetic. This was not his style.

The Second World War eventually transformed politics at State Council and ministerial level in Ceylon, but this took time. The outbreak of hostilities in Europe in September 1939 occasioned numerous changes. The British authorities armed themselves with draconian powers for use in emergencies and used their new powers of detention without trial to incarcerate several leading Marxists, including two members of the State Council, Philip Gunawardena and N. M. Perera. Taxes were increased, spending was cut on civil programmes (including some ministers' pet projects) and raised on military items. The government also assumed control of food and other essential commodities. This increased the powers of certain ministers – Bandaranaike for example supervised oil, fuel and eventually tyres and motor vehicles – and drew them into closer cooperation with the Governor.[114] But throughout the period before the Japanese attacked Britain's Asian colonies in December 1941, there was remarkably little diminution in the ministers' occasional disputes both with the colonial authorities and with one another. As usual, Bandaranaike was in the thick of most of these.

British preparations to deal with possible civil disorder revived bitter memories of the government's repression of innocuous Sinhalese politicians during the First World War and generated conflict both between the Governor and ministers, and among ministers. The dispute with the Governor was brought into the open at an early stage when Bandaranaike violated an informal agreement by revealing the government's plans for dealing with disturbances to the State Council and the press.[115] Conflict among the ministers centred around Sir Baron Jayatilaka who at Home Affairs dealt with internal security and who, in the view of his colleagues, was far too acquiescent towards the Governor. Jayatilaka, like D. S. Senanayake and several other leading politicians, had been jailed and threatened with execution in 1915, but he had become – as the Governor himself later wrote – 'played out . . . too senile, too casual,

---

[113] Postcards from Bandaranaike in *ibid.*, 4 and 24 November 1940. Sir Solomon recalled in his diary that Hopetoun House had 365 windows.

[114] See, for example, *CDN*, 7, 14 and 19 September 1939, 1 and 19 June and 29 August 1940, 21 June and 5 July 1941.

[115] *CDN*, 20 September 1939. See also, Report No. 1, 7 September 1939 in CO 54/971/11, PRO.

too lazy and too flabby to lead the Council . . .'[116] By subtly exploiting this situation, Senanayake was able to advance his cleverly disguised campaign to ease Jayatilaka out of office in order to achieve clear pre-eminence in the island's politics – a campaign which finally succeeded in 1942.[117] In December 1939, the Governor told the Colonial Office that the ministers persisted in their appetite for conflict, despite the outbreak of war 'because they don't think us in need of their help. Ceylon is out of the zone of hostilities and in a life that goes on much as usual they are behaving no better and perhaps a little worse then usual. They do not question the certainty of our victory.'[118]

Things changed somewhat after June 1940, with the fall of France and other grave reverses for the British in Europe. Senanayake and several ministers tempered their criticisms of the colonial authorities and joined energetically in the war effort. But Bandaranaike continued, in the Governor's words, in the 'self-appointed role of "opposition Minister" at all my conferences' with the ministers.[119] It was a situation that was unlikely to be tolerated for long, even by an enlightened Governor such as Sir Andrew Caldecott, and in early 1941 Bandaranaike gave him a chance to do something about it.

In 1940, several local councils under the jurisdiction of Bandaranaike's ministry had sought to make contributions to British war funds. It was soon discovered, however, that legal technicalities made this impossible and his Local Administration Committee came under pressure to change the law.[120] Before any action could be taken,[121] a fresh dispute between ministers and the Governor developed in February 1941, after the latter made it plain that he was prepared to use his powers to nullify State Council bills on Indian immigration if they impaired the war effort, British planting interests or relations with India.[122] This angered ministers who saw it as a curtailment of their authority on an emotionally charged issue.

Bandaranaike was particularly angry. He rose in the State Council to pour scorn on Churchill's claim that Britain was fighting as 'the outpost of civilization'. This, he said, was a civilization 'fraught with hypocrisy . . . which seems to consist of nothing but humbug'. Five days later at a

---

[116] Secret Reports, 'Things Ceylonese', 28 December 1939 and 18 February 1940 in CO 54/971/11 and CO 54/977/7, PRO.
[117] *CDN*, 16 and 28 September 1939. For more on conflict among ministers, see for example, *CDN*, 19 October 1939.
[118] Secret Report, 'Things Ceylonese', 28 December 1939, CO 54/971/11, PRO.
[119] Secret Report, 'Things Ceylonese', 20 August 1940, CO 54/977/7, PRO.
[120] *CDN*, 27 and 29 June and 4 July 1940.
[121] Bandaranaike to Caldecott, 7 April 1941, file 1, BP, and *CDN*, 14 August 1940.
[122] *CDN*, 12 February 1941.

mass meeting in Colombo, he accused the Governor of deceit and 'impertinence'. He then told a meeting in a village hall, attended by police agents who were now watching him closely,[123] that the Sinhala Maha Sabha would soon ask the State Council and the public to cut off aid to the war effort. Why should they 'sacrifice our blood and money' for rulers who were 'trying to ruin the existence of the Ceylonese'. He also announced that his local administration committee would prevent local councils from making gifts to war funds. On 19 March, without prior consultation with other ministers,[124] it imposed that ban and threatened to maintain it until the dispute over immigration was resolved satisfactorily. A few days later, police agents recorded Bandaranaike telling a Sabha general meeting that 'only a bloody revolution as happened in France' could solve the economic ills caused by British rule. He reportedly said that 'Differentiation between Hitler and the British Government would be like a choice between the Devil and his wife.' The meeting then resolved 'that further war assistance both by Government and public should cease'.[125]

In a letter to Bandaranaike on 2 April 1941, the Governor reminded him that he was a minister of the Crown and asked him how he reconciled that fact to these statements and to his committee's actions against grants to war funds. Bandaranaike initially replied with a bland denial that there was any incompatibility between these things, but it soon became apparent that Governor Caldecott would not let the matter rest there. It would, constitutionally and politically, have been nearly impossible to take Ceylon through the war without the ministers, so Caldecott meant to impose greater cohesion and discipline by confronting Bandaranaike and making an example of him. In mid-April 1941, he again wrote to say that the committee's action was probably illegal, certainly 'a gross abuse of its powers' and 'plainly incompatible with his oath to serve His Majesty well and truly in his ministerial office'. He instructed Bandaranaike 'as your ministerial duty publicly to notify forthwith, on your receipt of this letter' that his committee's action would be reversed at its next meeting. He added that some of Bandaranaike's recent statements were also 'plainly incompatible with your ministerial oath'.[126]

Bandaranaike appears to have taken this as an ultimatum carrying an implied threat of dismissal. Unbeknown to him and at that point to

[123] Secret Report, 'Things Ceylonese', 1 May 1941, CO 54/984/4, PRO.
[124] *CDN*, 9 April 1941.
[125] This material is available in a letter from Caldecott to Bandaranaike, 2 April 1941, file 1, BP. The correspondence was later released by Bandaranaike to the press. The hand of police agents is clear in the inelegance of the English sentences which could not have been verbatim quotations. See also, *CDN*, 20 March 1941.
[126] Caldecott to Bandaranaike, 13 April 1941, file 1, BP.

Caldecott as well, the Governor did not possess the power to sack a minister in such circumstances. Indeed the question of even the King's authority to do so was 'not free from difficulty and requires consideration'.[127] Nevertheless, in the week before the letter's arrival, Bandaranaike had hurriedly asked fellow ministers to stand with him in his defiance and had been rebuffed.[128] They did not approve of his action on war funds, had not been consulted before he took it and – given his ambition, lone-wolfery, talent and popularity – they would have been happy to see him leave office. Despite many threats over the years to defy the colonial authorities, to 'suffer' and to 'sacrifice', he could not bring himself to break with them and with the prestige and patronage that high office carried. The day after receiving the Governor's final letter, he capitulated.[129]

There followed a dramatic turnabout in Bandaranaike's behaviour, very similar to that described in chapter 4 after he had yielded to the superior authority of senior ministers. As Caldecott noted, he 'assumed the role of Governor's champion in the Board of Ministers', made speeches stressing that he 'wants us to win the war' and was 'extremely affable and courteous to me'.[130] For some time thereafter he remained, in the words of a Colonial Office mandarin, as 'never before . . . polite and tractable'.[131] In normal circumstances, this change might have proved temporary, but the Japanese attacks on British possessions in Asia which coincided with the bombing of Pearl Harbor provided more compelling reasons to assist the colonial power. The speed and scale of Japanese successes alarmed and astonished onlookers in Ceylon. Within three weeks Hong Kong had fallen, HMS *Repulse* and HMS *Prince of Wales* had been sunk and major enemy advances had occurred in Malaya, Burma and the Philippines. By mid-February 1942, Singapore had been taken and Ceylon was clearly on the front line. These events and the sensibly diplomatic efforts of Governor Caldecott had persuaded ministers to cohere into what Sir Andrew called a '*de facto* Cabinet'. They lent their 'co-operation and energy . . . far better than I dared to anticipate'.[132]

Within four weeks of that report, this '*de facto*' arrangement was formalized with the formation of a War Council consisting of the Governor, the ministers and representatives of the armed services.[133] It

[127] Secretary of State to Caldecott, 23 April 1941, CO 54/982/2, PRO.
[128] Secret Report, 'Things Ceylonese', 1 May 1941, CO 54/984/4, PRO.
[129] Bandaranaike to Caldecott, 14 April 1941, file 1, BP, and *CDN*, 17 April 1941.
[130] Secret Reports, 'Things Ceylonese', 1 May and 23 August 1941, CO 54/984/4, PRO.
[131] Note by Blaxter, 15 November 1941, CO 54/982/2, PRO.
[132] Governor to Secretary of State, CO 54/985/5, PRO.
[133] It should be noted that some officials in the Colonial Office wanted a Cabinet system in Ceylon at the outbreak of war. See Minute of the Secretary of State, 3 October 1939, CO 54/971/11, PRO.

was headed by the Commander-in-Chief, Admiral Sir Geoffrey Layton who became the supreme civil authority on 17 March 1942. This situation, which was to last for the duration of the war, generated profound political changes which – from the ministers' viewpoint – were of a decidedly mixed character. In some respects, their influence declined. Until then, they had enjoyed considerable freedom from interference from the Governor who, in Caldecott's words 'is outside the governmental machine until something goes wrong and then he is called in without any previous inkling to set things right . . .'[134] By contrast, Admiral Layton ran the War Council like a commanding officer and at times dealt summarily with ministers. Bandaranaike was one of the first to discover this when he arrived late to an early War Council meeting and received a curt dressing down from Layton.[135] Ministers also had to yield some of their powers over bureaucrats and their control of essential commodities to Oliver Goonetilleke, a talented Sinhalese civil servant who was given overall responsibility for the maintenance of supplies.[136]

Ministers also faced anxieties during the first half of 1942 about a possible Japanese invasion. In April, a Japanese fleet moved into the Bay of Bengal and in a week sank more than a hundred ships, including HMS *Hermes* only six miles off the shores of Ceylon. Colombo suffered a small but unnerving air raid by carrier-based planes and the port of Trincomalee on the east coast was heavily bombed. The public did not know that this left the RAF in Ceylon without a single fighter that could fly and that the British had not even a single division in South Asia that was fit to fight,[137] but at the very least, the ministers would have suspected as much. There is no evidence to suggest that any important politicians in Ceylon ever contemplated collaboration with the Japanese. Before the outbreak of hostilities with Japan, the youthful J. R. Jayewardene and Dudley Senanayake had made secret enquiries with a Japanese representative about the prospects for Ceylonese nationalists, should the British be driven out. But they were firmly reprimanded by a horrified D. S. Senanayake and nothing further came of it.[138]

It was also true, however, that the creation of the War Council yielded leading politicians several important gains. Ministers were empowered to act without obtaining the sanction of their Executive Committees of state

[134] Secret Report, 'Things Ceylonese', 18 October 1940, CO 54/977/7, PRO.
[135] I am grateful to Jane Russell for this information. See also, Bandaranaike to Chairman, Board of Ministers, 31 March 1942, file 1, BP.   [136] *CDN*, 6 August 1942.
[137] *CDN*, 7, 10–11 April 1942 and 4 April 1959; P. Mason, *A Shaft of Sunlight* (London, 1978), p. 166 and material in CO 54/985/5 and CO 54/985/8, PRO.
[138] Interview with J. R. Jayewardene, Colombo, 11 September 1980.

councillors. Some of them, including Bandaranaike, already enjoyed pre-eminence over their Committees,[139] but this change enhanced ministerial prestige enormously and marked a clear step away from the Donoughmore Constitution, towards Cabinet government. So did the colonial authorities' tendency in press reports to stress the collective doings of the War Council. Despite the fact that, under Admiral Layton, ministers had little choice but to support the cause, this change created the impression that the ministers' petitions for a Cabinet system based on collective responsibility had been granted. It would be impossible to retreat very far from this after the war. Layton also emphasized from the outset that he preferred to leave questions of civil administration to the Governor, the ministers and the State Council. This again led the ordinary citizens to believe that ministers had gained new powers, an impression that had some substance. These changes and the postponement of the election of a new State Council until after the war – a decision that was greeted with 'beatific relief' by many leading politicians[140] – effectively confirmed that, with one important exception, the existing ministers would remain in office for several years to come.

The exception was the Minister of Home Affairs and Leader of the State Council, Sir Baron Jayatilaka. His incapacities had been a major embarrassment for years and, with the island facing a palpable emergency, fellow ministers (almost certainly with discreet support from the British) overcame his stubbornness and persuaded him to go to New Delhi as Ceylon's representative. This had two important consequences. First, D. S. Senanayake who had long been the most formidable of the ministers was unanimously elected Leader of the State Council. The only other faintly plausible potential candidate was Bandaranaike. But support for Senanayake was so great that there was never any suggestion that a contest would occur – a point which has some bearing upon Bandaranaike's later claims to equal status with Senanayake at this time. Second, the Executive Committee of Home Affairs chose (at Senanayake' urging) A. Mahadeva, a leading Tamil, as Jayatilaka's successor at that ministry.

Had this occurred before December 1941, it would have constituted a reversal for Bandaranaike, Senanayake and the other ministers. By ending the Sinhalese monopoly of ministerial posts, it would have impeded the efforts of Bandaranaike – and, to a lesser extent, of Senanayake and others – to use chauvinism to build popular support. But by late 1942,

---

[139] This was not the rule, however. Governor Caldecott had noted in 1939 that the 'Executive Committees just won't allow the Ministers to be Ministers, but want all the power in their own hands'. Secret Report, 'Things Ceylonese', 7 September 1939, CO 54/971/11, PRO. [140] *CDN*, 11 February 1942.

Mahadeva's election[141] met with a cautious welcome. There were several reasons for this. On a personal level, Mahadeva was more polished and pleasant than most other Tamil politicians and his energy and intelligence made him a distinct improvement over his vain and senile predecessor. More crucial, however, was the marked decline, since the outbreak of war with Japan, in the importance of Sinhalese chauvinism which clearly affected Bandaranaike. The gearing up of the war effort had nearly eradicated unemployment among urban Sinhalese[142] who had previously been susceptible to denunciations of Indian labourers. The authorities, who now carefully controlled public meetings and processions,[143] would have taken a dim view of any inflammatory public speeches – particularly by ministers of the Crown.[144] And, in any case, there was far less need to excite people with parochialism or anything else now that it was clear that a fresh election to the State Council was several years away.

It was also likely that when the election finally occurred, the central issue would be Ceylon's advance towards independence rather than the communal question. In 1942 the British had not yet offered Ceylon the prospect of postwar self-government which had been set before Indian and Burmese leaders, but it was anticipated by ministers.[145] They also believed that the way to ensure it was to contribute energetically to the war effort and to demonstrate their capacity for fairness towards minorities, particularly the Tamils. Mahadeva's arrival provided a splendid opportunity to do so. The war with Japan and the creation of the War Council had substantially altered the political logic in Ceylon. For the next few years, expedience impelled Sinhalese politicians toward more statesmanlike, cosmopolitan postures.

After spending several years establishing himself as the arch-chauvinist among Sinhalese politicians, this change came as an inconvenience to Bandaranaike. During late 1942 and early 1943, he sought ways of restoring the political utility of communalism. He warned audiences of a plan – which he seems to have imagined – to make Ceylon part of India[146] and helped to prevent acceptance of an agreement with India over immigrant labour in Ceylon, partly because the persistence of the problem served to sustain communalist passions.[147] But it soon became

---

[141] He was elected Acting Minister in August, while Jayatilaka was abroad. He became Minister in early December 1942. *CDN*, 15 August and 3 December 1942.

[142] See, for example, *CDN*, 19 January and 1 February 1943. This remained unchanged throughout the war (*CDN*, 14 October 1944).

[143] *CDN*, 29 August 1942 and 9 January 1943.

[144] For an example of Bandaranaike's more temperate manner at Sinhala Maha Sabha rallies, see *CDN*, 24 February 1943.

[145] *CDN*, 28 March and 10 October 1942.   [146] *CDN*, 24 February 1943.

[147] *CDN*, 27 February 1943. One result of this was that India was able to force through an arrangement *less* advantageous to Ceylon than the original agreement.

clear that Sinhalese chauvinism was on the wane and he was left groping for a new strategy.

He never quite found it. In the remaining war years, he shifted to and fro between old themes and new, without ever locating a clear point of fixity. The Sinhala Maha Sabha continued to function, but it seemed deflated and confused. In 1942, for example, it backed the successful candidate in a State Council by-election in Negombo, but delight at his victory evaporated when he announced that he was not a Sabha member and that he was 'sorry' that it had supported him.[148] We have already noted that in the following year, the Sabha was embarrassed by revelations that their main allies in a by-election were G. G. Ponnambalam and other Tamils seeking the votes of Indian estate workers, against whom Bandaranaike had so often railed.[149] Now more than ever, the Sabha seemed to exist merely to aid the personal advancement of its leader. At various times during this period, Bandaranaike served up a utopian scheme for socialism in a federation of middle-Asian nations in which 'the brotherhood of man would be realised' – and then advocated, by turns, generosity towards Ceylon's minorities, old-fashioned Sinhalese chauvinism and the need to struggle against the British to achieve self-rule.[150] But he never managed to extract one theme from this motley tangle to serve as his principal rallying cry.

The end of the war in Europe and the election of the Attlee government in Britain in 1945 raised hopes of an early grant of a greater measure of self-government. In response, Bandaranaike began preparing the Sinhala Maha Sabha to fight an election which could not be far off. Arguing that the British Labour Party's victory had shown the trend of the times, and stressing that the Sabha was 'definitely socialistic', he borrowed far more heavily than before on Labour's welfare state programmes. He spoke confidently of the Sabha's electoral prospects and claimed that it now had 120 branches all over the island. But the fact that in June 1945 it was necessary for him to 'form' (not for the first time) a branch in as large a centre as Galle – the fourth-largest city – strongly suggests that most of these were moribund.[151] One long-standing member of the Sabha has stated that by 1945–46, it was 'in effect, dead'.[152]

It was at about this time – the latter months of 1945 – that D. S. Senanayake began to press the island's leading non-Marxist politicians,

[148] *CDN*, 20 July 1942.
[149] *CDN*, 11, 28 and 30 September and 4 October 1943. Bandaranaike also backed a leader of the Indian labourers against Sinhalese candidates in a neighbouring by-election. *CDN*, 16 October 1943.
[150] The quotation is from *CDN*, 11 December 1942. See also, for example, *CDN*, 15 and 24 February 1943, 12 and 17 February, 11 April, 23 June and 22 August 1945.
[151] *CDN*, 23 June 1945. See also, *CDN*, 4 October and 27 November 1945.
[152] Interview with I. N. W. Wijesinghe, Nayakakanda, 23 September 1980.

including Bandaranaike, to join a new, broadly based political party which would seek power at the coming election. Bandaranaike was reluctant to cooperate, not least because it meant accepting Senanayake as party leader and, after the expected electoral victory, as Prime Minister. But there were several reasons other than the organizational weakness of the Sabha for Bandaranaike to be even more uneasy about refusing Senanayake.

During the war, he had been unable to use political patronage to develop enough support to go it alone against Senanayake. Restricted spending on non-military items had adversely affected every sphere of government, but Bandaranaike at Local Administration had the smallest budget of any elected minister. His main political rivals, Senanayake at Agriculture and Lands and J. L. Kotelawala at Communications and Works, had respectively four and five times more to spend.[153] The patronage powers that he appeared to exercise over motor vehicles, fuel and tyres were in practice largely controlled by the Chief Civil Commissioner, Oliver Goonetilleke, whose influence was so great that the wartime administration was sometimes described as an 'Oliver-garchy'.[154] Goonetilleke was a close ally of D. S. Senanayake and sought to strengthen the latter's hand, most notably through their joint management of a vast network of cooperative societies which distributed many essential commodities during the war. These societies were run (often in a dubious manner) by 'a special set of people' in local arenas, notables who developed tenuous transactional links to Senanayake and Goonetilleke as a result.[155] Bandaranaike, who had still not succeeded in creating regional councils to link him to the grass roots, was forced to deal with elected councils at the local level through unsympathetic colonial bureaucrats. He therefore lacked the kind of reliable ties that Senanayake was developing.[156] Bandaranaike presided over island-wide associations of village, town and urban councillors (although his relations with major municipal councils were far from happy). But these

---

[153] In the financial year 1943–44 for example, the expenditure of the seven ministries headed by State Councillors was as follows: *Source: CDN*, 15 July 1944.

Education	Rs 29,292,123
Communications and Works	25,190,045
Agriculture and Lands	21,014,040
Health	19,775,808
Home Affairs	15,584,806
Labour and Industry	5,343,134
Local Administration	5,342,586

[154] *CDN*, 20 March 1943.

[155] *CDN*, 20 September 1944 and interview with a civil servant involved in the programme, Colombo, 21 September 1977.

[156] *CDN*, 14 September and 4 October 1944.

organizations possessed only modest substance and he was right to doubt their utility in a test of strength against Senanayake.

Another post which Bandaranaike held during the late war years which at first had seemed likely to provide useful political resources, yielded little except embarrassment. This was the presidency of the Buddhist Theosophical Society, which was mainly concerned with overseeing a large network of Buddhist schools. When Sir Baron Jayatilaka offered to pass this on to him, in 1942, Bandaranaike accepted gladly since it would help to dispel suspicion that he was a Buddhist by convenience, and since at election time, teachers at schools aided by the Society had been known to campaign for its President or his allies. However, in 1944, at the annual re-election of officers, after Bandaranaike's nominee for the key post of General Manager of Buddhist Schools had narrowly defeated the leader of the opposing faction, there followed unseemly accusations of chicanery with membership rolls.[157]

Things degenerated further the following year when the presidential election was preceded by accusations that Bandaranaike's faction had wrongly prevented the enrolment of seventy new members loyal to his opponents. He ruled this out of order and was nominated for re-election. When the name of his leading opponent (who was absent through illness) was proposed, Bandaranaike produced a letter from him declining the nomination. Another opponent was then nominated and just as the counting of ballots was completed, someone rushed in with a new letter from Bandaranaike's main adversary contradicting the original letter which later was proved to be a forgery. (It is unclear whether Bandaranaike knew it to be one, although this seems unlikely.) It was immediately announced that Bandaranaike had won re-election and the meeting erupted into disorder, with which it concluded.[158] Things grew even worse a year later in 1945. The annual meeting opened with a meditation from a Buddhist monk 'on the futility of quarrelling at meetings', but fresh accusations of meddling with membership lists led to a 'free fight' before the election could occur. 'Large crowds . . . surged outside the closed doors and thronged the open windows . . .' and within the hall there was 'smashed and overturned furniture, stampeding crowds, abandoned footwear . . . bloodshed and utter confusion . . . scenes reminiscent of gangster rule in Chicago.' Bandaranaike had to abandon the meeting and summon the police. He later joked about 'the blood-stained battlefield of higher Buddhistic education',[159] but he was mortified at these unedifying scenes. Within a month, he had resigned the presidency of the Society to save himself further embarrassment.[160]

[157] *CDN*, 1 July 1943 and 12 September 1945.
[158] *CDN*, 19 July 1944 and 12 September 1945.
[159] *CDN*, 18 June 1945.   [160] *CDN*, 6, 12–13 September 1945.

His troubles deepened in August 1945, when it became clear that the British had accepted D. S. Senanayake as the sole Ceylonese representative in the negotiations leading to constitutional reform[161] which meant, of course, that he would reap most of the credit for the advance towards independence. The British intended this to solidify his position as the pre-eminent politician of the day and by dealing with him alone, to minimize the communal antagonism that arose when constitutional reform was discussed, and that was how it turned out. They saw Senanayake as a formidable man whom they could trust, and they were correct on both counts. They had not always had such faith in him, however. During the 1930s, he had shocked some of the more supercilious European residents of the island by treating them as equals, a habit that sometimes led to quarrels.[162] His repeated efforts to erode the influence and privileges of British bureaucrats in Ceylon made him appear to harbour a 'hatred of the public services'.[163] This was largely understandable since, as Governor Caldecott wrote, the British civil servant 'still regards himself as, and indeed still largely is, a "Raja of Bhong"'.[164] But even sympathetic observers noted that colonial officials were Senanayake's 'pet aversions' and that he was 'a bit aggressive' towards them.[165] During the early 1940s, however, the opportunity to work with the more enlightened Governor Caldecott, and Senanayake's achievements and reliability as the leading Ceylonese on the War Council won the respect of British officialdom.

If they had not always trusted him, there had never been any doubting the force of his personality and his capacity to achieve practical results. At times, he was too aggressive for British tastes, using 'the language of the mud-buffalo' and acting like a 'village bully'.[166] But he was known to be

---

161 K. M. de Silva tends to emphasize Senanayake's individual role in negotiations from mid-1943 onward in his *A History of Sri Lanka* (Berkeley, 1981), pp. 453–56. But de Silva's own material suggests instead that his acceptance as, in effect, the sole negotiator did not become clear until August 1945. Before that, he was obviously the leading figure on the Board of Ministers, but the other ministers still played a major role.

For background material, see D. S. Senanayake, Report of Negotiations with O. Stanley and G. Hall, Successive Secretaries of State for the Colonies about Dominion Status, 9 October 1945 in file SA 36/1, Bernard Aluwihare Papers, University of Peradeniya Library. I am grateful to Jane Russell for directing me to this.

162 See, for example, the reference to his tiff with a planter on the highway in M. Roberts interview with Sir Richard Aluwihare, Mss. Ind. Ocn. S.174, Rhodes House, Oxford.

163 Secret Report, 'Things Ceylonese', 28 December 1939, CO 54/971/11, PRO.

164 Secret Reports, 'Things Ceylonese', 23 August 1941, CO 54/984/4 and 21 March 1940 in CO 54/977/7, PRO. In the latter file, see also note by Blaxter.

165 M. Roberts interviews with S. S. E. Fernando (p. 2) and Sir Richard Aluwihare (p. 43) – both of whom were Sinhalese, in Mss. Ind. Ocn. S.174, Rhodes House, Oxford. See also, for example, telegram no. 1838, 18 November 1946 in CO 54/955/1, PRO.

166 Secret Report, 'Things Ceylonese', 18 February 1940, CO 54/977/7, PRO.

relentless in his pursuit of an objective that he believed in, even if this meant refusing to listen to helpful advice.[167] And the objectives that attracted him were almost always limited and realizable, so that he became known as 'a doer of doughty deeds'.[168] In this respect, he stood in sharp contrast to Bandaranaike who often seized upon grand, unrealistic objectives because he found their utopian elegance aesthetically pleasing and useful for inspirational purposes at public meetings. Senanayake was, in his unpretentious way, intelligent enough to cope ably with any complex issue and he laboured mightily to master the details of every problem that arose.[169] This again contrasted markedly with Bandaranaike's quicksilver reactions, his intellectual arrogance and occasional laziness which alienated so many British officials and anglicized Ceylonese.

Senanayake's abilities seemed slightly surprising, given his rough-hewn appearance and his limited education. Even in his later years, he was a well-muscled, barrel-chested figure of a man who walked with a confident, rolling gait. He was a far more robust figure on the public platform than Bandaranaike. This had its effect upon the British, one of whom wrote that 'In spite of his . . . hedgelawry, and tiresome blustering he is big and vital and a man.'[170] Senanayake spoke simply, directly and insistently both in conversation and in public speeches. Unlike his elder brother, F. R. Senanayake – a Ceylonese nationalist leader whose premature death had opened the way for the younger brother to enter full-time politics – D. S. had not gone to England for study. He had attended St Thomas' College where he had excelled at cricket and boxing rather than studies and then turned to strenuous work clearing and developing his family's considerable lands. This helped to earn him the affectionate, virile nickname of 'Jungle John' – as opposed to 'London John', the label commonly applied to F. R. Senanayake.

Bandaranaike's upbringing in a highly anglicized environment, cut off from ordinary folk, and his time at Oxford had caused him to overcompensate by adopting 'native dress' for most public occasions, as well as Buddhism and Sinhalese chauvinism. Senanayake – a lifelong Buddhist and sometime man of the soil – felt less need to be demonstrative in these matters. In a reversal of Bandaranaike's habits, he

---

[167] M. Roberts interview with Sir Richard Aluwihare, Mss. Ind. Ocn. S.174, Rhodes House, Oxford. [168] *TC*, 20 January 1951.

[169] See, for example, M. Roberts interview with E. Rodrigo, pp. 41–44, Mss. Ind. Ocn. S.174, Rhodes House, Oxford.

[170] Governor Caldecott had to remind civil servants very forcefully of their constitutional responsibility to carry out their ministers' policies and to make available to ministers all relevant information, whatever their private views. There had been numerous occasions of non-compliance. See his statement in *CDN*, 17 September 1943.

Bandaranaike alongside his leader and rival, D. S. Senanayake, who was
Ceylon's first Prime Minister. Both have struck characteristic poses and both
are dressed in their usual manner for public occasions.

often wore 'native dress' at home, but always appeared in public in European clothes. He too made adjustments in his lifestyle to cater to popular expectations. He once told a luncheon companion that he knew that he would not get far in politics 'unless I linked it to the Buddhist religion . . . it meant I had to give up my two greatest – two most favourite pastimes. One was hunting and the other was beer.'[171] But he was far less inclined than Bandaranaike to appeal to crowds with calls for the uplift of Buddhism and the Sinhalese 'race', and he firmly opposed efforts to promote the use of the vernacular. He largely confined his chauvinistic doings to action against Ceylon's Indian labourers – of whom he was genuinely suspicious – and to efforts to colonize unoccupied lands with Sinhalese settlers.[172] This earned Senanayake credibility with Sinhalese voters, but it was sufficiently moderate to make him appear trustworthy to the British authorities.

The story of the negotiations leading towards self-government has been told ably in detail by K. M. de Silva[173] and need not detain us unduly. By July 1943, the British had sought to encourage Ceylon's ministers with various declarations promising full control of internal civil aministration and the adoption of the Westminster model after the war. By early 1944, under Senanayake's leadership, the ministers had presented a Draft Constitution conforming to the terms of those declarations.[174] The British then announced in July 1944 that a Commission would visit Ceylon to prepare recommendations for a new constitution. The ministers refused to have formal dealings with the Commission, led by Lord Soulbury, during its stay in Ceylon in early 1945 (although informal contacts were frequent)[175] because it had been empowered to go beyond their Draft by consulting minorities and other interests.

After the Commission returned to Britain to prepare a report, Senanayake proposed that he travel to London to be on hand to press for further concessions. It was at this point that the British indicated their willingness to deal with him individually by agreeing to this. Soon after he arrived, the Labour government was elected and the Japanese surrendered, events which encouraged him to ask for full Dominion

---

[171] M. Roberts interview with H. E. Newnham, p. 20, Mss. Ind. Ocn. S.174, Rhodes House, Oxford.

[172] See, in this regard, D. S. Senanayake, *Agriculture and Patriotism* (Colombo, 1935).

[173] K. M. de Silva, 'The Transfer of Power in Sri Lanka – A Review of British Perspectives', *Ceylon Journal of Historical and Social Studies*, iv, 1 and 2 (1974), pp. 8–19, and *A History of Sri Lanka*, chapters 31 and 32.

[174] De Silva, *A History of Sri Lanka*, pp. 451–54; CO 54/980, file 55541/5, PRO; and *Sessional Papers XVII – 1943* and *XIX – 1944*, first cited by de Silva.

[175] See for example, *CDN*, 27 February and 1 March 1945 and de Silva, *A History of Sri Lanka*, pp. 455–56.

status – a step beyond what the Soulbury Report proposed. His request was refused and he returned to Ceylon a disappointed man in September. But the British White Paper on reform contained enough encouraging references to an early grant of Dominion Status[176] and Senanayake's doings in Britain had been so extravagantly dramatized by his friends in the Ceylon press,[177] that he was received as a hero. The State Council, unaware that the British anticipated a long six-year delay before Dominion Status, accepted the White Paper in November 1945, fifty-one votes to three.[178] For the next few crucial months at least, Senanayake's pre-eminence in the island's politics was solidly assured.

It was under these circumstances that he urged most prominent non-Marxists, including leaders of minorities, to join him in forming a broadly-based, cosmopolitan political party. This idea was not in itself abhorrent to Bandaranaike. He had at times suggested it when he had talked of defying the British,[179] but he did so on the assumption that he would at least be a co-equal leader. Senanayake clearly intended to head the proposed new party. In August, Bandaranaike had been empowered by his Sinhala Maha Sabha to negotiate the formation of a united front,[180] but that was mainly to enable him to act swiftly should the need arise. Right through late 1945 and even after plans for the new party became public knowledge in December, he defended Sinhalese chauvinism and insisted that his Sabha was a strong, distinct political force.[181]

He was nevertheless under great pressure, in public and in private, to join the new party. The Lake House newspapers, which were closely allied to Senanayake, launched heated attacks on Bandaranaike and the Sinhala Maha Sabha as a dangerous body subverting much-needed national unity,[182] in order to give Bandaranaike a taste of the slanging he would encounter if he decided to go it alone. Senanayake even turned his failure to obtain Dominion Status to his advantage by arguing that a show of inter-communal reconciliation (through the new party) would reassure the British and hasten a grant of self-government. His friends in the press attacked Bandaranaike's communalist campaigns as being 'partly responsible for Ceylon not obtaining [a] better measure of constitutional reform'.[183] Senanayake's efforts to project himself as a

176 *Ibid.*, pp. 456–60.
177 See, for example, *CDN*, 24 and 28 July, 9 August and 19 September 1945.
178 De Silva, *A History of Sri Lanka*, p. 460.
179 See, for example, *CDN*, 11 April 1945.   180 *CDN*, 20 August 1945.
181 See, for example, 9 November and 24 and 30 December 1945, and 4 February 1946. The first suggestion in the English language press that a new party was developing appeared in *CDN*, 28 December 1945.
182 See for example, *CDN*, 19 January, 2 and 9 February, 25 March and 8 April 1946.
183 *CDN*, 12 March 1946.

unifier won many moderate Tamils, including Home Minister Mahadeva, to his side.[184] The more extreme elements in the Tamil Congress
appeared to have slipped badly after their unrealistic demand for '50–50' –
equal parliamentary representation for minorities and the Sinhalese
majority – had received short shrift from the British. After a fruitless
journey to London to lobby Whitehall for concessions, the Tamil
Congress leader G. G. Ponnambalam – Bandaranaike's old adversary –
was described and widely regarded in elite circles as a 'fallen Fuehrer'.[185]
In January 1946, Bandaranaike stoutly denied that the Tamil Congress
had gone into decline,[186] since he badly needed it as a bogie if the Sinhala
Maha Sabha was to fight on, but his words carried little conviction. He
was further unnerved by Senanayake's success not only in attracting
support from those who desired communal reconciliation, but in
reassuring important Sinhalese chauvinists as well.[187]

Meanwhile, in private he was being shrewdly lobbied by Senanayake
who excelled at face-to-face encounters. He reminded Bandaranaike of
the extent to which they had been seen in common endeavour in recent
years,[188] to show him how surprised the public would be if he refused to
join him. He seasoned this with flattery – to which Bandaranaike was far
from immune – saying that he needed him to serve as the brains behind
policy formulation and offering him the chance to draw up the party
manifesto. He said that the party and the nation needed his eloquence and
he asked him to act as their principal spokesman at the ceremonial
opening of the new legislature. He also offered Bandaranaike expanded
ministerial powers and the post of Leader of the House in the new
Parliament, which in effect (though not in name) would make him
Deputy Prime Minister. Senanayake added that he was an old man and
revealed that he 'had a disease'. After a year or two, he said, he would
retire from politics whereupon Bandaranaike would inevitably become
the premier.[189]

In reality, Senanayake had no intention of retiring early and he did not
expect that poor health would compel him to do so. He also planned to
minimize Bandaranaike's influence in the new government and to arrange

[184] *CDN*, 31 January 1946.
[185] *CDN*, 13 February 1946. Also, *CDN*, 21 January and 6 and 8 May 1946 and interviews
with numerous Tamil and Sinhalese political activists, Colombo, August and September
1978. See also, Report No. 1, CO 54/971/11, PRO.
[186] *CDN*, 30 January 1946.
[187] See, for example, *CDN*, 14 March 1946.
[188] Interview with two close aides to Bandaranaike at the time, Colombo, 2 September 1977.
[189] This account is based on interviews with seven persons – relatives of Bandaranaike and
close aides to both men – Colombo and Kandy, August 1977 and September 1978.
Senanayake suffered from diabetes, but there was no sign in 1946 that it would shorten
his life.

for someone else to succeed him. But Bandaranaike appears to have believed most or all of what he heard. He was prone to a certain *naïveté* when his ego was being massaged and Senanayake's statements that no one else could match Bandaranaike's intelligence and experience was objectively quite true. For good measure Senanayake added the untrue comment that J. L. Kotelawala – Minister of Communications and Works and, at that time, the only conceivable rival to Bandaranaike – wished to quit politics in a year or two.[190]

Here, as on numerous other occasions, Bandaranaike faced powerful counter-pressures within himself. He found it impossible to accept Senanayake's authority as legitimate, but he was also unable to make a complete break with it. His political resources – his ministerial patronage powers, his ties to various voluntary associations, and the flimsy Sinhala Maha Sabha – looked distinctly unimpressive. Both the prevailing climate of opinion among the elite and economic conditions (which made jobs plentiful) were inhospitable to the Sinhalese chauvinism with which he and the Sabha were identified. Interest groups among rural dwellers, to whom he might have turned for support against the anglicized elite of the new party, had only begun (rather imperfectly) to crystallize. Most villages were still inadequately linked with supra-local and national-level politics, despite advances in economic integration during the war. It was very risky to go it alone. By March 1946, Senanayake had agreed to allow members of the new party to retain their ties with communal organizations,[191] a concession that was plainly aimed at Bandaranaike and the Sinhala Maha Sabha. By early May it was clear that numerous members of the Sabha intended to join what was now called the United National Party, whether or not Bandaranaike did so. So, on 12 May, he proposed that they join the party and the Executive Committee of the Sabha unanimously endorsed the idea.[192]

Just as the new party was beginning to take shape and a new phase in Ceylon's political history was opening up, Sir Solomon Dias Bandaranaike, who represented another, bygone era, died in his eighty-fourth year. His funeral contained elements of both the old and the emerging orders. His cortège travelled a route lined with schoolchildren from the house at Horagolla to a mausoleum on a hilltop elsewhere on the estate which Sir Solomon had designed 'after a visit to Versailles where he saw a mausoleum that took his fancy'. The funeral service was of course Anglican, and the coffin was carried by family servants and headmen of the area. But among the pallbearers were also D. S. Senanayake and

---

[190] Interviews with the people mentioned in note 189 and with Sir John Kotelawala, Kandawela, 2 September 1977.
[191] *CDN*, 16 March 1946.   [192] *CDN*, 6, 8, 11 and 13 May 1946.

representatives of the Sinhala Maha Sabha. The white mourning garments of Bandaranaike and his Buddhist associates contrasted starkly with the black worn by the Europeans and westernized Ceylonese, including most of the Bandaranaike–Obeyesekere clan. Just before the coffin was closed, Bandaranaike, in 'native dress', 'bent low with clasped hands in obeisance to his dead father in Oriental fashion'.[193] Soon after the funeral, the son quietly saw to it that the animals in Sir Solomon's large menagerie were set free. This was both a concession to Buddhist sensibilities and an expression of genuine feeling, but his kindness turned out to be partly misplaced. Several of the creatures were disoriented by their sudden release and soon perished.

[193] Sir Solomon Dias Bandaranaike diaries, 1940–46, NASL; *CDN*, 1–5 August 1946; and interviews with three witnesses, Colombo, 7 and 9 September 1977.

6

HEIR PRESUMPTIVE, 1946–1951

Bandaranaike spent most of the next five years as D. S. Senanayake's subordinate, a role in which he found little comfort. He was frequently embattled – sometimes because he was unreasonable, more often because he was treated unreasonably. He was routinely offensive to and offended by ministerial colleagues. Despite this, he remained in the ruling party because through most of this period, he clung doggedly to the notion that he was heir presumptive to the leadership of the nation. As time passed and evidence mounted of a campaign within the Cabinet to undermine his position, however, it became increasingly apparent that it was mainly Bandaranaike who was doing the presuming.

In the first weeks of its existence, the new United National Party (UNP) swiftly developed into a catch-all organization for most members of the old State Council. This came as a disappointment to Bandaranaike who wanted the party to be a force for change. Senanayake had allowed him to turn the UNP Manifesto into a cautiously reformist document,[1] but Bandaranaike could see that both the party's leader and most of its members were deeply conservative in their views. Scepticism about the new party extended even to conservative newspapers which complained about its lack of outreach and organization which made it seem 'a political party of State Councillors making early moves to climb back into their seats on the back of an influential Leader . . .'.[2]

It is hardly surprising, then, that Bandaranaike soon began to distance himself somewhat from the UNP and to hint that he was keeping post-election options open. His speech to a sceptical Sinhala Maha Sabha conference in July 1946 went to the extent of suggesting (correctly) that the UNP was something less than a party. It 'was in effect a coalition Party' in which the Sabha would retain its distinct identity. He clearly

---

[1] See the first draft of the UNP Manifesto, with Bandaranaike's revisions in his own hand in file 2; and further drafts and revisions in file 14, BP.

[2] *CDN*, 8 June 1946. It was resolved that the UNP would establish 'an electoral association', a less cohesive thing than a party 'branch', in each constituency (*CDN*, 13 June 1946). But this was regarded by many as empty talk, and it did not occur in most constituencies during the 1940s.

preferred things that way, indeed he had even considered calling the new party the 'United Coalition Party'. It was necessary, he said, to have such a party since Ceylon's new Constitution could only work effectively if one party could command a solid majority in the new Parliament. So although objective conditions did not naturally give rise to this party, the Sabha had agreed, in the national interest, to assist in the artificial creation of a group which could provide stable government. He stressed that 'when it was no longer possible for them honourably to continue in that party, they would leave it', although he hoped that the need would not arise.[3]

He argued that his talks with Senanayake had convinced him that the UNP was not 'a caucus of his relatives and intimates', as some Sabha members feared. But to remind the UNP of the terms on which Bandaranaike had joined it, the Sabha passed resolutions calling for reformist policies in education, health, housing, conditions of labour and basic services. They also wanted 'progressive nationalisation' of important services such as transport and utilities. The old concern for Sinhalese revivalism surfaced in calls for teachers in vernacular schools to be paid on a par with their English-medium counterparts, for the 'fostering of national culture' and for the vernaculars to be declared official languages.[4] The emphasis here was notably on the uplift of *both* indigenous languages and not just on Sinhala. Bandaranaike was shifting his ground away from his parochial stance of the early 1940s to a more cosmopolitan reformist approach. He probably did so gladly, since he was almost certainly more at home with this new posture. But the main reason for the change was that it made political sense at a time when relative prosperity had temporarily eased Sinhalese unemployment and their suspicions of others, and when he expected to play a central role in a government that sought votes from minorities.

Bandaranaike believed that if the UNP pursued reforms and reached out more effectively beyond the small circle of State Councillors, it would both increase support for the party and strengthen his hand within it by allowing him to draw in people who would look to him as their natural leader. But in these formative months, he was so preoccupied with the in-fighting among UNP leaders that he made little headway on this front. His early success at gaining roughly equal representation for Sabha members on the new party's executive was soon nullified by a *de facto*

---

[3] UNP draft Manifesto, file 2, BP, and *CDN*, 29 July 1946. Bandaranaike delivered more or less the same message in his contribution to a collection of brief statements by various UNP leaders, published under the title 'UNP' (CO 54/992/2, PRO). His comments produced protests from fellow leaders of the UNP. He responded with a letter to the *Daily News* stating that 'the decisions of its executive are binding on those Parties' which combine to form the UNP. *CDN*, 1 August 1946. See also, *The Nation*, 18 May and 22 June 1946.   [4] *CDN*, 29 July 1946.

enlargement of the party leadership which left him in the minority.[5] He
and others managed to prevent his most robust adversary on the Board of
Ministers, the rightist J. L. Kotelawala (who was also Senanayake's
nephew), from gaining the key post of General Secretary. But he found
himself one of five party vice presidents which tended to obscure his
supposed status as the leader's principal deputy and political heir.[6] He was
also distressed to find that Senanayake did little to quell the ceaseless
factional squabbles in the UNP[7] which further undercut Bandaranaike's
standing as the party's number two.

His nationalist hackles rose when Kotelawala, with Senanayake's
approval, invited British planters to join the UNP and declared the party
to be 'exhilarated' at the positive response from several.[8] By September
1946 when this occurred, it was also possible to discern a tendency among
Ceylonese ministers and the British authorities to nibble away at his
official powers. Until mid-1946, state-financed house-building had been
his responsibility, but in July the main powers in this sphere were
transferred to another minister. Bandaranaike attempted to continue a
project for workers' houses, but found himself thwarted by the Health
Ministry's refusal to approve his plans for sanitation facilities.[9] Budget
expenditure estimates issued in July left him without the increases in
allocatable resources which most other ministers gained.[10] Then, in
September, his bill to provide a much needed link between national level
politics and the grass roots by creating an elected council in each province
was shelved.[11] This decision was far more important than it seemed, since
the creation of regional councils before the issue became enmeshed in the
Sinhalese–Tamil conflict might have helped prevent the deterioration of
relations between the two linguistic groups.[12] But, in 1946, no one
foresaw this. Bandaranaike's ministerial colleagues feared that their
departments would lose power to these councils, which he would
oversee.

All of this, and the unpredictable political outlook further inclined
Bandaranaike to maximize his options. He did so, characteristically, by
clinging onto any theme that might yield political advantage, no matter
how inconsistent it made him seem. In September, only a week after
Senanayake had said that 'there is no place for communalism under the

[5] *CDN*, 20 August 1946.   [6] *CDN*, 3 and 20 August 1946.
[7] See, for example, *CDN*, 21 August 1946.
[8] *CDN*, 26 August and 7 September 1946.
[9] *CDN*, 1 July and 3 September 1946.
[10] Most of his increase was consumed by pay increases to staff, *CDN*, 12 July 1946.
[11] *CDN*, 7 September 1946.
[12] I have set this argument out in detail in 'The Failure of Political Integration in Sri
Lanka', *Journal of Commonwealth and Comparative Politics*, xvii, 1 (March, 1979), pp. 21–46.

new Constitution', Bandaranaike resurrected his old communalist message. He reminded a crowd of 50,000 at Anuradhapura, a centre of Sinhalese assertiveness, of his devotion to 'the regeneration of the Sinhalese nation and the revival of Buddhism' and looked forward to the day when 'Sinhalese would be united under the Sinhalese banner'.[13] More important, and more worrying for Senanayake, were his dealings with Ceylon's leftists whom everyone viewed as the main threat to the UNP at the elections scheduled for mid-1947. During a spate of strikes by leftist unions in 1946, Marxist leaders had negotiated with the Board of Ministers via very cordial talks with Bandaranaike.[14] When he made great play of this in the State Council, Senanayake bristled visibly and commentators speculated that Bandaranaike, who was 'neither here nor there', might resume negotiations with the left after the election.[15]

Leftists might also have been forgiven for wondering where he stood, since, a week later, he was courting bus company owners – those energetic practitioners of free enterprise and gangsterism – with praise for their success at keeping their employees on the job during recent strikes.[16] Later in November, he slammed the left at a UNP rally, saying that 'there is no place for riots and bloodshed' in Ceylon and that in the Soviet Union 'they have killed millions of people'.[17] But suspicions persisted in UNP circles that 'our Bolshie brothers' might seek an alliance in the new Parliament with Bandaranaike.[18]

The island at this time was of course still a British colony, but Ceylonese ministers had long enjoyed very substantial control over internal affairs. As early as March 1945, the Governor's wife had complained privately of her husband's 'anomalous' position:

his powers as Governor are very limited & although he has a lot of office work it is of an elementary variety and very dull. He is dependent for inside information on his officers of State & his Ministers, who tell him as much as they wish him to know & although he is in a position to influence he is not in a position to rule. I don't know how long he will be able to stand the boredom of it.[19]

The possession of so much *de facto* power naturally made ministers impatient for a new advance toward self-government. It was that and the

[13] *CDN*, 7, 12 and 14 September 1946.
[14] *CDN*, 31 September and 2 October 1946. See also Bandaranaike's progressive rhetoric in *CDN*, 28 September 1946. [15] *CDN*, 2 November 1946.
[16] *CDN*, 6 and 9 November 1946. This earned him the public wrath of one leftist leader. *CDN*, 12 February 1947.
[17] *CDN*, 16 November 1946. [18] *CDN*, 21 December 1946.
[19] Lady Moore to Jan Smuts, 25 March 1945, Smuts Papers, University Library, Cambridge. See also, letters dated 14 August 1945 and 20 November 1947.

related concern about a forthcoming election which preoccupied politicians for a full year after mid-1946.

The ministers and incumbent state councillors were eager to go to the voters as early as possible in order to deny Marxist leaders, who had suffered wartime detention, the chance to rebuild their organizations. But the British authorities were so deliberate in drawing constituency boundaries for the enlarged legislature, in preparing lists of voters – half of which were printed in England – and in deciding how much power to cede to the Ceylonese that the election dates kept receding from May 1947 to June and then finally to August–September.[20]

The main beneficiaries of these doubts and delays were the leaders of the three Marxist parties. They were divided – then as always – by doctrinal and personal disputes, but they were nonetheless able to apply pressure on three fronts: by demanding greater social justice for poor people, by calling the unions which they controlled out on strike[21] to undermine the ministers' authority, and by condemning the advances towards self-government as slow and inadequate. On the first of these issues, Senanayake and his colleagues were reasonably confident. The fall in certain commodity prices in 1946 had forced ministers to cut 'an extravagant budget' that included numerous welfare state measures,[22] but their promises and to a lesser extent their achievements in education, health, housing and others areas[23] appeared to offer a sufficient defence against appeals for social justice. On the other two fronts, however, they were more vulnerable.

In each case, they turned to the British for help, with mixed results. Senanayake's anxiety about the growth of trade unions that were linked to leftist parties first became a major issue at the Colonial Office in October 1946, after a politically-inspired strike – one of many – by among others, government employees. Senanayake protested bitterly to London that high officials in Ceylon, who until recently had opposed public employees joining trade unions, now encouraged it. When he received no satisfactory response, he launched severe public attacks both against certain British bureaucrats whom he deemed incompetent or uncooperative, and against leftists whom he accused of attempting to demoralize the civil service in order to prevent the new Constitution from succeeding. Senanayake preferred that the colonial authorities and not his

[20] *CDN*, 2 July, 31 August 1946, 25 January, 22 April and 8 August 1947.
[21] V. K. Jayawardena, *The Rise of the Labor Movement in Ceylon* (Durham, 1972) and R. N. Kearney, *Trade Unions and Politics in Ceylon* (Berkeley, 1971).
[22] Lady Moore to Jan Smuts, 22 June 1946, Smuts Papers.
[23] See, for example, J. Russell, *Our George* (Colombo, 1981) and K. M. de Silva, *A History of Sri Lanka* (Berkeley, 1981), pp. 470–78.

ministers take action against the Marxists so that he would not bear the odium for repressive action.[24]

This placed the Governor and other officials in an unpleasant position. At one level, they believed the strikes to be 'wholly political', but they also acknowledged that the strikers had 'genuine and legitimate griev- ances'. They were at pains to ensure that 'his (Senanayake's) own position is not weakened', and they believed that 'he is right in regarding the Leftist political groups as a serious threat to his own United National Party . . .' On the other hand, they served a Labour government in Britain which was staunchly pro-union, and which contained back- benchers who were prepared to push hard in the House of Commons for more generous treatment of the left in Ceylon.[25] Creech-Jones, the Labour minister with responsibility for the colonies, nicely exhibited the ambiguous stance of his government in early 1947 when he first gave Senanayake the impression that he hoped the UNP would succeed at the forthcoming elections and then wrote to insist that he had no feelings on the subject at all. He was not prepared to save Senanayake the embarrassment of passing draconian emergency legislation for use against leftist strikers by ramming through an Order-in-Council in London, but when the Ceylon State Council's version of the legislation was found to contain two provisions that were more extreme than that which London had refused to pass, he permitted it to go through.[26]

After some hesitation, London gave Senanayake more fulsome assistance on the other, much more important issue, the granting of self- government to Ceylon.[27] As a result, the transfer of power here, far more than in any other South Asian nation, took the form of a transactional arrangement partly because the initiative in Ceylon lay with the British to a much greater extent than in Burma, India and Pakistan. Their hand was eventually forced by the momentum of events, but they were able to support a favoured successor here (as was often the case later, elsewhere in Asia and Africa). The successor in Ceylon was not so much a party as

---

[24] D. S. Senanayake to J. C. Howard, 28 September 1946; Howard to Senanayake, 1 October 1946; Senanayake to Howard, 12 November 1946; memorandum by the Chief Secretary, 12 November 1946; inward telegram, 18 November 1946, CO 54/995/1, PRO.

[25] Inward telegram, 18 November 1946; inward telegram, 25 November 1946; Howard to Sir C. Jeffries, 4 January 1947, CO 54/995/1, PRO. For Labour backbenchers' pressure to lift the ban on the Ceylonese Communist, Dr S. A. Wickremasinghe, see documents 284–295 in CO 882/30, PRO. On the difficulties of the strikers in the face of inflation, see *CDN*, 20 July 1947 and M. Roberts interview with Sir Richard Aluwihare, p. 27, Mss. Ind. Ocn. S.174, Rhodes House, Oxford.

[26] Creech-Jones to Governor, 6 March 1947; Governor to Creech-Jones, 4 June 1947; Governor to Creech-Jones, 8 June 1947; Creech-Jones to Governor, 14 June 1947, CO 882/30, PRO. [27] De Silva, *A History*, chapters 31 and 32.

one man, D. S. Senanayake,[28] whom they eventually came to prefer not only to the island's leftists, but to others – most notably, Bandaranaike.[29] It would have been impossible to exclude Senanayake – the State Council's most prominent figure – from the negotiations, but it was not necessary to deal only with him.

The decision to do so was made in order to safeguard important British interests. The colonial authorities were eager to see a successor government which would neither move against British planting, shipping and banking interests in Ceylon nor make large withdrawals from the island's share of the sterling reserves at a time when the British economy was in dire difficulty. They were anxious to see the new Ceylon government pursue a sympathetic foreign policy within a future Commonwealth which they still presumed would remain, in part, an alliance in which non-aligned nations like Nehru's India would have no place.[30] And – since India planned to deny Britain the use of its former bases – they were acutely concerned to retain access to Ceylon's naval and air bases. The island was seen by the British Chiefs of Staff as 'an essential link in our cable and wireless network of the Far East. It is also the centre of our Naval intelligence organisations for countries bordering the Indian Ocean.' Ceylon offered the 'only existing main fleet base between Malta and Singapore', without which 'our air routes to Australia and the Far East would be gravely endangered'.[31]

By early 1947, the British saw D. S. Senanayake as the Ceylonese leader most likely to ensure these interests. The island's leftists were patently hostile to all of them, and Bandaranaike was seen as 'The most brilliant and anti-British minister',[32] a man with at least tenuous ties to the leftists, and a wayward opportunist who might reject or go back on an agreement to advance his career. He was also the most prominent of the 'independence-minded' politicians,[33] those who wanted complete independence rather than something that stopped short of that goal. The other leading Ceylonese were so close to Senanayake that they posed no problem. Thus the movement of the British towards a deal with

[28] Senanayake also sought out individuals on the British side with whom he might forge transactional ties. See the discussion of Lord Soulbury, Ceylon's second Governor-General, late in this chapter and in chapter 7.
[29] S. Caine to Governor, 24 March 1947, CO 54/1001/3, and material in file CO 537/1994, and in minute no. 3 in CM 32(48), PRO.
[30] See, for example, Secretary of State to Attlee, 22 March 1947, CP(47)147, PRO. Also, R. J. Moore, *Making the New Commonwealth* (Oxford, 1987).
[31] Memo, Chiefs of Staff to Cabinet, 5 May 1947, CP(47)147, PRO.
[32] Lady Moore to Jan Smuts, 2 April 1947, Smuts Papers, University Library, Cambridge.
[33] Note for Webber, 19 March 1947, CO 54/992/2, PRO.

Senanayake was partly designed to exclude Bandaranaike from the proceedings.[34]

In early 1947, the British plans for Ceylon were so ungenerous as to constitute a major embarrassment for Senanayake and his party. The colonial authorities planned to offer not full self-government, but rather 'Dominion Status by evolution'. They also intended, though this was not yet public knowledge, to retain formal control of certain aspects of Ceylon's defence and foreign policy. This was far less than any Ceylonese leader could have accepted and it became acutely inadequate after the announcement in February that both India and Burma, whose leaders had not supported the British during the war, were to be given independence. Ceylon's Governor, Sir Henry Moore, who championed the cause of the ministers throughout the negotiations,[35] sent London an unvarnished picture of the reaction among Senanayake and his ministers: 'Bluntly they consider that loyalty to his Majesty's Government during the war . . . is obviously not a paying proposition, and that the rate of constitutional advance is governed not by the merits of the case but by the nuisance of the applicants.'[36] Creech-Jones then warned Attlee that 'as leader of the Moderate Party which is fighting the forthcoming elections . . . he [Senanayake] is seriously embarrassed by the considerable capital which his opponents are making out of the acceptance . . . of a status for Ceylon much inferior to that now accorded to India and Burma.' Britain, he wrote, must take 'action to prevent a serious deterioration in the political situation in Ceylon . . .'[37]

That was in March 1947. Senanayake promptly put forward suggestions for further constitutional advance, but in May the Attlee Cabinet refused to reach a decision, citing among other things 'the difficulty of acting precipitately in response to an overture from a party leader however distinguished on the eve of an election.'[38] The election was now set for August and September, and the next day an alarmed Governor urged London to make a firm announcement before 31 July when nomination papers were due: 'While I appreciate the Cabinet's hesitation

---

[34] For a taste of British distrust of Bandaranaike, see Lady Moore's characteristically intemperate remarks about him in Lady Moore to Jan Smuts, 10 April 1947, Smuts Papers.

[35] Sir Henry Moore to Jan Smuts, 28 December 1946; Lady Moore to Smuts, 2 April, 7 and 19 June, 2 and 15 July 1947, Jan Smuts Papers.

[36] The quotation is from a memorandum, Creech-Jones to Cabinet, 29 April 1947, CP(47)144, PRO. See also the references to the *White Paper on Constitutional Reform* in Senanayake to Secretary of State, 28 February 1947, CO 882/30, PRO.

[37] Creech-Jones to Attlee, 22 March 1947, CO 882/30, PRO.

[38] The quotation is from Creech-Jones to Governor, 7 May 1947. See also, documents 146–150 in CO 882/30, PRO.

in appearing to treat with a party leader . . . if this opportunity is missed, the demand for complete independence outside the Commonwealth will become so strong that Senanayake himself may not be able to resist it.'[39] In response, the Cabinet agreed in June to allow the Governor to announce that Britain now offered Ceylon 'fully responsible status within the British Commonwealth of Nations'. They also permitted Senanayake to claim that this implied the kind of full self-government which India was being given.[40]

During the negotiations leading to this, Senanayake had voiced three potential concerns in order to galvanize the British into early action. The first – that numerous state councillors, including some of his own supporters, might launch an agitation for self-government – appears to have had no substance whatever. The second – that unless Ceylon forged an agreement that kept it within the Commonwealth, it might be forced to become a client state of a power-hungry India[41] – appears to have been believed by Senanayake, even though it had no basis in fact. But the third – that his party might perform badly in the forthcoming election – was entirely justified.[42] The threat of a burgeoning Marxist opposition that was hostile to British economic and security interests was adroitly exploited by Senanayake and his associates.[43]

There was less to the announcement of the grant of Dominion Status than met the eye,[44] but it made it possible for Senanayake to present himself to the voters as the man who had won self-government for Ceylon and reconfirmed Bandaranaike's inferiority to his leader within the UNP hierarchy. Senanayake was further assisted by an obliging Governor Moore who told the State Council and the nation that 'it is to

---

[39] Governor to Creech-Jones, 8 May 1947, CO 882/30, PRO. See also in this regard, Lady Moore to Jan Smuts, 2 and 4 April 1947, Smuts Papers.

[40] The quotation is from Governor to Secretary of State, 13 June 1947. See documents no. 159–176 in CO 882/30, PRO. For evidence of subsequent close consultation with Senanayake on the contents of the constitutional instrument, see documents no. 200–203 in the same file. The agreements of defence and foreign affairs later enabled the Soviets to create embarrassing difficulties about the admission of Ceylon to the United Nations. This contributed to fears in the British Cabinet, which proved unfounded, that Bandaranaike might use this issue to launch a bid for the premiership. See in this connection the following PRO files: CM 76(48) minute no. 3; CP(48)204 and 281; CO 54/994/2 and CO 537/2039 and 2218.

[41] See the details of Creech-Jones' talks with Sir Oliver Goonetilleke in the memo from Creech-Jones to the Cabinet, 29 April 1947, CP(47)144, PRO. This concern was shared, rather naïvely, by the last Governor. See Sir Henry Moore to Jan Smuts, 28 December 1946, Smuts Papers.

[42] Senanayake to Secretary of State, 28 February 1947, CO 882/30. See also, notes by Webber, 5 February 1947, CO 54/995/1 and by Sidebotham, 20 March 1947, CO 54/992/2, PRO.

[43] De Silva, *A History*, p. 460 and exchanges in CO 54/995/1 and CO 54/992/2, PRO. See also, C. Jeffries, *OEG* (London, 1969), pp. 65–97.   [44] *CDN*, 31 October 1947.

your Leader's personal vision and statesmanship that your thanks are primarily due'.[45] Celebrations of self-rule in several centres across the country were turned by Senanayake into campaign meetings for the United National Party.[46] His previous achievements – which were impressive – had always been handsomely praised in most sections of the press, but with an uncertain election at hand he was now depicted in near-mythic terms. He was 'a farmer who is known to have planted coconut trees with his bare hands and talks to draught cattle to quieten the fiercer fellows, a miner who is said to have habitually swung a huge club to bring under control clashing sets of other miners . . .'[47]

Senanayake needed as much of this as could be mustered because his party was in ghastly disarray. He was, for example, unable 'to quieten the fiercer fellows' among the UNP elite who were doing harm to the cause. It is unlikely that the large number of voters who were beginning to be swayed by the carefully marshalled arguments of the parties of the Marxist left were much impressed by J. L. Kotelawala's outbursts against 'Red vermin'. His 'case' against them consisted of boasts that he had kept his province free of 'political vermin' for seventeen years. He added that he would see to it that the Buddhist priests who had campaigned for the left in his bailiwick (still quite a rare phenomenon in 1947) would be forced to disrobe – a comment that scandalized many pious Buddhists.[48] Nor was Senanayake able 'to bring under control clashing sets' of UNP leaders. His Health Minister, George E. de Silva, told a public meeting that several political associations, including the Sinhala Maha Sabha which was now part of the UNP, were 'diabolical' and that their organizers, including his ministerial colleague Bandaranaike, were 'enemies of the country'.[49]

Next to nothing was made during the campaign of one of the party's main assets, the social welfare programmes that ministers had created. Publicity for these could have helped to ward off attacks from the Marxist left, but two things prevented their use. First, given the lack of collective responsibility under the old Donoughmore Constitution, each such programme was seen by UNP leaders as the creature of one particular minister. Their jealousies of one another were too intense to allow them to claim these schemes as a collective achievement. The second impediment was the conservatism of several key UNP leaders – most crucially Senanayake himself – which caused them to regard these programmes with suspicion rather than pride. Little wonder, then, that

[45] *CDN*, 19 June 1947.
[46] See, for example, the account of a reception at Kurunegala, *CDN*, 9 July 1947.
[47] *CDN*, 16 June 1947.   [48] *CDN*, 8 and 13 September 1947.
[49] *CDN*, 4 June 1947.

Table 6.1. *Results of the 1947 general election*

Party	Candidates	Votes	% of votes	Seats	% of seats
United National Party	99	744,698	39.6	42	44.2
Marxist Parties					
Lanka Sama Samaja Party	28	204,020	10.8	10	10.5
Communist Party	13	70,331	3.7	3	3.2
Bolshevist Leninist Party[a]	10	113,193	6.0	5	5.3
Labour Party[b]	9	38,932	2.1	1	1.1
Tamil Congress[c]	9	82,499	4.4	7	7.4
Ceylon Indian Congress[d]	8	72,230	3.8	6	6.3
Independents and others	185	555,461	29.5	21	22.1
Total		1,881,364	100.0	95	100.1

Notes: [a] The full name of the party was the Lanka Sama Samaja (Bolshevist Leninist Party of India, Fourth International Group). Like the main LSSP, it claimed to be a Trotskyist party. Variants of it would arise in later years with various initials attached to the 'LSSP' root.
[b] The Ceylon Labour Party, led by A. E. Goonesinha, Bandaranaike's opponent in the 1926 municipal election, had a narrow base in the Colombo working class. Its leader had once been a leftist of sorts but had become a Sinhalese chauvinist by 1947.
[c] The All-Ceylon Tamil Congress was a party seeking votes from Ceylon Tamils on the grounds that the UNP's Tamil candidates would not represent the minority adequately. It was led by G. G. Ponnambalam, Bandaranaike's long-time sparring partner in State Council debates.
[d] The Ceylon Indian Congress appealed to the Indian Tamil labourers on the estates at the centre of the island.
Source: CDN, 24 September 1947 and CO 882/30, PRO; Ceylon Daily News, *The Parliament of Ceylon, 1947* (Colombo, 1947).

even their most ardent supporters in the press complained that the UNP put no 'clear-cut programme to the voters and that its candidates were therefore often unable to hold their own in debate with opponents'.[50]

The most vivid sign of the party's problems was its inability to ensure that only one UNP candidate stood for each of the ninety-five seats in the House of Representatives (the lower, powerful house in the new Westminster-style system). Party leaders were so reluctant to alienate potential supporters that anyone who chose to call himself a UNP candidate promptly became one. The results were often bizarre. In Polonnaruwa no fewer than five UNP candidates came forward. In Horowapotana, Hakmana and Galaha, three presented themselves, and in a great many constituencies two candidates claimed the UNP label. And yet several seats were not contested by the party. In only one did the total votes for UNP losers exceed those for a successful opposition candidate, but the party's confusing, fragmented appearance in so many areas surely cost it support.

UNP leaders made little effort to impose discipline upon candidates, partly out of complacency. They believed that, in most constituencies, one or the other of their candidates had a personal patron–client network of sufficient strength to prevail against opponents from the UNP and the opposition without the added advantage of an endorsement from the party's national leaders. Indeed, such an endorsement might have caused the official candidate trouble by persuading those who would otherwise use the UNP label to unite behind an opposition nominee. Prominent UNP members did this anyway in some places.[51] It was also true that national leaders of the party were sometimes uncertain about which of the multiple candidates in various constituencies was actually the strongest. By allowing both or all of them to stand, they could find out.

As Calvin Woodward has shown,[52] in 1947 the notion of political parties had still to take root and most votes were cast for individuals. Bandaranaike was one such. He faced an opponent for the first time, a candidate from the leftist Lanka Sama Samaja Party (LSSP), and he won easily with 87.2 per cent of the valid votes and the island's biggest majority.[53]

Insofar as party labels can be taken to mean anything, the overall result was as in Table 6.1. This was a sorry showing for the UNP. Its share of the popular vote cannot, of course, be taken seriously since many of these

[50] *CDN*, 13 and 17 September 1947 and 'UNP', a brochure in CO 54/992/2, PRO.
[51] *CDN*, 17 September 1947.
[52] C. A. Woodward, *The Growth of a Party System in Ceylon* (Providence, 1969).
[53] *CDN*, 24 and 28 September 1947. His was the largest majority in a single-member constituency.

votes were cast for nominal 'UNP' candidates who were actually opposing one another. Fully twenty-two of the forty-five members of the old State Council who stood were defeated, including the former Speaker, Deputy Speaker and three ministers.[54] The party's failure to win even a bare majority of the seats was highly embarrassing. Before the election, most people believed that the left was no longer an insubstantial force, that it now had pockets of strong support among urban labourers and in some rural areas where Marxist leaders had done effective work to aid the poor and/or where their families had long enjoyed eminence. But despite this, it was widely anticipated that the UNP would win 70 to 80 seats.[55] Instead, Senanayake was now forced to bargain with Independents and small parties to hammer together a coalition.

Three things saved the UNP from an even greater shock that might have made it impossible to form a government. Personal and ideological rivalries among leftists meant that they could achieve only an incomplete agreement on constituencies and no effective cooperation.[56] Second, most UNP candidates possessed superior financial resources and access to vehicles, especially buses – the use of which was now, in theory, illegal – and, in many cases, thugs to prevent opposition supporters from reaching the still-scarce polling stations.[57] Finally and crucially, the bizarre delimitation of constituencies inflated the number of so-called 'UNP' victors by making voters in the areas where the Marxist parties were strong count less – often far less – than votes in much of the rest of the island. Most Marxist seats were won in the Western and Southern Provinces, and yet the population per constituency in these provinces was the highest in the island, as Table 6.2 shows. When the sizes of actual constituencies are considered, the contrast is even more striking. The three largest single-member constituencies (a small handful elected more than one legislator) had 55,000 to 56,000 voters. The smallest, Polonnaruwa, had 5,839. Even if we set it aside, since it is far smaller than any other seat, there are still numerous constituencies with very small electorates:

---

[54] *CDN*, 24 September 1947. Well known UNP veterans like A. Ratnayake and George E. de Silva barely squeaked in.

[55] See, for example, the note by Webber, 7 August 1947, CO 54/993/4, PRO.

[56] A post-mortem organized by J. R. Jayewardene concluded that had the leftists cooperated, they would have won three more seats. Report of the Special Commission, typescript, file 173, J. R. Jayewardene Papers, Presidential Archive, Colombo.

[57] *CDN*, 26 July, 8 September, 11 October 1947 and 12 March 1948; and the accusations in Parliament by N. M. Perera and C. Suntheralingam (a member of the Cabinet!) in *CDN*, 27 November 1947. For more evidence on the importance of transport, see material on J. R. Jayewardene's 1943 by-election campaign in file 227, J. R. Jayewardene Papers, Presidential Archive, Colombo. For British officials' anxieties about irregularities, see Report of the Legal Secretary, 20 November 1946, CO 54/1000/8, PRO.

Table 6.2. *Variations in population per constituency by province, 1947*

Province	Average population per constituency (in thousands)
Western Province	93.4
Southern Province	80.2
Central Province	75.5
Sabaragamuwa Province	74.7
Northwestern Province	66.8
Northern Province	53.3
Uva Province	53.1
Eastern Province	38.8
North Central Province	27.9

Source: CDN, 29 July and 22 August 1977.

Vavuniya	11,099 eligible voters
Haputale	11,122
Madawachchiya	11,403
Anuradhapura	11,585
Horowapotana	12,758

In such places, a vote counted four or five times as much as a vote in the largest constituencies.

Before we leap to hasty conclusions about a plot aimed specifically at helping the UNP and scuppering the Marxists, we should note that two of those three largest constituencies were represented by none other than Senanayake and Bandaranaike.[58] The architects of the delimitation had sought in part to ensure that people in more remote, less developed areas would have greater representation because they were less able to defend their interests. But they also believed that these same constituencies would tend to return MPs with conservative views. Nor is there any doubt that this helped UNP candidates and Independents on the right or centre-right, the kind of people Senanayake needed to construct a majority. Had votes in the Western and Southern Provinces counted the same as those elsewhere, the Marxist parties and left-of-centre Independents would have done better.

Despite this, however, the election result flattered the parties of the Marxist left and provided misleading clues to the future development of

[58] *CDN*, 29 July and 22 August 1947.

the opposition in Ceylon. Since the only semi-plausible 'parties' listed in the result are the UNP and the three Marxist parties, it appears that the island's people were likely to face a choice between the rightists and centrists of the UNP and what one British official privately described, apparently without irony, as the 'Red Peril'.[59] This suited the UNP since the red scare could be used against virtually the entire opposition. This certainly occurred in 1947. Both Senanayake and Bandaranaike, for example, told a rally in Kandy that if the leftists won they would extinguish religion and annex the country to Russia.[60] But a closer examination of the election result indicates that at least a large handful of Independents in the new Parliament were people of the non-Marxist left, the centre-left. They were a varied group, but most of them favoured a growing role for the state in promoting social reform and at least a modest redistribution of wealth. Most opposed the westernized ways of many UNP leaders and preferred that the state promote Sinhala language and culture which entailed promoting Buddhism and Buddhist values.

Because they were simply 'Independents' with no party to turn to in 1947, they were largely invisible in the results table. Nor, despite an abortive attempt,[61] did they manage to create a new party of their own. Some drifted into the UNP where Bandaranaike and his Sinhala Maha Sabha colleagues shared many of their views. Others remained in obscurity on the opposition benches. But what the results failed to show, and what the UNP leaders failed to recognize, was that such people posed a greater threat than did the more visible forces of the Marxist left.

There were four main reasons for this. First, those on the centre-left were not afflicted by the personal and ideological divisions which constantly weakened and embarrassed the Marxists. It was also very difficult for UNP leaders to convince voters that the centre-leftists were godless reds, since they were pressing for more support for religion. Third, these people were far more inclined than were most of the Marxists to use the indigenous language, symbols and themes, so that they found it easier to inspire rural Sinhalese voters, including those in the small up-country constituencies who elected so many MPs. Most of the Marxists were too westernized, in their lifestyles as well as their ideologies, to compete effectively. (Indeed, in 1947, one leading Marxist politician had only just decided to begin learning Sinhala). Finally, because they sought a cultural and religious revival, and because the reforms that they

<hr>

[59] Note by Webber, 19 March 1947, CO 54/992/2, PRO.
[60] *CDN*, 22 August 1947. See also, *CDN*, 24 November 1947.
[61] *CDN*, 25–27 September 1947. They made limited efforts to cooperate in the new Parliament with the Marxist parties, but this amounted to very little. See, for example, *CDN*, 14 October 1947.

proposed fell short of radicalism, those on the centre-left could appeal to key elites in the villages where most of the votes were – teachers, priests, ayurvedic physicians and small businessmen. In 1947, these elites were not yet capable of asserting themselves politically, but their potential was beginning to become apparent. The Marxists tended to frighten those rural elites. Most of their support came instead from the semi-urbanized coastal belt running between Colombo and Galle.

Ironically, the UNP's poor showing assisted Senanayake in winning further concessions and cooperation from the British who feared that he might 'have some difficulty in implementing the agreements with the UK . . .' and who therefore believed it to be 'of first importance that nothing should be done which would give further ammunition to his opponents . . .'[62] Help from London was duly forthcoming on two important matters. First, it was discovered that a legal technicality barring servants of the Crown from seeking elective office might make all of those who had been Crown ministers vulnerable to law suits challenging their election in 1947. Ceylon's Parliament had the power to alter this, but since that would seem a crass effort by ministers to save their own skins, and since their grip on power appeared so tenuous, the British agreed to have the Privy Council make the change. They did so with great distaste and reluctance, believing that it was 'most unfortunate that we should have to trouble H[is] M[ajesty] over this matter of of legal trickery . . .'[63]

More crucially, the British continued to acquiesce in Senanayake's desire to omit from the final agreements on the transition any stipulation that minority rights must be respected by the Ceylon government. Before the election, London had reluctantly decided upon a policy of 'letting this sleeping dog lie',[64] partly because the outlook for the UNP was so uncertain. The disappointing election result ensured that the British would not raise the issue again.

Even before the UNP leaders had word of the result of the election, there had been speculation that Bandaranaike might 'drift to opposition'.[65] This was based less on worries about the capacity of the UNP to form a government than on doubts about his ability to maintain civility with several of Senanayake's close supporters. Many also suspected that he

[62] Howard to Roberts-Wray, 10 September 1947 and telegram no. 1146 of 5 September 1947, CO 54/993/4, PRO. See also, Minutes of a [Ceylon] Cabinet Meeting – Secret, 29 October 1947, file 10, BP.

[63] Note by C. Jeffries, 22 November 1947, CO 537/2212 and the material in CO 882/30, PRO.

[64] See the exchanges in CO 537/2220 PRO. The quotation is from a note by 'JJP', 11 July 1947.   [65] The quotation is from *ibid*. See also, *CDN*, 6 September 1947.

would be unable to tolerate for long the role of Senanayake's principal lieutenant, but this latter fear was exaggerated. The two men had lately worked and campaigned together without serious disharmony, thanks in part to the leader's efforts to woo Bandaranaike. Press barons close to Senanayake now tempered their familiar attacks on Bandaranaike with hymns to his promise as Ceylon's next leader,[66] and he was further encouraged when Senanayake told the press of his intention to retire from politics within two years.[67]

Even had these things not occurred, however, it is unlikely that Bandaranaike would have left the UNP. Through all the years of his tempestuous relationship with Senanayake, during which he had consistently failed to come to terms with the patent pre-eminence of the older man, Bandaranaike had just as consistently been unable to allow a complete break to occur between them. This was partly because Senanayake was such a formidable leader, but it owed more to Bandaranaike's lifelong ambiguity towards figures of authority. This became vividly apparent a few years later in his long and agonizing delay, in the face of great provocation, before leaving the UNP. It is true that in September 1947 he secretly met Marxist and centre-left MPs for very tentative talks about the formation of a non-UNP government. But he cannot have seriously considered such a possibility – partly because too many Independents in the new Parliament leaned to the right[68] and to Senanayake – but also because he was temperamentally disinclined to take such a step.

As Senanayake set about constructing a team of ministers that would command a majority, there was much speculation in the press about invitations to certain smaller parties to join a coalition.[69] Most prominent among these was the Tamil Congress which was led by G. G. Ponnambalam who had clashed so often with Bandaranaike in the old State Council. His appeals to Ceylon Tamils in the north and east to back an assertively Tamil party that would engage in 'non-cooperation' with UNP,[70] and not to trust the UNP's Tamil candidates, had produced victories for the Tamil Congress in seven of nine seats. After the defeat of

---

[66] Compare for example, *CDN*, 6 and 18 September 1947.
[67] *CDN*, 17 September 1947.
[68] See the accounts of twenty or so MPs who clearly stood left of centre, *CDN*, 25–26 September 1947. Descriptions of Bandaranaike's meeting with leftists arose in interviews with a close aide to Bandaranaike, Colombo, 7 September 1978 and with the most important leftist, N. M. Perera, London, 18 November 1978.
[69] See, for example, *CDN*, 6 September 1947.	[70] *CDN*, 26 October 1947.

so many of his minority candidates,[71] Senanayake could have given his new Cabinet the look of a government of national unity had he drawn in the Tamil Congress, and many observers believed that Ponnambalam's communalist bluster – like Bandaranaike's – was more a vehicle for his ambition than a matter of conviction. But the Tamil leader's outbursts against the UNP after the results came in[72] made it impossible to include them. Instead, two Tamil Independents who had defeated UNP candidates were given ministries.[73] The Ceylon Indian Congress – the party of the Tamil labourers of Indian origin which had won seven seats in central Ceylon – was not considered as a potential ally.

Senanayake's choices for ministerial posts did not please Bandaranaike. Only one of the latter's allies from the Sinhala Mabha Sabha was given a post of importance, some were shunted into minor roles,[74] and most were offered nothing. At the same time, Senanayake brought in a number of men who were either his old allies or promising youngsters who regarded Bandaranaike as an adversary. Oliver E. Goonetilleke, who as a civil servant had coordinated much of the war effort and then had acted as Senanayake's link-man in London during the negotiations over Dominion status, was given a seat in the Senate (the upper house and made Home Minister. J. L. Kotelawala, Senanayake's nephew who had had many bruising exchanges with Bandaranaike on the old Board of Ministers, was kept on at Works and given great prominence. George E. de Silva, the former minister who had lately called Bandaranaike an enemy of the country, was also included. So was the young, highly intelligent J. R. Jayewardene – an associate of Senanayake's son Dudley – who was given the immense burden of the Finance Ministry. (D. S. Senanayake himself kept Defence and Foreign Affairs.) Finally, in a move which touched off an avalanche of controversy in the press,[75] Senanayake gave his old Ministry of Agriculture and Lands – a crucial post – to his son Dudley.

As a result, Bandaranaike found himself somewhat isolated in a largely hostile Cabinet. His frustration was compounded by the treatment that he received from Senanayake. He had been promised that the Health

---

[71] G. G. Ponnambalam had trounced the UNP's A. Mahadeva, a minister in the old State Council, at Jaffna. Senanayake also saw a UNP Tamil badly beaten by the Tamil Independent, C. Suntheralingam at Vavuniya, and the UNP Muslim, A. R. A. Razik lose to the Independent Muslim, M. M. Ebrahim at Pottuvil.

[72] *CDN*, 24–26 September 1947.

[73] One of these two had been elected with Ponnambalam's support and his decision was intensely annoying to Ponnambalam. *CDN*, 13–14 October 1947.

[74] Interview with Sir Senerat Gunawardena, Colombo, 12 September 1980.

[75] See, for example, *CDN*, 13 October 1947.

186 *The expedient utopian*

Ministry would be added to Local Administration and that he would also be designated Leader of the House, a post that Senanayake had held until recently and which some took to imply deputy leader of the government. When appointments were first announced, he lost control of Fisheries which he had supervised in his State Council days and was given the Health portfolio while retaining Local Administration – although it was implied that this occurred not because he had earned it but because health and local government were linked in England. No mention was made of the post of Leader of the House.[76] Bandaranaike had to call on Senanayake and lobby vigorously for this,[77] an episode that did not bode well for a happy working relationship.

Throughout his time in office, Bandaranaike was frequently provoked and then placated in this way. He was not an easy colleague and did plenty to encourage this, but after some time the provocations so outnumbered the placations that there could be little doubt that he was under assault from within the government. In late 1947, however, the oscillations were still comparatively gentle. In November, Senanayake alarmed him by publicly withdrawing his promise 'to retire from Parliament next year'. He told a public rally that this was because he was so fearful of 'the plague that (is) spreading all over the world from Russia . . .'[78] and he promised that he would not relinquish office until the threat was destroyed, a mission that would presumably keep him at the helm for some time. Bandaranaike's dismay at this was soon soothed, however, by the invitation from his chief to deliver the main address at the ceremonies marking the formal transfer of power in February 1948. And so it went.

Bandaranaike was not the sort of man to keep his exasperation bottled up for long, and it soon surfaced in public displays of discontent with the government. The precise form that this took is revealing. He could easily have adopted the familiar themes of Sinhalese Buddhist parochialism. With urban unemployment now on the rise again in early 1948,[79] the presence of Indian workers in Ceylon was once again becoming an issue. Leading *bhikkhus* (monks) had begun asking that Buddhism be given great protection and prominence. Others were dismayed at the government's failure to make provision for the use of Sinhala as well as English in parliamentary debates and at the continued use of the Union Jack (as well as a provisional national flag) on public occasions even after Independence on 4 February 1948.[80] That he did not raise these issues,

[76] *CDN*, 23 September 1947.
[77] Interview with two close Bandaranaike aides, Colombo, 6 September 1978.
[78] *CDN*, 24 November 1947 and A. E. Goonesinha Memoirs, typescript, p. 139.
[79] See, for example, *CDN*, 6 March and 24 May 1948.
[80] *CDN*, 28 November 1947, 12 January, 2 March, 5 and 26 April and 17 May 1948.

that he chose instead to decry the government's failure to seek rapid social reform, suggests that of the two great themes that dominated his career, it was reform rather than parochialism that was closer to his heart.

He opened his campaign of criticism with an aggressively bombastic speech in March 1948 to a public meeting in Anuradhapura. He said that 'a tremendous social revolution, shattering all conventions, will overtake the country' over the next five years. The 'common man's day had dawned' and people were demanding 'clothing, food and land'. Unless the government acted, 'there would be a revolution'. If the nation's leaders were not prepared 'to do their duty by the people . . . they should get out'.[81] After this, many wondered if he was about to resign. He professed surprise at this speculation and said that he was simply seeking to create enthusiasm for a memorandum which he was presenting to Cabinet on how the cause of reform could be advanced. But in April he was on the attack again, speaking of his 'disillusionment' with the UNP's failure either to assist the poor adequately or to perform essential organizational work 'which is now being almost monopolised by the Marxist parties . . .'[82] The next day he showed open contempt for his Cabinet rival, Kotelawala, heaping sarcasm upon him at great length.[83]

This drew heavy fire from both right and left. Newspapers close to Kotelawala and Senanayake now stated openly what had been whispered for weeks: Bandaranaike 'feels he is excluded from the inner counsels [sic] of the government' and had chosen to become 'the Bad Boy of the outer Cabinet'. Marxists argued that if he disagreed so deeply with prevailing policy, he should do the decent thing and resign. One leftist MP claimed that 'When God created Mr Bandaranaike, He gave him the necessary organs, except for the backbone.'[84]

Although (as we shall see in chapter 7) the squabbling between Kotelawala and Bandaranaike was not entirely unwelcome to the Prime Minister, when it reached this intensity it clearly damaged the government.[85] Senanayake therefore took steps to bring it under control, but the dispute simmered on for years. In the process, both made major contributions to a devaluation of the language of political debate. Kotelawala – a bluff, insensitive reactionary – caused widespread amusement by claiming that 'my political philosophy' was 'Efficient Socialism' which had somehow to replace 'Primitive Capitalism'. He

---

[81] *CDN*, 6 March 1948.
[82] The quotation is from *CDN*, 5 April 1948. See also, *CDN*, 8 and 15 March 1948.
[83] *CDN*, 6 April 1948. For another example from a later period, see Bernard Aluwihare Diaries, 25 April 1954, University of Peradeniya Library.
[84] *CDN*, 6–7 April 1948.
[85] See in this regard, A. E. Goonesinha Memoirs, typescript, p. 140.

characteristically left the meanings of both terms undefined. Bandaranaike usually offered more reasoned, informative comment – including, on one occasion, a cogent case for Keynesian economic policies. But his exuberance on the public platform often carried him headlong into the realm of fantasy, as when he informed the All-Ceylon Women's Conference that 'capitalist democracy . . . has reached its saturation point of exploitation and collapsed under its own weight'.[86]

By mid-1948, the suspicions toward Bandaranaike which most members of the Cabinet had brought into government had hardened into outright distaste. This was more or less inevitable given their deep differences on policy, but his manner in Cabinet meetings certainly hastened the process. He tended to arrive, tense and brimming with an idea that he felt compelled to expound passionately, early in the meeting, often in defiance of the day's agenda. Only when he had done this could he relax. As one fellow minister put it, 'We always waited for him to have his orgasm; then we could get on with things.'[87] But his troubles with most of the Cabinet team were overshadowed in the public eye by his dispute with Sir John Kotelawala (knighted in 1948) who had now emerged as his leading rival to succeed Senanayake. In mid-1948, Bandaranaike abandoned plans to accompany Senanayake on a foreign tour because in their absence Sir John would preside over the Cabinet, giving the appearance that he was number two. When the premier undertook the tour, Bandaranaike was given charge of Cabinet meetings, but he was pointedly denied the right to call himself 'Acting Prime Minister'.[88] And so it went. In the midst of all of this, a playful remark was made in Parliament to the effect that neither Bandaranaike nor Kotelawala was the true heir apparent, but that it was actually Senanayake's son Dudley. Bandaranaike was seen to smile broadly at such an unlikely suggestion, and the press treated it as a little light relief.[89] They should have been more circumspect.

Despite the initial refusal of the Tamil Congress to join the government, Senanayake continued his efforts to draw them in, on the theory that G. G. Ponnambalam, like his old adversary Bandaranaike before him, would find that his appetite for power outweighed his communalism and his penchant for stinging rhetoric. With the Ceylon Tamils firmly on board, the ruling alliance would appear to be something very close to a

---

[86] Quotations are from *CDN*, 10 February and 26 July 1948. For other examples, see *CDN* 8, 13 and 15 March, 3, 5, 10 and 15 April, 21 and 29 May, 21 June and 1 September 1948.   [87] Interview with J. R. Jayewardene, Colombo, 11 September 1980.
[88] *CDN*, 3 and 10 July and 29 September 1948. See also, 29 May and 10 August 1948.
[89] *CDN*, 29 July 1948.

government of national unity, and it would be able to withstand all but the most disastrous reverses at the next election. In August, the Tamil Congress entered the ruling coalition, gaining only one ministerial post: Industries and Fisheries for Ponnambalam.

There were, however, clear signs of disquiet among some Tamil Congress MPs and Independent Tamil ministers, over three pieces of legislation which the government was preparing, one of which was made public just after Ponnambalam joined the Cabinet.[90] These bills were aimed at Tamils of Indian origin, nearly all of whom were labourers on tea estates in the central highlands of the island, a group that stood at one remove – geographically and socially – from the Ceylon Tamils who mainly resided in the Northern and Eastern Provinces and in greater Colombo. As Hugh Tinker has explained, these bills effectively prevented most Indian Tamils from obtaining Ceylonese citizenship and disenfranchised them.[91]

This was not the first time that a predominantly Sinhalese government had sought to move against Indian Tamils. In the early 1940s, strict interpretation of electoral laws had meant that less than 20,000 of the 141,899 Indian Tamils who had been on the voting rolls in 1941 continued to qualify.[92] Despite this and the physical intimidation of Indian voters at the 1947 election,[93] seven Indian Tamil MPs were returned from Central Province constituencies. This left them with by far the worst per capita representation in the House.[94] But the new

---

[90] *CDN*, 23 and 30 August, 4, 8 and 15 September 1948. Eventually a second Tamil Congress man was named as a junior minister, *CDN*, 18 December 1948.

[91] The three pieces of legislation eventually became the Citizenship Act (No. 18 of 1948), the Indian and Pakistani Residents (Citizenship) Act (No. 3 of 1949) and the Ceylon (Parliamentary Elections Amendment) Act (No. 48 of 1949). The long-running controversy of the citizenship of estate Tamils is too complex and extensive to be dealt with in detail here. See H. Tinker, *The Banyan Tree* (Oxford, 1977), pp. 39 and 47, and *Separate and Unequal: India and the Indians in the British Commonwealth, 1920–1950* (Vancouver, 1976), pp. 339–40.

[92] Tinker, *The Banyan Tree*, p. 38.

[93] See, for example, the uncontested evidence from Gampola, *CDN*, 11 March 1948. Also, interview with Sir Senerat Gunawardena, Colombo, 9 September 1978.

[94] The breakdown provided at the time (*CDN*, 15 November 1947) was as follows:

Group	Population	Members of Parliament	Population per MP
Europeans	2,433	4	608
Burghers	33,671	3	11,224
Ceylon Tamils	804,950	13	61,919
Muslims	382,984	6	63,831
Sinhalese	4,515,198	68	66,400
Indian Tamils	732,258	7	104,608

government was still determined to exclude them from the electoral process, partly out of anti-Tamil bias, partly on the principle that 'foreigners' (many of whom had lived most of their lives in Ceylon) should not help choose governments, and partly because these seven seats would probably go to pro-UNP Sinhalese if the estate Tamils were excluded.[95]

This left Ceylon Tamil politicians facing a cruel dilemma. They could oppose the UNP, stand by the Indian Tamils and see the government ram the legislation through in their absence. Or they could work with the UNP and hope that Sinhalese leaders and voters would remember their cooperation and not turn on them. In the event, most of them chose the latter approach.[96]

As the 1940s drew to a close, quarrels among members of the UNP Cabinet continued apace. Ministers behaved as if the pre-independence system, in which each had had an independent power base, still existed. Indeed, to a limited extent it did since many of these ructions arose because agencies which different ministers controlled tended to conflict at the grass roots. In 1949, for example, the Home Ministry's new Rural Development Societies found themselves in competition at the local level with arms of no fewer than three other ministries: Cooperation, Industries and Local Administration. A little good will and coordination might have turned this into mutual reinforcement, but many ministers were too inclined to attack one another and to seek the abolition of rivals' agencies for this to happen very often.

The conservative press often paid special heed to Bandaranaike's very prominent part in these encounters. And in early 1949, the Lake House group – with which Senanayake and his close associate Sir Oliver Goonetilleke (knighted in 1948) had close ties – frequently hammered away at Bandaranaike's tardiness in bringing into being programmes that he had announced in grandiose terms. Some of this criticism was justified. Even his allies from that period concede that he had spells of laziness and inattention

---

[95] For example, the disenfranchisement of estate Tamils in one of them, Talawakelle, reduced the electorate from approximately 19,000 in 1947 to a mere 2,500 in 1951 (*TC*, 16 March 1951). The UNP leaders assumed that their tendency to win predominantly rural and Sinhalese seats would not change. In 1956, as we shall see in chapter 7, this assumption was proved wrong in many areas.

[96] Interview with a Tamil Congress leader of the period, Colombo, 17 September 1982. See also, *CDN*, 15 and 18 December 1948. Three of the seven Tamil Congress MPs opposed the government on the Indian and Pakistani Residents (Citizenship) Act. Subsequently, some Ceylon Tamil politicians who felt that their support for the UNP had gained them little, split from Ponnambalam to form a more assertive Tamil party.

to detail.[97] But many of his programmes were killed or delayed by opposition from other ministers.[98]

To be blamed for this naturally infuriated him. He was finding it more and more difficult to imagine Senanayake (who still showed no inclination to retire) annointing him as his successor, or his Cabinet colleagues welcoming him as their new leader. Accordingly, in mid-1949, he began taking a more independent line in public speeches than at any time since joining the UNP. In doing so, he stressed not only the cause of social reform, but the need for religious, cultural and linguistic revival. There was no small ambiguity in his speeches on this latter point. He tended to deliver them near Buddhist holy places – notably Anuradhapura, long a favourite platform – which implied a Sinhalese bias. But he also stressed the need to promote the use of both vernaculars.[99]

In August 1949, he went a step further by organizing and addressing a public meeting of his old Sinhala Maha Sabha, of which next to nothing had been heard since the formation of the UNP in 1946. He made caustic attacks on the government's failure to implement the reformist policies which he had written into the UNP Manifesto, on the failure of party leaders to consult the rank and file, and so on. Reporters were present and their stories enraged other ministers who resolved upon a 'showdown' at the next meeting of the UNP executive. Showdowns were difficult to arrange with the agile, elusive Bandaranaike, however. In a scene strongly reminiscent of his pre-independence dealings with Senanayake and the Ceylon National Congress, he told the executive that the press had grossly exaggerated his remarks which were nothing more than constructive criticisms. There was some truth in this, though not a great deal, and a sceptical party executive resolved to take no action against him 'on this occasion'.[100]

They promptly announced, however, that at the UNP's annual

[97] Interviews in Colombo with a civil servant who worked closely with him at that time, 9 August 1977, with A. P. Jayasuriya, 23 August 1977 and with another political ally, 7 September 1978.

[98] Interviews with two of Bandaranaike's aides, Colombo, 10 September 1977 and 16 August 1980. See also, for example, *CDN*, 21 and 26 March, 1 April, 4 June and 10 August 1949; and telegram Governor to Secretary of State, 27 June 1944, CO 54/986/5 (part 1), PRO.

[99] *CDN*, 2 and 12 October 1948, 26 January, 1, 9, 21 and 31 May and 22 September 1949. See also, *Ceylon Hansard* (1944), pp. 746 and 810–11; and R. N. Kearney, *Communalism and Language in the Politics of Ceylon* (Durham, 1967), p. 36.

[100] *TC*, 8 August 1948 and *CDN*, 16 August 1949; and an interview with a close Bandaranaike aide of that period, Colombo, 9 September 1980. See also, letters from Bandaranaike to Senanayake and Sir Ukwatte Jayasundera, dated respectively 15 and 12 August 1949, file 5, BP.

conference in September, they would bar from membership anyone belonging to other political associations – such as, for example, the Sinhala Maha Sabha. Amid much speculation that Bandaranaike might leave the government and revive the Sabha, the Lake House press weighed in with comments that he was unfit to succeed Senanayake, and that he was in 'the process of self-destruction'. The party conference duly passed the new rule, but Bandaranaike took little note of it and made a speech to the conference in support of the government.[101]

Matters did not rest there, however. His dismay over his prospects within the ruling party led him to keep open the alternative of the Sabha, no matter what UNP policy was. A month later, in late October, he told a large Sabha meeting that since Ceylon's independence had now been consolidated – a task for which the UNP had been essential – the Sabha 'could profitably abandon its dormant attitude of the past two years as its role for the future was becoming manifest'. He added that while he was firmly opposed to communism, he was worried about 'a trend towards Fascism or semi-Fascism which might creep upon us almost unawares, while the bogey of Communism is played up'.[102] This was principally a reference to Sir John Kotelawala's efforts to form a UNP Youth League, a group organized along militaristic lines amid talk of 'discipline' and the swearing of loyalty oaths to party and country. Some historians are inclined to dismiss this as a dose of comic opera, but this force – which wore green shirts, green being the party colour – was created (as Senanayake would later put it) for the purpose of 'resisting revolutionary elements'. And some UNP leaders engaged in violent rhetoric: Sir John's references to 'Red Vermin' for example, and J. R. Jayewardene's threat in late 1948 that if the Marxists used force, the UNP would reply with two kicks to one kick and two slaps to one slap.[103] So Perhaps Bandaranaike was right to stress that criticism from the opposition was valuable and to say that 'democracy can really be defended and fostered only by democratic methods'.[104]

His impatience with the government's conservatism was substantially justified, but the attitudes of his fellow ministers formed a complex

[101] *CDN*, 17 and 20 August 1949.
[102] *CDN*, 24 October 1949. See also, Bernard Aluwihare Diaries, 17–18 October 1946, University of Peradeniya Library.
[103] *CDN*, 9 October 1948 and 1 October 1949. See in this regard, *The Nation*, 5 January 1946; the maintenance in the postwar period of preventive detention powers (*CDN*, 1 May 1948); the Police Commission chairman's admission that the police 'are spying on certain suspicious groups' (*CDN*, 1 June 1946); and Senanayake's endorsement as 'an absolute necessity' the UNP Youth Corps, formed for the purpose of 'resisting revolutionary elements' (*CDN*, 2 October 1950).   [104] *CDN*, 24 October 1949.

pattern that must not be oversimplified. For example, while it is true that most of them – including the premier – were decidedly suspicious of change, several were not. Along with Bandaranaike, George E. de Silva and J. R. Jayewardene (among others) were eager to generate reform in certain spheres. But they did not make common cause as a reformist lobby in the Cabinet, in part because they were interested in different types of change. De Silva mainly sought to make resources available to disadvantaged groups,[105] while Jayewardene was preoccupied with increasing the use of the vernaculars (especially Sinhalese) so that ordinary people could have greater access to the workings of the state machinery. Bandaranaike had an interest in both sorts of change, but he was prevented from joining forces with these men by intense personal rivalries. Those rivalries – particularly that between Bandaranaike and de Silva – facilitated the government's continuing reliance upon and solicitude towards commercial and especially plantation interests; the plantations were being Ceylonized in this period as British-owned estates were sold to local buyers.

We must also remember, as we view this government as predominantly conservative, that many of these ministers played a role – both before and after independence – in developing programmes and public services that eventually helped to produce the high literacy and life expectancy and low infant mortality that have earned Ceylon such admiration throughout the world. The origins of these programmes can be traced in part to initiatives to provide services to labourers on Ceylon's tea plantations, in response to pressure from the Indian government for humane treatment of Indian workers.[106] Most of the Ceylonese ministers who then developed general welfare programmes were not philosophically committed to the redistribution of wealth. Rather, individual ministers from the late British period onward vied with one another to make a name for themselves as great, if somewhat paternalistic public benefactors.[107] By the late 1940s, most of their key programmes had been created, and most survived until 1956 – under UNP governments which, taken overall, were distinctly conservative in character – mainly as a result of inertia and the embarrassment which their elimination might cause. It was only after Bandaranaike came to power in 1956 that they were grounded in a

---

105 The Law Minister in the first UNP government made some modest but significant reforms. N. Tiruchelvam, The Popular Tribunals of Sri Lanka: A Socio-Legal Study, Harvard Law School doctoral thesis, 1973, pp. 148–49.

106 I am grateful to Ronald J. Herring for this information.

107 See, for example, *CDN*, 11 and 12 March 1947, and note by Sir Alan Rose, 14 June 1947 on the Education Ordinance in CO 54/996/5. For a discussion of the UNP's reliance on commercial and plantation interests, see, for example, the early sections of Marga Institute, *Welfare and Growth in Sri Lanka* (Colombo, 1974).

systematic commitment to 'socialism' which in effect meant moderate, welfare state reformism.[108]

Efforts during this first phase after independence to assist the disadvantaged were hindered by a severe lack of statistical data on the condition of the island's people. This was largely the result of a long-standing reluctance on the part of the British authorities to collect the kind of information which their counterparts in India had routinely gathered for decades. Despite earlier public complaints about this, ministers did not establish a statistical department until late 1948, and that did not produce a comprehensive effort at data-gathering. The scarcity of information, particularly concerning rural areas where most people lived – which for example entailed an ignorance of how much land was under various crops, or even how much land was potentially cultivable – persisted for some time.[109] Kandyan interests managed to persuade the authorities to mount an investigation into the condition of the peasantry in their area in the late 1940s, but ministers resisted pressure from within the UNP to expand it beyond that region – where British estates could be blamed for peasants' hardships – into a thoroughgoing survey of the entire island.[110] Ten years after independence, the national political elite still had no satisfactory island-wide statistical profile of the rural masses. Even the leftists did not seek to learn how severe the problems of landlessness and rural poverty were.

Given the lack of data and the conservatism of the first UNP government, it is not surprising that its land policies offered little new assistance to poorer rural dwellers. A small number of declining estates were acquired for landless and land-poor peasants and minor paddy cultivation schemes were developed. But, in the main, the government continued to rely on the colonization of unoccupied land which D. S. Senanayake had created in the 1930s, despite evidence that the beneficiaries were provided with such inadequate credit and basic resources that they often lost their land to money-lenders or clung onto it in 'appalling' conditions. The land question seldom surfaced in public discussion in this period, and the government's lack of interest was demonstrated by a long delay in passing a paddy lands reform bill which in any case had too few teeth to produce significant change.[111]

---

[108] See for example, *CDN*, 25, 27 and 29 July and 7 and 14 December 1946, and 19 February 1947.

[109] *The Nation*, 9 January 1943. See also, *CDN*, 26 July 1947, 12 November 1948, and M. Roberts interview with Sir Richard Aluwihare, pp. 21–23, Mss. Ind. Ocn. S.174, Rhodes House, Oxford.

[110] *CDN*, 3 February 1949. A survey of landlessness was eventually produced in 1952, but it was based on a sample that was too small to be satisfactory.

[111] The quotation is from a touring official of the government of Malaya, *TC*, 22 February 1951. See also *CDN*, 29 November and 1 December 1948, and *TC*, 8 February and 10 April 1951.

Budgetary constraints and problems with domestic food production go part of the way towards explaining the conservatism of the government. Many of the expensive welfare programmes had developed in the late war years when conditions drove prices for commodities produced in Ceylon very high. During 1946, however, certain key prices fell sharply and this, together with the failure of successive rains, produced a period of stringency lasting nearly four years. By 1950, however, things had eased considerably and yet no major renewal of schemes for social welfare and reform ensued.[112] Financial stringency does not suffice, therefore, to explain the government's reluctance to promote change.

Ministers, for example, resisted appeals to pay greater heed to the plight of seriously disadvantaged (and numerically powerful) caste groups, which could have been accomplished without major expenditure. Leaders of two such groups, the *Wahumpuras* and *Bathgamas*, had appealed to the pre-independence delimitation commission for multi-member constituencies in areas where their castes were heavily concentrated, since that was the only way that they could realistically hope to gain representation in Parliament, given the intimidation which they routinely suffered at the hands of other castes. This was opposed, however, by UNP leaders – including, on this occasion at least, Bandaranaike.[113] He appears to have done so in order to present a united front with his ministerial colleagues, since he shared neither their knowledge of [114] nor their prejudice against these castes, but he did so all the same. Indeed he only allowed his natural inclination to give those castes a more equitable role in politics – by, for example, seeking to increase the number of polling stations so that they could not be prevented from voting by roadblocks[115] – after he left the ruling party in 1951 and needed their

---

112 See letters, Lady Moore to Jan Smuts, 14 August 1945 and 22 June 1946; material between 30 October 1947 and 23 January 1949 in CO 537/1994, PRO and *CDN*, 5–7 June, 4 and 14 December 1946, 26 January, 5 March, 16 May 1947, 21 April 1948, 7 January, 3 February, 13 and 15 July and 8 August 1949 and 17 July 1950.

113 *CDN*, 27 and 29 June 1946. On another occasion, he sought to arrange delimitation that would assist disadvantaged castes (*The Nation*, 10 January 1946). The leader of one such group was also a Vice President of the Sinhala Maha Sabha (*The Nation*, 18 May 1946).

114 When Bandaranaike set out to garner the votes of disadvantaged caste groups against the mainly upper caste UNP after 1951, his aides found that he had only a vague familiarity with the names, condition and numerical strength of poorer caste groups. All that he knew was that they were out there in considerable numbers and that they had been seriously under-involved in politics, partly because they had suffered intimidation and partly because they were apathetic towards politics dominated by the UNP. Interviews with Nimal Karunatilake, Colombo, 17 August 1978 and Sir Senerat Gunawardena, Colombo, 9 September 1978.

115 Sir John Kotelawala told the author that he and other UNP politicians had frequently set up such blocks at elections. Interview at Kandawela, 26 August 1977. See also, Jiggins, *Caste and Family*. For information on polling stations under the first UNP government see, for example, *TC*, 24 and 26 April 1951.

support to defeat the UNP. On at least two occasions during the first UNP government, other ministers refused requests in Parliament to investigate the conditions of disadvantaged castes.[116]

Nowhere was the government's conservatism more strikingly apparent than in their preservation of the traditional headman system which had been widely regarded since the 1930s as a reactionary anachronism that should be abolished. UNP leaders who before independence had viewed most headmen as stooges of the British now came to value their willingness to assist the new ruling party. Headmen had made something of a political comeback during the war thanks to new regulatory tasks that they were able to perform. Over the long term, their influence was bound to wane given the increasing penetration of specialized state agencies to the village level, the growing assertiveness of local-level elites and the increasing sophistication of ordinary rural folk. But for the time being, headmen offered UNP leaders a useful political prop and a further means of impeding change in rural areas. This was regarded with intense distaste by Bandaranaike and some other ministers.

In another effort to cultivate support at the grass roots, the UNP government had civil servants organize Rural Development Societies from 1948 onward. These bodies created opportunities for villagers to articulate their needs and views to government officials and, in the view of some politicians (there was confusion on this point) to supervise the use of modest government resources at the local level. By late 1948, a very large number of Societies had been created, even in remote areas.[117] The bureaucrats who established them found villagers to be rather timid at the first few meetings, but they soon shed their inhibitions and raised aggressive, critical questions. Some officials found this awakening inspiring, but other civil servants, headmen and UNP MPs who were accustomed to deference had become alarmed by it as early as February 1949.[118] The government nonetheless continued to encourage Rural Development Societies, in large part because they were supervised by the Home Ministry which was controlled by Bandaranaike's adversaries and which sought to turn them into counterweights to the Village Committees that Bandaranaike had been organizing since 1936 as Local Administration Minister.[119] This may have checked his influence in the

[116] *CDN*, 1 December 1948 and 20 October 1949.
[117] See, for example, *CDN*, 14 May, 6 and 11 August and 20 November 1948.
[118] See, for example, *CDN*, 1 and 3 February 1949. Also, conference with three civil servants who had been involved with the development of Rural Development Societies, Colombo, 1 September 1980.
[119] See, for example, *CDN*, 7 March, 28 May and 19 December 1949. Bandaranaike later stated that he believed that the Rural Development Societies were created to 'clip my wings' (*CDN*, 16 February 1959). Also interview with A. Ratnayake, minister in charge of them, Colombo, 2 September 1977. See also, Bandaranaike's comments on this in Parliament, *Ceylon Hansard* (1954) cols. 364–6 and 368.

short term, but it also greatly facilitated the politicization of key village-level elites – school teachers, *bhikkhus* (Buddhist monks), ayurvedic physicians, small landholders and the like – who ultimately coalesced in 1955–56 to oust the UNP and bring Bandaranaike to power.[120]

These elites had not yet crystallized into self-conscious interests. This is clear from their failure to achieve much on issues that later became central: the need to encourage the use of Sinhala, and the highly westernized ways of prominent UNP leaders which were offensive to Buddhist sensibilities. The government gave them plenty to complain about, particularly on the language issue. The absence of stenographic and translation facilities in Parliament made it impossible at independence for MPs to speak in Sinhala or Tamil. In April 1948, a member was ruled out of order when he insisted on reciting a stanza in Sinhala, and it was not until July that the first speech was permitted in the language of the island's majority. It was, characteristically, Bandaranaike who made it. He decided hurriedly to do so, when he got wind of a plan by leftists to jump in ahead of the government.[121] As early as March 1948, J. R. Jayewardene – who had been the first politician to ask that Sinhala be the sole official language[122] – had wanted to make his annual budget speech in the vernacular but was thwarted by the lack of stenographers. The authorities dragged their feet to such an extent that three years later, he was still unable to do so.[123]

This extraordinary delay owed much to D. S. Senanayake's refusal to support greater use of the vernaculars, partly because he felt it would divide the nation by making it more difficult for Tamils and Sinhalese to communicate,[124] and partly because he was a conservative member of the most highly anglicized political elite in the non-western nations of the Empire/Commonwealth. On one occasion during this period, a deputation of *bhikkhus* called upon the Prime Minister and asked for greater support for Sinhala, lest the Sinhalese 'race' be destroyed. He responded contemptuously, saying that if the Sinhalese had survived several centuries of alien rule, they were hardly likely to crumble under a democratic system in which they formed a 70 per cent majority.[125]

This incident shows Senanayake to be both admirable and insensitive. The *bhikkhus*' request was couched in the naïvely exaggerated terms that

[120] This is abundantly clear from oral accounts by several civil servants involved with the Societies. For signs of discontent among vernacular schoolteachers, see *CDN*, 22 June, 11 July and 3 and 9 August 1946.
[121] *CDN*, 14 and 28 November 1947, 5 April and 29 July 1948.
[122] *Ceylon Hansard* (1944), pp. 746–811.
[123] *CDN*, 17 May 1948 and *TC*, 17 February 1951.
[124] See, for example, *CDN*, 25 September 1948.
[125] M. Roberts interview with Sir Richard Aluwihare, p. 45, MSS. Ind. Ocn. S.174, Rhodes House, Oxford.

were characteristic of their political utterances throughout the period
covered by this volume, and it is therefore not surprising that the premier
should greet it with sarcasm, as most members of the westernized elite
continued to do until 1955–56. But he should have offered them a more
considered response. He should have seen that they were men who were
unused to criticism or disagreement, who were politically inexperienced
and accustomed to deference, and that the extreme terms in which they
conveyed their message were therefore to be expected. He should also
have seen that they were raising an issue on which many Sinhalese felt
deep exasperation.[126] His failure and the failure of his two successors as
Prime Minister – Dudley Senanayake and Sir John Kotelawala – to do so,
allowed popular anxiety on this matter to fester into a grave danger to
public order and civility.

To buy time on the language question, the government established an
official commission in October 1948 to study the use of the vernaculars in
the administration of justice. At that juncture the authorities were still,
astonishingly, debating the wisdom of translating the laws of the land
into Sinhala and Tamil.[127] As late as mid-1949, most postal and
telegraphic services were not available in the indigenous languages, and
by then it had clearly emerged that many government officials were
unable to speak either vernacular.[128] Cabinet meetings were of course
conducted in English, as indeed they continued to be throughout the
years covered by this volume – even after 1956 when Bandaranaike's
government declared Sinhala to be the only official language. Soon after
independence, Bandaranaike had ordered employees in his ministries to
correspond with the public only in the vernaculars, and he and men like
Jayewardene were clearly displeased with the slow pace of change. But as
members of a conservative Cabinet, they were unable to take much action
to defuse the quite significant public frustration on this matter.[129]

Meanwhile, the more anglicized members of the government persisted
with many of the manners, symbols and styles of the colonial era, storing
up resentments that would emerge in the Sinhalese Buddhist revival of
the mid-1950s. Official photos of the first Cabinet show only Jayewardene and Bandaranaike in 'native dress'. Buddhist criminals receiving the
death sentence still heard the judge say 'May God have mercy on your
soul.'[130] The Union Jack still flew, sometimes alongside what was still

[126] See in this regard, K. Malalgoda, *Buddhism in Sinhalese Society, 1750–1900* (Berkeley, 1976),
pp. 173–76; and J. Russell, The Ceylon Tamils under the Donoughmore Constitution,
University of Peradeniya doctoral thesis, pp. 197 and 469–75.
[127] *CDN*, 2 and 12 October 1948.
[128] *CDN*, 21 May and 11 June 1949.
[129] See in this connection 9 and 31 May and 22 September 1949, and the mounting signs of
public disquiet in the pages of the Sinhalese papers – for example, *Dinamina*, 1949–1951.
[130] *CDN*, 8 July 1949 and *TC*, 22 March 1951.

only a provisional national flag, on public buildings and 'God Save the King' was still played on official occasions. Ministers gambled openly at the race track and appeared in press photos quaffing cocktails, while at least one conducted very public flirtations with women – all of which offended Buddhist sensibilities.[131] It was a time when a leading politician could cheerfully invite the British 'to think of Ceylon as a little bit of England'. He promised that if war broke out, 'Ceylon will rival Australia as the first Dominion to rally to the side of the Mother Country.'[132]

This sort of thing helped to provoke scattered and uncoordinated appeals from Buddhist laymen and *bhikkhus* for indigenous ways and indigenous religion to receive greater support from the state, and even for Buddhism to be made the state religion. Bandaranaike gave these pleas his support, albeit intermittently and in ambiguous terms, but this did not entirely endear him to Buddhist interests, some of whom openly suggested that he was a self-interested latecomer to the faith.[133] He also had difficulty with another emerging interest group of like mind, the ayurvedic physicians. As Minister of Health, he was the one to whom they appealed for official recognition on a par with western-trained doctors. He made concessions to them, but in good conscience had to withhold a blanket sanction lest what one newspaper called the 'quacks and charlatans' among them gain undue approval. He was also in a position to direct resources to indigenous medicine, but this seemed to fuel still greater expectations and discontent with the minister rather than to win their affection.[134]

He therefore found himself, as part of a government whose anglicized character and conservatism offended him, to be a target of resentment from the very elements of society he most wished to cultivate. To make matters worse, by the beginning of 1951, he also found that his position within both the government and the ruling party had become

---

[131] *CDN*, 4 July 1947. In the matter of the flag see, for example, *CDN*, 5 and 20 January 1948.

[132] The speaker was Oliver Goonetilleke who was knighted five months later. In this connection, see, for example, references to broadcasts of the revels of 'liquor-sodden crowds' on New Year's Eve in *CDN*, 20 December 1949; and the complaints of a leading *bhikkhu* that D. S. Senanayake, who made his reputation in the temperance movement, was now facilitating drinking, *TC*, 9 January 1951. Also, *TC*, 22 and 26 January and 31 March 1951.

[133] *CDN*, 12 January and 2 March 1949, *TC*, 12 April 1951.

[134] *CDN*, 19 January 1949, 20 October to 4 November 1950 and 20 November 1950; *TC*, 6 and 7 March and 23 May 1951. Bandaranaike was a firm supporter of ayurvedic medicine in his public speeches, and he had some genuine sympathy for it since in his boyhood he had seen an ayurvedic doctor be of great help to his sister Anna. But he never committed more than a tiny portion of the Health Ministry budget to it. His main thrust was in expanding the rural hospitals scheme quite impressively and in preventive medicine, also to good effect. He scored a major success in the struggle against the causes of malaria which had ravaged the peasantry in the 1930s.

unenviable in the extreme. He was isolated and frequently affronted within the Cabinet, denied the resources to develop programmes at his ministries, and routinely reviled in every mass-circulation newspaper (all of which were controlled by the right). He also saw little hope of forcing a change in government policies. Three things appear to have kept him from resigning: his lifelong reluctance to break completely with those in authority over him, the grim prospects that awaited him in opposition, and the absence of any convincing alternative as a successor to the Prime Minister. Sir John Kotelawala was his most obvious rival, but his reputation (like Bandaranaike's) had suffered as a result of their frequent and very public clashes, and his image as a blustering bully made even his sympathizers hesitate to consider him as a future premier. Bandaranaike had – with good reason – a low opinion of Sir John's intellectual gifts, and he found it hard to imagine how others might take the man seriously.

He appears therefore to have been unsettled to learn in the first week of 1951 that another rival, Sir Oliver Goonetilleke, was returning from London to resume control of the Home Ministry. Sir Oliver was a Christian who had never faced the electorate (he sat in the indirectly elected Senate), but he was an immensely intelligent man with a near-legendary record both as an administrator and a political tactician. Within a few weeks, it was clear that Senanayake meant to invest him with major powers. He was given responsibilities that should by right have gone to Finance Minister Jayewardene, he began to act as the conduit for information from MPs to the premier, and it was widely put about that he would soon be named Deputy Prime Minister.[135]

That rumour was plainly intended to provoke Bandaranaike, but it produced little obvious reaction in the early weeks of 1951. He forced his angry Sinhala Maha Sabha supporters to restrain themselves and although he now sometimes referred to himself as the Sabha leader and spoke up for Buddhism, he was restrained almost to the point of timidity. By May, however, Goonetilleke had emerged as a potent figure, an important programme had been taken from Bandaranaike and given to a Cabinet rival, it was reliably rumoured that he would soon be stripped of one of his ministries and offshoots of the UNP Youth League appeared to be organizing within his constituency to oppose him at the next election.[136] Virtually everyone in the political establishment now saw his resignation as inevitable – everyone, that is, except the man himself.

During May, he allowed the Sabha's executive to hold a formal

[135] *TC*, 8 January, 20 March and 6 April 1951. For evidence of Bandaranaike's anxiety on this matter, see the comments on it that appeared in his Sinhala newspaper's first issue in June 1951. For more on Sir Oliver, see Jeffries, *OEG* and V. H. Gunasekera, *The Life and Times of Sir Oliver* (Kandy, 1981).

[136] Interviews with A. Ratnayake, Colombo, 9 September 1977 and Sir Senerat Gunawardena, Colombo, 18 September 1978. See also, *TC*, 4 April and 16 May 1951.

meeting for the first time in years, at which they made plans for an 'annual' conference in June. He then began a series of hard-hitting speeches advocating socio-economic reform and the uplift of vernacular languages and Buddhism. This provoked fierce attacks in the press, which accused him of 'Bandaranarchy' – of being at war with himself over whether to preach reform or parochialism – and of failing in his duty to resign if he was so displeased with the government. His 'inaction' as a minister was condemned, and his largely accurate complaint that fellow ministers had thwarted several of his best programmes was dismissed as a lame alibi. Things deteriorated further at a Sinhalese Merchants Chamber banquet, when Bandaranaike included in an introduction of the Prime Minister an attack on civil servants 'who like Oliver Twist, are always asking for more'. This was clearly a reference to the ambition of Sir Oliver Goonetilleke whose subtle political machinations had earned him this nickname. Senanayake responded by saying that he knew that it was inappropriate to address this Sinhalese audience in English, but that since Bandaranaike had set the example, he would follow.[137]

Bandaranaike's dismay with civil servants stemmed mainly from a bitter and very public struggle with his Director of Medical and Sanitary Services who in his view was guilty of insubordination on a grand scale. He believed that the Director had been put up to this by Senanayake and his associates. There is no direct evidence that this was true, but it is sufficiently consistent both with the style of Sir Oliver and with the concerted campaign to force Bandaranaike out of the government, that his suspicions probably had substance. Nor does it seem an accident that at the height of this controversy, the civil servant in question received from King George VI a high ceremonial office in the Order of St John.[138] This was almost certainly arranged through the intercession of leading Ceylonese, and no one was as well-connected in London as Sir Oliver. It could hardly have been plainer that Bandaranaike must resign, to retain what was left of his dignity.

Yet still he dithered. When the Sinhala Maha Sabha finally met in early June, it was widely expected to transform itself into an opposition party under a new name. Many members were impatient for this, but Bandaranaike was at pains to stress that he offered the UNP no threat or ultimatum, and that he still sought to change the ruling party from within by persuading it to accept the resolution passed by the Sabha.[139] This and his willingness over the next four weeks to try time and again for a

[137] *TC*, 1, 23–26 and 30 May 1951 and *CDN*, 23 February 1951.
[138] Interview with two of Bandaranaike's aides at that time, Colombo, 22 August and 3 September 1980. Also, *TC*, 25 May, 6 and 30 June 1951 and *CDN*, 4 July 1951.
[139] Interviews in Colombo with A. Ratnayake, 9 September 1977 and A. P. Jayasuriya, 21 August 1977. See also, *TC*, 31 May and 9 June 1951; and *Ceylon Hansard* (1951), cols. 1535–36.

compromise, despite no sign of encouragement from the ruling party, indicates how reluctant he was to take his leave.

At its conference, the Sabha passed resolutions advocating social reforms, greater attention to indigenous culture, language and medicine, aid to Sinhala-medium schoolteachers, and support for Buddhism and Buddhist institutions. They also indicated in more ambiguous terms a readiness to assist Tamil. When Bandaranaike tried to put these to a meeting of the UNP executive committee on 5 July, he was ruled out of order and told that the resolutions 'were intended to create disruption in the country'. He was further informed that party rules forbade *any* initiatives from the Sabha, despite several precedents to the contrary. He had not a single supporter on the UNP executive. Soon thereafter, the Sabha leadership met at his home and agreed that it was impossible to remain within the UNP 'except under humiliating circumstances that do not accord with elementary self-respect or decency'. Bandaranaike then astonished his colleagues by proposing that they accept the UNP ban on resolutions from the Sabha and that he propose them in his personal capacity. They, however, found their position within the ruling party to be so hopeless, and their leader's temporizing so excruciating, that they refused to agree.[140]

This, in one important sense, was an 'event'. It was the only occasion on which Bandaranaike's hand had ever been forced by subordinates within one of his political associations. Nor did such a thing recur until he became Prime Minister, and then only rarely. Leaders of Ceylon's major parties – that is, Bandaranaike and the pre-eminent figures in the UNP – maintained clear ascendancy over their political associations, allowing them little autonomy or corporate substance of the kind which India's Congress Party had long since developed. The leaders also possessed such exalted family and caste status that their subordinates could only consider asserting themselves in times of extreme emergency. But for the members of the Sinhala Maha Sabha executive, just such an emergency existed in July 1951.

Bandaranaike, with surpassing *naïveté*, nevertheless persuaded them that one more appeal for reconciliation should be sent to the Prime Minister. Predictably, it elicited yet another flat rejection. So on 12 July, amid great tumult in Parliament, Bandaranaike took his seat on the opposition benches. His carefully crafted speech, which was both grand and grandiose, was intended to show that his resignation was a matter of conscience and self-sacrifice rather than of political necessity. He began, significantly, by likening the decision to part ways with D. S. Senanayake

[140] *CDN*, 7 and 9 July 1951.

to his decision in 1926 to disregard his father's objections and enter politics. On that earlier occasion:

I was faced with a most difficult decision involving not only personal relations with those whom I would not wish to displease but also certain sacrifices and hardships for myself. It would seem that I am faced with a similar decision once again now.

He said that he had joined the government and the UNP to ensure stability in the initial phase of self-government, and to try to make the new regime more progressive and effective. He had succeeded in the first aim and failed in the second. There had, he claimed, been no change from the thinking of the last quarter-century of British rule. Frustration was mounting in the country, so despite his personal affection for many in the government, he felt that it was his duty to the people to go into opposition. After quoting Lincoln, Acton and Milton, he concluded by saying that by resigning, 'I have conquered myself.'[141]

The speech was pompous and self-serving, but it was also brave. We now know, of course, that his exit from the government eventually profited him greatly, but the outlook in 1951 appeared bleak. It was possible to discern signs of promise for a leader and a new party offering a mixture of moderate reform and Sinhalese Buddhist revivalism. The Marxist parties were so thoroughly fragmented and so unwilling to couch their message in terms that would appeal to the mass of rural dwellers who decided elections that they had little hope of taking power, but popular discontent had still yielded them enough votes to suggest that a pragmatic centre-left party might succeed. Free education, other social welfare programmes and institutions such as Rural Development Societies were catalysing voters' expectations and assertiveness, with which the stodgy UNP leadership seemed ill-equipped to cope. By 1951, enough disgruntlement had surfaced within village-level elites – school-teachers, ayurvedic physicians, *bhikkhus* and small-scale entrepreneurs – to give opposition parties hope that these groups might crystallize into an effective new base. Certain disadvantaged castes – notably the numerically powerful *Wahumpuras* and *Bathgamas* – were another potential source of support. And the list of possible successors to D. S. Senanayake was decidedly uninspiring. All of this was discernible in 1951 but, amid so much countervailing evidence, Bandaranaike and his close associates did not pay it much heed. Resignation seemed, to him and to them,[142] to promise little other than grim adversity, defeat and eventual obscurity.

---

[141] *CDN*, 13 July 1951.
[142] Interviews with a large number of Bandaranaike's associates in Colombo, 1977 and 1978.

7

OUTCAST, 1951–1956

When he crossed the floor, Bandaranaike expected to take a substantial number of MPs with him. He had never abandoned the fiction that his Sinhala Maha Sabha formed the largest component of the UNP. Several nominal and not-so-nominal Sabha members had been given attractive positions in the government, but Bandaranaike still believed in their overriding loyalty to him. He also knew that numerous government MPs were angry because promises of patronage to their constituencies had gone unfulfilled, yet on the day of his resignation not a soul followed him across the floor. When no one budged from the treasury benches over the next forty-eight hours, an alarm went out to Sabha members and rallies were hastily staged to protest the inertia of two of his closest associates: A. Ratnayake, Minister of Food, and A. P. Jayasuriya, Junior Minister of Posts. This had some effect and on the third day after his resignation, five members – including Jayasuriya and George R. de Silva, Junior Minister at Justice and Bandaranaike's cousin, but excluding Ratnayake – had joined him. A sixth crossed over two days later, but he had too few supporters to become the new Leader of the Opposition. The UNP, in the worst eventuality imaginable, still had a majority of five or six.[1]

However secure that may sound, it touched off a brief panic among leaders of the ruling party. They recalled two MPs from visits overseas and Independents were frantically promised no UNP opposition at the next election if they would remain neutral. Ratnayake was offered an early promotion to the Home Ministry, while R. S. S. Gunawardena, Bandaranaike's friend from boyhood, was promised the embassy in Rome. Money certainly changed hands in several cases. MPs were plied with gifts of up to Rs10,000 and wavering ministers drew as much as Rs30,000 plus offers of full campaign expenses at the next election. The security of the government's position was confirmed in the late July when the Second Reading of the budget was carried, fifty-three votes to

[1] *CDN*, 13, 16, 17 July 1951.

thirty-eight.[2] Bandaranaike tried to salvage some advantage from the situation by returning to the theme of renunciation, but his position was unenviable and he was mercilessly lampooned, as when one writer, concocting a fictitious Cabinet of leading politicians, named him as 'Minister of Supreme Sacrifice'.[3]

Once the dust had settled, ministers began to turn their minds to the possibility of an early election. It made sense to force Bandaranaike to the polls before his new party could develop itself and forge ties to other opposition groups, but the ruling party itself was far from ready for a major test. On paper, it had 500 branches and 50,000 members. Sir John Kotelawala's Youth Front – which included everything from altruistic students to gangs of street toughs – was said to contain a further 50,000. But these figures were greatly inflated and the party organization barely existed beyond the parliamentary group. There were not even any district committees functioning. Political spoils had been distributed too intermittently and irrationally, according to the whims of a few leading figures, to draw large numbers of influential followers in intermediate and local power centres into transactional ties with the party as the Congress in India was doing. Indiscipline was widespread. One MP (and possibly more) was even allowed to hold membership both in the UNP and in Bandaranaike's party for over three months.[4]

To fill in the time while they strengthened their organization, UNP leaders mounted a sustained, often vicious, campaign against Bandaranaike. His erstwhile aide Ratnayake was particularly cruel, claiming in Parliament that his former leader was so consumed by his desire for the premiership that he could not concentrate on anything else. Others saw Bandaranaike as the dupe of the leftists who 'had joined the enemies of the country'. They would use him 'to place Ceylon under Moscow's tyranny' and then discard him. He 'had lost all control of himself . . .'.[5] Senanayake, who had taken over the health and local administration portfolios, professed to find that Bandaranaike's slack handling of these departments had left them in a dreadful state. As we have seen, there may have been some substance in these criticisms. But the Prime Minister, who as head of Cabinet shared the responsibility for such maladministration, blatantly exaggerated. Actions such as Senanayake's move to abuses against mental patients were advertised as correctives to curb

[2] *CDN*, 13, 17, 20, 27 July; 10 August 1951; 4 March 1952. Also interviews in Colombo with A. Ratnayake, 29 August 1977 and a former UNP MP, 19 August 1978.
[3] The quotation is from *CDN*, 14 July 1951. See also TC, 7 August 1953.
[4] *CDN*, 3, 13 August, 1, 9 October, 14 December 1951; *TC*, 29 May 1952.
[5] *CDN*, 18, 24, 25 July, 10 August, 9, 17 October, 24 December 1951, 25 January 1952.

Bandaranaike's misdeeds when in reality they were extensions of his reforming policies. He also deserved a share of the credit for an historic achievement, the eradication of mosquitoes, which led to a sharp decline in deaths from malaria.[6] Many of Bandaranaike's supposed omissions had been caused by his Cabinet colleagues' refusal to grant him the power to implement his plans. When Senanayake took charge, funds which Bandaranaike had long sought were suddenly released to fund the abolition of charges for hospital admissions and new programmes for local government.[7]

Bandaranaike, who could outdo the entire UNP at verbal abuse, surprised nearly everyone – perhaps including himself – with his serenity in the face of these attacks. His criticisms of former colleagues were oddly muted and they were only a minor element in his speeches during the latter half of 1951. He seemed a changed man – less tense, less bitter – more at ease with himself and his new role. This was no pose. For the first time in a quarter century in politics, he was free of the authority of a superior, he was fully his own man. He was no longer subject to reprimands within the secrecy of Cabinet meetings or to furtive conspiracies among ministers and bureaucrats. Their attacks upon him intensified after his resignation, but the were much easier to bear. They were what an opposition leader expected. By resigning, Bandaranaike forced his opponents to play by the rules. They now had to tackle him in public debate, on the ground where his talents and resources could be deployed most effectively. His new-found serenity and the more gracious and mature attitude that it engendered, could only develop fully when he had achieved supreme authority in 1956. It then became one of the principal marks of his premiership – a source of both strength and weakness. But during these years in the wilderness the first signs of it gradually won him respect and eventually made him seem a reasonably tolerable candidate for national leadership.

Soon after crossing the floor, he announced that he would establish a new 'centre party' into which the Sinhala Maha Sabha would merge.[8] At first, he intended to name it the 'Social Democratic Party', but on

---

[6] J. Jiggins, Family and Caste in the Politics of the Sinhalese, 1947–1971, University of Ceylon, Peradeniya, doctoral thesis, 1973, p. 113. See also *Ceylon Hansard* (1951), col. 1523.

[7] See, for example, *TC*, 27 July, 13, 23, 31 August 1951.

[8] In this chapter, the emphasis will fall heavily upon communalism. But it should be stressed that even the man who, more than anyone else, saw Bandaranaike as shockingly wayward and opportunistic in this period, had to concede that he consistently supported reformist measures. In the Bernard Aluwihare Diaries, contrast 21 March 1954 with entries for 19, 28 February, 16 March 1954, 18, 19 October 1955.

3 August 1951, an informal meeting of about forty people at his home resolved to call it (in its English version) the Sri Lanka Freedom Party. The formal founding occurred a month later.[9]

Bandaranaike spent the latter half of 1951 and much of 1952 doggedly touring, speaking, meeting people throughout the Sinhalese majority areas – trying to generate a following in time for an early election. He concentrated his efforts in areas where neither the UNP nor the leftists were solidly entrenched. These were mainly inland areas, away from the belt running down the west coast where urbanization, Catholicism and the leftist parties had all left their mark. They included parts of the Central, Sabaragamuwa and Uva Provinces, but most especially the entire North Central Province. The six predominantly Sinhalese constituencies there were all on or close to the line which separated Sinhalese and Tamil majority areas, and along which communal sensitivities ran high. Bandaranaike's effort to relocate the modern urban clutter away from the ancient Buddhist sites at Anuradhapura had earned him a reputation as a defender of Sinhalese Buddhist interests. He also expected to include among his party's candidates the province's Land Commissioner, C. P. de Silva, who was a popular figure among thousands of Sinhalese colonists whom he had settled on land there.

When Bandaranaike took his case to Anuradhapura, he was greeted by the largest public meeting 'in modern times'.[10] He also turned to groups whose interests he had served, especially to local board members and Buddhist leaders. He found plenty of sympathy among both, but suspicions of past inconsistencies and pessimism about his prospects kept most of these people from joining the new party. His few significant successes in these first months came among chauvinistic Buddhist laymen whose singlemindedness had rendered them too extreme for the UNP, and among the leaders of national associations of local boards who had always been close to Bandaranaike. He also picked up a few prominent politicians and barristers – categories which partially overlapped – including three independent, vaguely socialist MPs. But all of these people had been active in national-level politics for some time. He knew that to make real headway, he had to mobilize people of influence in towns and villages – people who had remained aloof from local politics because the complacent, over-centralized and poorly-organized UNP had offered them no opportunities for substantive participation. He also

---

[9] *CDN*, 16, 23 July, 4 August 1951; *TC*, 24 August 1951. Also, 'Rules of the Sri Lanka Freedom Party' in fragment of a document lent by M. P. de Zoysa.
[10] *TC*, 21 September 1951. See also, *TC*, 28, 29 September, 8, 23 October, 15, 16 November, 19, 24 December 1951, 23 January 1952; *CDN*, 19 January 1952.

had to attract the support of economically and socially depressed but numerically strong caste groups that the UNP had ignored or intimidated in previous elections.[11]

His style of campaigning was appropriate to the task. He moved relentlessly from district to district in a battered old Austin that he was too frugal to replace, seeking out local notables in their towns and villages. He wore 'native dress' and spoke informally to small groups of ordinary folk in village clearings. His abhorrence of caste prejudice enabled him to mix freely and eat with people, regardless of their status. This was in striking contrast to the style of nearly all UNP leaders. Their touring usually consisted of visits in fleets of expensive cars to government rest houses where they held court, usually in western dress, for a limited number of local notables. These usually included large landowners, important headmen of the area and prominent *mudalalis* – rich entrepreneurs who were important because of their wealth, their status and their ability at elections to muster transport and, on occasion, thugs (usually from among their employees). All of these groups consisted mainly of members of high castes.

But if Bandaranaike's style was right, style alone was not enough and it was mainly upon style that he relied. Organization-building was clearly secondary to the display of the leader's good humour and rhetorical flair. A visit to an area usually entailed a public occasion where a local 'branch' of the SLFP was formed. But in most cases, these bodies expired soon after the meeting broke up. Most of those that survived did not send representatives to higher level units of the party or influence the selection of parliamentary candidates. Many of the new 'branches' withered for lack of communication from the party's central office which itself had a somewhat fugitive existence.[12] Fortunately for Bandaranaike, the ruling party was also in a wretched state. So although his tireless touring in late 1951 and early 1952 won his SLFP little more than wide publicity and a small number of promising recruits from outside the national political elite, and although he developed not so much an organization as a following, this did not place him at a severe disadvantage. All parties in Ceylon were highly over-centralized and those with organizations – namely the Marxist parties – were far too doctrinaire to gain mass support.

Bandaranaike was driven on in his relentless travels by the knowledge that a general election was not far off. His prolonged indecision over resignation had postponed the break until quite late in the life of the first

11 *TC*, 17 August, 10, 14, 19 September 1951.
12 Interview with A. P. Jayasuriya, Colombo, 6 September 1977; Aluwihare Diaries, 12, 14 April 1952; report by K. A. Albert Perera in Aluwihare Papers.

Parliament. At best he had only eighteen months – until January 1953 – to create a credible force. But he knew that he was unlikely to be given so much time. Within days of the founding of the SLFP, Sir John Kotelawala – Minister of Transport and Works and the UNP propaganda chief – had sent a circular to every car or truck owner in Ceylon urging them to offer their vehicles to the ruling party for an imminent general election. His action was, characteristically, highly improper since he had taken addresses from the Transport Commissioner's register of vehicles. Recipients of the circular included – in addition to Bandaranaike and other opposition politicians – thousands of government employees, which also made it unlawful. But this and the UNP's cultivation of village headmen in the hope of gaining their (illegal) assistance in the election campaign suggested an early dissolution of Parliament and a snap election.[13]

In response, Bandaranaike sought negotiations with left parties for electoral alliances, but found them, as usual, hopelessly divided. There was no more bitter feud in Ceylon politics than that between the two incarnations of the Lanka Sama Samaja Party (LSSP), which claimed to be Trotskyists. The Stalinist Communist Party added a further, truculent complication. Bandaranaike soon realized that he had better settle terms with the most promising of these, the LSSP group led by N. M. Perera. Negotiations were well under way in November 1951, but Perera's delusion – so typical of minor party leaders in Ceylon – about his party's prospects beyond its narrow base among trade unionists and his personal followers, prolonged discussions for several months.[14] Nevertheless, despite a mounting flood of government largesse – drugs, milk, land, housing, radios, books, food, etc. – the ruling party had encountered such difficulty in constructing anew an electoral organization that, by March of 1952, it seemed possible that Parliament would be allowed to run for a further year.[15]

On the 21st of that month, D. S. Senanayake went for his usual morning ride on Galle Face Green. At 6.50 a.m., his horse made one slow pass along the sea front, then turned and moved into a fast canter. The Prime Minister then appeared to lose control – as a result of a stroke it was later believed – and slipped slowly from the saddle. He somersaulted forward several times and landed face down, unconscious and bleeding from the nose. He was rushed to hospital where he regained consciousness only briefly. He died the following afternoon.[16] The ceremonies leading to

[13] *TC*, 6, 7, 18–20 September 1951. In two weeks, 4,000 people offered the UNP their cars.
[14] *TC*, 2 November 1951, 1, 22 February 1952.
[15] *TC*, 14, 27 December 1951, 19, 25 January, 27 February and 7 March 1952.
[16] *TC*, 21, 22 March 1952; H. A. J. Hulugalle, *The Life and Times of Don Stephen Senanayake* (Colombo, 1974), p. 252

burial bespoke the respect and affection for Senanayake which existed throughout the political elite and the island at large. As the body lay in state in the Prime Minister's residence over half a million people queued, somtimes for hours, to pay their respects. When the coffin was brought to Parliament for a last farewell, opposition MPs carried it up the long staircase into the building, with Bandaranaike leading the way. The funeral procession was observed by nearly a tenth of the island's population.[17] But before Parliament could reconvene to offer eulogies, a successor had to be chosen.

At first glance, the leading candidate appeared to be Sir John Kotelawala who had held ministerial rank since 1936. He was deputy leader of the UNP, had done more organizational work for the party than any other minister and personally controlled the party's million rupee fund. He had succeeded Bandaranaike as Leader of the House and was the nephew of the late Prime Minister, although his boyish impulsiveness had often led him into situations which seemed embarrassing to everyone but himself. The only other plausible candidate, D. S. Senanayake's son Dudley, was far younger and had been in the Cabinet for less than five years. He had preceded that with four years of energetic work in the Ceylon National Congress, but it had been work that had alienated his father somewhat. He had the closest family tie of course, and had held the crucial portfolio of Agriculture and Lands which his father had passed on to him – a decision which had caused a 'furore' given Dudley's inexperience.[18] But on more than one occasion he had shown an odd diffidence, even a melancholy aversion to politics. In purely objective terms, another minister – J. R. Jayewardene – a more distant relative in the Senanayake clan, might have been judged the best man for the job. He had an acute mind and a well-deserved reputation for hard, meticulous work as a political strategist and Minister of Finance. But his aggressive instinct for the jugular in political quarrels made him seem an unlikely candidate for the role of statesman. Unlike his rivals, he had long urged official status for Sinhala and had worn 'native dress' – and unlike Bandaranaike, he wore it on all occasions – but in the UNP of 1952, these were not assets. He was not considered for the succession.

In the event, the quality of the candidates had little bearing on events. D. S. Senanayake, who had known for some time that a severe heart condition threatened an early demise, had arranged things in advance. He had informed the Governor-General Lord Soulbury that in the event of his death, he preferred that his son Dudley be called to form the next

[17] *TC*, 24 March, 20 May 1952.   [18] *CDN*, 13 October 1947.

government. Soulbury owed his high office to Senanayake[19] and was not above bending his own impartiality. When the Prime Minister's accident occurred, Soulbury was in England on holiday, but he had left instructions with the Chief Justice who was acting in his stead to summon him at once if the premiership fell vacant. It took him five days to reach Colombo. Most people still expected that Sir John would be called. Soulbury's plane landed at midday on 26 March and he drove straight to Queens House. After ninety minutes in which he held no consultations of any substance with any legislator, Dudley Senanayake arrived to be invited, at forty-one, to become the youngest Prime Minister in the Commonwealth. Soulbury's debt to D. S. Senanayake had been discharged.[20]

For several days, Sir John sulked on his estate while the conservative press barons strained to justify the choice. They recalled that the sons of Gladstone, Salisbury, Lloyd George and Ramsay MacDonald had held ministerial posts, omitting to mention that none had been premiers. The public belief that Dudley was a reluctant politician was met with pieties. He had thrown off his diffidence because he 'realised his mission in life was to save country-folk from false doctrines and to restore them the means of a decent life'. Soulbury became a hero who had saved Ceylon from the machinations and parochial sentiments within Parliament. He 'knew what was going on behind the scenes, but he also knew what the country wanted and he did the correct thing'.[21] Within a few days, Sir John was once again attending meetings in an unchanged Cabinet as Leader of the House. The succession had passed off smoothly.

Speculation immediately began about an early election, particularly in view of the 'continuous and rapid deterioration' in the price of tea over several weeks. Coconut prices were also seriously depressed, rubber prices had fallen slightly and the island's economy was faced with 'a serious crisis' which would soon hit the common man.[22] To prevent the opposition from gearing up their electoral machinery, UNP leaders denied election rumours and announced that the obliging Soulbury would resume his holiday on 2 April. The opposition relaxed somewhat.

[19] Soulbury acknowledged these things, albeit rather coyly. See Hulugalle, *The Life*, pp. 253 and 262. Several sources close to D. S. Senanayake indicate that the understanding was quite clear cut.

[20] See Sir John's letter to Soulbury concerning the breach of British parliamentary convention, to which the Governor-General never responded. J. L. Kotelawala, *An Asian Prime Minister's Story* (London, 1956), pp. 79–80. Bandaranaike was close to the mark when he described this as 'the culmination of a long, shabby and discreditable intrigue' in SLFP, *Annual Conference Souvenir 1953* (Colombo, 1953), p. 12.

[21] *TC*, 24, 27, 28 March 1952; *CDN*, 27, 28 March 1952.

[22] *TC*, 3, 4 April 1952. See also 28 March 1952.

The Governor-General would hardly leave the island if Parliament were soon to be dissolved. And yet, within a few days, it became clear that he had done precisely that, as Dudley Senanayake called for dissolution and a general election eight weeks later at the end of May 1952.

The opposition found it impossible to unite against the UNP, and remained divided in two loose alliances – the Communists together with one LSSP faction, and Bandaranaike's SLFP together with the other. Conflict between these two opposition blocs was constant, and *within* each bloc unity proved impossible to maintain. This was particularly true of Bandaranaike's own alliance. A minority faction within the NLSSP, to which he was linked, was deeply suspicious of him and complained openly that he was 'notorious for his vacillation and slippery tactics'.[23] Despite announcements as early as February that a common slate of candidates had been agreed, he had to hold at least three meetings with his allies after the election had been called, and even then failed to avoid contests with his supposed allies in nearly a dozen seats. Almost half of these were lost to the UNP as a result, but the island-wide effect of making the UNP seem the only clear-cut, cohesive alternative probably cost the opposition even more dearly.

The ruling party fought a very curious campaign. Almost nothing was said at UNP rallies or in pro-UNP newspapers about the government's achievements in the four years since independence. When comments were made, they tended to be apologetic as when the premier claimed that the government could 'not undo in four years what the foreigner had done in 450 years. It should therefore be given more time.'[24] Ministers found that people's expectations of the government had been pitched so high that crowds were often unenthusiastic even about the government's more significant accomplishments. This pattern of high expectations and inevitable disillusionment has recurred at every subsequent election.[25] But in 1952, the ruling party overcame it, thanks to intimidation, a near-monopoly of buses, its illegal use of the resources of state,[26] the divisions

---

[23] *TC*, 5, 8, 9, 19 May 1952; *CDN*, 14 May 1952. Bandaranaike's alliance also included, in theory more than in practice, the tiny non-Marxist Republican Party.

[24] *TC*, 9 May 1951. See also 20 May 1951.

[25] This trend was clear even before D. S. Senanayake's death. See, for example, *TC*, 20 May 1952. Interviews with two prominent UNP strategists of the day, Colombo, 17 August and 11 September 1978. For a discussion of the cycle of expectation and disillusionment at post-1952 elections, see J. Manor, 'The Failure of Political Integration in Sri Lanka', *Journal of Commonwealth and Comparative Politics*, xvii, 1 (March, 1979), pp. 21–46.

[26] In addition to its mobilization of headmen and more senior government employees, large quantities of UNP election leaflets were clearly printed at the 'Government Press'. See the packet marked 'Government Publications' in General Box I for 1947, 1952 and 1956 in the Election Literature Collection, University Library, Peradeniya.

in the opposition and three successful campaign themes: emotional references to the memory of their fallen leader, severe personal attacks on Bandaranaike and the red scare. The last of these, which was presented with surpassing crudity, dominated the campaign.

In analysing this election, it is as important to notice who did *not* participate as who did. Several interest groups that took an aggressive part in the crucial election campaign against the UNP four years later had not yet crystallized in 1952. Members of these groups also regarded the possibility of an opposition victory as so remote that they stuck to their hope that the UNP would meet their needs. The rural poor (including depressed caste groups), ayurvedic physicians, vernacular teachers, the officers and employees of local boards and others found precious little encouragement in the government's policies, and even found themselves sneered at and treated as figures of fun by UNP leaders and their allies in the press.[27] Champions of a Buddhist revival – both laymen and many, mainly younger, members of the clergy who were so essential to Bandaranaike four years later – also felt frustrated and were made the butt of establishment jokes. The jokes were usually aimed at 'religion', not at Buddhism and certainly not at the revered Buddhist clergy – but since Buddhism was the only resurgent religion, the message was clear.[28] A limited number of *bhikkhus* (monks) were active in the 1952 campaign – a development which caused surprise and comment because it breached their accepted code of conduct – but they tended to work for the insignificant Republican Party or, less often, for the UNP. The ruling party also had the aid of the Roman Catholic hierarchy which reminded the faithful that it was a sin to support Marxist parties or their allies, including the SLFP.[29]

For UNP leaders, the result was an improvement over their position after the 1947 election and before the dissolution of Parliament, when they had held forty-two seats. Even without the backing of six members to be nominated, they had a majority of thirteen in the scarcely imaginable event that the motley opposition would combine against them. The Tamil Congress, which had won four seats, was allied to the ruling party, and gave it an even safer margin. And yet beneath their euphoria at the prospect of five secure years in power, the more discerning among them

[27] For the sneers see, for example *TC*, 5 February, 19 March, 12 April 1952. For signs of frustration and some crystallization among these groups see, for example *CDN*, 1 August 1951, 8, 15 January 1952; *TC*, 19 September 1951, 23 January, 2, 6, 12, 26 February, 25 May 1962.

[28] See *TC*, 19 March 1952. Also, interviews with two journalists and one politician, Colombo, 6 August 1977, 15 and 21 August 1978.

[29] See *TC*, 14 December 1951 and 17 May 1952. Also interviews in Colombo with one Buddhist and one Roman Catholic priest, 8 and 16 September 1980.

Table 7.1. Results of the 1952 general election

Party	Seats won	% of seats won	Votes	% of Votes
United National Party	54	56.8	1,026,005	44.1
Sri Lanka Freedom Party	9	9.5	361,250	15.5
Nava Lanka Sama Samaja Party	9	9.5	305,133	13.1
Communist Party/Lanka Sama Samaja Party	4	4.2	134,528	5.8
Tamil Congress	4	4.2	64,512	2.8
Federal Party	2	2.1	45,331	1.9
Labour Party	1	1.1	27,096	1.2
Republican Party	1	1.1	33,001	1.4
Buddhist Republican Party	0	0	3,987	0.2
Independents	11	11.6	326,783	14.0
Total	95	100.1	2,327,626	100.0

Source: G. P. S. H. de Silva, *A Statistical Survey of Elections to the Legislatures of Sri Lanka, 1911–1977* (Colombo, 1979).

might have felt faint misgivings.[30] The improvement in the UNP's share of the popular vote, from 39.8 per cent to 44.1 per cent was pleasing, but after five reasonably prosperous years in power without a single major opposition party and with the advantage of the nation's grief for D. S. Senanayake, they might have hoped for a popular majority. A closer look at the result shows that, as votes for Independents declined, other parties garnered 9.80 per cent more of the total vote than in 1947, which was more than double the gains for the UNP (4.27 per cent). Five of the UNP's victories had a distinctly hollow ring about them, coming as they did from the tiny Kandyan constituencies in which Indians and numerous others had been disenfranchised. MPs from these places found themselves representing electorates of between 2,912 and 9,279, while most of their colleagues represented many times those numbers. Nor could the UNP take comfort from the emergence of a non-Marxist opposition party, Bandaranaike's SLFP, as the second largest vote-getter, with its base among rural electors who held the key to victory in a country where the overwhelming majority lived in villages.

The result offered little cheer for the parties of the left. In a time when parties in general were making substantial gains in votes at the expense of Independents, the Marxist parties' share had actually *declined* from 20.54 per cent in 1947 to 18.89 per cent in 1952.[31] So had their share of the seats, from eighteen to thirteen. Nor could they blame this loss entirely upon contests between leftist or opposition parties, since they lost most of their seats in straight fights with the UNP. They had been thrust further back upon the hard core of their support among urban and semi-urban trade unionists in the Western and Southern Provinces and among the personal and family followings which a few leftist leaders had developed in and near their constituencies.

Bandaranaike's SLFP was disappointed that its total of seats had merely remained constant, but for a party without organizational substance or financial resources, that had been in existence for only ten months – a party very heavily dependent on the industry and attraction of its leader – the result was far from disastrous. It had polled a respectable if unspectacular 15.52 per cent of the popular vote. If it had lost several of its former seats to the UNP, it had also ousted five UNP incumbents. The voters' tendency to turn against incumbents – a pattern that intensified in

---

[30] Indeed, J. R. Jayewardene, the most acute analyst among UNP leaders, clearly felt them. See UNP, 'Report of the Special Committee on Party Reform and Reorganization', 1960, pp. 3–4 in file 173, J. R. Jayewardene Papers, Presidential Archive, Colombo.

[31] The disenfranchisement of Indians who lived in Sabaragamuwa Province explained part of this, but only a tiny part.

later elections – boded well for the future of a young opposition party. The variety of seats in which it had done well was also encouraging. If it had less success than expected in the North Central Province where only the former Land Commissioner, C. P. de Silva, won at Polonnaruwa, it could link that to its success at holding nearby Dambulla in the northern part of the Central Province. These seats were won by attracting some high caste (*Goyigama*) votes along with substantial backing from two other important groups. The first were colonists who had come from other parts of the island – mainly Kandyans and C. P. de Silva's fellow *Salagamas* from the coastal belt – to settle on lands in this area. The second were the members of less exalted castes who saw the UNP as a *Goyigama* party and voted in greater numbers than ever,[32] as the increase in participation from 61.3 per cent in 1947 to 74.0 per cent in 1952 suggests. Their growing involvement was explained partly by their increasing assertiveness and awareness of national politics, and partly by a modest decrease in the use of intimidation by UNP leaders who were sometimes too confident to bother.[33]

The support of members of underprivileged castes was also crucial in SLFP victories over UNP incumbents in three other Central Province seats which demonstrated that the UNP was vulnerable in Kandyan areas. Muslim votes aided the SLFP in two of these constituencies and helped to elect the party's lone Muslim candidate in one. This lent credence to the SLFP claim to be more than a Sinhalese Buddhist party,[34] as did its hair's breadth failure (by fifty-four votes) to oust the incumbent at Chilaw. It fielded a candidate of the locally powerful Roman Catholic community in this constituency on the coast north of Colombo. Elsewhere in the low country, SLFP men defeated the UNP incumbents at Gampaha, just north-east of Colombo near Bandaranaike's own constituency, and well to the south in Baddegama near Galle where non-*Goyigama* votes were again crucial. These successes were achieved despite the huge advantage which the UNP enjoyed in its access to cars, fleets of buses, thugs, money and illegal but widespread assistance from headmen and government officials. This array of SLFP victories in widely varied areas and based on

---

[32] Interviews with leaders of depressed castes from the area, in Kandy and Matale, 2 and 4 September 1980, and with UNP campaign organizers, Colombo, 12 and 16 September 1980.

[33] But see, *CDN*, 11, 17, 19–20 and 27 June, 8, 28 July, 8 August 1952 and *TC* 21 October 1952; and Bernard Aluwihare Diaries, University of Peradeniya Library, 15–18 May 1952.

[34] Almost from the formation of the SLFP, a Tamil (A. C. Nadarajah), a Muslim (Badiudin Mahmud), and a Sinhalese Roman Catholic (J. C. Munasinha) had figured prominently in it. Nadarajah resigned in 1955 when Bandaranaike decided to support Sinhala as the only official language. Interviews in Colombo with A. C. Nadarajah, 9 September 1977 and Badiudin Mahmud, 1 September 1977.

support from divergent groups was a promising beginning, even if they still had to pin their hopes for ultimate victory upon future errors by a strengthened UNP.

The SLFP's performance in the election enabled Bandaranaike to be chosen Leader of the Opposition when Parliament convened. But despite this new responsibility, the period between mid-1952 and mid-1955 was one of the quietest periods of his adult life. In some ways it was enjoyable. He had time for tennis with other members of the Bandaranaike–Obeyesekere clan, for his greyhounds and for his family which now included a son, Anura, in addition to his daughters, Chandrika and Sunethra. There was also time for reading, and he began to fashion new adventures for his Sinhalese Sherlock Holmes, John Ratsinghe.

And yet his enjoyment at being free of the burden of official papers and the authority of a superior was heavily outweighed by a growing frustration over the loss of influence and ministerial status, and his sense of isolation as the daily stream of petitioners dried up and large crowds no longer gathered to hear him speak. It was profoundly galling to see men whom he regarded as his inferiors enjoying the power and, even more crucially, the adulation which attended high office. He seemed to perceptive observers to withdraw into himself, to brood, to grow tense and more inclined to lose his composure over petty things. It was in this period that he made a mildly unseemly scene before the family when a cousin beat him at tennis. At a Kennel Club show, he embarrassed himself by turning angrily on a boy who was competing against him. His own detective writing from this period dwells far more than the earlier stories upon horror, violence and the grotesque – the sort of images that appealed to him at another low point, in his early days at Oxford.[35] It was a bad time and he needed all of the grim forbearance that he had learned as a child under his tutor Radford, as a student facing racial prejudice at Oxford and as a leader-in-waiting for more than two decades in politics to survive it.

The new government – with numerous 'Independent' MPs (many of whom had failed to gain UNP tickets and had stood for election anyway) joining it and with nominated MPs and members of allied parties supporting it – soon commanded seventy votes in a House of ninety-nine,[36] and was obviously well-entrenched for the lifetime of Parliament.

[35] This is based on interviews with numerous relatives and close associates of Bandaranaike. Images of horror are to be found in 'The Horror of Mahahena', written at this time and first published in *The Times of Ceylon Annual 1956*, Colombo, 1956.

[36] *CDN*, 7 June 1952. On rejected UNP candidates standing as Independents see UNP, *Annual Report of the Hon. The General Secretary, 1951–52*, p. 16 in file 161-2, J. R. Jayewardene Papers, Presidential Archive, Colombo.

As a result, Bandaranaike cut back drastically on political work outside
Parliament and, since he had always outweighed the importance of his
party's flimsy organization, the press was soon complaining that 'Very
little is heard from the Sri Lanka Freedom Party.' Its decline was matched
by all opposition groups which seemed mere 'election parties' that faded
rapidly after polling day.[37] Even within Parliament, he played only a
minor role. In September 1952, he was granted six months leave of
absence from the House and although he did not fully take it, his
appearances were less frequent and uncharacteristically restrained.

1952 and early 1953 saw a modest upsurge in pressure from groups
bearing grievances against the island's westernized elite. These groups
had never been entirely absent from public life. Soon after independence
D. S. Senanayake had faced and spurned demands from poorly organized
vernacular teachers, local board members and others to revive Buddhism
and rescue the Sinhala language and the Sinhalese 'race' from 'peril'.[38] But
it was not until 1953 that this set of issues began to find their way onto the
centre of the political stage.[39] They emerged as semi-coherent pleas from
a motley array of different interest groups which, taken individually, were
poorly organized and, taken collectively, were only very loosely linked to
one another. Buddhist teachers and parents complained of the threat of
Christian schools to their children's beliefs and sought government
funds. Practitioners of indigenous medicine, though divided over the use
of techniques from western medicine, sought higher status and government patronage. Mainly Buddhist campaigns against drink, gambling and
animal slaughter surfaced in several parts of Ceylon but in this period
remained rather localized and unconnected with one another. An urban
housing shortage generated protests, while clerks and minor public
employees began to come together and press for concessions.[40]

The greatest pressure developed behind efforts to extend the official
use of the island's indigenous languages. There was a widespread, rather
unfocused popular discontent over the exclusive use of English in most
banks, in trials in district and higher courts, and the need to communicate
with most government offices including many local boards and police
agencies through the language of the ex-colonial power. These sentiments gained their clearest expression from teachers in vernacular-
medium schools who sought parity in status and salaries with those in

[37] *TC*, 22 August 1952.
[38] Interview by Michael Roberts with Sir Richard Aluwihare, Mss. Ind. Ocn. S. 174, Rhodes House, Oxford.
[39] *Dinamina* and *CDN*, November 1952 to February 1953. Even the *Times of Ceylon* which was resolutely out of touch with non-English speakers, began to take notice of this groundswell in this period.
[40] *TC*, 6 February 1952, 3, 31 January, 3, 25 February, 2, 28 March, 6, 15 April 1953.

English schools, and from small numbers of younger Buddhist monks.[41] But these groups were prevented from becoming a coherent force by one great source of confusion. Some, indeed most at this time, sought to promote the use of both Sinhala and Tamil rather than English, but many Sinhalese who wanted their language to gain at the expense of English also regarded the Tamil minority and its language with suspicion.[42]

Public protests from groups other than the opposition parties were something new to the UNP government and, after a comfortable election victory, it was in no mood to yield to them. Most of these pressure groups got little more than a polite hearing, if that. On the language issue, ministers pointed to the creation in mid-1952 of an Official Languages Department, to implement the report of a Select Committee on National Languages which had called, fully four years before, for advance towards official status for Tamil and Sinhala. But this Department was poorly funded and did little more than coordinate the work of translators. In a classic delaying tactic, yet another commission was tardily appointed to investigate the problems attending a language changeover. Fears about the government's sincerity were fuelled by events such as Sir John Kotelawala's tactless speech in 1952 before Buddhist monks who were sympathetic to wider vernacular use. In Ceylon the changeover from English would be gradual, he said, lest they repeat the mistakes of Thailand where 'many educated persons were thrown out of employment with the undesirables (coming) in(to) power . . .'. Students from vernacular-medium schools faced daunting barriers in university admissions and employment. Even in Parliament, members wishing to speak in the vernaculars had, until mid-1953, to give prior notice to the Speaker. They faced stricter time limits than when they used English and had no facilities for translation.[43]

Bandaranaike attempted to give a lead to this groundswell but without much success. The varied interests voicing complaints were too disparate to be led. In 1953, people had usually organized themselves only within their own locality and lacked ties to people with similar grievances in other areas. Alliances with other embryonic interest groups who shared their exasperation with the government were even rarer. Bandaranaike's links to potential leaders of this array of protests, most especially to prominent Buddhist monks, were improving but still far from satisfactory.[44]

[41] *TC*, 12 February, 18, 24 July 1952, 2, 5 January, 9 February, 2, 13, 19, 31 March, 23 May 1953.
[42] *TC*, 12, 26 February, 12 April, 28 June, 26 July, 29 August 1952, 9 January, 2 February, 2 March, 4, 20 May, 27 July 1953.
[43] The Kotelawala quotation is from *TC*, 5 February 1952. See also *CDN*, 6 June 1952; *TC*, 2, 30 July, 19 August 1952, 27 January, 10, 31 March, 24 May, 1 August 1953.
[44] *TC*, 1 December 1952, 13 January, 10 February, 29 March, 6, 15 April, 11 May 1953.

In mid-1953, the clamour over language, religion and other issues was overtaken by another controversy – a serious assault on the ruling party. The issue that triggered it was the price of rice, but the nub of the matter was not so much the issue itself as the form of protest used to dramatize it and the Prime Minister's inability to cope. Until 1952 Ceylon's economic position had been reasonably comfortable and the government had been able to please diverse interest groups. Private firms, in which foreigners still played a predominant role, were not burdened with heavy corporate taxes. Nor were income and sales taxes a major burden for middle-class Ceylonese. Prices for crucial exports stayed high enough to allow the government to sustain significant social welfare programmes, partly through deficit financing. The most costly of these were the system of free education and a subsidy on rice, the main staple in the Ceylonese diet. In 1952, however, world prices fell and they fell faster on key exports than on rice which was imported in huge quantities. The island's external assets declined by Rs 350m in 1952, a fall of nearly 30 per cent, and in the early months of 1953 the trend accelerated alarmingly. In March alone, assets fell by Rs 112m. Much of the problem was of the government's own making. Its so-called six-year 'plan', which was accurately described as 'farcical', earned the contempt of everyone from the World Bank and British planters to the Trotskyists. It involved almost no change of procedure from pre-independence times, set no spending priorities and brought no coordination between government departments. It failed even to promote private enterprise which ministers favoured. The government was also lax in the collection of taxes so that tax arrears in early 1953 equalled the island's total revenue in the last year before the war. By July 1953 the mounting deficit presented UNP leaders with a stark choice between imposing heavy taxation on the middle class and the corporate sector or cutting expenditure. They chose the latter and their axe fell heavily on the rice subsidy which was running at Rs 150m per year. They had left it too late to apply it gradually and the cut, plus extensive hoarding, nearly trebled the price of rice within a matter of weeks.[45]

The decision was hugely unpopular. Opposition parties mounted a joint protest meeting on Galle Face Green with Bandaranaike presiding and drew 200,000 people, one of the largest crowds ever assembled in the island. Bandaranaike sought to organize a united protest campaign and to link the upsurge of anger to the language issue, but he soon lost the initiative to the leftists. They called for a *hartal*, a general strike attended by a closure of all businesses, which was the first serious attempt in Ceylon's

[45] *TC*, 2–15 April, 18 May, 8, 16, 31 July 1953. 'Ceylon: An Economic Survey', *The Economist*, 14 February 1953, pp. 453–60.

history of organized extra-parliamentary action aimed at coercing the legislature. It was bound to lead both the authorities and the protesters into uncharted waters, and it posed a problem for Bandaranaike. His cooperation with the leftists in Parliament had inspired constant UNP attacks on him as a revolutionist and a dupe of the reds. Support for the *hartal* would have lent credence to the smear, so he held back, hoping to establish himself in the public mind as a moderate alternative to the ruling party.

Leftist mythology paints the August *hartal* as a unified, broadly popular movement which shook the foundations of UNP rule.[46] There is little substance in this. It was a rather muddled affair of limited scale and the UNP was shaken less by the *hartal* itself than by their own mishandling of it. No event involving the left parties was complete without a ritual squabble among them[47] and this time it arose over an issue of surpassing banality, the date of the *hartal*. Trade unionists and opposition groups lent uneven support and although protests reached a fierce pitch in Colombo and the leftist strongholds along the coast southward toward Galle, they were far more restrained elsewhere. The government invited trouble when it overdramatized the event in the days preceding it by issuing threats and arranging for provocative headlines like 'Enough Tear Gas' to appear in friendly newspapers. Having gone to the extent of declaring a state of emergency in the Western and Southern Provinces on 12 August, the day of the *hartal*, they failed to deploy adequate security forces in potential trouble spots. As a result, police were often badly outnumbered by angry crowds. They behaved contemptuously and brutally towards people in many areas and when trouble ensued, they quickly became alarmed and opened fire repeatedly. By conservative official estimates, on 12 and 13 August, 21 people were killed, 175 were seriously injured, over 380 were arrested and 40 police were hurt. Substantial damage resulted from arson, often in public buildings, and from attacks upon buses and rail lines.[48]

Leftist leaders, recognizing that they had forced the government into a miscalculation, called for a return to normality after the first day of action. Within a few days, disruptions had dwindled into insignificance, but the main reverberation from the *hartal* was still to come. The first sign of this came on 18 August when the Prime Minister appeared in Parliament looking distraught and, after moving an amendment, 'felt faintish' and retired to his room. It was said that he had missed breakfast, but in the

[46] See, for example, Colvin R. de Silva, *Hartal!* (Colombo, 1953).
[47] See the material presented in chapter 6.
[48] *CDN*, *TC* and *Dinamina*, all 24 July to 17 August 1953. Interview with J. R. Jayewardene, Colombo, 11 September 1978.

days that followed he continued to give the impression of a man badly
shaken by events. His discomfort increased as Bandaranaike and the
eminent lawyer, S. Nadesan, led devastating assaults in the two chambers
on the government's conduct during the *hartal* and on the draconian
public security legislation which it had rushed through Parliament.
Bandaranaike's delivery, which was unusually careful and restrained,
carried immense authority. He had been to the scene of a police firing in
his own constituency during the *hartal* and was clearly suppressing his
fury. He used the incident to demonstrate the government's 'compla-
cence and incompetence' before the troubles and its 'panicky measures'
during and after them. He detailed quite accurately a 'reign of terror' that
police had visited upon people since the firing, to intimidate witnesses
against them. Villagers were threatened and 'mercilessly beaten'. They
'had to be protected from the violence and hooliganism of the
authorities'.

The Prime Minister's response was limp and unconvincing. He had
been so traumatized by the crisis that a chronic stomach ailment which
was brought on by stress returned with a vengeance. He lost weight
alarmingly. His emotional state was such that he experienced physical
difficulty in signing emergency orders. On 20 August, he was plunged
further into depression when overzealous police fired on a taxi and killed
no less than the retired Chief Clerk to the old State Council. In the last ten
days of August, he was seldom seen in public. Rumours spread that he
was close to an emotional breakdown and UNP leaders were soon
jockeying for position should a succession struggle arise. The premier
appeared, clearly with some difficulty, for a no confidence debate at the
beginning of September, only to find the opposition leader in crackling
form once again. Bandaranaike's litany of the government's failures was
brilliantly presented. When he was criticized for neither endorsing nor
condemning the *hartal* and its violence, he turned the attack against the
government's own violence and stunned the House by recalling that his
own constituents had been 'shot down like dogs'.[49]

The Prime Minister weathered the debate and announced a national
tour to revive UNP confidence, but stories persisted that he was sick and
that he found the burdens of office loathsome. It became increasingly
apparent that a 'bitter rivalry' was developing over the succession
between Sir John Kotelawala and J. R. Jayewardene. In the third week of
September, Dudley Senanayake decided to resign but then relented. He
announced that he would have two weeks rest and quiet at Nuwara Eliya
while Sir John managed Cabinet affairs. On 11 October, he returned to

---

[49] *TC*, 18–19 August; 1 September 1953. T. D. S. A. Dissanayake, *Dudley Senanayake of Sri
Lanka* (Colombo, 1975), pp. 31–33.

Colombo for talks with the Governor-General on his future, but during the discussion fell violently ill once again. He resigned the following day and soon left for a holiday in South India where he was reported to be reading Dale Carnegie's *How to Stop Worrying and Start Living*. He was succeeded by his first cousin, Sir John Kotelawala.[50]

Dudley Senanayake's moodiness and his gentle, hesitant manner which bespoke a certain vulnerability endeared him to many people in Ceylon, but it equipped him badly for national leadership. He was too frail emotionally, in this first spell as premier at least, to withstand the stresses of office. In common with many members of the island's political elite, he held an oddly paradoxical view of the mass of his countrymen. On one hand, he avoided any change in the highly over-centralized character of the political system and opposed most programmes which made substantial concessions to disadvantaged groups. He was also prepared to countenance the systematic intimidation of those groups at election time. On the other hand, he was paternalistic enough to support some social welfare measures such as universal education and subsidies on food. This paternalism bred an occasional soft-heartedness which in this instance appears to have led Dudley Senanayake to err on the side of laxity in his preparations for the *hartal*. As a result situations arose that inspired brutality from the police. This traumatized Senanayake and drove him into bouts of severe melancholy. It left his party looking distinctly shaky and opened the way for a successor who, in his very different way, was also deeply unsuited to the task and the time.

The cliché most often used to describe Sir John Kotelawala in this period – a cliché that he relished and cultivated – held that he was the 'strong man' of Ceylon. This phrase had two meanings. The first was that of the tough, virile man about town. Sir John initially attracted attention in politics by threatening to 'thrash' any British planter who 'tries any nonsense' during the 1931 election campaign, and he claimed to have won numerous fist fights over the years. He was also known as 'Asia's foremost play-boy politician', the card-playing two-fisted drinker in the white dinner jacket with an eye for the ladies. This had a certain appeal among a limited constituency of westernized urban dwellers. At public appearances in the capital, he was often greeted by 'a glitter-group of faded beauties' known as the 'purple brigade' from their habit of wearing saris of his favourite colour.[51] His carefree ways led him grinning onto page one in a series of bizarre press photographs with the likes of Indian film starlets (popularly viewed as women of dubious repute), a nightclub

[50] *TC*, 21–28 September, 2, 13, 27 October 1953. Dissanayake, *ibid.*, p. 33.
[51] D. B. Dhanapala, *Among Those Present* (Colombo, 1962), pp. 42–45, 49 and 58. Even today, aging upper-middle-class ladies still bear spontaneous witness to his sex appeal.

entertainer known as 'the telepathic Jason' and a professional wrestler called 'The Hooded Terror'. Even a sympathetic writer noted that the 'brawn' and 'courage' of this 'political King Kong' was accompanied by a penchant for 'strutting' and 'jutting out his chest', by 'a colossal vanity' and 'simplicity' that led him to use 'banned words' and the 'crude jest' with 'barbaric splendour'.[52] It is possible that Sir John possessed intelligence but lacked the sensitivity to display it, but the record suggests that he lacked both.

The sense of fun that he undoubtedly possessed has led people to view him as an amiable oaf, a benign force in Ceylon's politics. But the second sense in which he was a 'strong man' calls this into question. Sir John's very considerable fortune was mainly derived from his plumbago (graphite) mines and for over two decades the labourers from his mines and others served repeatedly as a private force to intimidate opponents. As the same sympathetic commentator wrote:

He was all for democracy. But it was a curious kind of democracy.

Once he asked me what – after he had done so much for his constituency if there came a stranger as his rival at the election claiming his caste as his qualification – what was he to do? And then gave the answer: 'I will prevent those castes from voting. I will then be elected. And this is Democracy!'[53]

For Sir John, this was no hypothetical comment. In 1936, he had mustered his miners and elephants to intimidate members of depressed castes seeking to vote in the campaign that brought Dudley Senanayake into the State Council.[54] That was not an isolated instance.[55] Another writer who was partial to him could write quite blandly, as if it were a common occurrence, of an occasion on which he was 'collecting toughs', 'massing his plumbago miners from the Kahatagama Mines to march to Ratmalana aerodrome' to mount a 'demonstration' before no less a figure than the Governor-General.[56] Sir John was also the main link between the UNP and the bus owners who were responsible for many acts of violence and fraud at election time.

The change of Prime Ministers helped the ruling party to allay some of the suspicions generated by police indiscipline and over-reaction during

[52] *Ibid.,* pp. 46–48, 50–52; *TC,* 24 August 1951; 13 December 1952. Aluwihare Diaries, 21, 27 April 1955. Notes on 1937 visit by Kotelawala in CO 54/950/7 and Report no. 5, 22 January 1940 in CO 54/977/7, PRO.   [53] Dhanapala, *Among Those Present,* p. 49.
[54] Election petition, Dedigama constituency, 1936, lot 81/2609, NASL. See also, Dissanayake, *Dudley,* pp. 7–8. J. Jiggins, *Caste and Family in the Politics of the Sinhalese, 1947–1976* (Cambridge, 1979), p. 72.
[55] J. L. Fernando, *Three Prime Ministers of Ceylon – An 'Inside Story'* (Colombo, 1963), pp. 44 and 46. This was consistently substantiated in two dozen interviews with Sir John's former allies and adversaries, 1977 and 1978.
[56] *Ibid.,* p. 44. See also, S. W. R. D. Bandaranaike, 'The Opposition in a Democracy', *Community* (Colombo, July 1954), p. 74.

the *hartal*. There were few Cabinet changes, but the sight of a new and undoubtedly forceful premier saved the UNP considerable embarrassment in the short run. Over the longer term, however, Dudley Senanayake's departure took a heavy toll on the party. When it eventually sank in among the electorate that he had quit because he had lost his nerve, the government and the UNP forfeited its air of unshakable solidity. Sir John soon showed that he was as robust a leader as his uncle, Senanayake, but he often hurtled headlong into extreme embarrassments. This second generation of leaders in what wags now called the 'Uncle Nephew Party' seemed to lack the sound judgement of the first. As these opinions took popular root, it ceased to be unimaginable that another person and party might govern. For most people in 1953, this was not so much an idea as a vague feeling at the back of the mind. Much more was needed before it could begin to cohere around anyone in particular, but its birth was a major event.

Indeed, it was the main advantage which Bandaranaike gained from the *hartal*. And, not for the last time, it was an advantage gained by good fortune rather than his own initiative. His decision to stand aloof from the leftists' *hartal* in order to emphasise that he offered a more moderate alternative to the ruling party had been partly successful. But the *hartal* had generated such excitement that the left seemed to represent the main threat to the UNP, and this continued to be true during 1954 and much of 1955. This had certain advantages for Bandaranaike. The UNP and its backers in the press were so preoccupied with the Marxists that they were poorly prepared for a challenge from Bandaranaike and company. But as a man who enjoyed public attention and knew it to be essential to political success, Bandaranaike found this an exasperating period.

By the end of 1953, a recovery of export prices had improved the economic outlook so that the price of rice could be reduced somewhat and supplies increased. But if this soothed some of the grievances that had fuelled the *hartal*, the trauma of that episode continued to preoccupy the new premier, who had always fiercely opposed the left. In his first broadcast to the nation, he declared that 'one of my foremost duties (will be) to stamp out Communism from this country'. A few weeks later, he promised to raise an 'army of the youth' who would wear shirts of green (the UNP colour) 'to fight back red violence by delivering two slaps for one slap, two kicks for one kick . . .'. He barred socialists like Cheddi Jagan from the island, attacked a Burgher leader of Ceylon's Communists on grounds of his race and alarmed even the conservative press by threatening to appoint only his party's supporters to public service posts.[57]

---

[57] Quotations are from *TC*, 16 October and 23 November 1953. See also, *TC*, 26, 27 November, 8 December 1953.

By mid-1954, publications originating from countries deemed to be Communist 'sympathizers or fellow-travellers' were being seized by customs authorities and summarily burned, including books addressed to the libraries of the Colombo Museum and the university. In early 1955 Communist and UNP thugs figured prominently in a parliamentary by-election. The public was informed that the Prime Minister had been reading Trotsky in order to stay one jump ahead of 'the artifices of Communist subversion'. He provided the major embarrassment at the 1955 Bandung Conference by lecturing Chou En-lai on 'red colonialism' and by suggesting ignorantly that Taiwan should be to China as Ceylon was to India. When Nehru intervened to cool tempers, he was 'told off' by Sir John'.[58] Early 1955 also brought what Bandaranaike described with only mild understatement as 'a strike of a few garage hands'. Sir John saw in it the beginnings of a new *hartal* and used it as an excuse to start training picked employees from essential services in the use of arms for future emergencies. By then he had developed a new Public Security Department which amounted to a force of police answerable only to him, outside the control of the Inspector-General. Its activities included the gathering of intelligence on opposition politicians – including many non-Marxists – by telephone-tapping and other clandestine and illegal means. It is probable that some of its doings were more sinister than that.[59]

All of these things formed a pattern which posed a palpable threat to civil liberties and which has been overlooked by observers who are amused at Sir John's amiable bumbling and rhetorical gaffes. Had the left been capable of mounting a serious challenge to the UNP, the reaction might have maimed or destroyed the liberal processes which existed in Ceylon amid elite dominance, but it was capable of no such thing. The year 1955 brought a fresh spate of arcane Marxist squabbles, defections and lone-wolfery and Sir John's illiberal instincts were never fully provoked. This main historical significance of his pursuit of the red peril lies not in the damage it did to others but in the blindness it inflicted on the premier himself. He was so preoccupied with subversion on his left

[58] Quotations are from *CDN*, 17 July 1954, 5, 30 March 1955. See also, *CDN*, 7 July 1954, 1, 8, 22 March 1955.
[59] Numerous press reports through late 1955 indicate that the government was opening mail, arming paramilitary units from among its employees and assuming powers to break strikes. Police excesses in an operation to stop traffic in cannabis were widely experienced. On these matters and the Public Security Department, see *CDN*, 22, 26 April 1955; F. C. Scharenguivel Papers; Aluwihare Diaries 1 April and 1 August 1955; interviews at Colombo with an official involved in that Department's operations, 29 August 1977 and another involved in dismantling it after Bandaranaike's election, 4 September 1980. See also, the 'Confidential' police report on Bandaranaike, file 15, BP; *Ceylon Hansard* (1955), cols. 2151–52; and materials from 1954 in file 442, J. R. Jayewardene Papers, Presidential Archive, Colombo.

and with formal party politics that he ignored a less formally organized but more dynamic and broadly-based set of forces welling up from below, from outside the party system. A prompt and sensitive response could have turned it to his advantage and prevented it from becoming poisonous to the nation's social well-being. But he failed in this and passed the advantage and the responsibility for dealing with it to Bandaranaike.

This set of forces was the same cultural, linguistic and religious groundswell that had begun to send tremors up to the national level before the *hartal*. In that earlier phase, it had been very loosely integrated, consisting of a spate of localized complaints from half-formed local interest groups on a broad range of issues that were themselves often imperfectly related. As they began to force themselves upon leaders' attention again in late 1953 and early 1954 when the dust had settled after the change of leadership, it would still have been an overstatement to describe them as a 'movement'. The most that can be said is that at that point most of these various and disparate groups shared grievances against the westernized, mainly English-educated people who were predominant in the national political elite.

Most important, because of the reverence in which they were held by villagers, were the *bhikkhus* – mainly younger monks with little connection to the heads of the great *nikayas* (chapters or sects), but often with close ties to certain *pirivenas* (Buddhist centres of higher study) from which they had emerged in large numbers during the late 1940s and early 1950s to serve villages that previously possessed local priests who were 'more animist or Hindu than Buddhist'.[60] They were joined in campaigns for greater official aid to Buddhist institutions by a modest number of ardent Buddhist laymen who operated in both the Sinhalese and westernized idioms. Vernacular school teachers, practitioners of indigenous medicine, members and employees of local boards, vernacular writers, young people (not only students but youths educated in the vernacular and frustrated by their prospects) and campaigners against gambling and drink completed the list of groups to be found in most areas, including Tamil districts. To these must be added a few smaller groups that had begun to crop up in certain limited areas: small shopkeepers and entrepreneurs whose aspirations were threatened by large Sinhalese, British or Indian firms; consumer groups and – more timidly but in the long run more crucially – groups of poorer peasants and members of

---

[60] 'B. M.,' 'A "People's Government": Social and Political Trends in Ceylon', *The World Today*, xii, 7 (July 1956), pp. 284–85.

depressed castes such as the *Wahumpuras* and *Bathgamas*. Some of these
categories overlapped to a limited degree, but not enough to provide
strong or numerous links between them.

Their grievances were not new. Most of them had been quietly
simmering for years, in some cases for decades.[61] Nor was it new that
people should sporadically articulate them and take action to dramatize
them. What *was* new was the incidence and intensity of their appeals and
the organization of issue-oriented voluntary associations for sustained
pressure. People were beginning to understand and operate within the
logic of open, representative politics and, in so doing, were changing
what had been an alien imposition into something more fully their own.
This was not easy since the national political elite had, since the 1930s,
maintained the highly centralized character of the political system and
prevented the development of strong local boards or substantive
transactional bonds between the national level and intermediate and local
levels.[62] But, despite this, the groundswell from below proceeded. It is
difficult, on the incomplete evidence, to put firm dates on the change. But
it appears that between 1949 and 1952 voluntary associations were
developing in many local arenas (particularly outside the more remote
Kandyan areas) and that between 1952 and 1954, imperfect ties were
developing between similar associations in various local arenas. Certainly
by the end of 1954, broadly representative associations of teachers,
ayurvedic physicians, *bhikkhus* and writers were making common cause.
Throughout 1954, their doings assumed an increasingly dominant place
in most Sinhala papers and by the end of that year even readers of the
English press had vivid evidence of the clamour almost daily. A sensibly-
managed government would have responded urgently, and some in the
UNP – mostly notably J. R. Jayewardene – stressed this repeatedly. But
Sir John and most of his colleagues could not be roused.[63]

Mismanagement and inaction born of inefficiency, internal wrangles
and over-confidence had marked UNP rule from the start, and after the
deceptively easy election victory of 1952 and despite the *hartal*,

[61] *Dinamina*, August–December 1953; and interviews with two *bhikkhus* who played
leading roles in these events. See also D. C. Vijayavardhana, *Dharma-Vijaya or the Revolt
in the Temple* (Colombo, 1953); U. Phadnis, *Religion and Politics in Sri Lanka* (London,
1976); K. N. O. Dharmadasa, The Rise of Sinhalese Language Nationalism: A Study in
the Sociology of Language, Monash University doctoral thesis, 1979; K. Malalgoda,
Buddhism in Sinhalese Society, 1750–1900 (Berkeley, 1976) and numerous other works on the
history of these grievances.
[62] This is set out more fully in Manor, 'The Failure of Political Integration'.
[63] This is based on readings from two English and two Sinhala papers and from interviews
with numerous local board members and civil servants who were then in rural areas. See
especially, *CDN*, 1 December 1954. See also, material in the second part of file 305 and
file 442, J. R. Jayewardene Papers, Presidential Archive, Colombo.

complacency reached monumental proportions. Many government departments left sizeable funds unspent and pledges on agrarian reform, housing, schools, irrigation and reform of the headman system went unfulfilled. The extension of credit facilities and the planning, coordination and execution of economic development programmes were woefully mishandled. Ministers insulated civil servants, who were disinclined to pursue programmes to promote change, from MPs who might have lobbied for such things. As late as November 1955, officials were still able to refuse to see MPs. Legislation was sometimes imprecise, with unhappy consequences, while other laws were ignored or inadequately enforced. UNP legislators grew increasingly inaccessible, cut off from public contact by corrupt middlemen. Their self-satisfaction sometimes ran to breathtaking callousness.[64]

The cultural and linguistic upsurge was fuelled by the UNP government's inertia and bungling on sensitive issues. It was not until five years after independence that such basic laws as the Rural Courts Ordinance, the Motor Traffic Act, the Workmen's Compensation Ordinance and all acts governing local boards were translated into the vernaculars from English. Non-Christian witnesses in courts had to swear oaths of an objectionable nature unchanged from colonial times. It was still illegal in 1953 to transact business at banks in Sinhala or Tamil, the Education Department appeared to be conniving with schools reluctant to introduce vernacular teaching as promised by the UNP,[65] and so it went. Sir John had begun his premiership with an assault on colonial remnants by ending the practice of flying the Union Jack and playing 'God Save the Queen' on official occasions. Revivers of indigenous culture took heart from this, but they soon realized that the Prime Minister's aim was only to annoy Lord Soulbury who had ignored his claims in the succession to D. S. Senanayake. The bemonocled Governor-General was 'very much peeved' at this and within a year had decamped for Hampshire.[66]

Sir John's lifestyle and public indiscretions soon made him a symbol of westernized crudity in the eyes of campaigners for indigenization. His well-publicized penchant for jodhpurs by day and dinner jackets by night, for cocktails and extravagant entertainments, seemed alien and offensive to many Ceylonese, particularly to the Buddhist clergy. He seemed game for anything. It took scathing editorials in the press to dissuade him from

---

[64] See the comment by a minister on infant mortality in *TC*, 20 July 1953. See also, *TC*, 2, 9, 10, 13 March, 1 May, 1, 24 July, 4 August, 3 September, 19 November 1953, 6, 25 January 1954; *CDN*, 12 June, 3 August, 8 December 1954, 8 January 1958; Aluwihare Diaries, 24 November 1955.

[65] *TC*, 28 April; 4 May; 27 July 1953; 8, 9, 12 December 1954.

[66] *TC*, 31 October; 12 November 1953.

riding to a reception in a chariot pulled by sixty girls. In July 1954, he outraged pious Buddhist opinion by attending a barbecue where a calf was roasted on a spit, an incident which became part of the island's folk memory and haunted him ever after. As the Buddhist upsurge gained momentum in 1955, Sir John blithely described it as 'madness' and blamed the monks for the decline of the faith.[67] He seemed to represent all that the revivalists loathed, and this forced them to seek champions from outside the government.

No one was more impatient to step into this role than Bandaranaike. He had been auditioning for the part since 1937 and was quick to lend his voice to the rising clamour, but he was to be kept waiting a little longer. Most leaders of the cultural-linguistic revival had initially hoped to win the backing of the UNP government. They reacted angrily to Sir John's brusque rejection and for a time poured scorn on all politicians. A *bhikkhu* in Matale put it plainly in January 1955 when he railed at the 'so-called political leaders of this country' whose knowledge of indigenous language and culture was 'quite deficient'. They 'must be ousted forthwith' and replaced by men new to politics, chosen from among the vernacular revivalists.[68]

It was soon apparent, however, that this was unworkable. The revivalists lacked the skills, contacts and public notoriety of established politicians. Yet even then they hesitated to turn to Bandaranaike. Despite his position as Leader of the Opposition, his long-standing efforts on behalf of Sinhala and Buddhism and his links to several *bhikkhus* active in the revival, he was distrusted by many (probably most) activists. He had never lived down his family's Christianity and close association with the British. To many he was still a Donoughmore Buddhist. This impression gained credence from his habit of appearing often in western dress, his waywardness over the years on so many issues and occasional flashes of Oxonian snobbery, as when he had corrected a minister's English pronunciation in Parliament in December 1953.[69] A year later, Bandaranaike had admitted under oath during a trial that 'I can read Sinhalese, but not very fluently.' To save time, he had articles in a Sinhala paper that he published read to him before going to press. Despite his considerable ability as an orator in Sinhala, linguistic revivalists attacked him bitterly for this admission.[70]

---

[67] See, for example, *TC*, 1–4, 10 December 1953, 17 July 1954; *CDN*, 9–10 August 1954, 21 February 1955 and interview with Sir John Kotelawala, Kandawela, 6 September 1977.   [68] *CDN*, 3 January 1955.   [69] *TC*, 12 December 1953.

[70] The quotation is from *CDN*, 19 December 1954. See also *TC*, 12 December 1953; *CDN*, 13 January; 24 February; 14 March 1955. It must be stressed that there were numerous other members of the national political elite who shared Bandaranaike's difficulties in reading Sinhala. See, for example, Bernard Aluwihare Diaries 28 April and 14 May 1952, University of Peradeniya Library.

Most of them were inclined to turn to Dudley Senanayake before Bandaranaike. Although still a nominal Vice-President of the UNP, Senanayake privately regarded its leadership as 'vile'. He began making disgruntled noises from retirement in late 1954 and, by early 1955, he had launched a campaign for total prohibition, an issue dear to most cultural revivalists. This helped to give the revival greater visibility and focus, and as late as May 1955, Buddhist activists appeared to prefer Senanayake to Bandaranaike as their leader. But his protracted indecision over whether to be fully in or out of the ruling party exasperated potential followers. By late 1955, most of them had drifted away.[71] This left Bandaranaike. But even then, he needed a vivid gesture to overcome the hesitations of many revivalists. This led him to the most fateful decision of his life, which can only be understood against the background of the burgeoning revival.

During 1955, the year in which the cultural and linguistic upsurge acquired irresistible force, it became clear that the dominant issue which drove it forward was that of language. Religion – which is to say Buddhism – ran it a close second, but Buddhism as an issue alienated not only the Tamils but large numbers of Sinhalese Christians.[72] Language was crucial. The varied interests that had a share in the movement (and by late 1955, it had begun to attain the coherence of a movement) had varied grievances. But there was one complaint that all of them shared, one complaint that formed a part of the particular grievances of teachers, *bhikkhus*, local councillors, ayurvedic physicians and others – the injustices done to the vernacular. That statement, however, raises further problems because there were two vernaculars. Was the struggle being waged for both against the privileged status of English or for Sinhala, the language of the majority, alone? Until well into 1955 there was no clear answer to this question. In its early stages, the campaign against English had clearly predominated. In 1952 and early 1953, even *bhikkhus*, Sinhala writers, and teachers – people who might have been expected to seek preferment for Sinhala alone – tended to appeal on behalf of Tamil as well. It was common to see Tamils and Sinhalese working in tandem and reinforcing one another's demands. Bandaranaike's SLFP had, from its

[71] *CDN*, 10, 18 July 1954, 25, 28 February, 26 March, 9, 12, 14 May, 13, 20 June 1955. On Dudley Senanayake's opinion of the UNP leadership, see Aluwihare, Diaries, 2 June 1955. On the absence of any firm tie between Bandaranaike and *bhikkhus* as late as October 1955, see Aluwihare, 13 and 16 October 1955. Secret negotiations between Bandaranaike and Senanayake on a possible electoral alliance continued until late 1955 (Aluwihare, 25 November to 1 December 1955). But Bandaranaike rightly saw that Senanayake had dithered too long.
[72] For the historical background to this, see Dharmadasa, The Rise of Sinhalese Language Nationalism, pp. 335–40.

inception, promised official recognition for both vernaculars and in mid-
1952 his suggestion that all Sinhalese school children should be taught a
smattering of Tamil aroused little comment from Sinhala revivalists. In
March 1953 Tamil and Sinhalese MPs, including Bandaranaike, joined
forces to make vernacular speeches in Parliament in protest at the status of
English.[73] At about that time, however, a student campaign for
Buddhism had begun to gain momentum. Its main thrust was anti-
Christian, but any stress upon Buddhism also implied opposition to
Hinduism and soon quickened mass awareness of the Buddha's mandate
to the Sinhalese to guard the purity of Buddhism. The xenophobia that
this aroused tended easily towards anti-Tamil feeling and, in early 1953,
the appeal that Sinhala alone should be the national language had begun
to gain ground.[74]

Thereafter, the two themes – the uplift of both vernaculars against
English and the uplift of Sinhala alone – could be heard amid the revival
from which both drew strength. Efforts for the two vernaculars
outweighed those for Sinhala for many months yet and, had the
government responded forcefully to these legitimate grievances, much of
the heat could have been taken out of the Sinhala chauvinist campaign
which gradually gained force. But no response came and soon opposition
politicians were having to tread carefully round angry Sinhalese bigots.
Bandaranaike was no exception. There is no doubt that he preferred to see
both Sinhala and Tamil recognized as state languages, but when
confronted with a crowd that had eyes only for Sinhala, he temporized. In
April 1953 he told one such gathering that 'Sinhalese is the language of
the majority of the country. The unemployment and economic problems
can be solved to a great extent by making Sinhalese the state language.'[75]
The sleight of hand artist was at work here. He gave the crowd what they
wanted but did not explicitly say that *only* Sinhala should be recognized.
Tamil was simply never mentioned.

Despite such moments, Bandaranaike's preference for both vernaculars showed through in most of his and his party's stands in 1953 and
1954. But, in the latter half of 1954, that view was overtaken by a popular
demand for Sinhala as the only state language.[76] This theme was adopted

[73] *CDN*, 13 July 1951, 4 April 1952; *TC*, 26 February, 12 April, 2, 24, 26, 29 July, 12, 19
August, 1 December 1952, 2, 7, 10 February; 2, 13, 26 March 1953. On the SLFP
language policy, see also *Daily Mirror* (Colombo), 24 January 1971 and D. S.
Senanayake's comments on the SLFP's predecessor, the Sinhala Maha Sabha, *Ceylon
Hansard* (1951), col. 1544.
[74] *TC*, 6 April 1953; *Dinamina*, March–April 1953.   [75] *TC*, 16 April 1953.
[76] *Dinamina*, August–November 1954; *CDN*, 4, 7 December 1954. On Bandaranaike's
preference for the recognition of both vernaculars, see *Ceylon Hansard* (1953),
cols. 997–98.

by many within the SLFP and Bandaranaike, who opposed it, played for time. In December 1954 a special party committee which he chaired was formed to study the 'Sinhala only' question.[77] He managed to prolong its sittings for nine months, but during that period the outcry for Sinhala intensified. Its emergence as the dominant issue in the revival was mainly the work of activist *bhikkhus* and a small handful of ardent Buddhist laymen. Unlike teachers and students working in the vernacular, practitioners of indigenous medicine, local board members and others in the revival, the *bhikkhus* and most lay campaigners shared little common interest with Tamil counterpart groups. The *bhikkhus* also possessed far more evocative power than any other revivalist elements because of the great reverence in which Buddhists hold their clergy.

Throughout 1955 Bandaranaike continued to have difficulty persuading revivalists that he should be their leader. Their view of politicians was vividly expressed by a leading activist *bhikkhu* who complained that 'Today the drunkard, the hypocrite and crook had first place in society . . .' No one could accuse Bandaranaike of being a drunkard or a crook – those were references to the ruling party – but he could not free himself of the suspicion of hypocrisy, of feigned enthusiasm for the common man's language and religion.[78] A decision to become the first major politician to lend his voice to the mounting cries for Sinhala as the only official language clearly offered some hope of overcoming this suspicion so, at the end of September 1955, the Sri Lanka Freedom Party met and unanimously endorsed their leader's call for 'Sinhala only'.

It is for this that the party conference is remembered, but the resolutions passed there were carefully worded to allow a very substantial role for Tamil. Both Sinhala and Tamil would be used in Parliament and all laws would be promulgated in both languages. Sinhala would be the language used by all courts, government offices and local boards 'except in the Northern and Eastern Provinces where the language should be Tamil' and the medium of instruction in schools would be the language of the local majority. Although the resolutions rejected parity for the two vernaculars, the SLFP had accepted something very close to it.[79] The headlines read 'Sinhala only', but the small print contained a rather different message. This had serious repercussions when the party came to power.

[77] *CDN*, 7 December 1954.
[78] The quotation is from *CDN*, 6 September 1955. See also, for example, *CDN*, 24 February; 12 September 1955.
[79] *CDN*, 24 September 1955. Tarzie Vittachi's claim in *Emergency '58* (London, 1958) that provisions for the reasonable use of Tamil were left out of the Sinhala version of Bandaranaike's election manifesto is false. See Mahajana Eksath Peramuna, *Prakashanaya* (Colombo, 1956), p. 2.

This pattern ran through most of Bandaranaike's speeches between this party meeting and the general election in April 1956. He usually passed some quiet comment early in his speech promising Tamil fair treatment, and as his later actions as premier demonstrated, he meant it. But these remarks were soon forgotten amid the white heat of his rhetoric about the plight of Sinhala. After a lifetime of tailoring his speeches to the tastes of the crowd, he was not about to change, particularly when his hearers responded with unprecedented enthusiasm. His difficulty was that their fervour ran to hysteria and bigotry and in seeking to make himself their leader, he allowed himself to follow them part of the way down that road. Even before his party's endorsement of 'Sinhala only', he had stated publicly that parity 'would result in the disappearance of the Sinhalese language' and had played to the Kandyan fears of Tamil estate workers by describing them as 'a source of danger'. Both notions were absurdities, but they were popular absurdities, so he lent his voice to them. The fantasy that unless 'Sinhala only' were adopted, Sinhala and indeed the Sinhalese 'race, religion and culture'[80] would somehow 'vanish' became part of Bandaranaike's litany from the public platform.[81] The crowds that grew intoxicated with his supremely skilful presentation of this message could be forgiven for failing to notice his equivocations on the future role of Tamil.

An elitist assumption lay behind Bandaranaike's actions here. In telling the throng roughly what they wanted to hear while reserving to himself the right to interpret the finer shades of meaning in his remarks, he assumed that he would be free to adjust or even reverse his course once the crowds had melted away. Until then, this had been a safe assumption. The political system had been highly centralized, and the politicization and mobilization of the mass had been rather limited. People at the apex of the system therefore had abundant freedom to manoeuvre. But things were changing, particularly as increasingly large groups were drawn into the excitement over the language issue. Bandaranaike welcomed this. It meant that Ceylon was becoming more fully a democracy and this was something he genuinely sought. But he naïvely failed to realise that mass politicization on this issue and the growth of democracy might intrude upon his freedom, once in office, to ram through a reasonably even-handed policy towards the two vernaculars. The great scale and intensity of the movement was changing the rules of politics.

The SLFP decision for 'Sinhala only' gave the movement its first major

---

[80] The polyglot character of the Sinhalese renders them a linguistic group but not a race. The reader will recall that even the Bandaranaikes acknowledge Tamil and European ancestors.
[81] *CDN*, 15 September, 3, 12 October, 2, 8, 18, 24 November 1955, 4 January 1956; *Dinamina*, December 1955, 1–9 January 1956.

ally in the realm of formal politics and began a gradual process by which Sinhala activists accepted Bandaranaike as their leader. It also brought the Sinhala campaign greater attention from the national press in all languages and gave a modest fillip to the efforts of enthusiasts in outlying areas to organize themselves and forge links to activists elsewhere. Activist *bhikkhus*, now more than ever in the public eye, planned an all-island rally on the issue. On 11 October 1955, a Communist Party meeting at Colombo Town Hall to support parity for the two vernaculars was disrupted by *bhikkhus*. The anti-Communist press reported that Communist red shirts 'mercilessly thrashed . . . slapped and kicked them about, mauled them with chairs and forcibly dragged them out . . .'. A woman wearing a red sari 'jumped at one of the monks and plucked off his robes'. A crowd of outraged Buddhists then stoned the Town Hall and 'ran amok', smashing up Muslim and Tamil shops.[82] Any attack on the clergy was deeply offensive to most Buddhists and reports such as this drew an ever-widening circle of people angrily into the movement. By mid-October, the language issue was becoming increasingly prominent even in the most loyal UNP English papers.

The Prime Minister, whose failures to respond to legitimate grievances on many issues, including that of language, had contributed to the emergence of narrow extremism, remained remarkably unmoved by the mounting excitement. Most of his UNP colleagues in Parliament were ready to compromise with the movement, but Sir John dismissed the 'Sinhala only' demand as 'a mockery'[83] and at the end of October left on a month-long foreign tour. It could not have been more ill-timed. In his absence, the 'Sinhala only' campaign burst forth in full fury. Mass meetings throughout the Sinhalese districts drew together SLFP and other politicians, *bhikkhus*, vernacular teachers, local board members and others into a loose front for action bound together less by organizational ties than by shared ardour. Anti-English and anti-Tamil feelings tended to merge amid the excitement over the need 'to fight', even 'to sacrifice their lives' to make Sinhala the state language and end the threat 'to destroy the Sinhalese race and their culture'. Increasingly prominent members of the Buddhist clergy, including the head of the Amarapura sect, became active in the movement. Members of parties supporting parity for the two vernaculars, including the UNP and two of the three main leftist groups, defected or threatened to defect in growing numbers to 'Sinhala only' parties.[84] These included the SLFP, the Bhasa Peramuna – a 'party' hastily formed by a few of Parliament's more transparent

[82] *CDN*, 12 October 1955.
[83] See *CDN* for the first three weeks of October 1955, particularly the 15th and 19th.
[84] Quotations are from separate meetings on a single day. See *CDN* and *Dinamina*, 25 October to 25 November 1955.

opportunists – and the Vipla Lanka Sama Samaja Party (VLSSP), the Trotskyist faction led by Philip Gunawardena. SLFP members pressed Bandaranaike to abandon the electoral pact that he had begun to forge with the other Trotskyist group because its pro-parity stand had now become politically poisonous.

Bandaranaike's oratory became increasingly shrill. He deplored the 'show of violence' of often apparent in revivalist rhetoric, which suggested venomous emotions beneath the surface.[85] But he then came close to fomenting them by denouncing UNP leaders as 'treacherous of their race and language', by claiming that parity would mean 'disaster for the Sinhalese race' and by playing upon feelings of inferiority which were very real, at least among Sinhalese from in or near urban areas: 'With their books and culture and the will and strength characteristic of their race, the Tamils (if parity were granted) would soon rise to exert their dominant power over us.'[86] Such sentiments were in keeping with and helped to stir the soaring revivalist emotions, which soon generated downright hysterical rhetoric, as when a *bhikkhu* in Matara called for a boycott of Tamil shops in these terms: 'It is not necessary actually to assault the Tamils. If ten to fifteen youths of Matara get together and with knives move about on the public road, that alone will make the Tamils run back to the North.'[87] As the pitch and force of the movement rose at public meetings throughout the Sinhalese areas, the majority of the ruling party's MPs firmly resolved, for their own political survival, to adopt 'Sinhala only' at the first opportunity. They had the full support of J. R. Jayewardene, their leader in Sir John's absence and the man who in 1945 had introduced a motion in the State Council to make Sinhala the only official language. But he and they could do nothing with the Prime Minister overseas. Frantic efforts were made to warn Sir John of the crisis before his return and, to reinforce the message, a crowd from the UNP Youth League met his plane with cries of 'Sinhala only'. But before his Cabinet colleagues could confer with him, he left them aghast on the tarmac by denouncing these 'dangerous slogans' which marred the good name of Ceylon abroad. 'If there is a problem', he said, 'it will solve itself.'[88]

Within hours, Sir John's advisers had enlightened him on the momentum which recent events had acquired and almost immediately he accepted a strategy that they had hammered out. A special conference of the ruling party would be summoned at which 'Sinhala only' would be

---

[85] This had been apparent even during the earlier, pre-*hartal* upsurge of linguistic revivalism. See, for example, *TC*, 2, 7 February, 18, 28 March, 4 May 1953.
[86] *CDN*, 8, 24 November 1955. For examples of violent language used by *bhikkhus* campaigning for 'Sinhala only', see allegations in *CDN*, 7 January 1956.
[87] *CDN*, 12 November 1955.   [88] *CDN*, 26 November 1955.

adopted as policy. An immediate general election would then be called to ask for a popular endorsement of the 'Sinhala only' decision. The UNP might thus turn the movement to its own advantage. Having resolved upon this strategy, however, the Prime Minister frayed the nerves of his colleagues by dragging his feet. The party conference would not meet until mid-February 1956,[89] which meant that the UNP would remain officially committed to a gradual transition to both vernaculars for another twelve weeks and that an election could not occur until April.

It was soon clear that the ruling party was paying a grievous price for this delay. A massive procession of Sinhala schoolteachers which marched down the west coast to the Kataragama shrine in the extreme south was greeted repeatedly at mass meetings along the way organized by local *bhikkhus* and 'Sinhala only' committees. Another huge march of *bhikkhus* made its way to Kataragama by a different route, then turned and wound its way across up-country districts invoking 'divine blessings for Sinhalese only' before mammoth crowds. Still another proceeded from Kotte to Kandy bearing banners, relics and sacred texts. More localized marches in many areas also achieved impressive results.[90] These processes stirred popular support for the movement and cemented ties between teachers, *bhikkhus* and others who had previously been only loosely linked – ties which proved crucial in the coming election. Some UNP politicians tried to associate themselves with these demonstrations, but with no public pro-Sinhala signal from the Prime Minister, they made little headway. Bandaranaike's impassioned speeches and his close ties to a few of the leaders of the marches gained him greater success. But his reluctance to abandon an electoral alliance with two leftist parties that favoured parity for both vernaculars still prevented him from taking undisputed leadership of the movement. At the end of January 1956 the Sinhala upsurge was still not firmly linked to any political party.

The movement was likely to support whichever party presented the most credible and unambiguous commitment to the cultural revival and to 'Sinhala only'. The Prime Minister hastily arranged to be photographed in appropriately reverential postures with *bhikkhus*, but this had little effect when he also continued to appear in his dinner jacket hoisting cocktail glasses. His great attempt to seize headlines as a Buddhist benefactor – his receipt of a sacred scripture from leading *bhikkhus* – was swamped by the massive outpouring of grievances at the presentation on the same day of the report of a Buddhist Commission which severely indicted the government.[91]

---

[89] *Ibid.* [90] See, for example, *CDN*, 2–6 January 1956.

[91] Buddhist Commission of Inquiry, *The Betrayal of Buddhism* (Colombo, 1956). The quotation is from Weerawardana, *Election 1956*, p. 171. See also, *CDN*, 6 February 1956; D. C. Vijayavardhana, *Dharma-Vijaya or the Revolt*; and in Sinhala, Walpola Rahula, *Bhiksuvagē Urumaya* (Colombo, 1946).

A few MPs in the ruling party told Sir John that distrust of the government's intentions was so great that it was vital to make Sinhala the sole official language *before* the election. A mere promise would not be believed. He would not comply, partly out of stubbornness, but also because Bandaranaike had neatly boxed him in on this front. The 'Sinhala only' resolution which already awaited action by Parliament stood in Bandaranaike's name. If the change were made before the election, much of the credit would go to the opposition leader. Bandaranaike knew that Sir John would never accept this and told every available crowd that the government's promises were false.[92] This and Sinhala activists' suspicions of the ruling party nullified the impact of Sir John's much heralded announcement on 17 February of his promise of 'Sinhala only'. Parliament was dissolved a few days later and an election called for the first week of April.

During this same period, Bandaranaike came under still greater pressure to discard his electoral pact with leftists favouring parity and to forge a new one with groups pledged to 'Sinhala only'. He was extremely slow to do so, partly because he was less aware than were colleagues nearer the grass roots of the strength of popular feeling on this issue and partly because he was suspicious of his potential new allies. Chief among these were Philip Gunawardena and W. Dahanayake. The former was an immensely capable Trotskyist, but his extremely aggressive manner made him seem a troublesome colleague. The latter was the supremely wayward lone wolf in a political system which excelled at producing such creatures. Only six weeks earlier, Dahanayake had formed a new 'party' which included a leading Tamil MP, but by mid-February as leader of the Bhasa Peramuna, he was saying that the Tamils were 'deadly enemies' of the Sinhalese. A few years before, he had been Bandaranaike's most constant and vicious critic. But whatever Bandaranaike's reservations about these men, the force of the language issue was unabating. Leading activists among the clergy with impressive numbers behind them had formally coalesced into an organization called the Eksath Bhikkhu Peramuna to campaign for 'Sinhala only' candidates in the coming election. So on 22 February it was announced that a common front of the SLFP, Gunawardena's VLSSP and others including Dahanayake's newly formed 'party' would fight the election, mainly on 'Sinhala only'. The front was led by Bandaranaike and called the Mahajana Eksath Peramuna (MEP). They had left it late, but by then leading *bhikkhus* and lay activists had abandoned the UNP and concluded that 'Only Mr Bandaranaike has

[92] *CDN*, 3, 31 January; 2, 3 February 1956.

the intelligence and education to administer the country satisfactorily' and to institute 'Sinhala only'.[93]

The election of 1956 has been discussed in great detail on several occasions.[94] What follows is a review of the most crucial elements of that story, including some which have gone unremarked in earlier accounts. Despite the excitement surrounding the language issue, Bandaranaike and friends were not optimistic about their chances. The UNP appeared to hold most of the cards. Most newspapers gave it much fuller and more sympathetic coverage and it had massive financial resources, thanks to large contributions from rich individuals and firms – including numerous foreign companies. Once again it illegally mobilized government employees.[95] It also retained its huge advantage in transport for polling day – including both private cars and fleets of buses – and ministers saw to it that this advantage mattered. The Election Commissioner had recommended a substantial increase in the number of polling stations, but the government scotched this idea so that a very large proportion of voters remained in need of transport. The opportunities to impede voters travelling on foot to the polls remained great. Polling stations were often located in areas of strong support for the ruling party, which usually meant among higher caste voters.

The election was to be held on three separate days and the Election Commission was persuaded to schedule supposedly safe UNP constituencies for the first day, to give the ruling party the best possible start. Village headmen again aided the UNP, both in preparing voters' lists and in active campaigning. New voters were allowed a mere fortnight in which to register, and while facilities for scrutinizing voters' lists had improved, they were still inadequate. The ruling party also found it far easier than its opponents to recruit eminent people as candidates. Accounts in the press seemed to show that the Prime Minister had turned the 'Sinhala only' theme to his advantage and as late as a fortnight before polling day, Bandaranaike confided to friends that he expected defeat. He had half-decided to call on Sir John after the election and ask to be named ambassador to the United Nations.[96]

[93] *CDN*, 18 February 1956. The speaker was L. H. Mettananda, a key activist. There is no elegant translation of *Mahajana Eksath Peramuna* (Great People's United Front). The translation of *Eksath Bhikkhu Peramuna* is United Bhikku's Front.
[94] The most valuable of these is W. H. Wriggins, *Ceylon: Dilemmas of a New Nation* (Princeton, 1960). See also, Weerawardana, *Election 1956*.
[95] See, for example, Bernard Aluwihare Diaries, 25 May 1956, University of Peradeniya Library.
[96] Weerawardana, *Election 1956*, chapter 6, especially p. 130. *TC*, 12 March 1953; 23 January 1954; *CDN*, 10 February 1956. Interviews at Colombo with A. P. Jayasuriya, 19 August 1977; Nimal Karunatileke, 26 August 1978 and R. St. L. P. Deraniyagala, 10 September 1978.

This is not surprising when we consider the depressing state of Bandaranaike's party which was seriously short of money, manpower, confidence and substance. Until 1956 he had paid nearly all of the party's expenses from his own pocket. The election was bound to cost far more than he had on hand, but he so loathed asking for contributions that he even forbade his closest aides to appeal to rich relatives. Rather diffidently and late, he applied for a mortgage of Rs200,000 on his Colombo home, but UNP leaders forced government lending agencies to reject it. (A loan was of course approved *after* the election.)[97] Nor was the SLFP able to attract many candidates with the money to fund their own campaigns.[98] Most of its nominees were rather impecunious people: former government employees, advocates, teachers and the like, known to Bandaranaike from Sinhala Maha Sabha days. The story that he stationed agents outside the premier's residence to waylay unsuccessful seekers of UNP tickets is probably apocryphal, but it conveys a sense of the prevailing atmosphere. The SLFP had extreme difficulty in finding reliable candidates for several seats, and its nominees – while usually from the constituency – were often obscure figures. This and the still quite flimsy party organization[99] bred demoralization. Two SLFP MPs – including one of Bandaranaike's two main deputies – and more than one party branch, defected to the UNP as the election approached.

The election campaign of March 1956 was essentially a continuation and intensification of what had gone before, with the language issue dominating the discussion. UNP leaders occasionally trotted out the red scare, Bandaranaike's inconsistent record and the inability of the opposition to form a stable government, but each was used to show why Bandaranaike would not be able to enact 'Sinhala only'. Bandaranaike reminded voters of UNP corruption, price rises, unemployment and police excesses, but for both main contestants the campaign was essentially an occasion to prove their enthusiasm for 'Sinhala only'. The Prime Minister began the campaign confidently, asking for sixty-five seats to give him a two-thirds majority, but by the middle of the month,

[97] General Manager, Bank of Ceylon to Bandaranaike, 16 February 1956; Manager of Ceylon Savings Bank to Bandaranaike, 23 April 1956, file 16, BP and interview with A. P. Jayasuriya, Colombo, 19 August 1977.
[98] They did, however, gain campaign workers who turned against the UNP when its candidates would not or could not pay them extravagantly. No such largesse was expected of the SLFP. See, for example, Bernard Aluwihare Diaries, 23, 25 March 1956, University of Peradeniya Library.
[99] Interviews in Colombo with A. P. Jayasuriya, 19 August 1977, Badiudin Mahmud, 22 August 1977 and Nimal Karunatileke, 20 September 1980. See also, Aluwihare Diaries on Bandaranaike's personal and financial dominance of the party, 14 July 1954; 3 June and 4, 6 November 1955; on overall organizational problems, 7, 30 April 1954 and 4 June 1955 and on problems in maintaining ties to non-*Goyigamas*, 28 February 1954.

such visions had evaporated and the UNP was on the defensive as never before. It had become clear that several thousand *bhikkhus* were campaigning vehemently for Bandaranaike's MEP. These mainly young monks were trained speakers, held in great reverence by villagers. A favourite theme was to turn the government's effort to aid Buddhism on its head. Instead of praising the UNP for funding the forthcoming celebrations of the Buddha Jayanthi which marked 2,500 years of Buddhism, they excoriated the Prime Minister for calling a divisive election on the eve of this sacred event. They revived the millenarian visions often associated with Buddha Jayanthi, and likened their movement and Bandaranaike's opposition front to the cleansing force that was expected to sweep away things alien and impure.

Their speeches often ran to extremes. Throughout much of the Kandyan region and beyond, *bhikkhus* showed photos of scaffolding erected on the great Temple of the Tooth in Kandy. This had been put up as part of the restoration scheme paid for by the UNP government, but *bhikkhus* claimed that it showed the temple being dismantled. Tales of UNP leaders' drinking and the 'sins of Kotelawala with his women and (his eating of) flesh' were caricatured as an attack on the Buddhist faith.[100] Coming from supposedly puritanical *bhikkhus*, whose sensibilities were thought to be extremely tender, these stories deeply shocked villagers. Sir John could only rail impotently against 'fire-spitting *bhikkhus*' and 'Yellow-robed men hired for five rupees a day who go about spreading the foulest language.'[101]

Polling was scheduled for 5, 7 and 10 April and by the 6th it was clear that a major upset was at hand. On the first day, Bandaranaike's MEP gained twenty-three seats from the UNP and held five others to give it twenty-eight of the thirty-seven seats at risk. Six out of seven UNP ministers were beaten, the only exception being the Prime Minister himself. The momentum which the UNP expected to gain from these 'safe' seats went instead to Bandaranaike, and after the final two days' polling, his MEP finished with a clear majority of forty-nine out of ninety-five, not counting Independents who would join him and six members whom he would nominate.

There were 2,616,759 votes cast, representing 69.0 per cent of the electorate. Despite winning more than a quarter of the vote, the UNP gained a mere eight seats. The multiplier effect, which had given them a majority of seats on a minority of the popular vote in 1952, now worked similarly for the MEP. The former ruling party also suffered because the anti-UNP vote was less divided than ever. When Bandaranaike, with

[100] The words are those of an unsuccessful UNP candidate. Bernard Aluwihare Diaries, 2 April 1956.   [101] *CDN*, 30 March; 1 April 1956.

Table 7.2. *Results of the 1956 general election*[102]

Party	Seats won	% of seats won	Votes	% of votes
Mahajana Eksath Peramuna	49	51.6	982,228	37.54
United National Party	8	8.4	718,164	27.44
Nava Lanka Sama Samaja Party	14	14.7	274,204	10.48
Communist Party	3	3.2	119,715	4.57
Federal Party	10	10.5	142,036	5.43
Tamil Congress	1	1.1	8,914	0.34
Independents	10	10.5	352,928	13.49
Others	0		18,510	0.71

Source: Dr Silva, *A Statistical Survey.*

[102] R. G. Senanayake, who won two seats, is sometimes counted as a member of the MEP. In fact, he joined the MEP only *after* the election and did not use the party symbol. He is therefore counted here among the Independents. The MEP put up fifty-eight candidates. They can be disaggregated as follows:

	Total candidates	Successful
SLFP	43	37
VLSSP ('Trotskyist')	6	5
Independent MEP	6	5
Bhasa Peramuna (Language Front)	3	2
Total	58	49

The previous experience of MEP candidates was as follows:

	Newcomers	Stood unsuccessfully before	Ex-legislators	Unknown	Total
SLFP	20	11	11	1	43
Others	1	1	8	5	15

The pre-eminence of the language issue and other grievances over questions of religion was clear from the success of MEP candidates in areas with large Christian populations such as Chilaw and Ja-Ela, and from the victory of a Christian candidate on the SLFP ticket over the eminent Buddhist. A Ratnayake in predominantly Buddhist Wattegama. (*Sources: CDN,* 7 April 1956; de Silva, *A Statistical Survey*; and interview with A. P. Jayasuriya, Colombo, 19 August 1977.)

great fanfare, had formed the MEP by joining forces with those committed to 'Sinhala only', he had quietly maintained much of his old electoral agreement with left parties seeking parity for the two vernaculars. His party therefore clashed with the Communists in only two constituencies and with the NLSSP in only six. This helped these two left parties to increase their share of the seats as well, despite a decline in their share of the votes. The MEP made its gains almost entirely at the expense of the UNP.

The MEP's ability to attract votes from non-*Goyigama* caste groups resulted in almost no change in the caste composition of the new Parliament. Bandaranaike and his colleagues were seen – with some justice – to be more sympathetic to other castes and to poorer *Goyigamas*, even though their candidate slate was indistinguishable on caste grounds from that of the UNP.

The assertion that Bandaranaike and his SLFP-dominated front *won* this election, while not false, is true only in a limited sense. Two other statements reveal a greater part of the truth. The first is that Sir John Kotelawala and the UNP *lost* the election. Enough has been said of Sir John's colourful blunders, but the UNP was also afflicted by serious organizational weakness. It had plenty of hangers-on and seekers after spoils, but its effective organization still consisted mainly of MPs and their small personal coteries. Political resources rested with individual ministers who usually distributed them largely on impulse. Patronage thus reached MPs only haphazardly and its distribution to people beyond Parliament was inconstant and ineffective. Important decisions were made by a small handful of men at the apex of the party, who seldom consulted lesser leaders, let alone the rank and file. All of this and the heavy concentration of power in the political system at the national level, to the detriment of institutions at intermediate and local levels, made it impossible for the UNP to knit large numbers of influential people across the island into firm, transactional alliances.[103]

UNP leaders had grown complacent after the election victory of 1952, and 'taking things easy' in organizational work became a habit. The so-called 'branches' of the party fell into a sorry state. Sir John publicly conceded in 1953 that 'many . . . exist only on paper' and 'perhaps' met once a year. Many failed even to send in the nominal Rs 10 annual affiliation fee. In mid-1954 he found that the party branch in Kandy, the second most important city in the island, 'was totally inactive – except for the sign-board'. Little improvement followed for, in September 1955, the

---

[103] This view of the UNP was confirmed by, among others, Sir John Kotelawala, interview at Kandawela, 30 August 1977.

Table 7.3. *Caste of Sinhalese MPs*

Election	Goyigamas	Salagamas	Karavas	Duravas	Wahumpuras	Bathgamas	Others
1947	48	4	9	1	1	1	4
1952	57	4	8	1	1	1	3
1956	56	4	8	2	0	1	3

Source: J. Jiggins, *Family and Caste in the Politics of the Sinhalese, 1947–1976* (Cambridge, 1979), p. 127.

party had to 'open' branches at Kandy and several other major centres.[104]
This near-absence of party structure outside of Parliament allowed
indiscipline to remain a deeply serious problem, which was compounded
by the rivalries and resentments that grew out of the two succession
crises. The most damaging of these saw Dudley Senanayake and his
cousin R. G. Senanayake leave the UNP. This left the ruling party devoid
of leaders bearing its founder's name, a point emphasized to great effect
by its opponents.[105] The UNP could still muster impressive crowds and
displays of 'muscle' by green-shirted Youth Leaguers. But for a party
which had controlled the machinery of state for nearly a decade, its
structure was remarkably fragile and its support base grossly
underdeveloped.

During the early 1950s, the UNP had also acquired a distinct odour of
corruption, partly through inaction in pursuing wrongdoers and partly
through active connivance. The evidence served up by the pro-UNP
press alone makes lurid reading. The ruling party was implicated in
corruption in municipal politics, in the sale of Senate nominations to
major contributors, in soliciting funds from public servants, in the
occasional use of influence to gain the release of people on serious
criminal charges and in favouring higher castes in the distribution of
goods and services.[106] Its links to entrepreneurs operating outside the law
became almost legendary. It seemed to be 'the age of the racketeer
contractor' as materials for public works projects vanished and were
resold on the black market. Despite government promises, inadequate
action was taken against a 'car racket', against illegal gambling dens on
race days, and – on a larger scale – against the profiteering and thuggery
of bus owners. Sir Oliver Goonetilleke was made Governor-General in
the teeth of allegations from several sources that he was involved in
misdeeds in the Central Bank. A number of other prominent politicians
and civil servants were very plausibly charged with irregularities.[107]
These reports were matched in the experience of villagers by corrupt
practices among headmen who controlled rice ration books and access to
most government services, and by widespread theft of goods and funds

[104] Quotations are from *TC*, 22 August, 28 November 1953, 14 June 1954 and 1 September
1955. See also *TC*, 9 September, 9 November 1954; *CDN*, 4 June, 2 July 1954.
[105] For indiscipline, see *CDN*, 9 June 1952, 16, 18, 22, 27, 30 July, 13 August 1954, 14
March, 15 June, 10 October 1955; *TC*, 3 March 1955. On other matters, see *TC*, 26
August 1952; *CDN*, 8, 12 July, 14 August 1954, 28 March 1955.
[106] See, for example, *TC*, 26 January, 1 August, 28 October 1952; *CDN*, 17 July, 4 August
1951, 16 January, 4 March 1952.
[107] The quotations are from *TC*, 17 October 1953 and 27 July 1951. See also, *TC*, 27 July,
16 August 1952, 20 February, 20 November, 2 December 1953.

from cooperative societies, often by local notables who were leading UNP supporters.[108]

Policies which UNP leaders initiated to increase their popularity sometimes had the opposite effect with quite devastating results. Universal free education, introduced in 1947, created opportunities for study that gave rise to unprecedented appetites among students which the economy and an establishment strongly biased towards the English-educated could not satisfy. Subsidies on essential commodities were intended to generate popular support, but they were an inefficient means of doing so since they could not be selectively allotted to potential backers. People soon took subsidies for granted and forgot that they were there – until the government raised the price of rice. That action more than any other reminded people that the national government impinged upon their lives, that even everyday affairs in local arenas had acquired a national dimension. Another important initiative which went badly awry, and which has gone largely unnoticed, was the creation of the Rural Development Societies.

They had been set up after 1948 to promote voluntary community projects in the villages and to provide a counterweight to Bandaranaike's Village Committees. After he resigned from the Cabinet, the Societies were kept going as potential aids to future UNP election campaigns, but many of them instead became centres of lively debate which took to lobbying forcefully for government aid. When their expectations could not be fulfilled, many grew resentful and criticized astonished officials. Instead of fitting into the network of pro-UNP forces in rural arenas, the Societies often clashed with village headmen and wealthy magnates who formed the basis of the ruling party's power. Ministers were out of touch with officials on the ground and thought the Societies to be rather innocuous. They even encouraged *bhikkhus* to join hands with the Societies and thereby quickened the popular upsurge of the mid-1950s. By 1952, there were over 5,000 Societies embracing a huge membership. In Galle District alone it ran to 90,000.[109]

Rural Development Societies, like the universal franchise and the system of free education, worked imperfectly, but all three of these things gradually eroded the basis of UNP rule. They did so not by reducing the wealth and clout of the UNP's magnates and headmen, but by changing

---

See, for example, *TC*, 29 March 1952, 11 February, 7 August, 11 December 1953; *CDN*, 4 March 1952, 7 December 1954.

CDN, 19 July 1951, 17 July, 4 August 1954; *TC*, 25 July, 17 September 1951, 1, 15, 19 January, 12 March 1952. Interview with A. Ratnayake, successor at the Home Ministry to Sir Oliver, Colombo, 2 August 1977, and four former District Revenue Officers who worked with the Societies, Colombo, September 1978.

villagers' habits of mind. They began to shed their former deference and increasingly embraced the egalitarian assumptions which underlay the universal franchise and free education. They began to articulate resentment over the government's failure to develop programmes to keep pace both with its own rhetoric and with the changes which the franchise, free education, Rural Development Societies and the like had generated.[110] One further point is in order. No thorough study of economic change in Ceylon's villages in this period has been done, but on present evidence, the villager's growing political maturity does not seem to have resulted from any marked change in his economic condition.[111] In this instance, politics seems to have enjoyed primacy as an agent of change.

The second important statement that needs to be made about this election is that Bandaranaike owed his victory very substantially to people outside his party, people who backed him reluctantly, because no alternatives existed. It is, for example, highly misleading to accept the widely held view that his oratory played a major role in galvanizing the movement. There were still in the 1950s frequent flashes of the deadly 'retort Bandaranaceous' and of what even his opponents called his 'crushing power of invective'. But by then his speeches had all too often become stale, rather antiquated in their stylized over-elaborations – even if he was speaking in English, in which he was far more effective than the Sinhala which had to be his mainstay in 1955–56.[112]

The five main groups that delivered victory to Bandaranaike have been enumerated – local board members, ayurvedic physicians, vernacular teachers, young people with bleak prospects[113] and *bhikkhus* – but they

---

[110] For example, the government failed miserably to live up to promises of aid to the landless. (See *CDN*, 7 May 1957 in the light of the *Report of the Kandyan Peasantry Commission, Sessional Paper XVIII – 1951.*)

   The UNP leaders did not realize the impatience of ordinary citizens, even in rural areas, partly because they were too complacent and partly because their party organization was so weak that it was a resounding failure as an information-gathering instrument. It is true that unemployment had grown worse in towns and even in villages outside the main urban concentrations in 1954. (See, for example, the Bernard Aluwihare diaries, 15 January 1955.) It also probably continued to do so. A severe drought over 30,000 acres in the Eastern and North Central Provinces also had some importance (although the MEP put up no candidates in the Eastern Province). But see Economist Intelligence Unit, *Quarterly Economic Review of Ceylon*, no. 9 (February, 1955), pp. 1 and 5; no. 10 (May, 1955), pp. 1, 405; no. 11 (August, 1955), p. 6; no. 12 (November, 1955), Appendix 1; and no. 13 (February, 1956), p. 4.

[111] Interview with Nimal Karunatileke, Colombo, 22 September 1977. *TC*, 2 March, 11 May, 11 July, 1–7, 21 October 1953; *CDN*, 19 January; 17 July; 18 December 1954; 10 January; 21 February 1955.

[112] *CDN*, 17 May 1947. See also, for example, *Ceylon Hansard* (1953), col. 995. Comments on his increasingly stuffy oratory by the mid-1950s come from Gooneratne, *Relative Merits*, p. 157.

[113] On younger voters, see for example, A. L. Wood, 'Political Radicalism in Changing Sinhalese Villages', *Human Organization*, xxiii, 2 (1964), p. 102.

deserve further discussion.[114] Of all these groups, only the members of local boards had a sustained prior association with Bandaranaike, but the strength of his ties to these people has been exaggerated. In sixteen years as the Minister overseeing local government, he was unable to develop strong transactional alliances with large numbers of local board members. In part, he failed because he had neither the inclination nor the skill to be a good distributor of patronage, but mainly because financial stringency and the opposition of his fellow ministers prevented him from obtaining the substantial funds needed to forge such alliances. The most that can be said of most local board members is that they regarded Bandaranaike with a certain, far from compelling, sympathy. After 1952, the UNP had imposed severe cuts in grants to local boards. Their powers to raise revenues were so limited that they were heavily dependent on grants from the national level and nearly all electricity, drainage, water and housing schemes had to be abandoned. It soon became clear that UNP leaders had set out to harass local boards because they regarded them as a source of support for Bandaranaike. The Minister of Local Government was armed with new punitive powers and local boards were temporarily deprived of powers they had long possessed.[115] Board members' efforts for Bandaranaike at the 1956 election were less the result of sympathy for him than of anger at the UNP.

Ayurvedic doctors who backed Bandaranaike at the election also did so mainly out of exasperation with the UNP. The Health Ministry's 1955 white paper on *ayurveda* had been designed more to control indigenous medicine than to aid it. It sought to dictate the content of ayurvedic medicine, to impose state control over teaching institutions and to force aspiring doctors to learn English. It also required government agencies to employ only graduates of the College of Indigenous Medicine, despite

---

[114] K. N. O. Dharmadasa (The Rise of Sinhalese Language Nationalism) has shown that by late 1955, it was unnecessary for Bandaranaike to integrate these groups into a single, loosely-knit movement. It had also been unnecessary, since the late 1940s, to shape the content of popular Sinhalese consciousness. By then, the 'ideology of ethnicity had been largely accomplished', and 'integrated interpretation of the collective past had been developed', as had 'a definitive image of Sinhalese-Buddhist hegemony on the island and defence of Sinhalese people and Buddhism against South Indian invaders' (pp. 398–99).

It should, however, be emphasized that this ideologization had nonetheless occurred quite recently, within the twentieth century, and was not ancient and immutable. See R. A. L. H. Gunawardena, 'The People of the Lion', *Sri Lanka Journal of the Humanities*, v (1979), pp. 1–36.

One of the reasons Bandaranaike had had difficulty linking up with this Sinhalese revival was that it was far more cultural than economic in its focus, and in the 1930s and 1940s, he had tended to stress economic elements – particularly the Indian Tamil presence – first. By 1955, he had shifted firmly to a cultural emphasis.

[115] *TC*, 31 January 1955; *CDN*, 14 and 19 March, 24 May, 14 September, 1 October 1955.

the fact that only 500 of Ceylon's 200,000 practitioners had attended the college. All of this left ayurvedic doctors 'up in arms' and subsequent amendments of policy did little to win back their support.[116]

The grievances of vernacular-medium schoolteachers are already familiar, but two points need emphasis here. First, the schoolteachers who were active in the election campaign were also mainly motivated by anger towards the ruling party. In 1951, it had promised to initiate a gradual but steady changeover from English to the vernaculars as media of instruction, beginning in 1953, but official inaction in preparing vernacular texts made it impossible to meet this schedule. By the end of 1954, vernacular teachers saw clear signs that the government was actively conniving to stifle their expectations. Protests and scattered acts of defiance forced Sir John to issue a new plan for the transition to vernacular education in early 1955. But this rejected the recommend-ations of a pro-vernacular majority in an official report on the problem and seemed an outright betrayal. A few weeks later, vernacular teachers were granted more pay, but they were still earning less than their English-medium counterparts. The UNP's refusal to train more vernacular teachers, or to provide enough facilities for teachers using English to switch to vernaculars, created deep bitterness. It was that emotion more than devotion to Bandaranaike that roused them for the election.[117]

The reader will have noted that these comments have referred to *vernacular* teachers, not Sinhala teachers. The distinction is important. The bitterness towards the government was shared by Sinhala-medium and Tamil-medium teachers alike. Both groups had to suffer inferior pay, schools with inferior facilities and – most crucially in this intensely status-conscious society[118] – inferior status. Both groups knew that until they were placed on an equal footing with English-medium instructors, their promotion prospects would be wretched. Both groups protested vigor-ously. Many Sinhala-medium teachers were well aware that they shared a common interest with their Tamil counterparts. Many of them, overcome by intense frustration, plunged into the bigoted extremes of the Sinhala revival, but many others gave way to 'Sinhala only' reluctantly, expressing fears that it might alienate their Tamil colleagues. They acquiesced to 'Sinhala only' because they believed that the UNP offered them no hope and had to be brought down. Common interests with Tamil counterparts were also shared by three other groups who campaigned for Bandaranaike in 1956: local board members, ayurvedic doctors and students educated mainly in Sinhala who faced far more

[116] *CDN*, 7–11 December 1954, 7 January, 4, 12 April, 9, 13, 19 May 1955.
[117] See, for example, *TC*, 20 June 1953; *CDN*, 7 December 1954, 1, 10 June 1955.
[118] *CDN*, 1 December 1954, 19, 25 May, 27 July, 9 September 1955, *TC*, 20 July 1953.

severe unemployment problems than English-educated youths.[119] This
left only one major group among Bandaranaike's supporters in 1956 who
were not parted from natural Tamil allies by the 'Sinhala only' issue – the
activist *bhikkhus*. Unfortunately for the island's social cohesion, they were
by far the most powerful force in the movement that delivered the
election to Bandaranaike.

Finally, what does all of this tell us about the mass character of
Bandaranaike's 1956 election victory? It is often described as a revolution,
with the linguistic movement providing the vehicle by which the masses
entered Ceylon's history, at last and for good. It is difficult to accept this
view. There is no question that Bandaranaike's MEP polled a mass vote,
nor can we doubt that the language movement generated popular
excitement, perhaps even mass excitement among the Sinhalese. But the
generation of that excitement and of the MEP's mass vote was largely the
work of these five groups – local board members, ayurvedic physicians,
Sinhala-medium schoolteachers, educated youths and *bhikkhus*. Far from
being 'the masses', these groups constitute a set of village-level elites.
Some are even inclined to call them a rural middle class, although that
term overstates their cohesion. But they were not ordinary villagers. Four
of these groups (leaving aside the youths) tended to possess high status
within the village and to receive deference from fellow-villagers. Most
members of these four groups (and according to numerous witnesses,
most youthful activists) came from locally pre-eminent castes. It was
common for ayurvedic physicians, local board members and schoolteachers to possess modest plots of land. *Bhikkhus* controlled village temple
lands which they sometimes exploited for profit. This usually did not
make them wealthy, but it bolstered their elite standing in relation to most
of their fellow-villagers who were comparatively less secure
economically.

If members of these groups – and here we can include the youths – did
not constitute a rural middle class, they at least shared middle-class
aspirations and grievances which were probably alien to most village
dwellers. These aspirations caused them to look beyond the village to
supra-local and national arenas, to urban or semi-urban areas. In large
measure, this tendency and their connections to associations and informal
networks of interaction (however flimsy) that reached down into the
village from those arenas made them people who were *in* the village but
not wholly *of* the village.[120] When they are considered alongside the

---

[119] See, for example, the testimony of a District Judge and a school principal to the Sasana
Commission, *CDN*, 21 May 1958.
[120] These comments are based on a wide range of interviews with scholars and participants
in the events under study. Of special importance were interviews with Sharon Mayne,

westernized, prosperous urbanites in Parliament before the 1956 election or even alongside the UNP's wealthy backers in the hinterland, members of these five groups seem humble figures. But when they are viewed alongside common villagers, they clearly fall within the upper-middle stratum of village society.

The popular response which these village elites helped to generate came in substantial part from the middle and lower strata of rural society. In terms of caste, Bandaranaike's MEP drew heavy support from non-*Goyigamas*, including underprivileged groups like the numerically powerful *Wahumpuras* and *Bathgamas*. These were the groups which, at previous elections, had suffered intimidation. This and apathy at the depressing choice before 1956 among candidates who did not represent their interests had caused many, and in some cases most of them to abstain at previous elections.

In 1956, Bandaranaike sought their support quite explicitly. Although he was largely ignorant of the size, location and internal structure of the depressed castes, his lifelong abhorrence of caste discrimination had long been apparent from his unpretentious style on tour. He specifically encouraged these groups not to be intimidated by toughs. Many of them responded,[121] thanks to their increasing awareness of supra-local politics, the new assertiveness that many had acquired in the expanded school system and the Rural Development Societies, and the sense of old verities passing away amid the popular intoxication with the language movement. In the event, they encountered less intimidation than in previous

---

9 September 1978 and Gananath Obeyesekere, 21 August and 6 September 1978, all in Colombo. See also, *CDN*, 1, 2, 7, 14 August 1939; 16 August 1940; 6 March 1957; M. Roberts, 'The Political Antecedents of the Revivalist Elite within the MEP Coalition of 1956', Ceylon Studies Seminar, typescript, 1970.

[121] It should be said that from the existing statistics, it is not possible to *prove* that increased depressed caste participation carried the MEP to power in 1956. An analysis of figures from the constituencies known to contain large *Wahumpura* and *Bathgama* populations reveals that while four showed an increase in voter turnout between 1952 and 1956, five showed a decline which exceeded the decline in national turnout from 70.7 per cent to 69.0 per cent, and one a smaller decline than the national average. In only six of the ten constituencies did the increase in the number of registered voters between 1952 and 1956 exceed the rate of increase nationally (15.8 per cent). Given these figures, it is nonetheless possible that (a) the depressed caste voters who had previously supported the UNP turned to the MEP, or (b) that an increase in depressed caste votes was masked by a decrease in high caste votes. Impressionistic information collected by Janice Jiggins and the author strongly suggests, however, that the latter explanation is more credible. A great deal of oral evidence indicates that the *Wahumpuras* were particularly avid in their opposition to the Senanayake clan and to Sir John as a member of it.

The ten constituencies mentioned above are Kegalle, Ratnapura, Matale, Kurunegala, Anuradhapura, Hambantota, Nivitigala, Wariyapola, Kalawewa, and Mawanella. *Sources:* J. Jiggins, *Family and Caste*; and interviews with Nimal Karunatileke (the successful SLFP candidate at Matale), Colombo, 22 and 26 September 1978.

elections, partly because many complacent UNP leaders[122] failed to organize it. More crucially, many village headmen – whose annoyance at the government's failure to defend their interests had led to a slackening in the time-honoured structure for social control in rural parts – failed to provide the UNP with essential local-level assistance.[123]

It is well known that by drawing these disadvantaged groups more fully into the political process, Bandaranaike and his allies contributed to the medium-term stability of the political order.[124] But what is often overlooked is that by providing these groups with a champion at the apex of the Sinhalese status hierarchy, Bandaranaike ensured that their resentments would not be turned against the prevailing *social* order. So even as the Sinhala revival threatened social cohesion among the Ceylonese, the change of government that it produced helped to conserve it among the Sinhalese.

By reaching down below the social stratum on which the UNP based its power, to mobilize people in lower strata, Bandaranaike and his allies found new political resources which carried them to power. In the process, he neatly turned the tables on the Senanayake clan, of which Sir John was a member. In the early decades of the century, the Senanayakes and their allies had ousted the Bandaranaike–Obeyesekere-led Anglican elite from pre-eminence by mobilizing elite Sinhalese Buddhist groups that had not previously participated in national politics. However, in speaking of 'mobilization' in the 1956 election, great caution is called for. People responded more as a result of the emotional force of the issues involved and the evocative power of the symbols and slogans presented than the strength of the organization making the appeals. The *bhikkhus*, teachers, ayurvedic doctors and others were thrown very loosely and imperfectly together by the excitement of the revival. When victory was achieved, their 'organization' – such as it was – quickly began to disintegrate. Bandaranaike, who perceived these groups (particularly the *bhikkhus*) as allies who might turn on him when their wildly inflated expectations were inevitably frustrated, made no effort to prevent this. He tried to forge links between his party and some leading figures from these groups, but this was mainly to ensure against their disaffection. Next to nothing was done to sustain the mobilization either of the voters or of the village elites that had galvanized them.

---

[122] See UNP, Report of the Special Commission', file 173, J. R. Jayewardene Papers, Presidential Archive, Colombo.

[123] This is based on numerous interviews with candidates, observers and government servants then working in rural areas.

[124] It can be argued that the insurrection of 1971 demonstrates that 1956 also helped to sow the seeds of *long*-term *in*stability.

This was not the result of a desire on Bandaranaike's part to exclude the common man from the political process. On the contrary, he genuinely hoped and even believed that his reformist government could enable someone of humble origins to succeed him one day as Prime Minister.[125] But he did not see that it was necessary to create new organizational structures to make that possible. As we shall see in Chapter 8, he rather naïvely believed that a new era of greater opportunity for ordinary folk could, without enormous effort or difficulty, be ushered in by a concerned, reforming government. One result was that Bandaranaike, by simply not asking himself whether he should alter the over-centralized character of the political system, tended somewhat unconsciously to manipulate symbols and slogans as a *substitute for* rather than as a *means to* sustained political mobilization.

The election of 1956 was the first in which issues, party programmes and hence parties clearly outweighed personalities.[126] The central issue, the status of Sinhala, acquired much of its emotional force from popular discontent on a wide range of other issues.[127] The failure of the UNP to deal sensibly with those discontents, or with the Sinhala revival when it arose, places far more of the responsibility for the emergence of anti-Tamil bigotry upon the old ruling party than has been attributed to it. Bandaranaike, however, also bears a considerable share of that responsibility. He never abandoned his desire to aid both vernaculars, as his *sotto voce* comments during the campaign on provisions for the use of Tamil suggest, but the main thrust of his campaign speeches contributed to the fervour and to the dangerously unrealistic expectations of Sinhalese chauvinists. Bandaranaike the opportunistic candidate, then, did much to encourage the emergence of the bigotry with which Bandaranaike the curiously naïve, utopian Prime Minister was unable to cope.

[125] Interviews at Colombo with two Bandaranaike lieutenants, 27 August 1977 and 9 September 1980.

[126] For more on this, see C. A. Woodward, *The Growth of a Party System in Ceylon* (Providence, 1969).

[127] This is a major theme in Wriggins, *Ceylon: Dilemmas*.

8

ARBITER, 1956–1959

Bandaranaike's early days in power witnessed abundant changes in style. Some were rather contrived, but all bespoke the Prime Minister's determination to offer ordinary people a responsive, liberal government that was sensitive to their needs and values. Members of the new Cabinet were required to be sworn in wearing 'national dress', attire which for some of them was unusual enough to provoke jokes from their leader. The government announced that imperial honours would no longer be awarded and that Ceylonese debutantes would cease to be presented at Buckingham Palace. Fruit juice replaced liquor at official functions which – in accordance with Bandaranaike's restrained tastes – were far less lavish than before. The new premier continued the customary weekly breakfast-time press conferences, but the menu was indigenized. Sir John's famous Anglo-Ceylonese egg-hoppers were replaced by *kiribath* (a milk and rice dish), although Bandaranaike spoiled the effect somewhat by wearing a western suit and eating it with a spoon rather than his fingers.

More radio time was devoted to Sinhala at the expense of English, though not of Tamil, and concern was shown for the anxieties of Tamils by emphasizing the need to ensure 'the reasonable use of Tamil' once Sinhala was made the sole official language. Other minorities were reassured to see a Muslim chosen as Speaker, a Burgher (a person of European ancestry) as Attorney General, a Christian as Chief Whip, and a Christian and a Muslim as ministers in a Cabinet of fourteen in which for the first time no Tamil served.[1] The caste composition of the Cabinet changed little,[2] but Bandaranaike sought to reassure depressed caste

[1] *CDN*, 13–26 April 1956.
[2] The differences between the new Cabinet and the last UNP Cabinet were as follows:

	Goyigama	Karava	Salagama	Muslim	Tamil	Total
UNP Cabinet	10	1	0	1	2	14
MEP Cabinet	9	2	2	1	0	14

Source: J. Jiggins, Family and Caste in the Politics of the Sinhalese, 1947–1971, University of Ceylon, Peradeniya doctoral thesis, 1973, pp. 133–34. Jiggins mistakenly omitted the MEP's Muslim from her count.

groups by appointing one of their number to a seat in Parliament and a few others to high bureaucratic posts – although the *Bathgamas* gained much more from this than the *Wahumpuras*.[3]

It was announced that the first Speech from the Throne would be in Sinhala rather than English until it was learned that the Governor-General, Sir Oliver Goonetilleke, could not read it well enough, even if roman letters were used. The very fact that Sir Oliver (a Christian and a pillar of the old UNP) was allowed to retain his post indicated that Bandaranaike's liberality extended not only to supporters but to former foes as well. Even Sir John Kotelawala benefited when he was allowed to bend currency regulations to purchase a farm in England.[4]

Bandaranaike's immense, indeed excessive generosity soon generated problems, but for the present, the change of government was greeted with exuberance by common folk. On the day the new Parliament opened, people from distant villages crowded into the galleries and when the proceedings ended, they pushed their good-humoured way onto the floor of the House. With cries of 'Now we are the government', they took turns sitting in the Speaker's chair. 'From the well of the Chamber they gazed upwards into the galleries and from the galleries the remaining MPs and guests looked back at them.'[5] For this moment of mild bewilderment at least, it seemed (in a much-used phrase) that *ape anduwa* – 'our government' – had arrived.

It is impossible in a single chapter to provide an exhaustive account of this or any premiership. Instead, this discussion will focus on a few crucial elements in the story. The two great themes which dominated Bandaranaike's career from the late 1930s onwards – Sinhalese parochialism and cosmopolitan reform – will hold centre-stage. As Prime Minister, Bandaranaike generally sought to placate and contain the former while promoting, somewhat cautiously, the latter. He did so because he was at heart no communalist and because he was anxious and uncertain about the Sinhala revivalists, especially the *bhikkhus*. His delight in his landslide victory was tempered somewhat by the suspicion that it owed more to the doings of these groups than to his efforts and those of his party. As one political aide put it, 'he had tried so many things to get to the top and now he was a little shaken to find that it was someone else who had put him there'.[6] It was difficult to devise a strategy for

[3] *Ibid.*, pp. 143 and 255, and J. Jiggins, *Caste and Family in the Politics of the Sinhalese, 1947–1976* (Cambridge, 1979), p. 14. For further material on the background of MEP legislators, see Ceylon Daily News, *The Parliament of Ceylon 1956* (Colombo, 1956); and M. R. Singer, *The Emerging Elite: A Study of Political Leadership in Ceylon* (Cambridge, MA., 1964).

[4] Interview with Sir John Kotelawala, Kandawela, 22 August 1978.

[5] *CDN*, 21 April 1956.

[6] Interview with Nimal Karunatilake, Colombo, 6 September 1978.

dealing with the *bhikkhus*. He had had close ties to a few of them for many years, but the great mass of activists had turned to him only very recently. They were too poorly organized to put forward representatives and the formal revivalist association, the Eksath Bhikkhu Peramuna – which was itself an *ad hoc* body – had never spoken for more than a minority of activist monks. Soon after the election, it was riven by severe factional squabbles, and some of its leaders alienated many *bhikkhus* and Buddhist laymen by criticizing the high priests of the two great chapters based in Kandy. Bandaranaike also saw that many *bhikkhus* had wildly unrealistic and occasionally millenarian expectations, extravagant notions of their own importance and a hard-eyed, zealous intolerance of any other viewpoint.[7]

Bandaranaike was, as always, unusually susceptible to the dictates of whatever role he happened to find himself in, and in 1956 he found himself the leader of a heterogeneous nation which could only be governed effectively by cosmopolitan means. He regarded social and political reform as a cure for parochialism and for civic disharmony in general. To promote such reform among some of his more reluctant ministers, he found it useful to have the Marxist leader Philip Gunawardena and one of his colleagues – Fisheries Minister William Silva – on hand. But to keep them in check, he had also intentionally given them less ministerial power than they had hoped for, as if to remind them that his SLFP had won enough seats to form a government of its own.[8] As things eventually developed, reforms were enacted too slowly and conflict within the Cabinet over reforms undermined the government's authority, so that there was little hope that progress on this front could ease communal tensions. And to compound the problem, at crucial moments Bandaranaike proved to be an inconstant cosmopolitan. In part this occurred because he took dangerously uncritical satisfaction in his recent success, as when he expressed unguarded delight to an interviewer that 'I have never found anything to excite the people in quite the way this language issue does.' But the main explanation was his weakness in the face of pressure from Sinhalese bigots. That was the most costly example

[7] This is apparent in the more scurrilous stories that people spread about the UNP at the 1956 election. See, 'Report of the Special Commission on Party Reform and Reorganisation', appendix C, file 173, J. R. Jayewardene Papers, Presidential Archive; see also Bernard Aluwihare Diaries, 17 March 1956, University of Peradeniya Library; and *CDN*, 17 August 1959.

[8] Some have suggested that Gunawardena and Silva cleverly wrung more out of Bandaranaike than he wished to give them, but accounts from both Marxist and SLFP sides suggest that the Prime Minister held the upper hand throughout. This is based on interviews with (among others) Prins Gunasekera (who accompanied Gunawardena in the first round of negotiations), 26 August 1978 and A. P. Jayasuriya (Bandaranaike's Home Minister), 2 September 1977, both at Colombo.

of a general and quite astonishing tendency to make unwarranted concessions to almost any group that demanded them. This inclination, which was to prove his political undoing, arose out of an eccentric notion of what constituted legitimate authority, and of what posture he should adopt as Prime Minister.

He chose for himself the role of arbiter, both in the narrow sense of a mediator resolving small-scale disputes – an activity to which he devoted an inordinate amount of time – and more broadly, as the magnanimous bestower of largesse, soothing the nation's discontents. In this second role, he sought to be a latter day Solomon finding a judicious balance between Tamils and Sinhalese, between rightists and leftists in his deeply divided government. And yet when pressured from one quarter or another, he yielded so much so quickly and guilelessly – in the belief that mere magnanimity would somehow generate harmony – that he squandered his own authority. This made it impossible for him to arbitrate effectively, to promote reform adequately, and for the centre to hold in the disputes between Sinhalese and Tamils, and between right and left.

For most Afro-Asian leaders of this generation, arrival at the top of the 'greasy pole' – as Bandaranaike, quoting Disraeli, called it[9] – occasioned a great swelling of the ego. Most of their countrymen were still quite unfamiliar with the new political process, and were therefore – at least for a time – unable either to assert themselves effectively within that process or to devise alternatives to it. For a limited period, while the rules of politics were being absorbed by the masses, the leader had great freedom of action and immense opportunities for creativity or abuse. Since most people tended to perceive the political process through the person of the leader, he had a great educative task to perform. But the relative absence of restraints allowed him, if he was so inclined, to shape political institutions around himself and his personal appetites. Human nature being what it is, most were so inclined. The need in many new nations for an evocative figure to provide coherence and focus while the political system took shape and gained acceptance also impelled national leaders to allow themselves to seem larger than life. Many began to believe their own propaganda and that often led, eventually, to their downfall.

Bandaranaike and his ego experienced a distinctly different sort of liberation in 1956. His resignation from the ruling party five years earlier had freed him from the authority of superiors which he had never been able to accept as legitimate. His rise to pre-eminence ended the infuriating

[9] Interview with R. St. L. P. Deraniyagala, Colombo, 1 September 1980.

ordeal of seeing at the helm of affairs men whom he believed to be his inferiors. As a consequence the spite and the abrasive, sometimes wanton pursuit of narrow advantage that had often surfaced in the past – not least in the 1956 election campaign – drained away almost completely.

While most other Afro-Asian leaders projected themselves as symbols of the new political and social order, Bandaranaike actually scaled down the rhetoric of self-advertisement. Consider, for example, his favourite image of his role in the transition from the old order to the new.

I feel that I am in my own small way both a nurse and a midwife. I am a nurse at a deathbed. I realize at least that the thing is dying. I would like to see, as should be the case at every deathbed, that the death is reasonably peaceful and dignified. It shocks me equally that anyone should try artificially to galvanize the dying thing into life and that anyone should place his hand at the throat of the dying thing and squeeze out the life that is already fast ebbing.

I am also, I feel, a midwife at a birth. I would like that birth to be auspicious and painless as far as possible . . . I am not impatient to drag the living thing before its time out of the womb with instruments and bring forth to the world something grotesque and distorted. I am also not prepared to strangle that life in its womb.[10]

He casts himself here not as the embodiment of the new order but in an instrumental role, crucial for a time, but ultimately a rather marginal figure. Nor did he aspire to an interminable spell in power. After many years of often undignified struggle to arrive at the pinnacle, when he reached it, he wanted nothing so much as a reasonably early retirement. He hoped to hold power for a few years until the common people had emerged into the political arena sufficiently to take up their birthright. He would then move on to a well-earned rest, perhaps as a ceremonial President under a new republican constitution. He would reside among the ruins at Anuradhapura and complete his epic novel, *Karma*, which could never receive the time it deserved while he remained a full-time politician.[11]

This may seem a remarkable change in a man who had pursued power for so long, often with the gloves off, but it was not entirely illogical. In part, he was conforming, mostly unconsciously, to the British liberal tradition of restraint in the use of power, and respect for precedent and the institutions of state. It was easier for him to do so than for most other Asian and African leaders since in Ceylon (like India) institutions were

[10] M. A. de Silva, *The Thoughts of S. W. R. D. Bandaranaike* (Nugegoda, n.d.), pp. 54–55. See also, *CDN*, 11 March 1957.

[11] Interviews with several close associates of Bandaranaike, Colombo, 1978 and 1980, and an interview with Lord Garner (an acquaintance of Bandaranaike who met him in Canada during his premiership and heard of these aspirations from him) in London, 6 November 1979. See also, W. L. Fernando, 'Personal Reminiscences of the Late Mr S. W. R. D. Bandaranaike', *Radio Times* (Colombo), xxi, 24 (1970), pp. 7–8.

well-developed and well-integrated with elites that possessed at least tenuous links with the mass. But his reckless generosity as Prime Minister went far beyond British political custom and owed more to his own peculiar view of what constituted legitimate authority. With the possible exception of Warden Stone, no superior to whom he had been subject had ever enjoyed legitimacy in his eyes – not Sir Solomon, Radford, Ceylon's British Governors, Jayatilaka, D. S. Senanayake or his successors. He saw legitimate authority as a rarity which could only be attained through acts of great magnanimity. Bandaranaike's ambiguous relationship with his father probably played a central role in the development of this view since in adopting it, he was reacting against Sir Solomon's coercive ways within the family, even as he conformed to the old mudaliyar's practice of showing clients and petitioners the fulsome generosity that they expected of someone in his position.

His notion of legitimate authority also appears to have rested on the assumption that human nature was essentially benign, so that the task of a leader was to foster that goodness through acts of inordinate concern and kindness. He believed that he could thereby produce a society which would be broadly equitable and in which a spirit of sharing, tolerance and common interest would yield the kind of harmony that he envisioned in his lyrical reference to the Garden of the Hesperides which precedes the preface to this book and which he again recalled as Prime Minister. This was a noble, utopian vision, but it was utterly unsuited to the mundane, petty realities of running a polity – particularly a polity riven by communal animosity that had been fuelled by the bearer of the utopian vision.

This post-election change of view quickly became apparent. He emphasized the need for 'fairplay to all' in Ceylon society and made sure that reporters noticed that he was accompanied by his Tamil secretary and a Burgher official when he visited Radio Ceylon to make his first broadcast to the nation. He stressed that the change in the official language would not threaten the jobs of non-Sinhalese civil servants[12] and astonished close associates by telling self-deprecating jokes to reporters, something which the old Bandaranaike had never done, either in public or in private.[13] Before long, he began to carry magnanimity to

---

[12] On these incidents, see *CDN*, 12, 13, 17 and 24 April 1956. This gave a rather misleading impression since in practice, Bandaranaike quietly reduced the number of Tamils in higher bureaucratic posts quite markedly. He also cut back *Goyigama* representation from roughly one-half to roughly one-third and gave Karavas and Salagamas a great many more high posts, with a much smaller number of appointments going to Duravas, Muslims and Bathgamas. Jiggins, *Family and Caste*, p. 253.

[13] *CDN*, 5 May 1956. The comment on the old Bandaranaike is based on dozens of interviews.

excess. In May 1956, eighteen men of the Ceylon artillery went on hunger strike in the northern town of Mannar, apparently demanding that the army train them as jockeys. Instead of disciplining them or dealing with them through an intermediary, the premier flew personally to the scene. He sat with the men for an hour, explained that the army had no race horses and resolved the dispute.[14]

To have done this at a time when many long-suppressed grievances – real and imagined, weighty and spurious – were being set before 'our government' was to inflate what were already dangerously unrealistic expectations and to risk the rapid dissipation of his authority. Yet Bandaranaike revelled in the role of conciliator and healer, and he made a great show of receiving aggrieved deputations, some of which spoke for tiny, eccentric interests which should either have been politely spurned or dealt with by his ministers. Hunger strikes became something of a national pastime and could be relied upon to trigger a response from Cabinet level, as when the Home Minister rushed to Welikade prison to treat with fasting inmates. By the end of May, it had reached absurd proportions. On a single day, a driver for the Irrigation Department undertook a fast in Minipe, demanding to see a minister about non-receipt of a bonus while a prisoner at Anuradhapura jail climbed to the top of a bo tree and refused to come down, insisting that the Prime Minister 'call over and speak to him'.[15]

All of this might have been more entertaining had it not intruded upon the most important issue of the day – the 'Sinhala Only' Bill. Bandaranaike had convened a special committee of his legislators, including hard-liners on the language issue, to draw up the bill. It met at his home where he was able to steer through a draft that included numerous safeguards for minorities, partly by introducing them too late for hard-liners to study them properly. To preserve unanimity, he agreed to drop a clause permitting correspondence with government departments in English and Tamil. But he succeeded characteristically in having it both ways by obtaining a verbal understanding that letters in English or Tamil would be answered in those languages.[16] On 22 May, the draft was presented to the entire MEP parliamentary group where he encountered stiff resistance from Sinhala revivalists whose extreme views had been encouraged by his own campaign rhetoric. Nonetheless, by making a few minor concessions, he managed to win another unanimous endorsement.

The matter might have ended there, but the following day a university

[14] *CDN*, 10 May and 27 July 1956.
[15] *CDN*, 16, 21–22, 26 May 1956. See also, *CDN*, 18 February 1957.
[16] *CDN*, 17 and 23 May 1956.

teacher and long-time SLFP member went on hunger strike within the precincts of Parliament, demanding to address legislators on the evils of the draft bill. His statements, like those of other Sinhala extremists, were consistently hysterical. He claimed that a clause permitting local authorities, after a two-thirds vote, to use Tamil or English was 'worse than parity and calculated to make Ceylon a part of Madras in six months and an attempt to commit murder in the dark'. Such preposterous remarks might have been studiously ignored, but instead the premier sent Cabinet Ministers to plead with him to abandon his fast. In response the man asked why, if the Prime Minister could fly to Mannar to meet eighteen common soldiers, he could not walk downstairs in Parliament to meet one of his own 'supporters'. In a fit of misplaced liberality, Bandaranaike then agreed over the objections of Cabinet colleagues to reopen the matter with the parliamentary party and to let the extremist address the meeting. The occasion was a disaster. The extremist's speech (in English until, at MPs' insistence, he switched to Sinhala), whipped up sentiment that forced Bandaranaike to drop two key clauses permitting local boards to use Tamil and English, and candidates for government service to sit examinations in those languages. Bandaranaike announced that provisions for the 'reasonable use of Tamil' would come later, when emotions had cooled, but he had stumbled badly and the editorial pages insisted that 'THE PREMIER MUST GOVERN' and 'LET THE PILOT STEER.'[17]

This triggered a strong Tamil reaction. Federal Party leaders had whipped up feeling against the bill for weeks and on 5 June, the day that it was introduced in Parliament, a complete *hartal* (suspension of normal business) was held in Tamil-majority areas. Two hundred Tamils converged on Galle Face Green next to Parliament. Police barriers blocked their way to the House and Bandaranaike's appeal for calm to a Sinhalese counter-demonstration plus an opportune cloudburst prevented serious violence. But the debate was conducted amid 'the sounds of rampaging mobs along the road past the barricaded Parliament'. Small, mainly Sinhalese bands roved through Colombo stoning restaurants, looting a few boutiques and destroying two cars. The following morning 'looting mobs' reappeared in the Colombo Pettah (market area) and police opened fire on three occasions, wounding seven. Official estimates for these two days counted 87 injuries, 113 arrests and 43 looted shops in the capital where all demonstrations were thereupon banned. Two days later, violence and arson broke out in the Eastern Province ports of Trincomalee and Batticaloa. In the latter city, violence following a

[17] *CDN*, 17, 23, 26, 29–31 May and 2 June 1956.

demonstration by 10,000 Tamils provoked police firing which caused at least two deaths. Bandaranaike then banned a large Federal Party march on the city. In Jaffna, a sniper opened fire on police attempting to make an arrest.[18]

Incidents took place in several outstations, but the worst violence occurred in Gal Oya, an area of the heavily Tamil Eastern Province which had been colonized by Sinhalese settlers under D. S. Senanayake's land development scheme. Sinhalese toughs – inspired as always by fantastic rumours – seized government cars, bulldozers and high explosives and for a few days terrorized the Tamil minority in the colony. Scores of Tamils, certainly well over one hundred, were massacred and hundreds more were driven into hiding. The army was sent in to quell disturbances and three senior ministers were rushed in to calm Sinhalese colonists. Gal Oya was by far the worst episode of communal violence in modern Ceylon's history to that time, but although it left many people mildly stunned, its effect upon the public consciousness was rather muted. The press and the government both severely understated the death toll and the extent of the campaign of terror. Gal Oya's remoteness and the brief duration of the violence cushioned its impact. Even those who knew the full, horrific story were inclined to see Gal Oya as an eccentric place, on the margins of national life. A colony of uprooted Sinhalese in a Tamil-majority area seemed particularly explosive. Ministers and the Colombo establishment in general assured themselves that such events could not happen in mainstream areas. They were encouraged in this view by a patent decline over the next few months in the potential for communal violence. A Tamil march on Trincomalee led by the Federal Party two months later passed off without incident.[19] But ministers' response to the Gal Oya killings was nonetheless a naïve, complacent and ultimately costly misjudgement.

For several months after the troubles of June, Bandaranaike studiously minimized public discussion of the language issue. He appealed repeatedly for tolerance and good will in speeches, while privately assuring Tamil community leaders of his determination to secure fair treatment for them. The day after the 'Sinhala Only' Act took effect in July, he quietly issued a *Gazette* notification stating that any language other than Sinhala could continue as before in official use until further notice.

---

[18] *CDN*, 6–9 and 14–23 June, 12 July 1956; and Bernard Aluwihare Diaries, 5 June 1956, University of Peradeniya Library.

[19] *CDN*, 14–23 June 1956 and T. Vittachi, *Emergency '58*, London, 1958 p. 20. See also, Gal Oya Development Board, *Annual Report, 1957–57* (Colombo, 1958), p. 1; *Administration Report of the Inspector-General of Police, for 1956* (Colombo, 1957), pp. A10–A17; and *Administration Report of the Government Agent, Batticaloa District, for 1956* (Colombo, 1957), p. A176.

This nullified much of the new act and eased Tamil anxiety. A month later, leading Tamil politicians in the Federal Party threatened 'direct action' if their demands for a federal state and an end to 'Sinhala Only' were not granted. But their fear that the Prime Minister was winning over moderate Tamils caused them to give the government a full year, until August 1957, to accede to the ultimatum. The ruling party's most virulent Sinhalese bigot, K. M. P. Rajaratna, who had proved an embarrassing Junior Minister of Posts, mercifully resigned. Within a few weeks, the defections of three MPs – including a Tamil and a Muslim – to the ruling party indicated that the violence of June and Bandaranaike's quietly moderate policy on the language issue had not yet weakened his position too seriously.[20]

The new government faced such high expectations that it would have caused disappointment even if it had moved rapidly and forcefully to introduce changes of real substance. In failing to do so, it compounded its difficulties in dealing with those expectations, with extremists on both sides of the language issue and with its opponents. Some important changes were made, mainly on the orders of Bandaranaike who quickly proved to be far more innovative than most of his Cabinet colleagues. The Public Security Department which had begun to seem an ominously intrusive police force responsible only to the premier under Sir John Kotelawala, was placed under the control of the Inspector-General of Police who had orders to dismantle it. Armed paramilitary units made up of 'volunteers' from the public service were disbanded. The death penalty was suspended for a period of three years. The first steps were taken toward the normalization of relations with Communist countries, the closure of British air and naval bases in Ceylon, and the adoption of a non-aligned foreign policy. The free midday meal for schoolchildren was restored, and subsidies reduced the price of rice and sugar, and so on.[21] But these changes were outweighed in the public mind during 1956 by serious omissions.

Complaints about delays in the passage of the 'Sinhala Only' Bill[22] were unfair if predictable, given Bandaranaike's campaign pledge to make the change within twenty-four hours. Hopes of swift action on several other issues dear to the hearts of Sinhalese revivalists were dashed by tardiness and tokenism. Those who sought the prohibition of liquor and gambling were pleased at the closure of the bars in the Lower House and the

[20] *CDN*, 13, 19 July, 13, 22 August, 4 September and 16 and 23 October 1956. See also, material in file 308, J. R. Jayewardene Papers, Presidential Archive, Colombo.
[21] *CDN*, 19–21 and 27 April, 3 May and 11 August 1956.
[22] See, for example, *CDN*, 5 May 1956.

legislators' hostel, but they were annoyed when Bandaranaike would only say that total prohibition was a long-term goal and when the Home Minister would not go beyond an acceptance 'in principle' of the need to ban horse racing.[23] Those who wanted major programmes to encourage Sinhalese culture – including the new Minister of Cultural Affairs and his revivalist advisors – were sorely disappointed by the Prime Minister's delaying tactics,[24] and inaction on the promise to convert Buddhist *pirivenas* (centres of higher study) into universities produced protests.[25] The leisurely pace at which the adoption of the vernacular was urged upon civil servants at the district and provincial levels and the delay until September of the publication of even the government *Gazette* in Sinhala (or, to be more precise, of just one section of it) also angered many.[26]

The government's dilatory ways also had an impact in the areas which concerned groups other than Sinhalese revivalists. Pledges to overhaul or abandon the old headman system appeared to be contradicted by the Home Minister's assurances to headmen in October. The nationalization of the bus system eventually occurred *in toto*, but during 1956, ministers seemed to prefer a piecemeal plan that would require eight years. The non-appearance of programmes to aid unemployed and underemployed secondary school graduates, some of whom had worked for the MEP at the 1956 election, caused further distress.[27] Delays even extended to matters of importance within the ruling coalition. Despite repeated statements in press editorials and by Bandaranaike that Trade Minister R. G. Senanayake should resign one of the two parliamentary seats which he had won in April, the latter took no action. In December, the MEP found itself unable to finalize its candidates list for the important Colombo municipal election until only five days before polling.[28]

There are several explanations for all of this. First, ministers did not manage their time well, mainly because they allowed the petitioners who constantly waited upon them at home, at the office and on the road far too much access. In receiving these people, ministers were playing a role very like that of the old quasi-feudal seigneur of British and Dutch Ceylon, bestowing largesse from the verandah of his *walauwa* (grand family residence). It was a role which appealed to them immensely and which most of them regarded as essential to their political survival. On this latter point they were mistaken since survival in a mass polity actually depended on the systematic, institutionalized and rather impersonal distribution of goods and services to a wide array of interests. Their random dealings

---

[23] *CDN*, 24 and 27 August 1956.
[24] Interviews with the Minister's principal aide and a long-time revivalist, N. Q. Dias, Colombo, 6 September 1977. [25] *CDN*, 12 November 1956.
[26] *CDN*, 6 September, 17 October and 6 December 1956.
[27] *CDN*, 23–24 July, 12 September, 16 October and 13 and 24 December 1956.
[28] *CDN*, 8, 10, 18 May, 4 October and 6 December 1956.

with petitioners were a distraction from that and a largely unproductive diversion of spoils. It reached the point where even Bandaranaike's hard-headed deputy and Leader of the House, C. P. de Silva, confessed in August 1956 that he had to follow the crucial budget debate mostly through printed accounts because so much of his time was consumed by petitioners.[29]

Many delays were also caused by civil servants who were un-sympathetic to the new government and unhelpful in planning and executing new programmes and in most cases by ministers who were inexperienced, incapable or usually both. There were some notable exceptions. Philip Gunawardena at Lands was brilliant and forceful, C. P. de Silva at Agriculture had vast experience as a civil servant and was very effective. In M. W. H. de Silva, Bandaranaike had found a capable and imaginative reformer, the finest Law Minister in the island's history.[30] Yet despite the contributions of other capable men at Transport, Finance and elsewhere, the Cabinet was in general unimpressive. The pool of hastily recruited MPs simply contained too few gifted or experienced people, and some who possessed those qualities and were made ministers lacked the emotional stability to serve constructively. Bandaranaike, a lifelong intellectual snob, was acutely aware of these weaknesses and sometimes showed his contempt openly. When a bumbling Cabinet colleague once quoted a man of letters in a speech to a public meeting, Bandaranaike turned to a journalist and said, 'You see, some of my ministers actually read books.' He later told an SLFP legislators' meeting that he 'pitied the ignorance' of Minister of Health Mrs Wimala Wijewardene,[31] one of the least able, least stable and least principled members of his team.

His concern about the abilities and the quite conservative attitudes of many of his ministers, and the excessive deference which some of them showed him – so that they would not even take minor decisions without his approval – and the emerging divisions between left and right within his Cabinet, impelled the Prime Minister to take more responsibilities unto himself than any single person could manage expeditiously. The inevitable result was further delay, and the problem was compounded again by his own liking for the role of arbiter which entailed both the depletion of his personal authority and the expenditure of far too much time on trivial matters.

---

[29] *CDN*, 2 August 1956.
[30] See N. Tiruchelvam, The Popular Tribunals of Sri Lanka: A Socio-Legal Inquiry, Harvard Law School doctoral thesis, 1973. I am also grateful to Vijaya Samaraweera for information on this point.
[31] For the first incident, interview with Mervyn de Silva, Colombo, 16 September 1980. For the second, *CDN*, 4 September 1957.

The excitement over linguistic and communal issues had receded after the passage of the 'Sinhala Only' Act and the violence at Gal Oya in June 1956. Ministers thus had some justification for thinking that they had put this problem behind them, but they were mistaken. The insecurity of many Sinhalese and the exasperations of interest groups whose fortunes were linked to Sinhala had not been removed. Nor had the suspicions of Tamils. Their leaders in the Federal Party had promised direct action if fair treatment was not conceded by August 1957, but others in the Tamil majority provinces were not prepared to wait that long. In December 1956, they began defacing newly introduced motor vehicle number plates on which the Sinhala character for 'Sri' (as in Sri Lanka) had replaced English lettering. Vehicles bearing the new plates were often stoned or waylaid in Tamil areas and the Tamil parties were joined by left opposition parties in rallies against what was an ill-considered innovation at a time when the Prime Minister was seeking to ease Tamil fears. Demonstrations and intimidation mounted, but the authorities restrained police lest they provoke serious trouble. On 4 February 1957, Independence Day, which Tamils observed with a *hartal* as a day of mourning, two Tamils were shot dead by a sniper as they tried to hoist black flags in Trincomalee, but the immediate deployment of heavy police and military forces prevented further incidents.[32] The anti-'Sri' campaign declined gradually over the weeks which followed and eventually petered out. Bandaranaike's restraints on the police, which established a dubious precedent for the future, had worked well in this instance and he pressed on with efforts to develop an understanding with Tamil leaders.

The anti-'Sri' protests predictably incensed the more extreme Sinhala chauvinists, most notably a small and rather loose association of literati and *bhikkhus*, the Sinhala Jatika Sangamaya. In March 1957, they threatened to organize anti-Tamil strikes and boycotts. This group, on its own, posed no serious threat. Bandaranaike still had the support of the main *bhikkhus*' organization on the language question and an earlier protest by the extremists in the Sangamaya had ceased abruptly when a little government patronage was sent their way.[33] Their re-emergence on this occasion only caused anxiety because of rumours that they were joining forces with the old ruling party, the UNP. Word reached Bandaranaike of a conspiracy to create disturbances in order to provide the Governor-General, Sir Oliver Goonetilleke (a former UNP master-strategist), with an excuse to declare a state of emergency and dismiss the

[32] *CDN*, 22, 24–28 December 1956; 8, 21–26 January, 4–6 February 1957. Also, *Administration Report of the Government Agent, Batticaloa District, for 1957* (Colombo, 1958), p. A195.   [33] *CDN*, 22–23 March 1957.

Bandaranaike as Prime Minister, taking a break from a parliamentary debate,
looking out to sea from the front steps of Parliament. (Courtesy of
Associated Newspapers of Ceylon Limited.)

government. The premier apparently half-believed the rumours since
both Sir Oliver and J. R. Jayewardene, who was managing the affairs of
the UNP, seemed capable of such things, and he issued unusually fierce
warnings about his readiness to take drastic action to scotch any
disturbances.[34] Nothing came of this, indeed it appears that the rumours
were begun by no less than the Governor-General himself to create an
opportunity to deny them and solidify his position with Bandaranaike
who had come under heavy pressure to dismiss him.[35] Sir Oliver had long
been something of a specialist in such byzantine machinations.

[34] *CDN*, 4, 18 and 22 February 1957.
[35] *CDN*, 15 February and 22 March 1957, and interviews with two of Sir Oliver's close
associates, Colombo, 11 and 16 August 1980.

In March 1957, with the approval of leading *bhikkhus*, Bandaranaike unveiled a three-point plan to reassure Tamils and persuade the Federal Party to cease preparations for direct action in August. First, he offered his long-standing proposal for regional councils which would replace intermediate-level civil servants and provide a link between local boards and the national level. This was now advertised as a means of giving Tamil-majority areas a degree of autonomy. Second, he suggested amendments to the Constitution to safeguard fundamental rights for minorities. Third, he promised provisions for the reasonable use of Tamil within the scope of the 'Sinhala Only' Act.

In taking this line, he was naïvely flirting with serious trouble. The Sinhala chauvinism which he had helped to catalyse during the 1956 election and which had prevented him from including concessions to Tamils in the 'Sinhala Only' Act had not evaporated in the intervening months. By linking his regional councils scheme – an essential step towards genuine elite–mass integration – to the communal issue, he was placing one of his most important and creative ideas in dire jeopardy. Regional councils legislation had been ready in draft form since the previous August. He would have been wiser to enact it quietly and *then* use its provisions to draw Tamils into an agreement. To delay enactment amid the general inertia of his government and then to assume blithely that he could force it through against the wishes of Sinhala chauvinists were grave miscalculations.

His complacency about how much inconsistency he could get away with was further apparent in his frontal and very public approach to the problem. Had he been more sensitive to the force of anti-Tamil feeling among the Sinhalese, he would have proceeded more furtively in negotiating with Tamil leaders. By publicising the details of his offer so early, he gave extremists in both linguistic groups time to mobilize against accommodation. Bandaranaike's *naïveté* here sprang from something noble – a rosy, indeed a utopian vision of what Ceylonese society might become – which all too easily gave way in his mind to a firm expectation of how it would all turn out. But however noble its origins, it led him into serious risks, of which he was woefully unaware.

He managed to avoid disaster on the communal/linguistic issue during 1957. Extremists on both sides did their worst. Among the Tamils, Federal Party leaders rejected his proposal as 'absurd', as 'a smoke screen' to hide a vicious assault on the minority. They proceeded with plans for a campaign in August, 'to force Mr Bandaranaike to throw 25,000 of our people in jail'. Among the Sinhalese, the usual extremist claque was joined by the official voice of the UNP, now under the influence of J. R. Jayewardene, a tough pragmatist and seeker after leverage. While Dudley

Senanayake maintained a moderate tone, Jayewardene dealt in what even a pro-UNP English paper described as 'hysteria and acrimony'. Fears of the Indian Tamil tide were raked up, Bandaranaike's departure from earlier pro-Sinhala postures was vilified and Sinhalese extremists were drawn into the UNP publicity machine. An official resolution of the party's executive accused the Prime Minister of perpetrating a 'colossal fraud' in that he 'is now showing an extraordinary concern for the exaggerated claims of a small Tamil clique of the most virulent communal-minded and violently anti-Sinhalese politicians . . . under whose complete personal influence Mr Bandaranaike has now come.'[36]

This was an ironic reversal of the roles which Bandaranaike and the UNP leaders had played in late 1955. Then he had mobilized Sinhalese chauvinism to defeat a UNP government attempting to sustain an evenhanded approach to the two linguistic groups. Now from opposition the UNP, or a sizable part of it, sought to disrupt his efforts to restore and institutionalize a balance and an understanding between Tamils and Sinhalese. This was an important moment in the island's political history. It marked the first cycle in a pattern which has recurred as a central and poisonous feature of the political process at critical junctures. The party in power strives to foster communal accommodation. The major party in opposition manipulates Sinhalese parochialism to wreck that attempt. The wreckers failed in 1957, but this – like subsequent setbacks – was only temporary.

Despite hostile early reactions, Bandaranaike persisted with his effort to forge an agreement with the Federal Party. In Parliament, he proposed that the 'reasonable use of Tamil' should entail the right of Tamils to study in their language 'to the summit of the educational system', the right to take public service examinations in Tamil, the right to correspond with the government in Tamil and the right for local boards to correspond with the government in Tamil and the right for local boards to transact business with the central government in Tamil. Federal Party leaders countered with demands for citizenship and the franchise for estate Tamils, an end to Sinhalese colonization in Tamil areas, parity for Tamil as a national language throughout the island, and an autonomous Tamil state within a federal framework. Bandaranaike organized an intensive publicity drive in Tamil areas to undercut the Federal Party plan for an August agitation. When the Federalists pressed ahead, he made well-publicized plans for a tough response.[37]

In late June, after much posturing on both sides, negotiations began

---

[36] Quotations are from *CDN*, 23 March, 20, 27 April, 8 May and 15 June 1957. See also, *CDN*, 18 May, 5–6 and 13 June 1957.

[37] Quotations are from *CDN*, 5 June 1957. See also, *CDN*, 20, 26 April and 3 May 1957.

between Bandaranaike and the Federalists led by S. J. V. Chelvanayakam. They continued intermittently for over a month. The Tamils
demanded regional control over lands, agriculture, fisheries, industries,
education and health. Bandaranaike countered with vague and decidedly
limited promises of extended powers for regional councils. On this they
proved remarkably flexible and indicated a desire to conclude an
agreement before August. Bandaranaike gave ground where it cost him
least, on Sinhalese colonization in Tamil areas, and by mid-July a
settlement seemed likely. Talks intensified as the deadline for the Tamil
agitation drew near and, on 25 July, on the very eve of a Federal Party
conference to decide what action to take, Bandaranaike and Chelvanayakam arrived at a pact and the agitation was called off.

   The Federalists publicly conceded that they had failed to gain parity for
Tamil and the abrogation of 'Sinhala Only'. They had no more than an
assurance of Bandaranaike's 'early consideration' of the status of estate
Tamils. The selection of settlers on colonized lands was awarded to
regional councils – a gain for the Federalists. But they had accepted a
good deal less than a federal system of government. Regional councils in
Tamil areas would be permitted to 'amalgamate' and 'collaborate' with
one another even across provincial lines, and they would possess certain
powers over agriculture, education, etc. – two provisions which alarmed
Sinhala chauvinists. But these powers were still to be specified by
Parliament, as were the new councils' taxation powers which seemed
likely to be quite limited. On these points, the Tamil leaders were in effect
relying upon Bandaranaike's promises. On balance, the negotiations had
clearly gone the Prime Minister's way.[38]

   The Bandaranaike–Chelvanayakam pact provoked a predictable
chorus of protests. Well-known Sinhala extremists and J. R. Jayewardene of the UNP labelled it a 'betrayal of the Sinhalese'. Dudley
Senanayake announced that the pact was an 'act of treachery' which
would mean the 'partition' of Ceylon. He was 'prepared to sacrifice my
life' to stop it. The Sinhala newspaper of the UNP took up the campaign
in such scurrilous terms that its pages seemed to 'reek of racialism'. A
motley alliance of Sinhalese hysterics, including several *bhikkhus* and a
few academics and professional men, threatened a hunger strike before
the premier's residence and a 'satyagraha' to oppose the pact. But when
Bandaranaike drew huge crowds sympathetic to the pact, the threat was
abandoned. G. G. Ponnambalam, Bandaranaike's old Tamil sparring

---

[38] Quotation is from *CDN*, 26 July 1957. See also, *CDN*, 10, 15 and 24 July 1957. Also,
   interview with J. R. Jayewardene, Colombo, 11 September 1978. The text of the pact
   can be found in R. N. Kearney, *Communalism and Language in the Politics of Ceylon*
   (Durham, N.C., 1967), appendix II, pp. 144–46.

partner, described the agreement as an 'abject surrender' to the
Sinhalese.[39] But in both Tamil and Sinhalese areas the agreement had, in
general, a tolerably good reception.

There were three main reasons for this. First, the terms of the pact were
so undefined on crucial issues – particularly the powers of regional
councils – that opponents had few specifics to seize upon. Second, the
interest groups from which protests might have come such as Sinhala-
medium teachers, ayurvedic physicians and Sinhalese youths, were no
longer as capable of taking political action as they had been at the 1956
election. The organizations which had been hastily assembled to canvass
in the election had quickly crumbled after victory was achieved and even
their professional guilds had ceased to lobby effectively on their behalf.
As a result, few structures existed to voice the anger which was certainly
felt by many in these groups. Even the *bhikkhus'* organizations had
suffered serious fragmentation and had lost most of their former
substance. The least insubstantial of these were half-beholden to the
government for patronage received and anticipated.[40] Third, Bandaranaike's credentials as the principal champion of the Sinhala revival
among the island's political elite reassured many potential opponents
of the pact that it was no sell-out to the Tamils.[41]

In early October 1957, UNP leaders made a bid for the support of
Sinhala chauvinists by attempting to march from Colombo to Kandy to
protest against the pact. It would take five days and was advertised as a
pilgrimage which would culminate in an act of worship before the
Temple of the Tooth. Its leader, J. R. Jayewardene, like Bandaranaike
and many other prominent Ceylonese leaders (including some Tamils),
was no communalist bigot. But in what has been a central facet of the
island's tragedy, he found the temptation to use communalism to
mobilize popular support too tempting to resist.

The procession set out from Colombo on the morning of 3 October
with several hundred participants including a group of monks seated in a
flat-bed truck, constantly chanting. Dudley Senanayake paid a token visit,
walking a short distance with the marchers, but it was very much
Jayewardene's affair. At several points along the eleven miles covered on
the first day, they were met by jeers from SLFP members and from Philip
Gunawardena's supporters among the port labourers. Occasional skirmishes occurred, stones, firecrackers and harmlessly crude 'hand-bombs'

---

[39] Quotations are from *CDN*, 27 July, 2, 5 and 11 August 1957. See also, *CDN*, 26–29 July
and 30 September 1957; Bernard Aluwihare Diaries, 23 August 1958; and *Siyarata*,
July–September 1957.

[40] *CDN*, 26 and 29 July, 11 August, 14, 22 and 26 September 1957 and interviews with
several SLFP and *bhikkhus'* leaders of that period.

[41] See material in file 316, J. R. Jayewardene Papers, Presidential Archive, Colombo.

were thrown. Near the end of the day, a UNP van was overturned and set alight, but Jayewardene's claim that on Bandaranaike's instructions police gave them no protection was false. Police made three baton charges to disperse opponents of the march and of the sixteen people injured, only two were moving with the procession and one of those was a policeman. In Parliament, Bandaranaike made light of the affair, saying that it was led by a man to whom the idea of a pilgrimage had never occurred before.

On the second day, the procession had covered only three miles when it met with a large and menacing body of counter-demonstrators blocking the road. They were led by S. D. Bandaranayake, a second cousin of the Prime Minister and an SLFP Member of Parliament, but to describe him thus is to suggest far too close a link to the premier. He was an impetuous, eccentric maverick who stood far to the left of both his party and his leader. He had little patience either with party discipline or with the niceties of liberal parliamentary government. Threats of intimidation and violence rolled easily off of his tongue. He had been a prime mover in an attempt to create a large force of SLFP volunteers – an idea with which the Prime Minister had always been rather uncomfortable and which he had squashed once the pact with the Tamils had been forged. There was little about S. D. Bandaranayake that was not at least mildly embarrassing to the premier and that included their family tie, for the Prime Minister – unlike his widow in later years – had a marked distaste for involving relatives in politics.

Nevertheless, there is no doubt that the stalemate which developed on the Kandy road that morning was convenient for the premier. The marchers and their opponents were separated by a large contingent of police in riot gear. Jayewardene insisted that he should be allowed to proceed, but serious violence seemed inevitable. High police officials consulted the Prime Minister by telephone and, on the grounds that 'a serious breach of the peace was imminent', the police banned the march. Jayewardene asked that a procession of five persons be allowed to press on to Kandy, but the police did not feel that they could provide adequate protection and refused this as well.[42]

Four days later, UNP opponents of the pact with the Tamils rallied and worshipped before the Temple of the Tooth in Kandy. The *Mahanayakes* (high priests) of the great Asgiriya and Malwatte chapters presided and invocations were offered at the four *devales* (shrines) beside the temple to persuade the gods to destroy the pact. All of this was attended by noisy

[42] *CDN*, 30 September – 5 October 1957; material in files 301 and 302, J. R. Jayewardene Papers, Presidential Archive, Colombo; and Bernard Aluwihare Diaries, 16 January 1958.

counter-demonstrations which were met by repeated baton charges from police. Some stones and bottles were thrown and five persons were later hospitalized with injuries. But this attempt to undermine Bandaranaike's position came to little.

Throughout this period the Prime Minister toured the Sinhalese districts tirelessly to defend the pact. He attracted massive sympathetic crowds, some of which were counted in hundreds of thousands. He found them deeply sceptical of the UNP's effort to sell itself as the new guardian of the 'Lion Race'. Much fun was had at Jayewardene's expense and Bandaranaike's jokes sometimes succeeded in attaching popular suspicions of the UNP to Sinhala extremists in general. Within a fortnight, the protests had largely subsided and it was clear that, for a time at least, the pact was safe. But astute observers of the political scene were left with a certain uneasiness about the prospects for communal amity. A September by-election had seen a candidate sweep to a massive victory after a campaign consisting entirely of livid Sinhalese bigotry.[43] Fear and venom were there, just under the surface, and they might burst forth again at any time.

The tensions which had developed over the pact had only just begun to ease when an issue arose that would test the government's progressive credentials, its unity and its leader's authority. It involved Philip Gunawardena, the leader of the leftist component in the ruling MEP coalition and, therefore, arguably its second most prominent figure. He had a well-earned reputation for impulsive belligerence, intolerance and an inability to accept peers, not to mention superiors. And since he shared this last difficulty not only with his leader but with at least two other ministers, W. Dahanayake (Education) and R. G. Senanayake (Trade), Cabinet meetings were often turbulent. But, as we shall see, Bandaranaike still found him a useful colleague.

Philip Gunawardena was the same age as Bandaranaike, the son of a prosperous *Goyigama* estate owner and minor headman in the inland Kelani valley area of the Western Province. His father had been arrested with other Sinhalese nationalists during the troubles of 1915, condemned to death and then reprieved. Young Philip attended school in Moratuwa and at Ananda College in Colombo, the island's leading Buddhist secondary school. After a year at the University College, Colombo, he spent two years at the University of Illinois and a further three at the University of Wisconsin. He studied politics, law, labour problems and philosophy, and at Wisconsin – in the company of a friend from India

[43] *CDN*, 7–8 September and 9–26 October 1957.

named Jayaprakash Narayan – he became a radical socialist. Between 1925 and 1928, he worked in the American socialist movement and developed a reputation for brilliant, incandescent oratory. He was based in New York, but travelled on missions to Central and South America. In 1928, he moved to London where he worked within the Communist Party as a sometime theoretician and emissary to various parts of Europe, and then with Krishna Menon in the Indian League. His belief that Marxist theory had to yield very considerably to indigenous political and cultural patterns in struggles for national liberation led him in 1930 to join the Trotskyist fold.

Two years later, he returned to Ceylon and set to work with other leftists in a campaign to displace the wayward A. E. Goonesinha from the leadership of urban labour unions – a campaign which ultimately succeeded. In 1935, he joined with several other Marxist returnees from western universities to form the Lanka Sama Samaja Party. The following year, his support among labourers and poor peasants and his family's traditional eminence in the area enabled him to win the State Council seat for Avissawella, which he represented thereafter, with minor interruptions for an unseating and time in jail for political doings.[44] Although he was a quiet, almost shy man in private life, Gunawardena remained a combative fire-breather in public. He both suffered and perpetrated violent physical assaults at public rallies, and during the second State Council he engaged in dramatic clashes on and off the floor. When the young John Kotelawala once claimed in the State Council tea room that his wealth was the result of virtuous doings in former lives, Gunawardena tartly offered a less flattering explanation. Kotelawala promptly 'sprang over the table and struck the Member for Avissawella twice in the face'. When Gunawardena resisted, his assailant 'seized him by the hair and began striking his head on a chair'. D. S. Senanayake waded in to separate them. On another occasion, he had the better of things. He had told the House that G. G. Ponnambalam 'should be horse whipped', and when an altercation between the two men broke out in the corridor Gunawardena 'practised a strange jiu-jitsu hold on the Point Pedro prize-fighter (Ponnambalam), throwing him to the floor in an amazing fashion'.[45]

Because he was less infatuated with the parliamentary process than were other leftists, like N. M. Perera, and because he was prepared to engage in the rough and tumble of street politics, he seemed more than any other leftist to be – in the words of Governor Caldecott – 'a pukka scarlet'.[46] And yet he was less doctrinaire than the others and far less

[44] V. K. Jayawardena, *The Rise of the Labor Movement in Ceylon* (Durham, 1972).
[45] *CDN*, 19 April 1952, 3 March 1938 and 11–12 March 1939.
[46] Report No. 9, CO 54/977/7, PRO.

westernized in his lifestyle. He was the only leading Marxist to wear
'native dress' and was fully at home in colloquial Sinhala while, for
example, the Communist leader Pieter Keuneman did not begin to learn
that language until 1956.[47] Gunawardena's willingness to adapt his
Marxist beliefs to indigenous conditions led him naturally into the
linguistic revival in 1955–56. His flexibility, his keen intellect and the
respect which Bandaranaike showed him in the Cabinet added up to the
first major opportunity for the left in Ceylon's history.

Those who expected fireworks from Gunawardena as Minister of
Agriculture and Food were surprised at how little was heard from him in
public during the MEP government's first six months. Within the
Cabinet, he was prickly and offensive and did little to disguise his
contempt for most of his colleagues, but the rows that resulted were
largely unknown to the public. His main open quarrels – and they were
vicious – were in Parliament with opposition leftists.[48] Nor were
there early legislative initiatives from the departments under his
command. The only important innovation in agrarian policy during that
first half-year came from C. P. de Silva's ministry, a programme to
accelerate the distribution of Crown land among landless and land-poor
peasants, and to increase grants-in-aid to allottees which were crucial if
they were to develop the land.[49] It was not until October 1956 that the
broad outline of Gunawardena's main initiative in land policy, a Paddy
Lands Bill, was announced.

If his presence in the Cabinet provided an opportunity for a leftward
advance, the Paddy Lands Bill provided the crucial test of the extent of
that opportunity. In essence, the bill set out to accomplish five things –
first to give ownership rights on rice lands to tenants and share-croppers
who worked it, including the right to sell or give the land to others. As a
concession to opponents, Gunawardena agreed that a small sum would
be paid on each crop by former tenants to former owners. Second, it
sought to raise the wages paid to agricultural labourers on those lands.
Third, it sought to create Cultivation Committees consisting entirely of
persons actively cultivating paddy land (thus excluding absentee landowners and owners relying wholly or mainly on the labour of others).
The powers bestowed on the Cultivation Committees were considerable,
and gave them decisive influence over most of the important aspects of
agrarian relations. With non-cultivating landowners excluded, the
Cultivation Committees were intended to become struggle committees,
structures within which the lower-middle stratum of rural society could

[47] Interview with two close associates of Keuneman, Colombo, 20 September 1980.
[48] *CDN*, 7 July and 21–22 September 1956.
[49] See for example, *CDN*, 19 April, 5 May, 2 August 1956 and 12 January 1957.

develop solidarity, confidence and the will to assert itself.[50] The fourth
expectation was that this *lower-middle* stratum – ex-tenants and share-
croppers now converted into owner–cultivators – which would dominate
the Committees, would through its power over agricultural wages forge
links to the *lowest* stratum of rural society, the landless labourers. This
would have the effect of politicizing the landless, whom Gunawardena
and other leftists regarded as a rural 'proletariat' possessing enough latent
revolutionary energy to generate further changes in the agrarian order.
Finally the bill established firm ties between the relevant minister
(Gunawardena) and this new political force at the grass roots. It gave the
Ministry major powers to make important rulings on the status of persons
and land and to requisition animals, tractors and implements from their
owners to ensure their availability to former tenants. The reforms under
the bill were to be reinforced by the creation, through separate
legislation, of multi-purpose cooperatives in every village. These would
be under the same minister, would replace the various forms of existing
cooperatives which tended to be controlled by wealthy people, and
would provide the less privileged groups on the Cultivation Committee
with a major source of economic power.[51]

The bill was not intended to affect owners of less than five acres who
spent most of their time in active cultivation. As even C. P. de Silva
conceded,[52] no fully reliable statistics existed on the distribution of lands,
but estimates from 1953–54 were as in Table 8.1. It is unclear from these
figures how many of the 96.8 per cent of the lands in plots of five acres or
less were held by tenants, owner–cultivators, etc. But similarly questionable figures from the following year indicated that 55.0 per cent of all
parcels of paddy lands were held by owner–cultivators, 28.7 per cent
were share-cropped and 13.7 per cent were leased.[53]

---

50 Committees had the power, in effect, to acquire and reallocate lands not justifiably held
under the Bill. They controlled the register of paddy lands and made the initial decision
on the status of persons and plots of land, decisions which could only be appealed to the
minister and not the courts. They were empowered to prevent or revoke evictions of
tenants which were illegal and to force former landowners to make machinery, tools and
animals available to former tenants. They could consolidate fragmented holdings. They
were given certain vague, open-ended powers which could be very broadly interpreted
and the minister reserved the right to bestow further powers on them, by decree rather
than by legislation. *CDN*, 4 and 29 October 1956.

51 *CDN*, 4 and 29 October, 15 November 1956, 8 and 21 February and 19 September 1957.
See also, P. Gunawardena, 'The Cooperative Development Bank Bill', *Ceylon Economist*,
iv, 4 (September, 1959), pp. 419–33. Interviews at Colombo with G. V. S. de Silva, 6
September 1977, Prins Gunasekera, 26 August 1978 and Nimal Karunatilake, 9
September 1980.   52 *CDN*, 29 October 1957.

53 The source of the extra 0.1 per cent here is unclear. Department of Census and Statistics,
A Report on Paddy Statistics (Colombo, 1955) and *CDN*, 29 October 1956. See also,
Report on the Survey of Landlessness, Sessional Paper XIII – 1952 (Colombo, 1952). The data
came from 108 villages.

Table 8.1. *Distribution of paddy lands
by size (%)*

Less than 0.5 acre	36.2
0.5 to 1.5 acres	44.9
1.5 to 2.5 acres	9.3
2.5 to 3.5 acres	3.9
3.5 to 5 acres	2.6
5 to 10 acres	2.4
10 acres and above	0.8

Source: Department of Census and Statistics,
A Report on Paddy Statistics (Colombo, 1955).

If these figures can be taken as a loose guide to agrarian conditions – and they probably can – they suggest that the Paddy Lands Bill should have affected a sizable minority of rice land holdings. But since 'leased' lands were of dubious status under the bill, since landowners with tenants could be expected to take evasive action in anticipation of the bill's passage and since such a vast majority of holdings were under five acres, it would be unlikely to transfer ownership of more than a tenth of paddy plots. It is thus impossible to see the bill as a revolutionary measure, as its opponents did. Nor were critics correct in claiming that it would lead to collectivization, massive intrusions by the minister in local arenas and declining production. Despite the hopes for collectivization which Gunawardena voiced in speeches, he knew that it would require far more drastic legislation than this – not to mention a transformation of peasant attitudes. The administrative machinery for ministerial intrusions did not exist and was well nigh impossible to create, so that the main hope for implementation lay at the local level with the Cultivation Committees.

As sponsor of the bill, Gunawardena's tactical position was un-enviable. He knew that most of his Cabinet colleagues were closely linked to paddy-owning interests and would therefore oppose it. He therefore felt compelled to break with normal procedure and publicize the bill before taking it to Cabinet, in order to generate popular pressure in its favour. He did this on public platforms throughout Ceylon in late 1956 and early 1957. The difficulty in this approach was that it also gave opponents of the scheme time to study it and to organize themselves, and it gave owners of paddy lands ample opportunity to evict tenants and replace them with wage labourers to whom the bill, in its original form, did not give rights of ownership. By December 1956, evictions were soaring and Gunawardena hastily added two new elements to the bill to meet the situation. He promised that its effect would be retroactive to April 1956, when the government took office and that wage labourers would also be given land ownership rights.

By early 1957, resistance to the bill had begun quietly to crystallize, particularly in the (mainly Kandyan) districts where paddy lands were of greater importance than rubber and coconut which were unaffected by the legislation. Several key figures and interests joined the opposition. Barnes Ratwatte, brother of Mrs Bandaranaike, headed the Paddy Landlords Association of Ratnapura District. Much of the island's paddy land was owned by Buddhist temples and this drew in the leaders of the great Kandyan chapters[54] and numerous village *bhikkhus* who saw a threat to the modest income of local temples. Signs of restiveness began to appear among two other elements of Bandaranaike's 1956 support base, ayurvedic doctors and vernacular school teachers, people who often owned modest plots of land worked by tenants or labourers. By April 1957, despite a low level of public protest, the lobbying of these groups forced Gunawardena into minor concessions but, between June and September, opponents of the bill within the Cabinet grew more active and joined forces with landowners' associations in the districts. Gunawardena had to suffer the embarrassment of seeing Marxists in opposition defend his bill against attacks from fellow ministers.[55] But, despite the rising tempo of contention, the Paddy Lands Bill did not become a major controversy until the threat of communal trouble had receded after the UNP's abortive march to Kandy in early October 1957.

By that time a clear cleavage had developed between Gunawardena on the left and several SLFP ministers who spoke for paddy landowners. The most prominent of these were R. G. Senanayake (the nephew of D. S. and a former UNP minister who was as unmanageable an ego as Ceylon politics has known), Wimala Wijewardene (the confused, unstable and assertive young widow who was on intimate terms with the Venerable Mapitagama Buddharakkhita, the head of the great Kelaniya temple, and who represented landed interests of the temples), and Stanley de Zoysa (the intelligent Finance Minister) who had been persuaded by low-country planters and wealthy Roman Catholic interests to make common cause with paddy landowners. Bandaranaike found it necessary but also useful to place himself between these rival groups, arbitrating between forces and maintaining the coalition.

[54] See *The Memorial of the Mahanayake Theros and Anunayake Theros of Malwatte and Asgiriya Viharas to His Excellency Sir O. E. Goonetilleke*, 8 February 1958, a copy of which is in file 76, J. R. Jayewardene Papers, Presidential Archive, Colombo.

[55] *CDN*, 7 December 1956, 30 January, 9 February, 6 March, 11 and 30 April, 18 and 22 June, 2, 9–10 July, 23–28 August and 4–12 September 1957.

This was true in two senses, on two levels. First, it was true in mundane personal and political terms. After a year and a half in office, Bandaranaike's early doubts about the intellectual calibre and managerial competence of many of his SLFP ministers had been abundantly confirmed. Gunawardena's constant criticism of other ministers' muddled thoughts and actions and the keen analytical edge that he brought to Cabinet meetings helped Bandaranaike – in the role of arbiter, the promoter of consensus – to correct some of the ministers' more serious weaknesses. Gunawardena also broadened the government's base, both in Parliament and in the country at large, particularly in urban areas where the SLFP remained weak. With the pact with Chelvanayakam still to be implemented, and with other ambitious plans including constitutional reform to follow, that broad base was essential.

Bandaranaike was probably surprised to discover over that first eighteen months how much, at the level of ideology or philosophy, he needed and wanted Gunawardena's presence in the Cabinet. Bandaranaike was certainly surprised to find that many SLFP ministers were far more wedded to the status quo than he was. His romantic, vague but deeply felt empathy for the disadvantaged and for substantive reform, and his contempt for the materialist self-indulgence of the island's upper-middle class consistently placed him to the left of most of his SLFP colleagues. Their conservatism was evident in the absence, after eighteen months, of any major 'socialist' or reformist initiative other than the nationalization of the buses. And that had less to do with a passion for public ownership than a desire to remove a major source of corruption, thuggery and UNP leverage at elections, as even Bandaranaike demonstrated when he welcomed nationalization by going to Peliyagoda – the bailiwick of a bus owner who was a notorious personal enemy.[56] At this second, philosophical level, Bandaranaike needed Gunawardena as a counterweight to the conservatism of most SLFP Ministers and as a clarifying intelligence amid their confusion. If Gunawardena's criticisms were usually abrasive, this suited the Prime Minister who once again could step in as the soothing, good humoured arbiter forging modestly progressive compromises without taking the blame for wrenching SLFP ministers out of their caution – a role which Bandaranaike found both personally satisfying and politically productive.

By late October 1957, it was clear that the controversy over the Paddy Lands Bill was nearing a climax. Earlier that month, stout resistance to the bill had surfaced at a meeting of the large SLFP executive. Most of the party's MPs had opposed the language pact with Chelvanayakam and had grown restless after the failure of Bandaranaike – who knew of their

[56] *CDN*, 3 January 1958. The Act was passed the previous October.

opposition – to consult the party before he concluded it. This seemed almost high-handed, given his tendency in his early months as Prime Minister to allow dissent from within the party to carry him some distance from his original views. When opposition arose to the Paddy Bill, he seemed at first to be his old pliable self once again. While defending Gunawardena and the bill, he conceded the need to suggest changes, as long as they did not alter it fundamentally, and agreed to chair a committee to draw up suggestions. Before this process could bear fruit, however, he met privately with Gunawardena to hammer out a list of amendments. These he suddenly revealed to the government's MPs on 29 October and, thanks to the element of surprise and his manipulative skills, he won acceptance of the amended version. He also persuaded them to allow *him* to revise the text of the bill, incorporating the amendments.

These deserve a moment's attention since they provide a revealing example of Bandaranaike playing off the two sides within his coalition against one another to produce the kind of moderate reform that he desired. All but one of the amendments were distinctly modest, but were designed to create the impression that major inroads had been made. One amendment, however, struck down an essential element of the bill. It required that up to one-quarter of the members of the crucial Cultivation Committees be drawn from among landowners not engaged in cultivation. This effectively emasculated the Cultivation Committees, for although landowners would only be a minority, their wealth and power would give them much greater influence than their numbers implied. Their presence would prevent the Committees from promoting solidarity among the deprived.[57] Bandaranaike had seen that Cultivation Committees were vital to the success of Gunawardena's plans since even the most committed bureaucracy could not hope to penetrate into many local arenas – and Ceylon's bureaucrats were far from committed to change. He also saw that this might eventually lead to polarization and conflict, which Gunawardena desired but which a gradualist like the Prime Minister wished to avoid. Bandaranaike therefore used the pressure from the right within the SLFP to wring this very painful concession from Gunawardena.

This action raises once again the questions of Bandaranaike's commitment to 'socialism' and of his government's power base and of the mass character of the election victory of 1956. If the Prime Minister had believed that his power rested on the great mass of the rural poor, if he

[57] *CDN*, 6 and 30 October, 2 and 4 November 1957. Also, interviews with G. V. S. de Silva, Colombo, 6 September 1977 and with three SLFP MPs of that time, Kandy, 19 August 1978.

had seen his government as an instrument of what many called (and still call) the 'revolution' of 1956, he would not have forced this change in the bill. His sympathies lay with the rural poor and he could mount trenchant, subtle arguments for 'democratic socialism' in the tradition of Anthony Crosland.[58] He also had no liking for landowners, despite the lobbying of Mrs Bandaranaike and her relatives which on this and every other occasion (as we shall explain in chapter 9) had no influence upon his political views.[59] But despite these sentiments, he forced the change in the bill because he rightly believed that it would alienate important village elites which had delivered the 1956 election to him – ayurvedic doctors, school teachers and *bhikkhus* – crucial intermediaries between his party and the rural mass.[60]

In practice, the bill in its original form would have left most of these people unaffected, but even their unwarranted fears were enough to make him draw back. He would not risk their temporary displeasure until, after a year or two, they realized that the bill posed no great threat. Bandaranaike genuinely desired to draw the rural poor, whom the bill sought to aid, into the kind of active political involvement that the village elites had engaged in at the last election – it was in his interest to do so – but not at the expense of the support of the village elites. These elites might all too easily defect to the UNP with its new-found enthusiasm for Sinhala chauvinism. It is clear from Bandaranaike's rhetoric that he saw no necessary contradiction between the interests of the village elites and the village poor. Provoking early conflict between them could wreck the careful, gradual effort 'to rise above those conflicts, to secure an ultimate harmony, an ultimate reconciliation'. He spoke constantly of this 'age of transition', of 'evolution' and almost never of revolution – hence the metaphor of the midwife. In his quest to realize his utopian (and unrealizable) vision of the people's entry into the perfect harmony of the Garden of Hesperides, the need to avoid severe conflict along the way was fundamental.[61]

Had the process of changing the Paddy Lands Bill ended with Bandaranaike's set of amendments, the result would have been a moderately progressive law on paper producing rather limited but not insignificant change in practice, and would have reaffirmed the Prime Minister's pre-eminence within the ruling coalition. But it did not end

---

[58] See, for example, the notes on the SLFP programme, dated 13 February 1958 in file 2, BP.

[59] These comments are based on a wide range of confidential interviews with Bandaranaike's close associates.

[60] The person who put this most clearly at the time was Sir Edwin Wijeyeratne, *CDN*, 29 October 1957.

[61] S. W. R. D. Bandaranaike, *Speeches and Writings* (Colombo, 1963), pp. 334 and 337.

there. The day after the amendments were accepted, twenty Kandyan MPs including three ministers petitioned Bandaranaike for further 'drastic' changes. Some of them threatened to resign from the ruling alliance if the bill became law. Bandaranaike hit back at a public meeting, but the Kandyans were soon joined by important low-country MPs and ministers who saw themselves as dependent upon landowning groups for electoral success. They complained that at the meeting of the parliamentary group the only person permitted to offer amendments had been the Prime Minister and they again asked for the chance to propose further changes.[62]

This brought Bandaranaike to one of the critical moments of his career. Had he stood his ground and asserted his authority, it is likely that he would have prevailed. An amended but not entirely toothless Paddy Bill could have been the first step in a series of incremental reforms which might have built a solid constituency for the ruling alliance among the less prosperous majority of rural dwellers. Had he stood firm, the delicate balance in the alliance between right and left could probably have been maintained for some considerable time. This balance was crucial since it allowed Bandaranaike both to check Gunawardena's more adventurous plans, which could never have been implemented within the context of the parliamentary system (although the original Paddy Bill does not fall under this heading), and to drag his conservative SLFP colleagues out of their inertia. It was also essential to his own continued authority over his government that he not yield. Yet he failed to see that he had reached such a critical juncture, and this failure of perception was grievously damaging. What he *did* perceive – or rather misperceive – was that to be legitimate, authority must be generous and availing. In that spirit, in a decision strikingly reminiscent of his indulgent treatment of Sinhala extremists in 1956, he agreed to reopen the question of amendments.

It appears that at this point events took a bizarre turn. The new text of the Paddy Bill, as amended by Bandaranaike, was released and to the astonishment of nearly everyone, it failed to contain most of the amendments agreed upon by the legislators. We shall probably never know precisely how this happened, but the apparent course of events was as follows. Before meeting their colleagues in Parliament, Bandaranaike and Gunawardena had agreed upon a limited list of amendments which nonetheless included the key change in the composition of Cultivation Committees. When he met the legislators, the Prime Ministers did not face them squarely with the limited changes agreed with Gunawardena but instead enlarged the list of amendments. His aversion to provoking displeasure by telling an audience hard truths showed itself here. He

[62] *CDN*, 31 October and 2 November 1957.

preferred to try to slide round the problem by later delivering only partially on his commitments. To his eccentric notion of what constituted legitimate authority must be added this breathtaking presumption about how much plain deception he could get away with. Many times in his career, he had changed course suddenly without being called to account because political structures were sufficiently undeveloped to allow this. On most of those occasions the constituencies to whom initial commitments had been made were too loosely organized or too remote from him and from the public eye to pressure him into keeping his word. In assuming that he could elude a commitment to parliamentary and ministerial colleagues standing at his shoulder, he was guilty of tactical folly.

The inevitable storm soon burst around him. Opponents of the bill demanded the reinstatement of the original amendments and then resolved to go further, to gut the bill and cripple Gunawardena politically. Backbenchers drew up ten further amendments, a deputation of six ministers and the Chief Whip pressed Bandaranaike for concessions and no less a person than his principal deputy and Leader of the House, C. P. de Silva, published a list of *thirty* new amendments. A group of thirty-two government MPs then secured a meeting with the premier and kept up the pressure. Delegations from a motley array of interest groups, real and imagined, streamed to his house with petitions against the bill. It is a measure of Bandaranaike's *naïveté* that he was surprised and distressed by this. All of these signs of dissent, he complained, 'are likely to be construed as a loss of confidence by members in the Prime Minister'.[63]

On 17 November, Gunawardena rallied his supporters. He insisted that Bandaranaike was the friend of the common man and would see this matter through. He rightly stressed that the bill's opponents were misleading the public when they claimed that it would end private ownership of land. He said that it would instead *secure* possession of land for those who worked it, and that the Prime Minister knew and applauded this. But the next evening at a meeting with SLFP ministers, Bandaranaike agreed to accept all of the initial amendments and several more besides, among which was one further hammer blow against the bill. A clause giving tenants security against eviction by landowners was cut out, a change which transformed the bill from a promising attempt to strengthen the hand of the rural poor to a source of widespread dispossession of tenants[64] and of painful ambiguities for many poorer

---

[63] The quotation is from *CDN*, 15 November 1957. See also, *CDN*, 6–19 November 1957. Also interviews with two members of the Cabinet, Colombo, 6 and 8 August 1980.
[64] C. P. de Silva himself conceded this later (*CDN*, 19 August 1959). See also, R. J. Herring, *Land to the Tiller* (New Haven, 1983).

villagers.[65] Gunawardena learned of the change from Bandaranaike the next morning. Having overcome their Prime Minister, jubilant SLFP ministers hastily soared into hyperbole about his vision and statesmanship, to limit the damage to his position. But damage aplenty had been done and it was exacerbated when Bandaranaike emerged from it all 'looking quite pleased', with a blithe air that was less a brave face after defeat than downright self-deception.[66]

The emasculation of the Paddy Lands Bill, which passed into law in February 1958, undercut not only the government's claim to be a vigorous force for reform, but also the Prime Minister's capacity to lead on other fronts. He found it harder than ever to energize ministers whose performance, or the lack of it, was alienating important elements of the government's social base. Vernacular school teachers were still waiting, two years later, after the MEP had taken power, for parity with English-medium teachers in salaries and conditions. The Buddhist Commission Report, a crucial rallying point for the clergy in the 1956 election, was given very leisurely treatment. An incompetent Health Minister snarled up plans to aid ayurvedic doctors. Programmes for secondary school graduates in difficulty were similarly mismanaged. The exasperation of these groups was bound to find an outlet eventually and a resurgence of communal tension in early 1958 provided it. Just as MPs' unease over the pact with Chelvanayakam had contributed to the crisis over the Paddy Bill, Bandaranaike's mishandling of the latter left him ill-equipped to cope with renewed communal polarization.

By February 1958, the Prime Minister was facing pressure from Tamils to embody the pact in legislation, as he had promised to do. When he assured them that draft bills on regional councils and on the use of the Tamil language were nearly ready, Sinhalese chauvinists in his own camp, some of whom had helped to gut the Paddy Bill and had thereby grown more assertive, promptly asked to examine them as well.[67] But these

---

[65] See in this regard, N. Sanderatne, 'The Paddy Lands Act of 1958', *South Asian Review* (January, 1972), pp. 117–36; G. H. Peiris, 'Land Reform and Agrarian Change in Sri Lanka', *Modern Asian Studies*, xii, 4 (1978), pp. 611–28; H. D. Dias and B. W. E. Wickramanayake, 'The Gambara System in Hambantota District', in S. W. R. de A. Samarasinghe (ed.), *Agriculture in the Peasant Sector of Sri Lanka* (Peradeniya, 1977), pp. 147–48; and J. Brow, 'Class Formation and Ideological Practice: A Case from Sri Lanka', *Journal of Asian Studies*, xl, 4 (August, 1981), pp. 708–9. Nonetheless, the Act *did* reduce the incomes of Buddhist temples with major holdings in paddy lands (See, for example, *CDN*, 5 and 13 August 1959).

[66] Quotation is from *CDN*, 19 November 1957. See also, *CDN*, 18–20 November 1957. Also, interviews with G. V. S. de Silva, Colombo, 6 September 1977, and with two members of the Cabinet, Colombo, 6 and 8 August 1980.

[67] See for example, *CDN*, 13, 22–23 February 1958.

matters received hardly any public attention in the first three months of 1958 because the government and the press were preoccupied with a spate of strikes and the continuing struggle between Philip Gunawardena and his opponents.[68] Even the main organization of activist *bhikkhus* concentrated almost exclusively on attacking Gunawardena.[69]

Then, at the end of March, as the Transport Ministry sent newly-nationalized buses into the Tamil-majority areas bearing licence plates with the Sinhala word 'Sri' on them, Tamil militants in the Northern Province again began defacing these plates. On 31 March, Sinhalese in Colombo started retaliating by smearing tar over Tamil letters on signboards. Within twenty-four hours, things in the capital had got out of hand. Two large groups of defacers, one of them led by *bhikkhus*, systematically combed the city, and even managed to obliterate the Tamil section of a sign in three languages on Bandaranaike's official Cadillac which read 'left hand drive'. The man responsible for that incident was arrested and armed police were sent to keep Sinhalese from a street of Tamil and Indian shops in central Colombo, but police were instructed to act with great restraint and so did little else to subdue miscreants. Extremists were permitted to stop vehicles crossing the main bridge into the city in order to deface Tamil lettering and two explosions occurred near a cinema. Numerous other incidents, including assaults on Tamil truck drivers, took place throughout the Sinhalese-majority areas[70] and it became apparent that some Sinhalese lawbreakers were presuming from the restrained posture of the police that 'our government' did not object to such doings.

Tamil leaders, alarmed by the fierce Sinhalese reaction, tried to stop the anti-'Sri' agitation and the Cabinet finally resolved to arrest and prosecute anyone damaging property. After police had opened fire and killed two members of a Tamil crowd that attacked a police station at which a bus had taken refuge, all meetings and demonstrations were banned, and police were put on alert. Tarring gradually declined over the next few days and – despite two stabbings and some looting of Tamil shops in Sinhalese areas – the streets were largely under control when Bandaranaike and Chelvanayakam met on 4 April to discuss the implementation of their pact.[71]

The talks went well enough for Chelvanayakam to travel to Jaffna four days later to seek a formal end to the anti-'Sri' campaign. Meanwhile, Sinhalese chauvinists demanded that the pact be scrapped. They included extremists who were inveterate enemies of the Prime Minister, including

[68] *CDN*, 1 February – 28 March 1958.   [69] *CDN*, 12–17 and 20 March 1958.
[70] *CDN*, 24, 28–29, 31 March 1958. See also, *CDN*, 24, 28–29 March 1958.
[71] *CDN*, 2–7 April 1958.

a *bhikkhu* who told a rally of 5,000 in Bandaranaike's constituency that the pact would 'lead to the total annihilation of the Sinhalese race'. Public protests also arose from the premier's own legislators and even from a government minister. When the Cabinet met on the morning of 9 April, a small group of ministers insisted that the pact be abrogated, but they lacked majority support, and Bandaranaike got through the meeting by making minor concessions.[72]

It then emerged, however, that several dozen *bhikkhus* had attempted to march on the premier's private residence in Rosmead Place and when a police cordon stopped them 100 yards from the house, they squatted in the street, pitched two tents and refused to move until the pact was abandoned. Bandaranaike returned home and, with several ministers who were his close allies, walked down to speak to the demonstrators. He told them of the Cabinet's decisions and refused to give way on the pact. The *bhikkhus* also stood firm and he returned home where he faced a critical decision. The squatters appeared ready for a very long siege. If, as seemed likely, it became necessary for the police to remove them, hysterical and politically damaging charges of brutality were sure to follow – no matter how delicately it was done. Bandaranaike had already had a taste of such hysteria, since his Health Minister, Mrs Wimala Wijewardene, was already in the street weeping over the *bhikkhus*' lack of shelter from the sun. But to agree to their demands was to squander most of his much diminished political capital. The situation cried out for gentle but resolute action to remove the *bhikkhus*, but when faced with such confrontations as Prime Minister, Bandaranaike had always yielded on the assumption that when tempers had cooled, he could still get his way by other means. And so, in the most grievous blunder of his career, he caved in.

He drove to the radio station and announced to the nation that the Bandaranaike–Chelvanayakam pact was dissolved. He then returned home and informed the *bhikkhus* of the announcement, but they demanded a declaration in writing. He refused, saying that it was unnecessary, and still they insisted. He then consented, but before they took their leave the *bhikkhus*' leader added further humiliation by asking that the Federal Party be banned, that demonstrators among the estate Tamils be sent back to India and that Tamil lettering be deleted from the official stamp that government employees used on correspondence. The premier explained that he had the power only to accomplish the last of

[72] *CDN*, 8–10 April 1958, and interview with A. P. Jayasuriya (then Home Minister), Colombo, 12 September 1977.

these, and promised to do so. At last the *bhikkhus* agreed to withdraw.
The newspapers reported all of this in detail.[73]

The following day, Tamil leaders predictably resolved to mount mass
civil disobedience in protest. They made plans for a conference on May
23–25 at Vavuniya, a town near the sensitive line that separated Tamil and
Sinhalese areas of the island, to formalize the start of the agitation.
Bandaranaike countered with an invitation to discuss bills to ensure the
reasonable use of Tamil and to establish regional councils, but his action
carried little force as Sinhalese extremists called for boycotts of Tamil
businesses, alleging that the anti-'Sri' campaign threatened 'the destruction of the chief race'.[74]

During most of late April and May 1958, prolonged and occasionally
violent strikes developed which both distracted public attention from the
communal conflict and contributed to a general sense of lawlessness as
strikers, employers in both private and public sectors, and police threw
off conventional restraints. Hardly anyone emerged with credit from this
episode. Opposition leftists called for the strikes mainly to erode the
government's authority, irresponsible ministers – Wimala Wijewardene
(Health) and W. Dahanayake (Education) – made the ludicrous charge
that the strikes were the result of a Tamil plot and many strikers suffered
bitter disappointment when leftist politicians who had achieved most of
their political aims called them back to work[75] without winning them
adequate financial gains amid serious inflation.[76]

Given the public's preoccupation with the strikes, when serious
violence between Sinhalese and Tamils began to occur in late May, it
came as something of a surprise. It unfolded in three overlapping phases.
The first extended from the night of 22 May until 25 May during
which serious incidents occurred mainly in and around two up-country
places: Polonnaruwa in the predominantly Sinhalese area of the North
Central Province and at Eravur in a mainly Tamil section of the Eastern
Province. The second phase extended from 25 to 29 May and was marked
by attacks, overwhelmingly against Tamils, throughout most of the
Sinhalese-majority areas. The third phase, between 26 or 27 May and 2 or
3 June, took place mainly in the Tamil-majority Northern and Eastern
Provinces. The violence there was directed against Sinhalese and against
government personnel and installations.

The first serious violence was touched off by an innocuous incident in

---

[73] *CDN*, 10 April 1958. The text of his written statement to the *bhikkhus* is in *CDN*, 26 July
1958.   [74] *CDN*, 11, 13, 17–18 and 22 April 1958.
[75] *CDN*, 16, 19, 22–30 April and 1–24 May 1958.
[76] See, for example, *CDN*, 8–10 and 13 May 1958 and *Ceylon Observer*, 9 May 1959.

Valaichennai, a mainly Tamil town on the east coast rail line. Sinhalese travellers inflated this into a Tamil atrocity and carried it forty miles westward along the railway to the mainly Sinhalese city of Polonnaruwa. This had an incendiary effect upon people there, and at about midnight on the night of 22–23 May, about 500 agitated Sinhalese met a train at Polonnaruwa station which was believed to contain Tamils. They found only one passenger on board whom they severely beat without allowing him to explain that he was not a Tamil.

On the next night (the 23rd) near Eravur, another train was derailed, resulting in three deaths. The train was then attacked and most of the injured were Sinhalese. Tarzie Vittachi implies without supporting evidence that this attack was of a piece with the previous incident and that it was the work of Sinhalese. But given the Tamil predominance in this area and the violent doings of Tamils which welled up there at this time, it seems far more likely that it was the work of Tamils reacting to the news of the violence at Polonnaruwa. On the following day, a truck and a car were blown up by dynamite blasts in Eravur. These and other daylight incidents appear to have resulted in the deaths of two persons, one of whom was a Sinhalese policeman. After dark on the 24th, a car carrying D. A. Seneviratne, a Sinhalese planter and former mayor of Nuwara Eliya, and two friends was waylaid at Eravur and Seneviratne was shot dead. It was later claimed that he was killed by personal enemies, but by that evening a pattern of Tamil-initiated violence was well-established in and around Eravur.[77]

Meanwhile, back in the Polonnaruwa area on the 24th, 'At every main junction large crowds of [Sinhalese] thugs gathered, halted vehicles that passed by and assaulted passengers who were in them.' These sometimes murderous attacks were directed against Tamils. They were accompanied by successful intimidation of Sinhalese merchants who had been asked by hard-pressed civil servants to provide food for Tamils in their care. On the evening of the 24th, the station was again invaded by a crowd of 'nearly a thousand' who assaulted numerous persons and wrecked property until armed police cleared the area. At Giritale, five miles to the north, several persons were grievously wounded that night by toughs. At nearby Hingurakgoda, a mute scavenger of indeterminate communal origins was brutally murdered, while there and at Minneriya – eight miles from Polonnaruwa – men were burned alive.[78]

On the 25th, police and troops who had been rushed to the Eravur area succeeded in restoring peace. The only major exception occurred that

---

[77] Vittachi, *Emergency '58*, pp. 34–37 and 51; *CDN*, 24 and 26 May 1958.
[78] Vittachi, *ibid.*, pp. 34–37; *The Times* (London), 27 May 1958 and *CDN*, 26–27 May 1958.

morning when a car carrying a Sinhalese policeman and friends was stopped and fired upon with the loss of three lives, including that of the constable. But on the 25th, the situation round the other major trouble spot – Polonnaruwa – deteriorated still further. Assault, arson and looting continued against Tamils in broad daylight in most towns in the area. Government bungalows believed to belong to Tamil officials were put to the torch and another murder occurred at Hingurakgoda. On the night of the 25th, large gangs of Sinhalese armed with swords, knives and clubs attacked settlements of Tamil labourers. A considerable slaughter ensued with several dozen deaths, although Vittachi's figure of seventy is probably an overstatement.[79]

It then became alarmingly clear that the violence was spreading in the Sinhalese areas. From a wide range of localities came reports of harassment of Tamils. Most incidents were rather minor, but the trend was clear. Until this point, it had been possible to see the clashes as a dose of vile but isolated local difficulty in two places which lay close to the line separating Sinhalese- and Tamil-majority areas. By the morning of 26 May, this view was no longer tenable. The government faced the distinct possibility of an island-wide conflagration. The time had come to crack down with all the resources available, the deployment of which required the declaration of a state of emergency. And yet the Prime Minister held back.

On 26 May, the day an emergency should have been declared,[80] the second phase of the disturbance began, with attacks on Tamils throughout the Sinhalese-majority areas. Incidents occured at intervals along the main road linking Polonnaruwa with Colombo. Very severe violence occurred in the capital itself[81] and spread – mainly in the form of the looting of Tamil shops – down the coast to Panadura, Galle and even to Weligama, near the southern tip of the island.

At several places, strangely naïve and revealing reactions occurred when police came to the aid of Tamil victims. In Kurunegala, *bhikkhus* led a procession through the streets to protest the arrest of a man who had

[79] *Ibid.*

[80] Bandaranaike was remiss in delaying the declaration by one day, but given the fragmentary reports that were reaching him and the isolated nature of the two centres in which violence occurred over the days preceding the 26th, it is unfair to claim that he held back for 'four terror-filled days'. R. N. Kearney, *The Politics of Ceylon* (Ithaca, 1973), p. 197.

[81] After a morning of scattered cases of arson, looting and theft by small gangs of Sinhalese, the afternoon saw trouble concentrated in the Fort and Pettah areas of Colombo. This became alarming during the evening rush hour when, within sight of Parliament, wild scenes occurred. People were dragged from cars and buses to be beaten, cars were overturned and burned. Clashes continued throughout the city late into the night. *CDN*, 27 May 1958 and *The Times*, 28 May 1958.

stoned Tamil shops. Their assumption was that with state power in the hands of men elected by the Sinhalese revival such things should be permitted. The same evening, a policeman was stabbed when he intervened to stop a murderous attack upon Tamils there. At two other places police had to open fire when their stations were attacked for similar reasons. In one case, the crowd of between 1,000 and 3,000 apparently did not believe that this government's security forces would fire upon them.[82]

On the evening of the 26th, Bandaranaike made a radio address to the nation to calm fears and stress the government's intention to act firmly. But he mistakenly said that the first serious incident had been the death of the Sinhalese politician Seneviratne in a predominantly Tamil area. It is likely that he was misinformed rather then wilfully dishonest in making this remark, but it convinced many Sinhalese (who by now were perpetrating nearly all of the violence) that the Tamils were to blame.[83] The next morning, attacks on Tamils resumed in many parts of Colombo. Hysterical rumours of Tamil atrocities against Sinhalese and cries of vengeance for Seneviratne were heard amid dozens of cases of maiming, murder, arson, rape and looting both in the capital and southward along the coast to Galle and Matara,[84] up country at Kandy and numerous towns in the Central Province and at Kurunegala, Polonnaruwa and even remote Badulla.[85]

Late on the morning of the 27th, as reports of the deteriorating situation poured in, Bandaranaike conferred with the Governor-General, Sir Oliver Goonetilleke, and agreed that the latter should declare a state of emergency at 12.15 p.m. This imposed extensive press censorship and a dusk to dawn curfew, and banned public meetings, processions and strikes in essential services. It mobilized the armed services and gave them and the civil authorities draconian powers of detention without charge, and of search and seizure. Two political parties were proscribed: the Federal Party which was the main voice of the Tamils and the Jatika

[82] *CDN*, 27 May and 9 July 1958; Vittachi, *Emergency '58*, pp. 42–44 and an interview with a senior policeman during 1958, Colombo, 9 September 1978.

[83] *CDN*, 27 May 1958 and *The Times*, 28 May 1958.

[84] The anti-Tamil violence along the coast between Matara and Colombo, where most of the killing probably occurred, is reported to have been mainly precipitated by the return of Sinhalese fishermen who had been attacked in the Eastern Province. Interview with a Sri Lanka Tamil scholar, London, 5 February 1980. For more on the role of rumour, see J. R. Jayewardene Diaries, 3, 8 and 9 June 1958, file 5, J. R. Jayewardene Papers, Presidential Archive, Colombo.

[85] *CDN*, 28–29 May 1958; *The Times*, 28 May 1959; and Vittachi, *Emergency '58*, pp. 47–49. See, by contrast, *Administration Report of the Government Agent, Kalutara District, for 1958* (Colombo, 1959), pp. A515 and A703–04.

Vimukti Peramuna, a collection of extravagant Sinhalese bigots, some of whom had defected from Bandaranaike's ruling coalition.[86]

These measures quickly had a major impact in most of the Sinhalese-majority areas. There were a few savage incidents over the next twenty-four hours, particularly in southern Colombo and (still) in and near Polonnaruwa. But within two days of the declaration of an emergency, apart from stray incidents, violence in the Sinhalese areas had ceased.[87]

The third phase of the troubles, however, was just reaching its peak as the Tamil-majority areas reacted. The violence there mainly occurred in and around the coastal cities of Jaffna in the Northern Province and Batticaloa in the Eastern Province.[88] On 25 May, accurate reports of the murder of two Tamil Hindu priests sheltering in a temple in Panadura, south of Colombo, swept through Batticaloa. By the 27th, at least a small number of serious attacks against Sinhalese had occurred there, including the murder twenty-five miles south of the city of perhaps a dozen Sinhalese fishermen who migrated to the east coast at this season each year. On 26 or 27 May, a party of servicemen was fired on ten miles south of Batticaloa and two were killed.[89] Several more such firings occurred on the 28th and 29th in the clearest documented expressions of anti-government feeling, and over the next seven days there followed unspecified incidents of armed resistance to a major troop build-up in this district.[90]

The same reports of the killings of Tamil priests circulated in Jaffna where several cases of arson occurred on the 28th. The next day, a crowd of over 100 Tamils attacked a Buddhist temple in the city. Police intervened to save the priest who was hospitalized and this provoked an attack on the hospital which was repulsed by police firing without loss of life.[91] Between 30 May and 1 June, every customs and excise station in the Kayts area (an entrepôt for trade with India) and some government offices were raided or demolished. In nearby Velvettiturai, severe attacks

[86] *CDN*, 28 May 1958; *The Times*, 29 May 1958; and Public Security Ordinance No. 25 of 1947 as amended by Public Security (Amendment) Act No. 22 of 1949 and Public Security (Amendment) Ordinance No. 34 of 1953.

[87] *CDN*, 29 May 1958; *The Times*, 29 May 1958; and Vittachi, *Emergency '58*, pp. 56–59 and 63–68.

[88] Vittachi's claim that the Governor-General and others deliberately exaggerated disruptions in Tamil areas at this time (Vittachi, *Emergency '58*, pp. 72–75) finds no support in numerous interviews with journalists, military commanders and politicians of various linguistic and party backgrounds.

[89] *CDN*, 29 May 1958 and Vittachi, *Emergency '58*, pp. 51–54. See also, D. Horowitz, *Coup Theories and Officers' Motives* (Princeton, 1980), pp. 112–13.

[90] On 1 June, three cases of arson and the dynamiting of empty houses were reported from Batticaloa. *CDN*, 2 June 1958; *The Times*, 3 and 7 June 1958.

[91] Vittachi, *Emergency '58*, pp. 59–61.

forced police to abandon numerous stations and concentrate forces in three places for their own safety. On 30 May, a group of toughs sailed to the island of Nainativu where stood a temple which was an important place of pilgrimage for Sinhalese Buddhists. They flattened nearly every building, dynamited the temple and dismembered the statue of the Buddha. This was potentially the most inflammatory incident of 1958, since it might have precipitated a general massacre of Tamils. Fortunately the government was able to maintain secrecy until calm was restored and the services had a tight islandwide grip. By 3 June, when martial law was imposed on Jaffna and Batticaloa Districts, order had been largely restored.[92]

Who took part in the violence and why did they do so? The available evidence yields only partial answers, but some of these are enlightening. The worst violence against Tamils in greater Colombo occurred in the southern portion of the city, sparked in part by rumours. Railway stations and bus depots in that area yielded tales of violence from throughout the capital and from further south, and at Ratmalana airport, passengers disembarked from Jaffna with stories of Tamil 'outrages' there. It was also here that Colombo's large Tamil minority tended to be found. Their numbers and prosperity had increased substantially over the previous two decades, causing resentment among the Sinhalese.

Their anxieties were neatly reinforced by a widespread belief that Tamils were more clever, diligent, devious and better organized than they were.[93] During the troubles of 1958 this helped trigger looting and the destruction of Tamil houses, much of it carefully organized locally.[94] The main targets tended to be Tamils of the highest *status* rather than those who were most conspicuously *wealthy*.[95]

Much of the violence in the Polonnaruwa area and elsewhere in the North Central Province where Tamils suffered was the doing of Sinhalese who came from large colonization schemes. Two groups from the colonies were responsible for most of this. The more active were labourers whose supervisors included Tamil officials. Under a government which had pledged to uplift the Sinhalese and had accelerated the distribution of land to Sinhalese colonists, these landless wage-labourers faced two cruel ironies. They had to take orders from and acknowledge the superior status of Tamils, and their future prospects were grim at a

---

[92] *Ibid.*, pp. 61–63 and *CDN*, 2–3 June 1958.

[93] See, for example, the statement of the Junior Minister for Home Affairs, *CDN*, 12 October 1952 or Bandaranaike's comments as quoted in A. J. Wilson, *The Politics of Sri Lanka, 1947–1973* (London, 1974), p. 25.

[94] Interviews with residents of the area and with military commanders, Colombo, September, 1978; Vittachi, *Emergency '58*, pp. 49–50, 55–58 and 99–101; and *CDN*, 27–29 May 1958.   [95] Vittachi, *Emergency*, pp. 99–101.

time when other Sinhalese, usually from more favoured castes, were gaining lands all around them.[96] The second group, which wrought far less havoc – they were less organized and lacked the labourers' access to and knowledge of heavy vehicles and explosives – consisted of Sinhalese squatters on or near colonies. They eked out a precarious existence on tracts which they knew might soon be taken from them, as indeed some were. By threatening violence a few months earlier, they had helped to scotch a government plan to settle Tamils at one colony. The memory of that and their insecurity and grievances led them naturally to join in the violence.[97]

Detailed evidence on those responsible for violence in Sinhalese-majority areas outside Colombo and the Polonnaruwa area is severely limited.[98] It is likely, but impossible to prove on available evidence, that interests which had suffered during Bandaranaike's two years in power contributed to the rioting in order to destabilize the government. Prominent among the candidates are former bus owners whose vehicles had been nationalized and retail traders, money-lenders and notables who felt threatened by Philip Gunawardena's proposal to create new and well-funded multi-purpose cooperatives.[99]

Since most of the violence in the Tamil-majority areas occurred after the emergency and press censorship, information on the identity of participants and the character of the violence is scanty. In Jaffna, educated youths who had earlier defaced number plates were active in the attack on the city's Buddhist temple and hospital and early attacks on Sinhalese shops. In some cases, however, police and troops traced looters of shops to the premises of victims' business rivals.[100]

The systematic raids on customs and excise stations in the Kayts area and on police outposts near Velvettiturai were neither communalist nor insurrectionary in character. Posts manned by Tamils and Sinhalese suffered equally and although this qualifies as anti-state violence, it was criminal in nature. The attacks were made by well-organized gangs acting on behalf of long-standing networks of smugglers. When they seized customs stations, they not only carried off arms and ammunition but also carefully destroyed documents dealing with past violations. It is also likely that one such gang mounted the highly organized, communalist

---

[96] See, for example, Colvin de Silva's speech in *CDN*, 9 July 1958.

[97] Vittachi, *Emergency '58*, pp. 64–65.

[98] *CDN*, 29 April–21 May 1958; Vittachi, *Emergency '58*, pp. 38–39 and interviews with military commanders, Colombo, September, 1978.

[99] *CDN*, 26 October 1957 and interviews with police and military officers, Colombo, August–September, 1978.

[100] *CDN*, 30 May and 2 June 1958 and interviews with military commanders, Colombo, September, 1978.

attack on the offshore temple at Nainativu, since the attackers possessed
boats and explosives and a sophisticated knowledge of both.[101] A mixture
of communal and criminal violence, then, predominated in the north. It
was not until the 1970s, when the security forces began heavy-handed
doings in Tamil-majority areas, that the Northern Province generated
widespread anti-state violence.

There are abundant signs that violence within local arenas was often
organized, but there is no solid evidence of a wider conspiracy. Ministers'
allegations[102] that there might be one were generated by anxiety and
confusion rather than belief, and they did not persist in these views.
Vittachi's suggestion of a possible conspiracy – which others have seized
upon[103] – remains unsupported by evidence.

Where does the responsibility lie for the avoidable violence of 1958?
Nearly every commentator on these events had laid the blame at
Bandaranaike's door. This is neither surprising nor wholly unfair since he
clearly bore a greater responsibility than any other person. He had, after
all, been seeking to manipulate parochial sentiments for personal gain
since the late 1930s, and his actions since becoming Prime Minister had
betrayed a particularly dangerous *naïveté*. He was naïve in thinking that
his communalist election campaign would not generate invidious
expectations among extremists and, when they then arose, in assuming
that hesitation and inaction would not inflame them. He was naïve in
squandering his authority and above all, in his 'kid gloves' response to
dangerous provocations.

And yet to pillory Bandaranaike alone is to mislead. The leaders of *every*
major party – with the possible exception of the Federalists – made
substantial contributions to this mournful episode. The well-nigh
moronic mishandling of Sinhalese grievances by Sir John Kotelawala and
his colleagues in the old UNP government had bequeathed to Bandaranaike an alarming situation. Once in opposition, UNP leaders ran a
scurrilous campaign in their Sinhalese newspaper and elsewhere in order
to woo the bigots from Bandaranaike's camp. Responsibility is also
shared by the leaders of the two left opposition parties: the Communists
and N. M. Perera's version of the LSSP. They scrupulously refrained
from communalist actions but, in April and May 1958, they had cynically
staged strikes while communal tensions ran high. They called the men out
without consulting them, suppressed many of the workers' grievances,
despite the fact that the strike caused severe distress among strikers who

---

101 *CDN*, 2–3 June 1958 and Vittachi, *Emergency '58*, pp. 61–63.

102 *CDN*, 27 May, 3 and 5 June, 9 July 1958.

103 For example, 'Zeylanicus', in *Ceylon between Orient and Occident* (London, 1970), p. 230.

feared dismissal; and then called the strikes off without consulting the men and without gaining any significant concessions.[104] This produced bitter frustration among strikers which in many cases found an outlet when the rioting began.

Bandaranaike had no monopoly on opportunism and cavalier manipulation from elite levels in the political system. These habits were shared by nearly everyone in the small national political elite and they flowed logically from the severely overcentralized character of the political system. The principal flaw in the system was the discontinuity between elite and mass, which existed within every party.[105] Had parties not been so undemocratic and overcentralized, the opportunism, insensitivity, *naïveté* and manipulative ways of political leaders would probably have been checked. Since these elite traits contributed to the violence of 1958, that violence was in part a product of this systemic imbalance.

Bandaranaike stands accused of several misdeeds in the fortnight after the declaration of the state of emergency. It is time that these claims were reassessed. Robert Kearney writes that after the declaration, 'Bandaranaike virtually abdicated to the governor-general the authority to deal with' the crisis.[106] Essentially the same point is made in a sarcastic, polemical manner by Tarzie Vittachi and, with far greater care, by A. Jeyaratnam Wilson.[107] Vittachi suggests that the outbreak of rioting left Bandaranaike paralysed and frightened, that he turned the country over to the Governor-General for the duration of the troubles and retired to the Orient Club to play billiards.[108] Wilson notes Bandaranaike's comment that 'It is only after constant consultation with me that any instructions are issued (by the Governor-General) on my instructions.'[109] But he is not convinced by it. He states, correctly, that the Governor-General issued orders to service chiefs and civil servants during the riots, and that in the early days of the emergency, he was 'permitted to set himself up as the nation's chief press authority', a role which involved him in, among other things, censorship.[110] Wilson again notes Bandaranaike's statement that this was entirely proper under the emergency regulations, as long as the Governor-General had the Prime

---

[104] See especially, *Administration Report of the Inspector-General of Police, for 1958* (Colombo, 1960), pp. A153–56. Also, R. N. Kearney, *Trade Unions and Politics in Ceylon* (Berkeley, 1971), p. 105; and interviews with two LSSP organizers involved, 3 September 1978.

[105] J. Manor, 'The Failure of Political Integration in Sri Lanka', *Journal of Commonwealth and Comparative Politics,* xvii, 1 (March, 1979), pp. 21–46.

[106] Kearney, *The Politics of Ceylon,* p. 67.

[107] Vittachi, *Emergency '58* and A. J. Wilson, 'The Governor-General and the State of Emergency: May 1958–March 1959', *Ceylon Journal of Historical and Social Studies,* ii, 2 (July 1959), pp. 160–81. [108] Vittachi, *Emergency '58.*

[109] Wilson, 'The Governor-General', p. 164. The quotation is from *Ceylon Hansard* (1958), col. 40. [110] Wilson, 'The Governor-General', pp. 164–69.

Minister's approval. But he argues on the basis of British constitutional precedents that Bandaranaike's view represented 'a complete misunderstanding of the constitutional situation'.[111]

Much of this is unfair to Bandaranaike. Witnesses who saw him receive the first reports that serious violence had spread beyond the two original flashpoints have said that he was deeply shaken for a moment, but that he quickly recovered his composure and never lost it thereafter.[112] Vittachi's implication that he was incapacitated by the news is false. So is the claim that he withdrew from involvement in the administration during the crisis. Two witnesses – one who was privy to daily doings in the Governor-General's residence and one who participated in the meetings between Sir Oliver and the chiefs of the security forces, and neither of whom is a Bandaranaike sympathiser – argued strenuously that the Prime Minister was involved constantly and forcefully in decision-making. They also insist that in the actual issuing of orders, he deferred to the Governor-General because he believed that the emergency regulations required this.[113]

Was he correct in that belief? If our yardstick is British practice, he was not. But if we consider what had happened in Ceylon since independence, things look different. In theory, the Governor-General was supposed to occupy a neutral, transcendent position akin to that of the British monarch, but the office was shaped nearly as much by the activist, rather autocratic traditions of the colonial governorship out of which it had evolved. We have seen how Lord Soulbury ignored British precedents and acted in a partisan manner in selecting a successor to D. S. Senanayake, and that was no isolated case during his time in office. It was, however, when Sir Oliver Goonetilleke succeeded him in 1954 that the era of the interventionist, partisan Governor-General began in right earnest. This highly intelligent, irrepressible man had long been the principal tactician and arranger of deals for the United National Party, and his elevation to the island's highest office brought little change in that. As Governor-General, he was particularly energetic as a liaison for the Kotelawala government first with the civil service (which he had effectively run for the British during the war and for D. S. Senanayake thereafter) and second with the largely pro-UNP press. Bandaranaike shrewdly kept him on after 1956 against all expectations because he was short of gifted ministers and needed Sir Oliver's talents and personal

---

111 *Ibid.*, p. 166.
112 Separate interviews with two of Bandaranaike's aides, Colombo, 9 September 1977 and 16 August 1978.
113 Interviews in Colombo with Diana Captain, 8 September 1980 and Royce de Mel, 22 August 1978.

intervention with civil servants, high military and police officers and press barons to win acceptance for the new government. Sir Oliver very obligingly played this role[114] and his actions during and shortly after the riots of 1958 were in reality an expansion of his role since taking up his office. Moreover, as Wilson has noted, Ceylon's Constitution gave the Governor-General a certain latitude to innovate in this way.[115] It is true that Lord Soulbury and Sir Oliver carried their innovations much too far, but they had established that pattern long before 1958.[116] Bandaranaike must bear much of the blame for the violence in 1958, since his misjudgements earlier and in the first few days of the rioting contributed to it. But during the fortnight or so following the emergency declaration, he was far less passive and his actions and omissions were far less reprehensible than they have been made to appear.

During the year which followed the riots of 1958, disputes between left and right tended to predominate over communal issues, but these two themes were now bound up with one another more closely than ever before, as the hubris and resentments of Sinhalese chauvinists lent added thrust to efforts by some of the rightists in the ruling MEP, for whom communal issues were of secondary importance, to break the power of the leftists within the government.

Bandaranaike emerged from the riots determined to act forcefully to prevent further disorder and to ram through legislation to reassure Tamils. The state of emergency was not lifted[117] and this provoked protests from all sides, but in the weeks following the violence, the threat of more trouble was real enough to justify the decision. Five policemen lost their lives in violent incidents in this period, for example.[118] In mid-July 1958, with press censorship and widespread curfews still in force, the Prime Minister (who by now had decided to discard the Regional Councils Bill as too provocative) presented the long-deferred bill to provide for the 'reasonable use' of Tamil, first to a government legislators' caucus and then to Parliament even though the SLFP

---

[114] The author collected a great many references to the interventions of Sir Oliver after the change of government in 1956 with the civil service, the military, the police and the press in interviews in Colombo, 1977–80.

[115] Wilson, 'The Governor-General', 179. See also S. A. de Smith, *The New Commonwealth and Its Constitutions* (London, 1964), pp. 81–82.

[116] Both Howard Wriggins and James Jupp appear to agree that Bandaranaike was not guilty of constitutional impropriety here. W. H. Wriggins, *Ceylon: Dilemmas of a New Nation* (Princeton, 1960), pp. 94–95 and 269; and J. Jupp, *Sri Lanka: Third World Democracy* (London, 1978), pp. 286–87.

[117] On Bandaranaike's tough stance, see Vittachi, *Emergency '58*, pp. 83–86. For details of the emergency provisions, see H. H. Basnayake (ed.), *The Legislative Enactments of Ceylon* (Colombo, 1958), pp. 218–22.   [118] *TC*, 6 September 1958.

Executive Committee had not approved it. At the caucus, where
something like a majority privately opposed the bill, only two or three felt
bold enough to raise questions and Bandaranaike silenced them with
invitations to meet him later for private discussions.[119]

Leaders of the Tamils' Federal Party who were still kept in detention –
albeit in comfort at the Galle Face Hotel – were asked to take part in
debates on the bill but refused in protest at their incarceration. Other
opposition parties, including the UNP, also boycotted the proceedings
because of the continued detentions and emergency measures. A modest
number of Sinhalese extremists on the government benches expressed
anger that Tamil leaders had not been treated more severely and that 150
young SLFP members accused of looting Tamil shops during the riots
had not been released. Despite all of this, however, the bill became law on
5 August 1958.[120] Bandaranaike then toured the island, making hard-
hitting speeches denouncing the 'thugs and loafers' who had attacked
Tamils and urging communal harmony.[121] He made it clear that
whenever possible, Sinhalese rioters – unlike those of 1956 – would be
brought to trial, and he obtained a unanimous vote expelling from the
ruling party a junior minister who had opposed the Tamil Bill. This and
the resignation of one more particularly wayward MP left the government with fifty-seven votes in a House of ninety-nine, and though as
many as five more were said to be considering a departure from the ruling
coalition, that would still leave the majority intact.[122] In the event, no
further resignations occurred and this convinced Bandaranaike that he
had been right to stand firm. The state of emergency remained in force for
several more months with far less justification than in the weeks
following the riots. But several of its more stringent provisions were
lifted and the Prime Minister soon eased things informally by returning,
part of the time, to his role as arbiter. He continued with the emergency
because he did not want to lift it before a tougher Public Security Act
could be passed, but also because it was politically convenient.

Bandaranaike's hard line against the rioters and on the Tamil Bill
aroused great resentment among many MPs and government supporters,[123] and this soon found an outlet. It had long been apparent that

---

[119] The formal title was the Tamil Language (Special Provisions) Bill. *CDN*, 12, 16 and 18
   July 1958. Also, interviews with two SLFP MPs of that time, Colombo, 6 September
   1980 and Kandy, 28 August 1980.   [120] *CDN*, 1, 2, 4 and 6 August 1958.
[121] See, for example, *CDN*, 12 and 26 August and 12 September 1958.
[122] *CDN*, 7 and 11 August 1958. The House normally contained 101 members, but one seat
   was vacant and R. G. Senanayake continued to hold the two seats that he had won in
   1956. Five of the government seats belonged to *appointed* members.
[123] See, for example, the letter accusing the Prime Minister of a breach of faith, from a
   prominent *bhikkhu* (one of those who had demonstrated before Bandaranaike's house in
   1958) to the editor of the *CDN*, 26 July 1958.

various Cabinet members were pulling in different directions, with the leftist Philip Gunawardena appearing to be the principal odd man out.[124] In September 1958, he made a characteristically unvarnished attack on 'racketeers' in yellow robes. He was mainly referring to the Venerable Mapitagama Buddharakkhita, high priest of the great Kelaniya temple and a potent (if nefarious) force within the SLFP, of whom we shall hear more. The attack aroused the wrath of activist *bhikkhus* who accused Gunawardena of seeking to undermine the influence of the Buddhist clergy.[125] The exasperation that Sinhalese chauvinists felt over Bandaranaike's cosmopolitan actions in the wake of the riots, and over the provisions of the Tamil Bill and the manner of its passage, appears to have ignited a number of discontents which had long been smouldering in the minds of other groups that had backed Bandaranaike at the 1956 election. This generated further pressure against the left.

It is ironic that many of these discontents, which rightist ministers now turned to good account, were the results of bungling and foot-dragging by those very rightists. Two are particularly worth noting. Wimala Wijewardene, the Health Minister, had so alienated ayurvedic physicians that their island-wide association asked Bandaranaike to transfer ayurvedic medicine to another ministry,[126] and W. Dahanayake at Education had created widespread anger among vernacular school teachers by failing to implement the decision to give them parity in pay with English-medium teachers and by frequently transferring teachers.[127] It also took the government until July 1958 to introduce a Sinhala telephone directory,[128] MPs could still give notice of motions or put questions to ministers in Parliament only in English,[129] the government had taken no action against what puritanical Buddhists regarded as 'immoral' publications,[130] and it was not until December 1958 that legislation was introduced to facilitate the use of Sinhala in the courts.[131] None of these

---

[124] From the period under discussion, see *CDN*, 19 August 1958 and *TC*, 6 September 1958.

[125] The quotation is from *TC*, 1 September 1958. See also, *CDN* 12 September 1958, for an example of activist *bhikkhus* attacking another leftist, see the campaign against Nimal Karunatilake, *CDN*, 26 July 1958.

[126] *CDN*, 3 April 1959. See also, *CDN*, 4 September and 14 November 1958 and 3 March 1959. When she finally – and rather belatedly – came out with a plan for ayurvedic medicine, she overcompensated so much in response to these criticisms that she was attacked for excessive generosity (*CDN*, 24 and 29 November 1958).

[127] *CDN*, 23 August 1958; 10 January, 3 and 21 March 1959. For other complaints, see *TC*, 6 September 1958 and *CDN*, 9 September 1958 and 24 January 1959.

[128] *CDN*, 8 July 1958.   [129] *CDN*, 17 September 1958.

[130] *CDN*, 10 September 1958.

[131] *CDN*, 18 December 1958. It should be stressed that, in contrast to the ministers responsible for the problems listed above, Law Minister M. W. H. de Silva was not a rightist.

things was Gunawardena's fault, but they lent an extra impetus to the campaign which arose against him in late 1958.

It arose primarily from within the Cabinet, since power was – as usual in the island's history – too highly centralized and links between the national level and the grass roots were too insubstantial[132] to permit the resentments of *bhikkhus*, teachers or ayurvedic doctors to determine events at the apex of the system, although they had a noticeable impact. The struggle began when Philip Gunawardena presented his Cooperative Development Bank Bill to fellow-ministers in late November 1958. Its main aim was to create a fund of 10m rupees (rising eventually to 300m)[133] to support the activities of hundreds of multi-purpose cooperative societies that his ministry had established all across Ceylon. With that sort of funding, these societies could have provided the beginning of a broad rural power base – something that had always eluded the left. They could also have provided poorer villagers with resources that had never come their way from existing cooperatives which were largely controlled by more prosperous rural dwellers.

The reaction to this bill among Gunawardena's opponents in the Cabinet was complicated. Almost all of them welcomed the damage that it would do to major wholesalers and traders, nearly all of whom backed the UNP. But the new cooperatives would also threaten small merchants in villages and towns, many of whom supported the SLFP.[134] Several ministers were sympathetic to help for the disadvantaged, but they were uneasy about the reaction of village elites – teachers, ayurvedic doctors, *bhikkhus* and the like, upon whom they felt partly dependent – to a redirection of resources. But all of Gunawardena's opponents were unanimous in their anxiety over the potential rural base that the bill would provide, for him and for the left.

Their opposition to it on political grounds was powerfully reinforced by the intense personal dislike which most felt for their leftist colleague. He had long behaved contemptuously toward most of them, and he had lately caused two of them – Health Minister Wijewardene and Finance Minister Stanley de Zoysa – especially acute embarrassment. His reference to 'racketeers' in yellow robes had called attention to the doings of the *bhikkhu* Buddharakita who – his calling notwithstanding – was widely known to have a carnal relationship with Mrs Wijewardene (a widow) and a business alliance with de Zoysa through whom he had

---

[132] For examples of such overcentralization in this period, see the pleas of villagers direct to Minister R. G. Senanayake, *TC*, 6 September 1958; the failure of the regional councils scheme, *CDN*, 1 November 1958; and the complaint of R. G. Senanayake about the unmanageable burden which floods of constituents' petitions placed on MPs, *CDN*, 3 February 1959.   [133] *CDN*, 20 March 1959.   [134] *CDN*, 28 March 1959.

sought government contracts for a shipping line. Gunawardena had further enraged de Zoysa by alleging that the latter's brother, a Deputy Inspector-General of Police, had plotted to overthrow the government – a charge which may have had some substance.[135]

It is hardly surprising then, that Gunawardena's bill met with stiff resistance round the Cabinet table, and by mid-December 1958, two of the ablest ministers – Maithripala Senanayake (Transport) and C. P. de Silva (Agriculture) – had carried the issue onto the public platform.[136] Gunawardena's position was made more uncomfortable by a rash of strikes which broke out in December. Most of these were begun by unions controlled by leftists in opposition, partly to embarrass him. To maintain credibility in the unions which *he* controlled, he had to allow *them* to strike as well.[137] This laid him open to the charge of destabilizing the government of which he was a member and his adversaries seized it with relish. Bandaranaike had at first attempted to forge a compromise within the Cabinet over the Cooperative Bank Bill. He persuaded Gunawardena to cede control over cooperatives for colonization schemes and for fisherfolk to other ministers.[138] This cost him relatively little since the vast majority of cooperatives fell outside these categories and since the Fisheries Minister was a fellow leftist.

Rightist ministers were not prepared to let things rest there, however. By the first week of 1959, several of them were threatening to resign unless Gunawardena was dismissed.[139] Leftist MPs within the governing coalition hit back,[140] but they were too heavily outnumbered to prevent another victory for the right in February.

This occurred at a meeting of the SLFP Executive Committee, a body which Bandaranaike had not convened for several months because he feared a backlash against the Tamil Bill. At the meeting, the party's General Secretary Nimal Karunatilake proposed (with Bandaranaike's support) that the SLFP form an alliance with the Marxist opposition parties in the upcoming Colombo Municipal Council election. This made short-term political sense since the SLFP was weak in Colombo as in all urban centres, the Marxists were strong there and if no alliance was formed, the UNP would probably win. But with the Marxist parties mounting strikes against the government, SLFP rightists found this unpalatable and – more to the point – useful in their campaign against the left. Education Minister Dahanayake launched a stinging attack against

---

[135] See, for example, *CDN*, 24 September and 22 and 29 November 1958.
[136] *CDN*, 8 and 13 December 1958.
[137] *CDN*, 22–23 and 29 December 1958 and 1 and 3 January 1959.
[138] *CDN*, 17 December 1958. [139] *CDN*, 5–6 January 1959.
[140] *CDN*, 6–7 January 1959.

the Marxist parties at the Executive Committee meeting and a bitter dispute ensued in which two people came to blows and one man had to be 'forcibly silenced' after interrupting the Prime Minister repeatedly. The Committee then rejected the electoral alliance. The right, led by the aforementioned *bhikkhu* Buddharakkhita who was a member of the Executive carried things further by seeking to oust Karunatilake as General Secretary. He was one of the SLFP's more left-leaning figures and although he had no solid political base, he had proved himself an intelligent young man, both as party General Secretary and as a junior minister. The high esteem in which Bandaranaike held him would have saved him a year earlier, but the premier's hold over his party had been eroded by the Paddy Bill controversy, the riots of 1958 and the passage of the Tamil Bill against the wishes of many party stalwarts. The SLFP Chief Whip, J. C. W. Munasinha, was elected over Bandaranaike's objection to replace him. Munasinha represented conservative Roman Catholic sentiment and his nomination by Buddharakkhita signalled further cooperation between propertied Roman Catholic and Buddhist interests.[141]

This opened the way to mounting disorder and indiscipline within the ruling coalition. Leftist MPs in the SLFP suggested that they might quit the party if Karunatilake were not reinstated. Their numbers were small, but their departure would leave the government with a tiny majority. As strikes continued, a rightist junior minister told a public meeting that the Prime Minister and his Cabinet colleagues were spineless. If they could not govern properly – by which he meant banning all strikes – they should resign.[142] He was crying out to be disciplined, but Bandaranaike could not move against him without risking a major revolt on the right. The Prime Minister had to give way on an important procedural matter in Parliament when Education Minister Dahanayake, and several other rightists publicly threatened to resign unless he did so.[143] In reaction to this, a junior minister from Gunawardena's party joined the opposition.[144] It appears that at this point Dahanayake – one of the most unrestrained egoists in a political system that produced them in quantity, and a man who in the early 1950s had been a consistently vicious critic of Bandaranaike – took it into his head that he had sufficient support to depose Bandaranaike and form a government. The premier cooly invited him to present his list of backers to the Governor-General, and when this was done, his ambitions were shown to have outstripped his support by a huge margin. Yet Bandaranaike felt unable to impose discipline even

---

[141] *CDN*, 2 February 1959. See also, 4–5 February and 2 March 1959. For the quotation, see 9 February 1959.   [142] *CDN*, 7 February 1959.   [143] *CDN* 13 and 21 February 1959.
[144] This was T. B. Subasinghe. *CDN*, 14, 18, 23 and 25 February 1959.

for this. Dahanayake was too well connected with other rightist ministers to risk it.

In mid-February the decisive battle within the Cabinet over Gunawardena's Cooperative Bank Bill commenced. A meeting of the ruling party's MPs degenerated into a bitter slanging match between left and right.[145] A further Cabinet meeting, three weeks later, in which Bandaranaike tried to promote accommodation, produced a further explosion. Among other things, one minister had called Gunawardena 'scum'. Bandaranaike proposed that government MPs should be asked for their views on the bill before the Cabinet came to a decision, an unprecedented step. He could see that the right, which had more than a two-to-one majority in the Cabinet, was totally unyielding and he was gambling that he could sell a compromise formula to MPs in general. He acknowledged that this was risky, since it might split the parliamentary delegation at a time when only six defections would destroy his majority. But he knew that to abandon Gunawardena's bill might also produce that number of resignations.[146]

In March and April, the stress under which Bandaranaike had been operating began to show. He allowed himself to become embroiled in an unseemly dispute over the dismissal of the Inspector-General of Police in which he appeared weak and vacillating.[147] The state of emergency was finally lifted in mid-March, but this brought more blame than credit to the Prime Minister because he had delayed so long before taking this action. He had maintained it in a less severe form for many months, but it seemed to most observers to be unnecessary and to set a dangerous precedent which has since led to more serious abuses.[148] And then, in an act of astonishing utopian *naïveté*, he proposed constitutional reforms that entailed the abandonment of the Westminster model and Cabinet government in favour of the more decentralized Executive Committee system that had existed before independence. His aim was to counteract excessive polarization – between Sinhalese and Tamils, and between government and opposition. He might have dealt more effectively with communal antagonism had he borrowed from European consociational models, but he was apparently unaware of these. In any case, when it became clear that next to no one in public life agreed with him, he dropped the idea amid speculation that he was losing his grip.[149]

---

[145] *CDN*, 18 and 25 February and 30 May 1959. See also, 27 February 1959.

[146] *CDN*, 26–27 March 1959. On Bandaranaike's efforts to build unity, see *CDN*, 17 and 24 March 1959.   [147] *CDN*, 28, 30 March and 1, 4, 7, 9 and 20 April 1959.

[148] *CDN*, 9–24 September 1958 and 13 March 1959.

[149] Interviews with numerous MPs from that period in Colombo, August 1978 and *CDN*, 11 March, 4 April, 2 and 6–7 May 1959, *The Observer* (London), 8 March 1959, *Manchester Guardian*, 4 April and 22 May 1959, *The Times* (London), 20 and 22 April 1959, and newspaper clippings in file 3, BP.

This only stiffened the resolve of the conservative ministers who were now consulting astrologers on the timing of their moves. Gunawardena, realizing that he was probably in a fight to the finish, announced that there would be no compromise on his bill.[150] As public exchanges between right and left grew even more rancorous and embarrassing, Bandaranaike – in a last attempt to maintain some sort of unity – proposed that after making 'adjustments' in the text of the bill, he would personally administer it when it became law. A few days later, while this offer was still being considered by both sides, Gunawardena threatened and insulted a senior civil servant, the Private Secretary to the Education Minister, at the entrance to Parliament. He had to be restrained by other MPs from attacking the man.[151] This proved highly convenient to rightist ministers, ten of whom announced on 6 May that they would attend no Cabinet meetings until Gunawardena was dismissed.

Despite desperate attempts by Bandaranaike to heal the breach and – belatedly – to crack down on indiscipline, the ministers' 'strike' (as it came to be known) continued.[152] The deadlock clearly had to be broken since the annual conference of the SLFP was scheduled for the 16th, when some of the more irresponsible rightists led by *bhikkhu* Buddharakkhita were to seek to replace Bandaranaike with Dahanayake as party leader. They had little hope of succeeding, but the mere fact that this was contemplated suggested how much had changed in a party that Bandaranaike had once dominated. He had taken this threat seriously enough to postpone the party conference once already, and there was no avoiding it a second time. So, on the eve of the conference, he announced a re-allocation of portfolios among his ministers. He took personal control of the departments of food, cooperatives and marketing which had previously been held by Gunawardena, who got fisheries which had been in the hands of William Silva, another Marxist minister. Silva was given excise. This had predictable results. As the SLFP conference opened, the 'striking' ministers announced their willingness to return to Cabinet meetings, and Gunawardena and Silva threatened to resign unless the changes were rescinded. When Bandaranaike refused, they joined the opposition, as did three other Marxist MPs and six leftists from within the SLFP.[153] The party's annual conference was a rowdy affair, but the hall had been carefully packed with Bandaranaike's supporters. The armed men whom one of his aides has stationed offstage – without the

[150] *CDN*, 27 March and 2, 10 and 18 April and 11 May 1959.
[151] *CDN*, 21–24 April and 1 and 6 May 1959.
[152] *CDN*, 7–9 and 12–15 May 1959. Also, interviews with A. P. Jayasuriya, 9 September 1977 and Maithripala Senanayake, 13 September 1980, both in Colombo.
[153] *CDN*, 16–19 May 1959.

Table 8.2. *Government and opposition in Parliament, mid-May 1959*

For the government	
Elected MPs	41
Nominated MPs	6
Total	47
Against	
LSSP (Gunawardena)	5
LSSP (N. M. Perera)	14
Federal Party	8
UNP	6
Others	14
Total	47

Source: CDN, 24 June 1959.

Prime Minister's knowledge – were not needed since no serious challenge to him arose.[154]

As the leftists crossed to the opposition benches, two independent MPs were persuaded to come over to the government, but for Bandaranaike the parliamentary arithmetic was still grim (see Table 8.2). In addition, there were two Muslim independents and three Communist Party MPs who had recently voted with the government. But after the departure of eleven leftists, the Communists were unlikely to lend continued support for long. Even if they did so, the Prime Minister faced the embarrassment of depending on MPs whom he had nominated. A clear majority of elected legislators now stood against him. To make matters worse, one of his MPs was undergoing intensive medical treatment in India, another was in Colombo Hospital and a third was overseas. Bandaranaike was in an exceedingly precarious, undignified position.[155]

The days that followed (and the nights) were filled with frantic, anxious negotiations. One defector from the SLFP was persuaded to return and offers of junior ministries and other enticements kept several potential floor-crossers on the government side.[156] But when new

[154] Interview with the aide in question, M. P. de Zoysa, Colombo, 19 August 1978. See also, *CDN*, 16 and 18 May 1959, and the material on the conference in file 3, BP.

[155] *CDN*, 20 May and 15 and 24 June 1959. See also, Bernard Aluwihare Diaries, 1 January and 20, 23 and 26 May 1959, University of Peradeniya Library.

[156] Interview with A. P. Jayasuriya, Colombo, 9 September 1977 and *CDN*, 4, 10 and 15 June 1959.

ministers were named on 9 June, 'at least three or four' MPs who had been left out were said to be on their way to the UNP and two others were considering an exit leftward. Further wheeling and dealing including two more junior ministerial appointments at the end of June prevented these defections,[157] so that when Parliament reassembled in early July, the situation was delicately poised. For the first time in Ceylon, all opposition parties had agreed to unite against the government after the Speech from the Throne.[158] At the eleventh hour, three opposition MPs – at least one of whom had been wavering between the two camps for weeks – left the island for a conference in Vienna. This appeared to tip the scale decisively against the opposition so that on the crucial day several others also stayed away and the government won, fifty votes to forty-one.[159] The margin of victory was deceptive, though. A wave of leftist-inspired strikes that had gripped the nation since May was sure to continue. They added to the already excruciating strain under which Bandaranaike was working and they dismayed conservatives on the government benches who kept threatening to defect even after the vote of confidence.[160] It seemed only a matter of time before the government would fall.

All of this exacted a heavy toll on Bandaranaike's equanimity. Over the years, he had shown himself to have a remarkably thick skin. His staunch refusal to acknowledge embarrassments and reverses – both in public and, probably, to himself – had earned him a reputation for self-deceiving complacency and even shamelessness, but it had also preserved the inner citadel of his self from trauma. His unfailing aplomb in the face of difficulty and disappointment was no charade. By mid-1959, however, so many things had gone wrong, so much of his authority had been lost and such dire political troubles assailed him that both his utopian visions and his mundane, short-term prospects stood in grave jeopardy. His dreams of being his people's benefactor, of creating lasting reforms of real substance, of an honourable retirement as the island's elder statesman – all of these things were at risk. The stress began to tell. He often appeared tense and emotionally exhausted, and he began to experience moments of despair and near panic.[161]

Throughout July and August 1959 he was desperately searching for an escape from his predicament. Although, as we shall see, he eventually

---

[157] The quotation is from *CDN*, 22 June 1959. See also, *CDN*, 10 and 29 June and 1 July 1959. [158] *CDN*, 1, 3–4 and 7–9 July 1959.
[159] *CDN*, 8–9 July 1959. The waverer was P. Tennekoon. On his indecision, see *CDN*, 6 June 1959. [160] *CDN*, 15 July 1959.
[161] This is based on numerous interviews with aides and witnesses, Colombo, 1978 and 1980.

decided upon an audacious political gamble, for the present there seemed
no rational way out. This brought him to an emotional and intellectual
crisis which appears to have had no precedent in his adult life. Since his
return from Oxford, Bandaranaike had remained resolutely, even
arrogantly, a rationalist. He had stuck firmly to the highly intellectualized, unemotional brand of 'Protestant' Buddhism that stopped
well short of what he saw as the distastefully superstitutious practices in
which many westernized Buddhists in Ceylon – including his wife –
indulged when confronted with painful dilemmas.[162] Mrs Bandaranaike
had travelled to the Lunawa temple south of Colombo – a booming
centre of such practices[163] – to fulfil a vow to the Kataragama god whom
she believed had performed favours for her. The Prime Minister
accompanied his wife, but agreed only to look on as she signified her
obeisance to the deity in what was essentially a Hindu ceremony that was
vehemently denounced by Buddhist purists.[164] This ritual was clearly
alien to Bandaranaike's rationalistic Buddhism and, more crucially, it
demanded that the devotee undergo the sort of personal submission to
the authority of the god which had once made Christianity unacceptable
to him.

By July 1959, however, things had changed. Bandaranaike, facing such
profound political troubles, turned – like so many other 'Protestant'
Buddhists in times of crisis – to the supernatural for a solution. On a tour
of the Southern Province, he was prevailed upon to visit one of the
'soothsayers down Matara way'. This phrase appears to refer to a woman
'light reader' who made her living by staring into a flame, going into a
trance and providing clients with diagnoses of their problems in
supernatural terms.[165] The Bandaranaike papers contain notes in English
from such an encounter which are unmistakably in his hand and which
were clearly written after the leftist ministers had been dismissed. Some of
these are only semi-legible, but most are clear enough to make telling and
at times chilling reading.

The document begins with an indication that in its initial phase, his
government had been able 'to clean up troubles' and that the 'Gods' were
also 'engaged in cleaning up'. 'Fit and right people were chosen of gods'
to govern. Bandaranaike is then informed that troubles which were

---

[162] G. Obeyesekere, 'Social Change and the Deities: The Rise of the Kataragama Cult in
   Modern Sri Lanka', *Man*, xii (1977), pp. 377–96.

[163] *CDN*, 5 and 30 August 1958. I am grateful to Gananath Obeyesekere for information on
   the Lunawa temple.   [164] See the collection of newspaper cuttings in file 13, BP.

[165] The phrase quoted here is that of the lobby correspondent of the *Ceylon Daily News* (21
   July 1959), but the visit was confirmed by a close aide to Bandaranaike, Colombo, 14
   August 1980.

foretold the previous year actually 'took place'. He hears of 'more trouble this yr. But I shall be able to overcome this.' These are 'Troubles for me and gods.' He is told that the 'Gods have given me power' and that 'Therefore' he bears a 'responsibility' to them. There follows a specific diagnosis of his difficulties. This begins with an important word, 'Hunian'. Its literal meaning is 'black magic', but it also refers specifically to a *mala yaka* or demon which was gaining popularity at this time among troubled people who turned to him to take destructive action against their enemies.[166] Bandaranaike is told that 'I had come under his influence', and that 'He is conflicting with the K. god.' This refers to the Kataragama god, the deity which presided both at the Kataragama shrine in the far south of the island and at the Lunawa shrine just south of Colombo, where Mrs Bandaranaike had fulfilled her vow. He is told that 'This conflict must be ended' because 'Ministerial trouble [was] due to this conflict.' The solution, 'What is needed', is recorded in rather garbled fashion, but it seems clear that he is to make certain offerings 'to Vishnu and . . . K.G.' (the Kataragama god) over a period of '21 days'. This will free him of his troubles. He then learns that 'Philip G.[unawardena was] also chosen by gods.' There follows a most arresting sentence, in the light of subsequent events: 'Blood will flow this year.' Bandaranaike is advised that 'This trouble will arise . . . out of ministerial trouble.'[167]

He appears to have taken this seriously, since in late July, he went to the Lunawa temple and participated in the very ceremonies he had so pointedly abstained from on that previous visit with his wife. He carried 'The gem-studded gold image of the God Kataragama on his head from the Devale [shrine] to place the statue on the chariot' at the start of the procession. Press photographs show this quite clearly. 'The Premier is surrounded by Kavadi dancers who preceded the statue' and, 'while the invocation was gone through, several people went into trance and danced both within and outside the Devale'. The chief incumbent of the temple invoked the blessing of the god 'on the Premier, the Cabinet and the country', and another *bhikkhu* added that 'there was no doubt that the Premier had been able to overcome all forms of opposition and maintain himself as Premier of the country due to the help he had received from the god Kataragama'.[168]

Those involved were well aware that many Buddhists regarded such doings at Lunawa as less than respectable, involving as they did pacts of

---

166 I am grateful to Gananath Obeyesekere for informing me on these matters. Also, R. Gombrich, 'From Monastery to Meditation Centre: Meditation in Modern Sri Lanka', typescript, 1979.
167 'Sea-Gull Exercise Book', file 8, BP. See also, notes on a horoscope, June, 1959, file 16, BP.   168 *CDN*, 20 July 1959.

an instrumental nature with deities of Hindu origin or with demons and, for some, ecstatic experiences. One of the *bhikkhus* made this plain when he lashed out at people who might criticize Bandaranaike for taking part in these ceremonies and then come to Lunawa themselves at night to worship the god secretly. The Prime Minister himself felt called upon to justify his involvement, saying that 'If we believe in the existence of gods, there is no harm in worshipping them and invoking their blessing.'[169]

For Bandaranaike, this represented a radical break with previous practice which must have been difficult for him. He had to overcome more than public embarrassment and his erstwhile personal preference for a more orthodox and intellectualized Buddhism. By bearing the image of the god on his head, he was performing an act of personal submission to the deity. Given his strong, lifelong aversion to acknowledgements of the authority of any superior, either human or divine, this must have been a traumatic experience for him. He could not have gone this far had the pressures and anxieties that he faced in mid-1959 not brought him very near the breaking point.[170]

There are at least two ways of viewing this, both of which have a certain validity. A western reader's initial inclination is to see it as a sign of at least a partial breakdown both of his emotional stability and of his rationalistic approach to political and personal life. But those who have considered such events from the perspective of the persons involved tend also to see them as logical solutions to problems which cannot be solved by the means available to coolly rationalist, 'Protestant' Buddhists.[171] By turning to this new 'solution', Bandaranaike was able to call upon resources which – at a conscious level – he had previously scorned and ignored. Indeed, if we recall certain things from his past, we can see that by engaging in these actions, he was consciously acknowledging a dimension of himself which he had long ignored. The figures of the murderous giant and the terrified dog in the ruins at Pompeii from his boyhood writings, his fascination during anxious times at Oxford with unearthly, sometimes morbid elements in fairy tales and the writings of Poe, and the images of horror and soullessness which are central to some of his detective stories[172] – all of these things indicate that in projecting himself (both to others and to himself) as a cool, imperturbable

---

169 *Ibid.*
170 I am grateful to S. J. Tambiah and Gananath Obeyesekere for help in interpreting this event.
171 Interview with Gananath Obeyesekere, Colombo, 8 August 1980. See also, Obeyesekere, 'Social Change'.
172 See, for example, 'The Horror of Mahahena' and 'The Adventure of the Soulless Man' in S. W. R. D. Bandaranaike, *Speeches and Writings*, pp. 491–528.

rationalist, he had suppressed an important side of himself which responded readily to the 'solution' offered by the light reader and the gods.

A month later, with the political situation as precarious as before, events took a sinister turn. During the weekly Cabinet meeting on 26 August, the usual refreshments – glasses of milk – were handed out to ministers shortly after midday. C. P. de Silva – the formidable Leader of the House and Bandaranaike's second-in-command – took a sip from his glass and began to gag violently. The Finance Minister, seated next to him, patted him on the back to relieve the coughing, but de Silva then collapsed completely. He was carried into the Prime Minister's room next door, but when it became apparent that he was completely paralysed, he was rushed to the Central Hospital. By that evening, he had managed some speech and two days later, he had become capable of very limited movement.[173]

The initial impression was that he had suffered a stroke. The morning before the Cabinet meeting, he had complained of feeling unwell, but neither he nor anyone in his family had a history of hypertension. Within twenty-four hours, this diagnosis was in doubt.[174] It appears that for several weeks thereafter, the cause of the paralysis remained a mystery. An eminent neurologist from Britain soon arrived in Colombo and, on 7 September, took de Silva to the Hospital for Nervous Diseases in London. There is some confusion on this point, but it was apparently there that tests revealed the cause to be 'acute toxic nephritis', that is, poisoning of the kidneys. The doctors were at a loss to explain precisely how such severe damage could occur, apparently so suddenly, but they were convinced that it could only have resulted from 'the intake of a toxic substance'.[175] Several of them eventually concluded that de Silva's glass of milk had been laced with cobra venom or some similarly deadly poison, but this did not become known to many members of the political elite until more than a month later,[176] and the interval is immensely important.

If this view is accurate – and despite the fact that no adequate criminal investigation was ever undertaken, it is difficult to avoid the conclusion that de Silva was given some sort of poison – how is it to be explained? Some people believe that it was a bungled attempt to assassinate the Prime Minister, that de Silva got Bandaranaike's glass by mistake. This

[173] *TC*, 26–27 August 1959 and *CDN*, 27 August 1959.
[174] Interview with de Silva's sister (a physician), Stella de Silva, Colombo, 23 September 1980 and *CDN*, 27 August 1959.
[175] Interview with one of his physicians, Colombo, 24 September 1980.
[176] Interviews in Colombo with family members and doctors connected with the case, September, 1980; and with two Cabinet members, A. P. Jayasuriya, 2 September 1977 and Maithripala Senanayake, 26 September 1980, both in Colombo.

view seems long on melodrama but short on plausibility since this method of murdering the premier would have put at risk other ministers at the Cabinet table who were more to the liking of the people who later conspired to have Bandaranaike shot. If – as is likely – de Silva was the target, a second possibility is that this was simply an isolated case of an enemy seeking to destroy him. Had this been the last attempt on the life of a minister in the Bandaranaike government, that would clearly be the most credible explanation. But since thirty days later the premier himself was gunned down, it is more likely that someone tried to murder de Silva as a prelude to an attack on Bandaranaike.

C. P. de Silva was a tough, intelligent politician with a certain independence of mind and a strong popular base, an administrator of skill and experience who was personally close to Bandaranaike. As Leader of the House, de Silva would automatically have become interim premier if Bandaranaike had died or become incapacitated. Anyone seeking the Prime Minister's removal in order either to gain greater influence over the government or to win ministers' acquiescence in corrupt actions – both of which were motives of those convicted of conspiracy to murder Bandaranaike – could not have relished the prospect of de Silva as successor. He would have been impossible to control and difficult to oust. We will probably never know precisely how this incident originated, but the conspirators in the assassination of Bandaranaike had good reason to seek the prior removal of de Silva.

Whoever developed suspicions about foul play in the case of C. P. de Silva, and whenever they developed them – both issues remain unresolved – they do not appear to have sent word to Bandaranaike in the month after de Silva's collapse.[177] When the Prime Minister travelled to his constituency a few days later to unveil a statue, unusual security precautions were in evidence. Armed police lined the street and as Bandaranaike walked in the procession he was flanked on both sides by constables. But these arrangements seem to have been inspired by the memory of an earlier bombing incident at that spot and by the persistence of the quarrel that lay behind it,[178] rather than by any more general concern for his safety. Bandaranaike had joked some months earlier about reports that someone was planning to 'bump me off'.[179] but he did not take them altogether seriously and no tightening of security took place on any other occasion after de Silva had been struck down.

---

[177] The rumour that de Silva had been poisoned only spread in the Colombo political elite *after* Bandaranaike had been assassinated. See for example, Bernard Aluwihare Diaries, 2 September 1959 (written on the page for 26 August) and 8 October 1959. See also, *The Times* (London), 28 September 1959.

[178] *TC*, 7 September 1959.   [179] *Daily Telegraph* (London), 6 August 1958.

During late August and the early weeks of September 1959, Bandaranaike busied himself devising and preparing the ground for an
audacious political gamble which he hoped would restore some of his lost
authority and a reliable majority in Parliament. He planned to attempt it
suddenly in October, immediately after his return from a visit to the
United Nations where he would address the General Assembly. He knew
that this trip, which was to begin on 28 September, would produce a brief
surge of popularity at home since even the more hostile mass circulation
newspapers always turned grudgingly rapturous when a Prime Minister
appeared at a great occasion overseas. He also needed a break from the
strain of keeping his government afloat. He had only recently had a close
call when he was forced to send the Assistant Sergeant-at-Arms chasing
up country in a fast car to fetch a wayward MP in time for an unexpected
vote in Parliament.[180] His journey abroad was also to include a brief stop
in Britain where he was to address the Oxford Union, an occasion which
he relished and which would yield further good publicity in Ceylon.

He was determined to use the short-term lift that this would provide to
attempt a surprise realignment of forces within Parliament. He planned to
dismiss, quite abruptly, a small number of the more undisciplined
rightists from his Cabinet and, simultaneously, to induct most of the
major leftist leaders into his ministerial team. Even if some of them did
not formally join the government, he expected them to back his centre-
left coalition during votes of confidence. He would also draw back into
the fold the small number of SLFP leftists who had gone over to the
opposition when Philip Gunawardena had been sacked.

He might have just managed to form a government on this basis,
although this was far from likely. It was decidedly unlikely that it could
have survived for long. He had lost so much authority that he was
probably finished politically. His apparent aim, however, was not to cling
onto power until the next general election in 1961 but to present the
electorate with an ambitiously reformist programme, enact and implement what little he could, and then call a surprise election to seek a
popular endorsement. His cultivation of leftist opposition leaders during
the first half of 1959 and several of his left-leaning comments and
initiatives in that period were based on the expectation that, at the next
election, voters – including newly enfranchised youth now that the
voting age had been lowered to eighteen – would swing further left.[181] He

---

180 Interview with a parliamentary official, Colombo, 22 September 1980. See also, *CDN*, 1,
6–9 July 1959.
181 See, for example, 22 October 1958. His expectation was probably incorrect, but it ought
to be said that the actual outcomes of the two 1960 elections do not fully disprove it. The
electorate in 1960 voted amid a confused, emotionally charged situation. They did not
face the kind of clear cut choice that Bandaranaike sought to present to them.

believed that even if his manoeuvre failed within Parliament, it would produce major benefits from the electorate at large.[182] It is unlikely that he would have succeeded, but given his unenviable position, it was as promising a plan as could have been devised.

He appears to have revealed his intentions to only a small handful of people – almost certainly fewer than ten – all of whom were close personal confidants with leftist leanings or contacts. Precisely whom he informed in Colombo is unclear, but on 23 September after opening the new market in Kandy, he took two such persons on a drive into the Royal Botanical Gardens. One of them, a key figure among the Kandyans in the SLFP, began by complaining about the dismissal of Gunawardena. The Prime Minister cut him short, explained his plan and asked if he would work among Kandyan MPs in the SLFP to keep them loyal once the switch occurred. Bandaranaike asked his other companion, an SLFP leftist who had gone into opposition with Gunawardena, to act as an intermediary to certain leftist elements while he was overseas. Both eagerly agreed.[183]

It must be emphasized in the strongest terms, however, that there is no connection between this and the violent events that occurred two days later. The people who knew of this plan were too few in number and too committed to him to have leaked the news to his enemies. Indeed, even at this writing, few people in the island are aware of the plan. There are some who might cite this incident to lend credence to their claims that although a lone assassin held the gun that killed Bandaranaike, 'history will record that . . . behind the arm that held it were ranged the forces of right reaction'.[184] But it is false to claim that persons involved in the assassination knew of his impending swing to the left.

Two days later, on the morning of 25 September, between ten and fifteen people – apparently the usual clutch of well-wishers – had gathered on the verandah of Bandaranaike's residence. The new American ambassador had been having a brief chat with the Prime Minister in the interior of the house and at about 9.30, Bandaranaike came out onto the verandah to see him to his waiting car. He then spoke briefly to two Ceylonese in western dress and asked them to go into the adjacent office and make copies of the documents which they had brought. As they did so, he turned to a *bhikkhu* nearby and bent forward for a moment, hands pressed together in front of him, in the customary worshipful posture. The *bhikkhu* then took his

---

[182] For an indication of his view, see for example, *CDN*, 10 July 1959.

[183] This is based on interviews with one of Bandaranaike's companions, Colombo, 6 September 1980 and with the son of the other, Kandy, 15 September 1980. See also Bandaranaike's wooing of the leftist MP, S. D. Bandaranayake, *CDN*, 5 August 1959.

[184] Reprint of a 1966 Bandaranaike Day radio broadcast by Maithripala Senanayake, *The Sun*, 26 September 1980.

leave and drove off in a waiting taxi. Bandaranaike then approached a second *bhikkhu* seated on the other side of the verandah and again offered his respects. As he bent forward, the *bhikkhu* rose from his chair, clumsily stepping on his yellow robe so that he could not stand fully upright. He took one or two steps forward, reached into his robes under his left arm, drew a pistol and began firing at Bandaranaike. The Prime Minister shouted and twisted away from his assailant who had got off four shots in this time, and fled shouting into the house. The *bhikkhu* followed, firing once or twice more until he was felled by a shot in the thigh and groin fired by a sentry from in front of the house. He was then held down by several persons.

Bandaranaike had been hit four times by 0.455 calibre bullets, once on the back of the left wrist, twice in the right side of his chest and once in the right hip. He had received chest wounds while twisting away from the gunman, so that both bullets travelled across the body in a right-to-left direction and downward, causing serious damage. He had suffered wounds to his liver, stomach, small intestine, transverse colon, large intestine, pancreas, spleen and right and left side of the diaphragm. Once the gunman was subdued, Bandaranaike sat down in a chair, clutching at his abdomen. Characteristically, he struggled to maintain a certain minimal aplomb and assured onlookers 'I am alright.' He was persuaded to lie down on a nearby bed and his sister-in-law, a physician, carried out a quick examination, assuring him that there were no wounds near the heart. Bandaranaike was then carried to his official Cadillac and driven to the General Hospital.[185]

He arrived at around 10 a.m., fully conscious and with a rapid but strong pulse. He played down his injuries to the surgeon who examined him, saying 'I'm not bad, I have received a few gunshot injuries.' It was clear that the wounds were very serious, but the doctor told him that he had seen worse cases pull through. As they took x-rays, Bandaranaike joked with the attendants. He was taken into the operating theatre where he insisted on dictating a message to the nation. A reporter from the *Ceylon Daily News* took it down, and when the chief surgeon protested at its length, for Bandaranaike was suffering serious internal bleeding, the premier informed him that 'I have always been known for making long political speeches.'[186] The statement, the authenticity of which is not to be doubted, was as follows:

A foolish man dressed in the robes of a *bhikkhu* fired some shots at me in my bungalow this morning. I appeal to all concerned to show compassion to this man and not to try to wreak vengeance on him.

[185] Statement by Dr M. Ratwatte, Bandaranaike Assassination Case, I.B. Extracts, vol. i, Bandaranaike Museum, Colombo; and *CDN*, 26 September 1959.
[186] Testimony by Dr P. R. Anthonis, Bandaranaike Assassination Case, vol. i.

I appeal to the people of my country to be restrained and patient at this time. With the assistance of my doctors I shall make every endeavour to be able to continue such services as I am able to render to my people.

I appeal to all to be calm, patient and to do nothing that might cause trouble to the people.

To those closely connected with me, to Mrs Bandaranaike and my children, to the members of the government and all my friends and well-wishers, I make a particular appeal to be calm and to face the present situation with courage and fortitude.[187]

The operation lasted for over five hours. Internal bleeding had indeed been profuse, as four pints of blood were found in the abdominal cavity and he received twenty pints of blood during the operation. He emerged from surgery with a good pulse and blood pressure. By evening, he was talking freely to Mrs Bandaranaike and her brothers and showing few signs of pain. He was then given a sedative to help him to sleep. Doctors observed a slight improvement in his condition that evening, but it was still described as 'grave'. He spent a relatively comfortable night, waking at 2 a.m. to express concern for his assailant and puzzlement about possible motives for the attack.[188] He does not appear to have believed that he was near death.[189]

At dawn he awoke and when doctors approached, he said 'ah you want to see my famous tongue'. When a surgeon told him he was doing well, Bandaranaike informed him that 'we politicians are a tough lot'. The Governor-General arrived at 7 a.m. and the Prime Minister's banter continued. He told Sir Oliver to cancel his trip to the United Nations because 'I don't feel fit enough.' At 7.30 he complained of feeling warm and asked to be sponged. Ten minutes later he suddenly 'became restless and cyanosed (blue) and gasped for breath'. His pulse started falling and he lost consciousness. At 7.45 he died.[190]

Bandaranaike's assassination was not the work of people seized, however perversely, with some great cause. He was not cut down because enemies considered him a dangerous left-winger or a reactionary, a Sinhalese chauvinist or an extreme cosmopolitan. He was murdered for petty, squalid reasons by people labouring under monumental delusions. The

---

[187] *CDN*, 26 September 1959; reprinted in C. Jeffries, *O.E.G.* (London, 1959), p. 143. Also interview with the reporter in question, I. N. W. Wijesinghe, Nayakakanda, 23 September 1980.

[188] Testimony of Dr P. R. Anthonis, Bandaranaike Assassination Case, vol. i; and *CDN*, 26 and 29 September 1959.

[189] This is important since it removes the basis for the nonsensical stories that his fear of death occasioned a secret reconversion to Christianity.

[190] Testimony of Dr P. R. Anthonis, Bandaranaike Assassination Case, vol. i; and *CDN*, 29 September 1959.

conspirators actually believed that they could kill the chief of state and then reap benefits when more amenable leaders helped them to escape detection. They were both vicious and curiously naïve, a combination of qualities that has arisen on several occasions in the island's modern history.

The prime mover in the conspiracy was the Venerable Mapitagama Buddharakkhita, the high priest of the great Kelaniya temple and a prominent figure in the 1956 election campaign and in both the SLFP and the government thereafter. He was a rightist who had encouraged conservative ministers to subvert the Paddy Lands Bill and to oppose Philip Gunawardena, but his main resentments against the premier were personal rather than ideological. We have already seen how Bandaranaike thwarted his attempt to start a shipping line that might have made huge profits from government contracts. That and Bandaranaike's refusal to allow him a major role in policy-making outraged Buddharakkhita,[191] but what rankled most of all was the Prime Minister's attitude towards several anonymous pamphlets which contained graphic (and largely accurate) allegations that the *bhikkhu* had a carnal relationship with his political protégé, Health Minister Wimala Wijewardene.[192]

Mrs Wijewardene had privately appealed to Bandaranaike to suppress these publications and to find and prosecute their authors. His response was simply to ask whether the allegations were not in fact true. Soon after that, a scurrilous Sinhala poem appeared alleging – falsely – an amorous link between Mrs Bandaranaike and one of the Prime Minister's aides. Investigations produced the strong suspicion that Mrs Wijewardene was the author and that it had been printed on a press owned by one H. P. Jayawardena, a close associate of Buddharakkhita. Bandaranaike then confronted her with the evidence and, in mid-1958, these matters were discussed by the Cabinet. Mrs Wijewardene emerged feeling humiliated and bitter – emotions which were shared by her paramour – but the Prime Minister did not dismiss her, perhaps because he believed that it was safer to keep her and Buddharakkhita within the governing elite.[193] After the assassination, she was initially accused of being part of the conspiracy, but was discharged for lack of evidence before the trial commenced.

---

[191] See in this connection, Bernard Aluwihare Diaries, 2 March 1958 and 11–15 May 1959; *CDN*, 9 July 1958, 11–15 May 1959 and L. G. Weeramantry, *Assassination of a Prime Minister: The Bandaranaike Murder Case* (Geneva, 1969), pp. 14 and 114–18.

[192] *Report to His Excellency the Governor-General by the Commission Appointed . . . to Inquire into and Report on Certain Matters Connected with the Assassination of the Late Prime Minister Solomon West Ridgeway Dias Bandaranaike, Sessional Paper III – 1965*, pp. 43–47.

[193] Bandaranaike Assassination Case, vol. i, pp. 1605–6 and 1611–12; Bernard Aluwihare Diaries, 4 February 1957; and interviews with two close associates of Bandaranaike, Colombo, 6 and 13 September 1980.

Those tried included two minor figures, both of whom were acquitted, and Buddharakkhita, his associate H. P. Jayawardena and the *bhikkhu* who fired the shots that killed Bandaranaike, the Venerable Talduwe Somarama. Somarama was an ayurvedic eye physician who appears to have obtained a teaching post at the College of Indigenous Medicine through his ties to Buddharakkhita. He was disgruntled at the government's lack of support for ayurvedic medicine – for which, ironically, the incompetent Health Minister Wijewardene bore much of the responsibility – and he may have been anxious about losing his job.[194] But he was probably motivated less by disgruntlement than by a sense of obligation to his patron, Buddharakkhita. He was told that the nation was deteriorating to such an extent that the Sinhalese people and their language and religion might have no future, a common theme in the comments of extreme communalists. Buddharakkhita added that it was essential that the Prime Minister be removed, so that 'we would then be free to fashion things as we wished'. Somarama was assured that he would be freed from jail in two or three weeks, once a change of leaders had occurred, because arrangements had been made 'with those whose assistance we need'. He was then provided with a pistol and instructions in its use.[195]

Somarama, Buddharakkhita and Jayawardena were all convicted and sentenced to death under a law that had restored the death penalty with retrospective effect. A Court of Appeal commuted the sentence on the latter two to life imprisonment since the law did not specifically include *conspiracy* to commit murder – of which they had been convicted.[196] Somarama was hanged.

In the intervening years there has been considerable speculation about a wider conspiracy. Most of it has consisted of wild myth and rumour but it is impossible to dismiss all of it out of hand. In 1963 during Mrs Bandaranaike's first premiership, a three-member commission of senior jurists from Ceylon, Egypt and Ghana investigated the possible involvement of six persons. They included Bandaranaike's Education Minister and, for a brief spell, his successor, W. Dahanayake; Health Minister Mrs Wimala Wijewardene; and two brothers of Finance Minister Stanley de Zoysa. The commission found that four of the accused neither had prior knowledge of the conspiracy nor assisted the conspirators in any way. The case of one of the de Zoysa brothers was not taken up because he was then facing charges of having conspired in a coup attempt against Mrs

---

[194] Bandaranaike Assassination Case, vol. i, pp. 12, 24 and 72.
[195] Weeramantry, *Assassination*, pp. 15 and 154–55. Quotations are from p. 155.
[196] *Ibid.*, pp. 308–11.

0 *The expedient utopian*

Bandaranaike's government. The commission found that Mrs Wijewardene had not been party to the conspiracy, but that she had had knowledge of it and had both failed to report it to the authorities and aided the conspirators in their efforts.[197] She was later tried, convicted and jailed for several years.

Since then, the matter has rested there. Certain items of evidence encountered during the preparation of this volume suggest but in no way establish that the conspiracy may have been known to at least one person other than the four who were convicted of various offences. It is particularly regrettable that no adequate investigation of C. P. de Silva's collapse in August 1959 has ever been conducted since the list of those who had access to the Cabinet room is quite short. But it is probably too late now to uncover conclusive evidence in this matter, so that this is almost certain to remain an open question.

[197] *Report to His Excellency.*

9

LEGEND

Bandaranaike's murder traumatized the nation. People reacted with astonishment and with genuine grief. Nearly half a million waited patiently, day and night, five deep in two six-mile-long queues for an average of seven hours to file past the body at the late premier's home and then at Parliament. Colombo – from the business district to the shanty towns – was a city draped in white, the traditional colour of mourning. Provincial towns were at a standstill.[1]

The island's politics, which have often been marked by callousness and viciousness, can at times produce immense outpourings of warmth and generosity. This was such a moment. Bandaranaike's shortcomings as Prime Minister were forgotten by many and became unmentionable by the rest. The air was thick with adulation that he could never have hoped for had he lived to face the dilemmas which his misjudgements and the ill-considered doings of his erstwhile allies had created. His assassination was likened to those of Lincoln and Gandhi. It was said that he had become 'a Bodhisatva' (a Buddha-to-be) and that he was 'now in the Devyaloka' (*Divyaloka*, a lower Buddhist heaven) 'silently inspiring and guiding us from the other world'.[2] A great deal of this was the sort of short-lived hyperbole that attends such occasions everywhere. But Bandaranaike has remained – thanks in no small part to the promotional efforts of his widow – a legend who led a life of sacrifice and struggle for the common man and for a new national identity.

It was as much the manner of his death, in which the theme of sacrifice acquired compelling authenticity, as his achievements in life that accounts for this. It is no accident, for example, that Bandaranaike Day, until recently a public holiday, falls on the day of his death rather than his birth.

[1] *CDN*, 28–29 September 1959 and *Daily Telegraph* (London), 29 September 1959.
[2] *CDN*, 28 September and 1 October 1959 and *Ceylon Hansard (Senate)* (1959), cols. 307 and 344. Several leaders used the term, but the principal voice in all of this was his successor, W. Dahanayake, who had created immense difficulties for Bandaranaike within the Cabinet.

The film biography which the government later made[3] begins and ends with the massive funeral and his interment in a monumental tomb on the family estate at Horagolla. This burial place, which is adjacent to the main Colombo–Kandy road, is still visited by large numbers of people. Some have even used it as a shrine, lighting lamps or candles – which to many Sinhalese denote a presence – and offering prayers or swearing vows to Bandaranaike.[4]

His story, with its ghastly end, has often been seen as a tragedy at both the personal and the political levels, although many Ceylonese – conditioned by the personalized politics that result from elite dominance of parties – perceive no distinction between the two. There can be no doubt that at a personal level – for Bandaranaike, his family and close associates – this was a tragic end. A man in his prime, with great gifts and a zest for life, was brutally cut down before his time. But was it a political tragedy?

His murder can only be seen as a tragic episode in political terms if it deprived him of an opportunity to achieve something significant. By mid-1959, he had lost so much power and credibility that he no longer had such an opportunity. The riots of the previous year, the polarization of society along linguistic lines and the chaos within his Cabinet virtually guaranteed that his bold move to the left would have led nowhere. In other words, Bandaranaike's failures had rendered him something of a tragic figure even before his death. Indeed, although it is a harsh thing to say, the assassination has obscured the wasted opportunities of his premiership by distracting attention from the disintegration of the political experiment that he had undertaken as Prime Minister. His murder and the legend which grew up around him thereafter did more to revive the fortunes of that experiment than could anything that he might have done had he survived.

Legends are, necessarily, uncomplicated. Legacies and assessments of leaders' achievements are more ambiguous. Bandaranaike can be credited with the creation of a party and an electoral coalition that in 1956 offered voters a realistic alternative to a dubious incumbent government. The ruling UNP was led by a man who sometimes exhibited a brutish contempt for basic human rights and the representative process, who sought to prevent participation by disadvantaged Sinhalese castes, and who was dangerously insensitive even to the concerns of village-level elites. Bandaranaike enabled both the disadvantaged and the village elites to express their alienation from Sir John and the UNP within the existing

---

[3] The English version of the film is entitled 'Portrait of Greatness'. I am grateful to the Sri Lanka government for arranging showings of the English and Sinhala versions for me in August 1978. [4] I am grateful to Gananath Obeyesekere for this information.

political structures, and thereby contributed mightily to the credibility and survival of representative institutions.

By creating a centre-left alternative and by then embodying his intention to seek greater social justice in new government initiatives and in popular symbols and slogans, Bandaranaike firmly institutionalized social welfare programmes that had enabled Ceylon to achieve such remakable results in infant mortality, life expectancy and literacy.[5] UNP leaders from the 1940s onward share in the credit for this, but the presence of a rival party on their left flank ensured that there would be no retreat from these programmes for nearly two decades.

Nor, by 1959, was this any longer the result of uncoordinated *ad hoc*-ism. In that year, Bandaranaike's government produced a cogent ten-year economic plan which Michael Lipton has described as 'a fundamental departure in development thinking' in that 'its emphasis upon and analysis of the need to relieve poverty and unemployment (even at the cost of "growth") was far ahead of western models of its time'.[6] That achievement is not nullified by the subsequent implementation of the plan under Mrs Bandaranaike in a manner that was far too heedless of the need to consider economic growth. Some of those later problems were inherent in Bandaranaike's excessive optimism about the capacity of poorer folk to use new opportunities to create wealth, but in the late 1950s such hopes were widely – and, at that time, understandably – shared in most of the emerging nations of Africa and Asia.

In 1956, Bandaranaike had attracted the votes of disadvantaged castes that had seldom participated in earlier elections. They supported him not because large numbers of his candidates were of less exalted status than those of the UNP – in general, they were not – but because he and they were seen to care more for the needs of ordinary people.[7] Once in power, he moved to ensure that even if the UNP tried energetically to prevent such groups from voting – as, in their complacency, they had largely failed to do in 1956 – this would be impossible. He ordered a marked increase in the number of polling stations so that such groups could vote close to home without the threat of the road blocks and intimidation of old, and by nationalizing the bus companies, he removed the main means of intimidation. His government also provided the poor with imaginat-ive, meaningful legal reforms including a legal aid programme and

[5] This is apparent from statistics on less developed countries in any recent *World Bank Development Report*, but see also, A. K. Sen, 'How is India Doing?', *New York Review of Books* (Christmas number, 1982), pp. 41–45; and 'India: The Doing and the Undoing', *Economic and Political Weekly* (Bombay), 12 March 1983, pp. 237–41.

[6] M. Lipton, *I.D.S. Bulletin* (April, 1975), p. 11.

[7] See in this regard, J. Jiggins, *Caste and Family in the Politics of the Sinhalese, 1947–1976* (Cambridge, 1979), p. 78.

tribunals to resolve disputes before they reached overburdened courts – thanks to an altruistic and creative Law Minister.[8] Wider use was also made of the vernacular in government offices. Though some labour unions abused the government's generosity, urban workers in several sectors gained improved wages, conditions and negotiating leverage. State-aided insurance, sickness benefit and retirement funds for many manual and clerical workers were created or bolstered.

Bandaranaike's adroit use of symbols and slogans to stress to ordinary people that this was a caring, responsive government both reinforced these reforms and compensated somewhat for omissions on other fronts. His adaptation of the Buddhist ideal of 'the Middle way' to describe his party's position between the Marxist left and the UNP right was particularly ingenious. His constant references to their era as 'the age of the common man' and as an 'age of transition' to a new, more fully democratic future were widely known and appreciated. He also had an acute instinct for the telling gesture, as when he picked a poor man from the crowd at the opening of a new bridge and had him cut the ribbon. Such incidents crystallized in the minds of many a belief in the intentions of the regime to back its promises with action, even if its delivery of tangible resources lagged badly, as it did in many spheres between 1956 and 1959.

Many of these changes – both concrete and symbolic – dismayed elites that had prospered under previous governments, but since one of their own stood at the helm of the new regime, their dismay was tempered by a certain reassurance that the Prime Minister was a gradualist who understood them. On certain important occasions – most notably the struggle over the Paddy Lands Bill – prosperous groups and their representatives within the government became alarmed and combined to thwart change. But numerous other reforms came quietly into being without public outcry, thanks in part to the Prime Minister's patrician status.

The government suffered far more from the truculence of Sinhalese Buddhist extremists and from Bandaranaike's staggering miscalculations in handling them. But we must not forget that he had inherited a well nigh impossible situation from his predecessors. By 1955–56, Sir John and the UNP had allowed so much resentment to build up that inflated demands from extremists were inevitable, and major concessions to Buddhism and Sinhalese language and culture were essential. Many of the steps that were taken in response – the 'Sinhala Only' Act and the conversion of Buddhist *pirivenas* or centres of higher study into universities and much else – were unavoidable and in large measure creative. Changes in foreign and

---

[8] N. Tiruchelvam, The Popular Tribunals of Sri Lanka: A Socio-Legal Study, Harvard Law School doctoral thesis, 1973, pp. 150–58.

defence policies – establishing diplomatic ties to Communist nations, the adoption of a non-aligned posture and the closure of British bases in Ceylon – also began to instil in people a new identity and sense of direction. As his most perceptive Tamil critic said after the assassination, 'under his rule the Ceylonese began to understand that they were first-class Asians, not third-class synthetic Europeans'.[9]

After the assassination, Bandaranaike's party – amid confusion and internecine strife – was forced to an election in March 1960, under the leadership of C. P. de Silva, much recovered from the previous August. The result was inconclusive and there followed another election, in July 1960, which was won by an SLFP-led alliance with Mrs Sirimavo Bandaranaike as its leader. (She held power until 1965 and again – after a spell of UNP rule – from 1970 to 1977, when the UNP again displaced her.) In what was a very tearful campaign, much was made in mid-1960 of her personal loss and of her husband's thwarted dreams. These themes proved highly effective and, in the years thereafter, she mounted a systematic effort to sustain and enlarge upon the Bandaranaike legend. It was in her interest to do so. The more the legendary Bandaranaike towered over the political landscape, the more important his widow became, since she had the closest tie to him. It is a trifle ironic that Mrs Bandaranaike should have had such a major impact on the island's politics after her husband's death because she had had only marginal influence during his lifetime.[10] As one close relative put it, 'In Solla's

[9] *Ceylon Hansard (Senate)* (1959), col. 314. On these changes, see S. U. Kodikara, *Foreign Policy of Sri Lanka: A Third World Perspective* (Delhi, 1982), and H. S. S. Nissanka, *Sri Lanka's Foreign Policy: A Study of Non-Alignment* (New Delhi, 1984).
[10] She sometimes drew large crowds to political rallies, mainly in her native Kandyan region, while Bandaranaike was busy campaigning elsewhere. But apart from some rather ineffectual lobbying against the Paddy Lands Bill, she had little involvement in the doings of government. Her publicists have subsequently sought, understandably, to create a different impression, but their accounts are misleading. Her main difficulty was her husband's male chauvinism. The following recollection may be slightly overblown, but by most accounts it accurately captures the relationship between the premier and his wife, as well as his ebullient insensitivity:

One day he [Bandaranaike] noticed that there was a delay in the tea being served and his stentorian voice rose above the murmur of voices: 'Sirima'.
A coy figure appeared at the doorway and asked: 'Why?'
Mr Bandaranaike said: 'What about the tea?'
A while later tea was served. But Mr Bandaranaike, the shrewd observer that he was, noticed something wrong and once again the stentorian voice rose: 'Sirima'.
A shy figure appeared at the door again. 'These gentlemen', he explained, 'drink tea with sugar. For the sugar to get into the cup, there must be some instrument. You have not put a spoon in the sugar bowl.'
And the dutiful wife went to fetch a spoon and Mr Bandaranaike quipped: 'We have to think for them too.'

Source: The Sun (Colombo), 7 September 1978.

[Bandaranaike's] time Sirima presided over nothing fiercer than the kitchen fire.'[11]

Nevertheless, she proved herself a forceful – perhaps too forceful – leader and her custody of his legend needs to be carefully assessed. Three of the changes which some people expected during his premiership have never fully materialized. The first was a departure from the traditional dominance which supreme leaders had always exercised over Ceylon's major parties. Bandaranaike himself had done nothing to dilute it. His eagerness for mass participation in elections did not imply a similar interest in turning decision-making within his party over to subordinates or the rank and file. This owed something to his suspicion of extremists in the SLFP, but the basic reason was his lifelong predilection to dominate any organization that he led. Mrs Bandaranaike did likewise after him, as did the UNP's leaders until the mid-1970s, when J. R. Jayewardene took some modest steps in that direction.[12] The conflicts and extremism that resulted, after 1977, from that change within the UNP[13] may suggest that elite dominance in the island's major parties was a good thing. But in ways too complex to explain here,[14] an earlier and more carefully planned decentralization might have helped to curtail Sinhalese chauvinism and the unrealistic political expectations that have always attended it.

The other two changes, unlike the first, had been actively sought by Bandaranaike. The first – the creation of elected councils at the provincial or district level – would also have diminished the power of those at the apex of the political system. But he welcomed this sort of decentralization since he felt that it would give ordinary people the chance to choose representatives to councils that were close to home and thus more accessible and observable than was Parliament in Colombo. He also knew that if regional councils had meaningful powers, they would go some way towards easing the alienation of Tamils and promoting accommodation between the two main linguistic groups, which was the other major change that he sought once he became Prime Minister. It was of course for that very reason – because regional councils were seen by Sinhalese chauvinists as a concession to Tamils – that no progress occurred on that front under governments led by either of the Bandaranaikes. A UNP government created District Development Councils in 1981, but Sinhalese extremists again ensured that their powers were inadequate. At this

[11] Y. Gooneratne, *Relative Merits: A Personal Memoir of the Bandaranaike Family of Sri Lanka* (London, 1986), p. 160.

[12] See the material in file 182, J. R. Jayewardene Papers, Presidential Archive, Colombo.

[13] J. Manor (ed.), *Sri Lanka in Change and Crisis* (London and New York, 1984), especially the chapter by Obeyesekere.

[14] J. Manor, 'The Failure of Political Integration in Sri Lanka', *Journal of Commonwealth and Comparative Politics*, xvii, 1 (March, 1979), pp. 21–46.

writing, Provincial Councils are being created, but it remains to be seen how much power they will be given. Mrs Bandaranaike was less committed than her husband to a liberal, cosmopolitan vision, and she was acutely aware of the political utility of Sinhalese chauvinism. So the accommodation between Sinhalese and Tamils which he had sought was not adequately pursued in her time.

After his death, most of the changes which SLFP-led governments *did* introduce were presented as tributes to this memory and as fulfilments of his grand design. Many of these would clearly have pleased him. The final abandonment of the old headman system, the changeover to the use of Sinhala in lower courts,[15] the provision of banking facilities and credit to ordinary villagers, and the land reform of the early 1970s – these and other programmes to assist the common man would have won his hearty approval.

Certain other things done in his name would probably have distressed him, however. The promises of far-reaching nationalization of private firms that appeared in his 1956 election manifesto were mainly concessions to his leftist allies. He welcomed the state takeovers of the buses, since it meant an end to a major source of thuggery, and of the Colombo port. He would also have supported some further extensions of state ownership, but it is unlikely that he would have wished it to embrace the tea plantations, and he would probably have opposed the complex array of state controls on the economy which his widow's governments imposed. He would certainly have resisted the nationalization of the major newspaper chains and the conversion of the print and broadcasting media into mouthpieces for the ruling party. And his refusal during his premiership to yield to Buddhist pressure to take over Christian schools[16] – which in his view would have intruded too much upon minority rights – suggests that he would also have opposed his widow's initiatives on that front. Many features of the republican Constitution of 1972 would have pleased him, but not its illiberal manipulation to put off an election by an extra two years. It would not have surprised him that, after that episode, the rival UNP indulged in similar abuses once it regained power in 1977.

Mrs Bandaranaike understood that her husband's overgenerous ways as Prime Minister had created major problems[17] and she was determined to be radically different. But there can be no doubt that he would have recoiled from many of the abrasive and often vindictive acts that occurred under her regimes, especially after the abortive 1971 insurgency by leftist

[15] For an amusing by-product of this, see D. R. Wijegoonewardane, *Legal Talk* (Colombo, 1961).   [16] See, for example, *CDN*, 15 August 1959.
[17] See, for example, *The Guardian* (London), 7 May 1980.

Sinhalese youth. Ministers' extravagant insecurities in that period led to
rampant nepotism – which Bandaranaike had scrupulously avoided – and
to spiteful, brutish treatment of both the opposition parties and the
Tamils of the Northern Province. The needless imposition in the north of
an ill-disciplined and frequently abusive army that was overwhelmingly
Sinhalese instilled much of the bitterness which later generated armed
resistance there. So did that government's patent discrimination against
Tamils in areas such as higher education. His bouts of chauvinistic
rhetoric notwithstanding, Bandaranaike had viewed the 'state' as an
arena within which all social groups ought to be able to compete on equal
terms, and as an agency from which all ought to receive evenhanded
treatment and protection, and he had believed that the 'nation' should
embrace all of the island's people. In the years since his death, these
notions have been largely overtaken, with the 'state' being seen as the
partisan instrument of the ruling party, and the 'nation' being equated
with the so-called Sinhalese 'race'.

Bandaranaike's story is a tangle of ironies and incongruities. He was born
at the pinnacle of the old Ceylonese social order, and yet he did more than
any other leader to draw rural dwellers into a sense of involvement with
democratic institutions. His overweening elitism led him to an abhorrence of caste prejudice and to vague but genuine egalitarian views. He
was steeped in western learning which he mastered and loved, and he had
great difficulty reading Sinhala, but it was he who first made Sinhala and
Sinhalese Buddhist culture central concerns of the state. He gave
Sinhalese Buddhists greater confidence in themselves and their culture,
even as he failed to prevent their insecurities from producing excesses,
and from becoming a firmly institutionalized element in the island's
politics. He was both a utopian idealist and an avid opportunist,
relentlessly pursuing short-term political gains. But after thirty years of
seeking supreme power in that manner, when he achieved it, he let it slip
heedlessly away. Given all of this, it is hardly surprising that he failed to
resolve the dissonance between the two themes that dominated his career:
Sinhalese parochialism and cosmopolitan reform. The incongruity
between them stands at the core of his life, legend and legacy.

He had hoped to use chauvinism as a means to achieve power,
believing that he could disarm it by making modest, long-overdue
concessions to Sinhalese Buddhist interests, and then by concentrating on
reform to remove social injustice and soothe the anxieties of would-be
communalists. He did not succeed, partly because the problems that he
had inherited were so severe, partly because his ruling coalition contained
too many contradictions, partly because his government functioned so

sluggishly, but very substantially because of the way Bandaranaike himself thought and acted.

Had he not squandered his power in reckless generosity to groups frivolous and nefarious, had he asserted his authority in the country and the Cabinet, there was a reasonable chance that tangible reforms, promptly and effectively delivered, could have captured the popular imagination and served as a potent and lasting distraction from anti-Tamil bigotry. There is no reason to suppose that his efforts *had* to fail. But fail they did, and they were never adequately revived by those who later acted in his name. As a result, the two themes remained as antagonistic after his death as before.

The Bandaranaike legend served to sustain and enlarge the already unrealistic expectations that had developed during his premiership both among those who sought greater social justice and among Sinhalese communalists. The legend, and the expectations that attended it, were so over-inflated that they eventually became destabilizing liabilities that bred cynicism among both reformers and chauvinists. When excessive state controls caused the economy to stagnate, that cynicism turned to anger – first among those who had hoped for reform, in the insurrection of 1971, and later in the communalist upsurge that followed the election of a UNP government in 1977. The first produced a harsh response from Mrs Bandaranaike that so undermined liberal practices that they could not be revived under the UNP regime that came after her. The second has led to ghastly civil war and has contributed to the maiming of democratic institutions.[18] Behind all of this – the memory of a lively democracy, the dream of a fairer society, and the vile reality of chauvinism that has blighted them both – stands the complex, inconstant visionary, Bandaranaike.

---

[18] Manor (ed.), *Sri Lanka in Change*, especially the chapter by 'Priya Samarakone'.

SELECT BIBLIOGRAPHY

Collections of papers

Bernard Aluwihare Papers, University of Peradeniya Library
Sir Solomon Dias Bandaranaike Diaries, NASL
S. W. R. D. Bandaranaike Papers, NASL
Commonwealth Election Literature Collection, Institute of Commonwealth
    Studies, University of London
George E. de Silva Memoirs, typescript, edited by Jag Mohan, Colombo
Election Literature Collection, University of Peradeniya Library
A. E. Goonesinha Memoirs, typescript, Colombo
J. R. Jayewardene Papers, Presidential Archive, Colombo
James T. Rutnam Papers, Colombo
F. C. Scharenguivel Papers, Centre for South Asian Studies, University of
    Cambridge
Jan Smuts Papers, University Library, University of Cambridge
Sri Lanka Oral History Transcripts, collected by Michael Roberts, Rhodes
    House, University of Oxford
Sir Edwin Wijeyeratne Papers, NASL

Dissertations

Dharmadasa, K. N. O., The Rise of Sinhalese Language Nationalism: A Study in
    the Sociology of Language, Monash University doctoral thesis, 1979
Gunawardena, R. D., Reform Movement and Political Organizations in Ceylon
    with Special Reference to the Temperance Movement and Regional
    Associations, 1900–1930, University of Peradeniya doctoral thesis, 1976
Jayasekera, P. V. J., Social and Political Change in Ceylon, 1900–1919,
    University of London doctoral thesis, 1969
Jayasinghe, K. H., Some Political and Social Consequences of the Extension of
    the Franchise in Ceylon, University of London doctoral thesis, 1965
Jiggins, J., Family and Caste in the Politics of the Sinhalese, 1947–1971,
    University of Ceylon, Peradeniya, doctoral thesis, 1973
Malalgoda, K., Sociological Aspects of Revival and Change in Buddhism in
    Nineteenth-Century Ceylon, University of Oxford doctoral thesis, 1970
Marasinghe, M. L., Law and Development in Sri Lanka: An Historical
    Perspective, 1796–1978, University of London doctoral thesis, 1981

Meyer, E., *Depression et malaria à Sri Lanka, 1925–1939: l'impact de la crise économique des années 1930 sur une société dépendante*, doctoral thesis, Ecole des Hautes Etudes en Sciences Sociales, Paris, 1980

Morris, W. W., *Patterns of Electoral Politics in Ceylon, 1947–1970*, University of Illinois doctoral thesis, 1971

Peebles, P., *The Transformation of a Colonial Elite: The Mudaliyars of Nineteenth-Century Ceylon*, University of Chicago doctoral thesis, 1973

Russell, J., *The Ceylon Tamils under the Donoughmore Constitution, 1931–1947*, University of Ceylon, Peradeniya doctoral thesis, 1975

Tiruchelvam, N., *The Popular Tribunals of Sri Lanka: A Socio-Legal Study*, Harvard Law School doctoral thesis, 1973

Wilson, A. J., *The Development of a New Elite in Ceylon, with Special Reference to Educational and Occupational Background, 1910–1931*, University of Oxford doctoral thesis, 1968

Newspapers and periodicals

Ceylon Daily News, 1925–1959
Ceylon Independent, 1930–1934 and 1936
Ceylon Observer, 1958–1959
Dinamina, 1952–1956
The Nation, 1942–1946
Samasamajist, 1954–1959
Times of Ceylon, 1951–1953
Tribune, 1956–1958

Official publications

Ceylon Hansard (*State Council Debates*, 1931–1947 and *Parliamentary Debates*, 1947–1959).
Planning Secretariat, *Papers by Visiting Economists* (Colombo, 1959).
Sessional Papers, 1931–1959.

Books and articles

Amunugama, S. and E. Meyer, 'Remarques sur la violence dans l'idéologie bouddhique et pratique sociale à Sri Lanka (Ceylan)', *Études Rurale*, xcv–xcvi (1984), pp. 47–62.
Bandaranaike, S. D., *Remembered Yesterdays* (London, 1929).
Bandaranaike, S. W. R. D., *The Government and the People* (Colombo, 1959).
 Speeches and Writings (Colombo, 1963).
 Towards a New Era: Selected Speeches of S. W. R. D. Bandaranaike made in the Legislature of Ceylon, 1931–1959 (Colombo, 1961).
 (ed.), *The Handbook of the Ceylon National Congress, 1919–1928* (Colombo, 1928).
Bechert, H., 'S. W. R. D. Bandaranaike and the Legitimation of Power through Buddhist Ideals', in B. L. Smith (ed.), *Religion and the Legitimation of Power in Sri Lanka* (Chambersburg, 1978), pp. 199–211.

Buddhist Commission of Inquiry, *The Betrayal of Buddhism* (Balangoda, 1956).

Corea, G., *The Instability of an Export Economy* (Colombo, 1975).

de Silva, G. P. S. H., *A Statistical Survey of Elections to the Legislatures of Sri Lanka, 1911–1977* (Colombo, 1979).

de Silva, K. M., *A History of Sri Lanka* (Berkeley, 1981).

(ed.), *Sri Lanka: A Survey* (London, 1977).

et al. (eds.), *Sri Lanka since Independence*, special double number, *Ceylon Journal of Historical and Social Studies*, iv (1974).

(ed.), *Universal Franchise, 1931–1981: The Sri Lankan Experience* (Colombo, 1981).

(ed.), *University of Ceylon History of Ceylon*, volume iii, *From the Beginning of the Nineteenth Century to 1949* (Peradeniya, 1973).

Dissanayaka, T. D. S. A., *Dudley Senanayake of Sri Lanka* (Colombo, 1975).

J. R. Jayewardene of Sri Lanka (Colombo, n.d.).

Farmer, B. H., *Pioneer Peasant Colonization in Ceylon: A Study in Asian Agrarian Problems* (London, 1957).

'The Social Basis of Nationalism in Ceylon', *Journal of Asian Studies*, xxiv (1965), pp. 431–39.

Fernando, T., 'Elite Politics in the New States: The Case of Post-Independence Ceylon', *Pacific Affairs*, xlvi (1973), pp. 361–83.

and R. N. Kearney (eds.), *Modern Sri Lanka: A Society in Transition* (Syracuse, 1979).

Gombrich, R., *Precept and Practice: Traditional Buddhism in the Rural Highlands of Ceylon* (Oxford, 1971).

Gooneratne, Y., *Relative Merits: A Personal Memoir of the Bandaranaike Family of Sri Lanka* (London, 1986).

Herring, R. J., *Land to the Tiller: The Political Economy of Agrarian Reform in South Asia* (New Haven, 1983).

Hulugalle, H. A. J., *The Life and Times of Don Stephen Senanayake* (Colombo, 1975).

Jayawardena, V. K., 'The Origins of the Left Movement in Sri Lanka', *Modern Ceylon Studies*, ii (1971), pp. 195–221.

The Rise of the Labor Movement in Ceylon (Durham, 1972).

Jennings, W. I., *The Approach to Self-Government* (Cambridge, 1956).

Jiggins, J., *Caste and Family in the Politics of the Sinhalese, 1947–1976* (Cambridge, 1979).

Jupp, J., *Sri Lanka: Third World Democracy* (London, 1978).

Kearney, R. N., *Communalism and Language in the Politics of Ceylon* (Durham, 1967).

Trade Unions and Politics in Ceylon (Berkeley, 1971).

The Politics of Ceylon (Sri Lanka) (Ithaca, 1973).

Kearney, R. N. and T. Fernando (eds.), *Modern Sri Lanka: a society in transition* (Syracuse, 1979).

Kotelawala, J. L., *An Asian Prime Minister's Story* (London, 1956).

Leach, E. R., 'Buddhism in the Post-colonial Political Order in Burma and Ceylon', *Daedalus*, cii (1973), pp. 29–54.

Malalgoda, K., *Buddhism in Sinhalese Society, 1750–1900* (Berkeley, 1976).

Manor, J., 'The Failure of Political Integration in Sri Lanka', *Journal of Commonwealth and Comparative Politics*, xvii, 1 (March, 1979), pp. 21–46.
(ed.), *Sri Lanka in Change and Crisis* (New York, 1984).
Meyer, E. and S. Amunugama, 'Remarques sur la violence dans l'idéologie bouddhique et pratique sociale à Sri Lanka (Ceylan)', *Études Rurale*, xcv–xcvi (1984), pp. 47–62.
Moore, M. P., *The State and Peasant Politics in Sri Lanka* (Cambridge, 1985).
Obeyesekere, G., 'The Great Tradition and the Little in the Perspective of Sinhalese Buddhism', *Journal of Asian Studies*, xxii (1963), pp. 139–53.
'Religious Symbolism and Political Change in Ceylon', *Modern Ceylon Studies*, i (1970), pp. 43–64.
'Sorcery, Premeditated Murder and the Canalization of Aggression in Sri Lanka', *Ethnology*, xiv (1975), pp. 1–24.
'Social Change and the Deities: The Rise of the Kataragama Cult in Modern Sri Lanka', *Man*, xii (1977), pp. 377–96.
'Sinhalese–Buddhist Identity in Ceylon', in G. De Vos and L. Romanucci-Ross (eds.), *Ethnic Identity* (Palo Alto, 1975), pp. 231–58.
Phadnis, U., *Religion and Politics in Sri Lanka* (London, 1976).
Roberts, M., *Caste Conflict and Elite Formation: The Rise of the Karāva Elite in Sri Lanka, 1500–1931* (Cambridge, 1982).
'Foundations of Sinhalese and Tamil Nationalism and Some Implications', *Ceylon Studies Seminar* (1973).
'The Political Antecedents of the Revivalist Elite in the MEP Coalition of 1956', *Ceylon Studies Seminar* (1970).
(ed.), *Documents of the Ceylon National Congress and Nationalist Politics in Ceylon, 1929–1950*, 4 volumes (Colombo, 1977).
(ed.), *Collective Identities, Nationalisms and Protest in Modern Sri Lanka* (Colombo, 1979).
Robinson, M. S., *Political Structure in a Changing Sinhalese Village* (Cambridge, 1975).
Rogers, J. D., *Crime, Justice and Society in Colonial Sri Lanka* (London, 1987).
Ryan, B., *Caste in Modern Ceylon: The Sinhalese System in Transition* (New Brunswick, 1953).
Samaraweera, V., 'Land as "Patrimony": Nationalist Response to Immigrant Labour Demands for Land in the Early Twentieth Century in Sri Lanka', *Indian Economic and Social History Review*, xiv (1977), pp. 341–62.
'Land, Labour, Capital and Sectional Interests in the National Politics of Sri Lanka', *Modern Asian Studies*, xv (1981), pp. 127–62.
Seneviratne, L., *Bandaranaike: A Biography* (Colombo, 1964) (in Sinhala).
Seneviratne, M., *Sirimavo Bandaranaike: The World's First Woman Prime Minister: A Biography* (Colombo, 1975).
Singer, M. R., *The Emerging Elite: A Study of Political Leadership in Ceylon* (Cambridge, MA., 1964).
Smith, B. L. (ed.), *Religion and Social Conflict in South Asia* (Leiden, 1976).
(ed.), *Religion and the Legitimation of Power in Sri Lanka* (Chambersburg, 1977).

332   *Select bibliography*

aiah, S. J., 'The Politics of Language in India and Ceylon', *Modern Asian Studies*, i (1967), pp. 215–40.
Vijayavardhana, D. C., *Dharma-Vijaya, Triumph of Righteousness or the Revolt in the Temple* (Colombo, 1953).
Vittachi, T., *Emergency '58* (London, 1958).
Warnapala, W. A. Wiswa, *Civil Service Administration in Ceylon: A Study in Bureaucratic Adaptation* (Colombo, 1974).
Weeramantry, L. G., *Assassination of a Prime Minister: The Bandaranaike Murder Case* (Geneva, 1969).
Wilson, A. J., *Politics in Sri Lanka, 1947–1979* (London, 1979).
Woodward, C. A., *The Growth of a Party System in Ceylon* (Providence, 1969).
Wriggins, W. H., *Ceylon: Dilemmas of a New Nation* (Princeton, 1960).
    The Ruler's Imperative: Strategies For Political Survival in Asia and Africa (New York, 1969).

INDEX

All-Ceylon Village Committees
 Conference, 69n, 82, 118, 207
Arunachalam, Sir Ponnambalam, 72
ayurveda and ayurvedic physicians, 118,
 139, 166, 183, 197, 199, 203, 213, 218,
 227–28, 247–50, 252, 271, 278, 281,
 284, 299–300, 317

Bandaranaike, Alix, 18
Bandaranaike, Anna, 40
Bandaranaike, Anura, 217
Bandaranaike, Chandrika, 217
Bandaranaike,Lady Daisy Obeyesekere,
 15–18, 21–22, 24, 26, 35, 55, 58, 65,
 67, 110, 142
Bandaranaike, Mrs Sirimavo Ratwatte,
 13, 97, 147–50, 217, 272, 278, 281,
 307–9, 315–21, 323–27
Bandaranaike, Sir Solomon Dias, 2–3, 11,
 14–32, 34, 36, 40–41, 56–61, 65–66,
 68–69, 82, 90, 95–96, 101–2, 111–12,
 149, 165–66, 203, 259
Bandaranaike, Sunethra, 217
Bandaranaike, S.W.R.D., assassination of,
 2, 310–11, 313–20, 327; and authority,
 2–4, 10, 20–24, 26–36, 40–41, 45, 48,
 51–52, 61, 65, 68–72, 92–95, 104–6,
 108–9, 111–12, 122–23, 126–27, 137,
 141–44, 151–54, 166, 168, 170, 176–77,
 183–84, 186–87, 191, 199–203, 206,
 217, 255–61, 279–84, 286–97, 306–7,
 309, 312, 320, 326–27; and British rule,
 3, 5–6, 57–58, 65, 69, 93–94, 97–102,
 105, 108, 110, 145–47, 151–55, 157–58,
 161, 164, 170, 174–75, 259; and
 Buddhism, 2, 4, 7–8, 11–12, 23n,
 110–15, 118, 129, 149, 159, 161, 167,
 186–87, 199–201, 203, 207, 216,
 227–28, 307–10, 322, 326; and caste, 1,
 2, 10, 48, 58–60, 64, 90, 97, 113, 123,
 144, 208, 216, 224, 250–51, 320–21,
 326; childhood and schooldays, 1,
 14–35, 93, 110–11, 142, 217, 309–10;
 and Christianity, 4, 7, 14, 17–19, 23n,
 34, 56, 69, 87, 97, 99, 110–15, 148,
 166–67, 207, 230, 252, 307–8, 315n,
 325; and class, 10, 59, 61, 64–67,
 69–70, 75–77, 103, 247, 250–52,
 280–81; and cosmopolitanism, 1, 9,
 136–37, 155–56, 169–71, 231–35,
 255–56, 269, 299, 315, 325–26; and
 expediency, 1, 5, 9–10, 12–13, 34, 52,
 70–71, 77, 81, 89, 112–13, 128–29,
 131–32, 135–44, 169–71, 195, 231–33,
 253, 256, 295, 298, 326; fiction writer,
 3, 113–14, 217, 258; and inconsistency,
 70–71, 77–81, 89, 92–95, 101, 116–19,
 123, 127–31, 135–44, 149–50, 152–54,
 156–57, 169–71, 191, 195, 201, 207,
 212, 230, 232–33, 240, 260, 268, 280,
 282–84, 303, 307–8, 326–27; land
 policy, 105–10, 277–84, 322, 325;
 language and language policy, 10,
 56–57, 69, 76n, 97–98, 113, 129–30,
 169, 186–87, 191–92, 197, 201–2,
 218–20, 227, 230–52, 254–64, 266–73,
 325–26; legal studies and practice, 42,
 56–59, 65, 70–71, 81, 87, 92, 112, 118;
 legend, 9, 13, 318–27; and the masses,
 1–2, 10–11, 75–77, 89, 92, 100, 103,
 108–10, 114, 116, 123, 135–36, 139,
 142, 144, 203, 228, 231–35, 238,
 246–47, 250–53, 255, 259, 280–81, 324,
 326; and moralism, 5–6, 10, 51–52,
 106; and the national political elite, 1,
 4, 57, 60–63, 68–69, 71–75, 77–82,

Bandaranaike (cont.)
89–90, 92–95, 99–104, 106–9, 122–23,
126–27, 137, 141–44, 152–53, 155, 161,
168, 170, 183–84, 186–88, 196–97,
199–202, 206, 208, 259; and 'native
dress', 95–97, 114, 129–30, 162–63,
166, 198, 208, 230, 254; in opposition,
1, 137, 151–52, 183–84, 202–53, 269;
orator, 5–6, 10, 12, 31–32, 34, 36,
43–48, 52, 54, 57–58, 67, 69–71, 80–81,
89, 92–93, 105–6, 108, 118, 122, 125,
129–31, 141, 144, 151–52, 156, 165,
186–88, 191, 206, 218, 222, 232, 234,
236–37, 247, 253, 260, 281, 326; and
Oxford, 1, 3, 7–8, 10–11, 29, 32,
35–55, 57, 59, 61, 82, 89, 110–12, 136,
161, 217, 307, 309–10; and the
paranormal, 1, 12, 47, 51, 114–15, 217,
307–10; and political organization, 63,
118–19, 122–23, 127–31, 138, 143–44,
146, 157–59, 165–66, 202, 207–8,
218–20, 228–29, 234, 240–53, 280–81,
283–84, 295, 324; as Prime Minister, 1,
2, 4, 9, 13, 34, 131, 137, 145, 165,
193–94, 202, 206, 234, 253–318,
320–27; and rationalism, 1, 11, 47,
111–15, 306–10; and reform, 1, 8, 10,
13, 86, 108–9, 116–17, 128, 131,
135–41, 145, 157–58, 165, 168–69,
186–87, 191–203, 206n, 234, 253,
255–56, 279–84, 306, 312–13, 315,
321–22, 326–27; and Sinhalese interests
and parochialism, 1–2, 4, 8, 11–13, 62,
90, 109, 117–18, 123–41, 155–57, 161,
164, 170–71, 186–87, 191–92, 197–98,
203, 207, 216, 218–20, 227–53, 260–64,
266–73, 279, 281–82, 284–99, 303, 315,
324–27; and snobbery, 1, 10, 15, 18,
29, 33, 38, 45, 60–61, 95–96, 108, 142,
217, 230, 257–58, 265, 279, 326; and
socialism, 1, 44, 50, 57, 109, 115–17,
123, 128, 135, 157, 169, 207, 279–81,
325; and status, 1, 10, 15, 18, 21,
30–31, 34–36, 38–39, 41–45, 54, 59–60,
65–66, 89, 101, 104, 136, 142–43,
164–65, 168, 191, 202, 217, 257–58,
322, 326; and utopianism, 1, 9–10, 34,
52, 128, 157, 161, 253, 259, 281, 303,
306, 326; and village elites, 1, 118,
158–59, 166, 182–83, 196–97, 199, 203,

207–8, 213, 218–20, 227–53, 255–56,
278–84, 299–300, 320–21
Bandaranayake, S.D., 272
Batuwantudawe, Charles, 91, 125
Bettelheim, B., 18n, 23, 27
Bhikkhus, *see* Buddhist clergy
Blackton, C.T., 77n
British rule in Ceylon, 2, 9, 14–15, 22,
26, 29, 41, 56, 72–73, 76–81, 91, 93–94,
98–110, 123, 126–27, 141, 143–47,
150–56, 160, 163, 170–77, 182–83, 194,
203
Brow, J., 284n
Buddharakkhita, Mapitagama, 278,
299–302, 304–5, 316–18
Buddhism, 7, 11–12, 14, 60, 69, 87, 91,
99–100, 129, 132–35, 139, 163, 182,
186, 199, 202, 207, 213, 218, 227–52,
264, 291–92, 322, 325; *see also*
Bandaranaike and Buddhism and
Buddhist clergy
Buddhist clergy, 2, 82, 87, 110, 113–15,
139, 147, 166, 177, 183, 186, 197–99,
203, 213, 218–19, 227–52, 255–56, 266,
270–72, 278, 281, 284–86, 291,
299–302, 307–9, 313–17; *see also*
Buddhism and Eksath Bhikkhu
Peramuna
buses and bus owners, 84–85, 88, 171,
180, 212, 216, 224, 239, 245, 264, 279,
293, 321, 325

Cabinet government, 126–27, 143,
153–56, 160, 168–70, 177, 184–87,
190–202, 205–6, 210–11, 225, 254, 256,
260–61, 263, 265, 273, 275, 277, 279,
299–305, 308, 310–13, 316, 318, 320,
327
Caldecott, Sir Andrew, 127, 131, 148–54,
160, 274
caste, 83–84, 86–87, 97, 119–21, 123,
132–33, 138–40, 148, 195–96, 202–3,
207–8, 213, 216, 224, 228, 239, 240n,
243–45, 250–51, 254–55, 259n, 273,
293, 320; *see also* Bandaranaike and
caste
Ceylon Indian Congress, 178, 185
Ceylon National Congress, 61–64, 71–75,
77–82, 86–87, 91, 93, 104, 110, 116,
118–20, 122, 138n, 140–43, 210

Ceylon Workers' Federation, 75–76, 82, 92, 115
Chelvanayakam, S.J.V., 270, 273, 284–86
class, *see* 'Bandaranaike and class'
Colombo Municipal Council, 64–70, 81, 90, 110, 301
Communist Party, 178, 209, 212, 214, 235, 242–43, 294, 305
Cone, M., 7n
constitutional reform, 76–81, 90–91, 104, 126, 141, 160–65, 171–77, 182–83, 303

Dahanayake, W., 238, 273, 287, 299, 301–4, 317, 319n
De Silva, A.E. (later Sir Ernest), 64–66
De Silva, C.P., 207, 216, 265, 275–76, 283, 301, 310–12, 318, 323
De Silva, C.R., 132n
De Silva, G.P.S.H., 120n, 213n, 242n
De Silva, George E., 177, 185, 193
De Silva, George R., 204
De Silva, K.M., 2n, 69n, 72n, 79n, 100n, 128n, 160n, 163, 164n, 172n, 173n, 176n
De Silva, M.W.H., 265, 299n, 322
De Zoysa, Stanley, 278, 300–1, 310, 317–18
depression and malaria, 88, 104, 106–7, 116–17, 121–22, 127, 134n, 156
Dharmadasa, K.N.O., 228n, 231n, 248n
Dharmapala, Anagarika, 115
Donoughmore Constitution, 76–81, 102–4, 116, 143, 145–47, 155, 177, 303
Eden, Anthony, 11, 41
Eksath Bhikkhu Peramuna, 238, 239n, 256, 285; *see also* 'Buddhist clergy'
elections and electoral reform, 2, 10, 64–68, 75, 77–79, 81–90, 103, 119–24, 155–57, 168, 172, 176–84, 195–96, 203–5, 208–9, 211–17, 223–26, 233–53, 279, 299, 312–13, 320–21, 323, 325
Erikson, E., 27n, 28n

Farmer, B.H., 106n
Federal Party, 242, 261–63, 266, 268–70, 286, 290, 298, 305

Gandhi, M.K., 58, 74, 95–98, 102, 117, 123, 131–32, 319
Gardiner, Gerald (later Lord), 46, 115n

Gombrich, R., 7n, 115n, 308n
Gooneratne, Y., 11n, 14n, 324
Goonesinha, A.E., 64–70, 75–76, 78, 86, 88, 90, 127, 178n, 274
Goonetilleke, Sir Oliver, 154, 158, 176n, 185, 190, 199n, 200–1, 245, 255, 266–67, 290, 291n, 295–97, 302, 314
Gunawardena, Philip, 122, 150, 236, 238, 256, 265, 271, 273–85, 293, 299–305, 308, 312–13, 316
Gunawardena, R.A.L.H., 133n, 248n
Gunawardena, R.S.S. (later Sir Senerat), 71, 74, 82, 112–13, 121, 140, 204

Hartal of 1953, 220–23, 225, 228, 236n
headmen and headman system, 11, 14–15, 26, 54, 56, 65, 83, 85–86, 88, 92, 101, 105, 116n, 120–21, 148–50, 166, 196, 208–9, 229, 239, 245–46, 252, 259, 264, 273, 325
Herring, R.J., 283n
Hindus and Hinduism, 133, 147, 227, 291, 307–9

independence, 68, 94, 156–57, 160–66, 171–77, 182–83, 185
India, 2, 6, 43–45, 54, 57–58, 60–62, 72, 74, 81, 88, 95–100, 116–17, 122, 128, 132, 137, 143, 149–51, 156, 173–76, 193–94, 202, 205, 258–59, 305
Indians in Ceylon, 80, 92, 95, 99, 117, 127, 129–30, 132–33, 137, 139–40, 144, 151–52, 156–57, 163, 178n, 185, 189–90, 193, 215n, 227, 248n, 269–70, 285–86

Jayasuriya, A.P., 204
Jayatilaka, D.B. (later Sir Baron), 71, 74, 91–94, 118–19, 125–27, 133, 137, 143n, 150–51, 155, 159, 259
Jayawardena, H.P., 316–17
Jayawardena, V.K., 127n, 172n, 274n
Jayawardene, J. R., 133, 154, 180n, 185, 192–93, 197–98, 200, 210, 215n, 222, 228, 236, 267–68, 270–73, 324
Jiggins, J., 60n, 123n, 195n, 206n, 224n, 245n, 251n, 254n, 255n, 259n, 321n
Jupp, J., 81, 297n

Kandyans, 72–73, 80, 88–89, 92, 97, 121, 148–49, 194, 215–16, 228, 241, 247n, 278, 282, 313
Kannangara, C. W.W., 92, 149
Karunatilake, Nimal, 301–2
Kearney, R.N., 172n, 191n, 270n, 289n, 295
Keuneman, Pieter, 275
Kotelawala, J.L. (later Sir John), 109, 119, 123, 139, 158, 166, 170, 177, 185, 187–88, 192, 198, 200, 205, 209–11, 219, 222–26, 228–31, 235–41, 243–44, 246, 249, 252, 254, 263, 274, 294, 296, 320–22

Labour Party, 86, 178, 214
labourers, *see* working class
land and land reform, 1, 74, 83, 90, 103, 105, 116, 134, 163, 194, 216, 229, 250–51, 275–84, 302, 316, 322; *see also*, Bandaranaike and land reform
language, 2, 4, 11, 88, 97–98, 100, 169, 182, 186, 193, 197–98, 218–20, 229–52, 254–64, 266–73, 275, 284–99, 301, 317
Lanka Sama Samaja Party (LSSP), and variants, 178–79, 209, 214, 236, 238, 242–43, 274, 294, 305
Layton, Admiral Sir Geoffrey, 154–55
leftists and leftist parties, 87–88, 107, 115–17, 122, 124–25, 127, 137, 150, 164, 171–74, 176–84, 187, 194, 203, 205, 207–9, 212, 214–15, 220–23, 225–26, 235–38, 240, 256–57, 273–84, 287, 294, 297, 299–307, 312–13, 320, 322, 325–26
Lipton, M., 321
Low, D.A., 102n, 122n

Macan Markar, H.M., 92
Mahadeva, A., 155–56, 165
Mahajana Eksath Peramuna (MEP), 233n, 238, 241–43, 250–52, 254n, 260, 264, 273, 275, 284, 297
Malalgoda, K., 198n, 228n
Manor, J., 6n, 102n, 140n, 143n, 170n, 212n, 228n, 295n, 324n, 327n
Marxists, *see* leftists and leftist parties
Meyer, E., 106n, 107n, 108n, 122n, 139n, 148n
Moore, Sir Henry Monck-Mason, 15, 171, 175

Moore, M., 106n, 109
Moore, R.J., 174
Morris-Jones, W.H., 81n
mudaliyars, *see* headmen and headman system
Munasinha, J.C.W., 302
Murray, Gilbert, 51
Muslims, 66–68, 73, 129, 134, 216, 235, 254, 263, 305

Nadesan, S., 222, 323
Nandy, A., 11n
nationalism: Ceylonese, 3, 5–8, 62–63, 68–69, 72–73, 95–104, 108, 129, 132, 140–43, 210
Nehru, Jawaharlal, 5–6, 12, 99, 132, 137, 226
Nissan, E., 134n, 135n
Nkrumah, Kwame, 5, 7, 13
Nyerere, Julius, 5, 7

Obeyesekere family, 2, 15–16, 26, 32, 48, 59–60, 65, 67, 69, 82, 92, 106, 108, 127, 142, 144, 148–51, 166–67, 252
Obeyesekere, G., 114, 132n, 251n, 307n, 308n, 309n, 324n
Obeyesekere, J.P., 16
Obeyesekere, Mrs J.P., 59, 82
Obeyesekere, Sir S.C., 16, 69
Oxford Union Society, 11, 36, 38, 43–48, 52, 70, 307

Panabokke, T.B., 92
parties and political organization, 2, 63, 72–75, 79, 86–87, 91, 94, 102–4, 118–20, 122–23, 137–41, 143–44, 157–59, 164–66, 168–69, 177–85, 201–3, 205, 207–9, 217–18, 230–31, 235–53, 264, 271, 295, 320; *see also* Bandaranaike and political organization
Pater, Walter, 49–52, 82
Peebles, P., 14n, 15n, 65n, 99n, 101n, 103n, 148n
Perera, N.M., 122, 150, 209, 274, 294
Phadnis, U., 228n
Political Study Circle, 82
Ponnambalam, G.G., 117–18, 131–32, 157, 165, 178n, 188–89, 270–71, 274
press, 9, 67, 80, 85, 87, 94–95, 128, 142, 150, 164, 168, 177, 179, 184, 185, 187, 192, 200–1, 211, 221, 223–25, 229–30,

235, 239, 245, 261, 269–70, 285, 287, 290, 293, 295–97, 312, 314–15, 325
Progressive National Party, 61, 77, 90
public security laws, 222, 226, 263, 298

'race' in Ceylon, 63, 99, 128–29, 132–33, 163, 197, 218, 234–36, 273, 286–87, 326
Radford, A.C., 27–29, 32–33, 38, 217, 259
Rahiman, W.M. Abdul, 66–67
Rajaratna, K.M.P., 263
Ratnayake, A., 204–5
Regional Councils, 103–4, 145–47, 158, 170, 268, 270–71, 284, 287, 297, 324–25
Republican Party, 212n, 213–14
riots, *see* violence
Roberts, M., 2n, 60n, 73n, 74n, 77n, 104n, 132n, 141n, 144n, 160n, 161n, 163n, 197n, 251n
Rogers, J.D., 135n, 139n
Rural Development Societies, 190, 196, 203, 246–47, 251
Russell, J., 87n, 97n, 128n, 130n, 131n, 132n, 138n, 139n, 154n, 160n, 172n, 198n
Ryan, B., 16n, 17n, 60n

St Thomas' College, 29–35, 52, 60, 110, 161
Samarasinghe, S.W.R. de A., 284n
Samaraweera, V., 106
Senanayake, D.S., 3, 29, 53, 60, 68–69, 71–72, 76, 82, 94, 102, 105, 107–10, 118–19, 125–27, 133–34, 137, 143–44, 148–51, 154–55, 157–94, 197–203, 209–11, 213, 215, 218, 225, 229, 245, 259, 262, 274, 296; Dudley, 119, 123, 139, 154, 185, 188, 198, 210–17, 220–25, 231, 245, 268–71
Senanayake, Dudley, 119, 123, 139, 154, 185, 188, 198, 210–17, 220–25, 231, 245, 268–71
Senanayake, F.R., 69, 161
Senanayake, Maithripala, 301
Senanayake, R.G., 242n, 245, 264, 273, 300n
Seneviratne, Charles (cousin Charlie), 18–19, 21
Silva, William, 256, 301, 304

Singer, M.R., 255n
Sinhala Maha Sabha, 117–18, 128–35, 137–41, 148–49, 152, 157–58, 164–70, 177, 182, 185, 191–92, 200–2, 206, 240
'Sinhala Only' Bill, 260–64, 266–68, 270, 322
Sinhalese interests and parochialism, 11, 90, 99, 125–35, 147, 155–57, 163–66, 169–71, 182, 193, 197–99, 203, 207, 210, 218–19, 227–53, 260–66, 270–73, 281, 284–99, 317–18, 322, 324, 326–27
Smith, D.E., 134n
social welfare programmes, *see* welfare state
Somarama, Talduwe, 317–18
Soulbury, Lord, 163–64, 210–12, 223–24, 229, 296–97
Sri Lanka Freedom Party (SLFP), 207–9, 212–18, 232–53, 256–57, 261, 265, 272, 278–84, 297–98, 300–2, 304–5, 312–13, 316, 322–25
Sri Nissanka, H., 115
State Council, 78, 89–98, 103–4, 108–9, 119–23, 128, 136, 138, 146–47, 150–57, 164, 168–69, 180, 236, 274
State of Emergency, 289–93, 295–98, 303
Stirrat, R.L., 133n
Stone, Warden, 30, 32–35, 42, 259
Straus, M.A., 16
strikes, *see* working class
Sunderam, Peri, 92

Tambiah, S.J., 16n, 17n, 309n
Tamil Congress, All-Ceylon, 178, 184–85, 189, 213–14, 242
Tamils and the Tamil language, 2, 61–62, 72–73, 80, 87, 92, 97, 99, 103, 117, 120, 125–36, 139, 147, 155–57, 165, 170, 178, 183–85, 188–90, 197–98, 202, 219, 227, 231–38, 249–50, 253–54, 257, 259–64, 266–73, 284–99, 301–3, 324–27
teachers (vernacular-medium), 118, 139, 166, 169, 183, 197, 202–3, 213, 218, 227–29, 231, 235, 237, 240, 247–50, 252, 271, 278, 281, 284, 299–300
Thomson, Sir Graeme, 104–5
Tinker, H., 189
Tiruchelvam, N., 193n, 265n, 322n

Unions, *see* working class
United National Party (UNP), 166–73,

United National Party (cont.)
175–85, 187–88, 190–97, 200–17,
220–31, 235–49, 252–53, 255, 266–73,
278, 281, 294, 296, 300–1, 305–6,
320–25, 327
universal suffrage, 2, 77–90, 110, 116,
136, 144, 246

violence, 2, 4, 68–69, 84–85, 88, 120, 180,
192, 208, 212, 216, 221–26, 235–36,
239, 245, 251–52, 261–63, 266, 271–74,
279, 285, 287–98, 302, 310–20, 325,
327
Vittachi, T., 288–89, 290n, 291n, 292n,
293n, 294–96

Washbrook, D.A., 99n
Waugh, Evelyn, 11, 46, 48n
Welfare State, 172, 177, 193–95, 203,

220–23, 263, 321–22; *see also,*
Bandaranaike and reform
westernization, 2–4, 7, 9, 11, 14–16, 19,
53, 56, 88, 95–101, 112–15, 142, 161,
166–67, 182, 197–99, 217–18, 223, 227,
229, 241, 250–51, 254–55, 274–75, 307
Wickremasinghe, S.A., 88
Wijewardene, Wimala, 265, 278, 284,
286–87, 299, 316–18
Wilson, A.J., 292n, 295–97
Woodward, C.A., 179, 253n
working class, 64, 66–67, 69, 75–77, 85,
90, 127, 130, 156, 169, 172–73, 180,
186, 209, 215, 221–22, 226, 229, 271,
287, 292–95, 301–2, 306, 322
World War II, 146, 150–58, 196
Wriggins, W.H., 6n, 85n, 239n, 297n

Young, Henry, 19